Palgrave Studies in Economic History

Series Editor
Kent Deng, London School of Economics, London, UK

Palgrave Studies in Economic History is designed to illuminate and enrich our understanding of economies and economic phenomena of the past. The series covers a vast range of topics including financial history, labour history, development economics, commercialisation, urbanisation, industrialisation, modernisation, globalisation, and changes in world economic orders.

More information about this series at
https://link.springer.com/bookseries/14632

Ramesh Chandra

Endogenous Growth in Historical Perspective

From Adam Smith to Paul Romer

palgrave
macmillan

Ramesh Chandra
Independent Economist
Glasgow, UK

ISSN 2662-6497 ISSN 2662-6500 (electronic)
Palgrave Studies in Economic History
ISBN 978-3-030-83763-1 ISBN 978-3-030-83761-7 (eBook)
https://doi.org/10.1007/978-3-030-83761-7

This Palgrave Macmillan imprint is published by the registered company Springer Nature Switzerland AG
The registered company address is: Gewerbestrasse 11, 6330 Cham, Switzerland

To the memory of my mother who died early because of cancer.

Preface

This book grew out of my first *Allyn Abbott Young*. In Chapter 4 of that book dealing with Young's growth theory, each of the authors who either figured as Young's inspirations (Adam Smith and Alfred Marshall) or who were inspired by Young (Nicholas Kaldor, Lauchlin Currie, Paul Rosenstein-Rodan, Paul Krugman and Paul Romer) received a cursory treatment. This book sprang out of my desire to give a fuller treatment to each of these authors than what they had received in my first book. The idea of endogenous growth is not new and goes at least as far back as Adam Smith. Smith viewed a competitive system as containing the seeds of its own growth. Young saw endogenous growth as arising from the very forces inherent in the system. This book takes a historical approach to the subject to see how far the later authors on endogenous growth were faithful to the original authors (Smith, Marshall and Young) on the subject, and how far they deviated from the earlier authors. Each author's approach to endogenous growth is discussed critically so that the reader understands the exact contribution of each contributor in relation to others clearly.

A lot of confusion prevails on the subject of increasing returns. While some authors view increasing returns as confined to manufacturing, others take a generalized approach to increasing returns. Whereas some view them as arising from the economies of scale at the firm or industry level, others see them as a macroeconomic phenomenon. While some see growth as predominantly arising from exogenous technical progress (which is like manna from heaven) as in the neoclassical theory, others see technical change as endogenous arising due to factors such as human capital formation and R&D expenditures to produce new knowledge. Some authors see an intrusive government in an anti-market framework as essential to the promotion of increasing returns, while others favour a pro-market approach. Smith and Young—the original authors—had a generalized notion of increasing returns and did not view them as confined to specific firms or industries even if they are large. This book therefore is an attempt to clear the confusion on the subject which has persisted for long. The attempt is to elaborate each approach as clearly as possible as well as the policies emerging from it. The approach of the book is mainly based on common sense; the empirical validity of each theory is presented wherever such information is available. In the final chapter an attempt is made to synthesize different strands, to separate the grain from the chaff, and to cull out the policy conclusions which pass the tests of sound theory, practice, and historical experience.

This book fills an important gap in the literature. There are a number of good books on endogenous growth covering one approach or the other. There is no single book bringing together all the different approaches in a critical manner and then distilling the essence of the subject in terms of both theory and policy. This book is aimed at theoreticians as well as practitioners of growth. It follows a simple style with almost no mathematics or diagrams. A few equations are presented in Chapter 9 but no attempt is made at algebraic derivation or manipulation. They are presented in a clear and straightforward manner where it was felt necessary to understand the theory and its implications. Thus the book can be of benefit to a large audience consisting of students, teachers, researchers, practitioners, and administrators who deal with policies on day-to-day basis. This book, it is hoped, will delight those who are sceptical of "blackboard economics" consisting of long algebraic equations, derivations, and manipulations.

With the outbreak of the coronavirus pandemic, and with various restrictions in place, most of us (except those involved with essential services) have had to face lockdowns and have been mostly confined to our homes. Operating from home has become a new buzzword. More time at home has forced many of us into thinking of creative ways of utilizing it. With time availability being less of a constraint than what it can be in normal times, this book has been that much easier to complete. At the same time, with the universities and libraries closed, I had to rely on internet purchases for most of the books and materials I required. This obviously meant incurring additional costs than would have been the case in normal times.

I am grateful to the editor of the series for reading through the book and giving his acceptance. I am indebted to Anthony P. Thirlwall for his comments on the chapter on Nicholas Kaldor. I would also like to thank the editorial team, particularly Ruth Jenner and Lavanya Devgun, at Palgrave Macmillan who helped in shaping this volume at different stages. Finally, I would like to thank my family for being patient with me while I worked on this project.

This book is dedicated to the memory of my mother who worked hard for the family but unfortunately met with an untimely death due to cancer.

Glasgow, UK
July 2021

Ramesh Chandra

Contents

CHAPTER 1

Endogenous Growth: Introduction

This book examines the theme of endogenous growth in historical perspective. The term endogenous growth has become fashionable in recent years after the publication of the works of Romer (1986, 1987, 1989, 1990),[1] Lucas (1988), Krugman (1990, 1993), Murphy et al. (1989), Shaw (1992), and Aghion and Howitt (1998) among others. This "new" growth theory retains the neoclassical supply-side production function framework, and introduces new innovations like human capital and new knowledge as additional inputs. Technological change which was exogenous in the neoclassical theory (e.g., Solow 1956, 1957; Abramovitz 1956) is now sought to be explained through these innovations. However, the theme of endogenous growth goes far back and can be traced to Adam Smith (1776) who emphasized the relationship between the division of labour and market size. Smith made the market exchange as central to his analysis and discussed the role of institutions and conditions which best promote it. Marshall (1890) built on the relationship and emphasized the role of industrial organization in this regard. He also introduced the distinction between external and internal economies, and the device of a representative firm through which they

[1] David Warsh (2006) points out that it was in Paul Romer's (1990) paper "that the economics of knowledge at last came into focus, after more than two centuries of informal and uneasy presence in the background" (p. xv).

R. Chandra, *Endogenous Growth in Historical Perspective*, Palgrave Studies in Economic History,
https://doi.org/10.1007/978-3-030-83761-7_1

are realized in the long run. Young (1928) built on Smith and Marshall and cast the relationship between the division of labour and market size in terms of cumulative causation and came to the conclusion that the division of labour largely depends on division of labour itself. For Young this is more than a tautology because the forces making for disequilibrium are more pervasive and deeply rooted than we commonly realize.

It is clear that a number of authors with varying persuasions have written on the subject of endogenous growth from Adam Smith to Paul Romer. But the definition of endogenous growth is different in different authors, as also the role played by the market forces vis-à-vis state policy. While Smith emphasized the motive power of self-interest within a competitive market framework as not only capable of taking the individual but the whole society to opulence, the new growth and trade theorists emphasize the role of artificial monopolies and privileges as the basis of increasing returns. While the Smith–Young framework emphasizes the role of real demand (i.e., the market size) in growth, the new growth and trade theories emphasize the supply-side factors such as new knowledge and human capital. Thus many questions arise. What exactly is endogenous growth? What is the role of demand-side factors vis-à-vis supply-side factors in growth? That is, is growth demand driven or supply constrained? Does the scarcity of resources (in the form traditional inputs of land, labour, capital, and now new knowledge and human capital) impose a formidable constraint on growth? What is the role of the market vis-à-vis the state in promoting growth? Put differently, what is the role of competition vis-à-vis intervention in fostering growth? These are some of the questions this book will try to answer.

Several authors are discussed in the following chapters in the context of endogenous growth but Joseph Schumpeter is not one of them. So we devote some attention to him right upfront. Schumpeter (1934, 1942) did not base his theory of economic growth on Smith–Marshall–Young framework—the original authors of endogenous growth which we consider. In this book we have taken up only those authors who built on this framework or quoted them explicitly to advance their own analyses. Schumpeter neither built on this framework nor quoted their ideas to advance his own. In fact he disliked some of the ideas put forward by Smith or Marshall. For example, in his magisterial *History of Economic Analysis*, Schumpeter (1954, p. 187) posited that Smith put too much burden on the division of labour as an explanation of growth, which no one before or after him thought of doing. Technical progress, invention of machinery, and capital accumulation are all induced by it. Schumpeter (ibid., pp. 184–87) also stated that neither Smith's idea of the division of labour nor any other idea contained in the *Wealth of Nations* was original to him. For Schumpeter, Smith's contribution was mainly that of coordinating the already existing material which job, being a methodical professor, he did perform well.

Schumpeter (1928) interpreted Marshall in static terms with there being no fundamental difference between Marshall's and Walras's analysis since the former was as static as the latter (Raffaelli 2003, pp. 119–21). From this it followed that Marshall's analytical devices aimed at going beyond static analysis—increasing returns, external economies, the representative firm—were misplaced. As Raffaelli points out, this biased reading of Marshall stems from Schumpeter's dislike of Marshall's evolutionary philosophy. Schumpeter also rejected all biological analogies since they conveyed the idea of continuous organic growth. His theory of creative destruction is based on disruptive change brought about by entrepreneurial leadership.[2] Schumpeter placed statics and dynamics in two separate compartments, and each required a separate set of concepts and tools to deal with.[3] For him progress was not automatic but was driven consciously by the creative innovation of the entrepreneur. Since

[2] The innovative producer plays such an important role that even consumer tastes are moulded or created by him. "[W]e must always start from the satisfaction of wants, since they are the end of all production, and the given economic situation at any time must be understood from this aspect. Yet innovations in the economic system do not as a rule take place in such a way that first new wants arise spontaneously in consumers and then the productive apparatus swings round through their pressure. We do not deny the presence of this nexus. It is, however, the producer who as a rule initiates economic change, and consumers are educated by him if necessary; they are, as it were, taught to want new things, or things which differ in some respect or other from those which they have been in the habit of using" (Schumpeter 1934, p. 65).

[3] In the static world of Walrasian equilibrium while there is consumer sovereignty, there is no leadership role for the entrepreneur, the rate of interest and that of profit is zero and there are no innovations or qualitative changes. In the dynamic world, the entrepreneur has a leadership role in innovation, consumer tastes are actively influenced by him, and the rates of interest and profit are positive. New ventures are financed by bank credit as they cannot be financed by the revenues of the stationary circular flow. See Elliot (1983, pp. xvi-xvii). Further, the capitalist process cannot be understood by abstracting from money. Money is not a factor of production but a distinct agent which stands between the entrepreneur and factors. Bank credit is used to buy the *existing* means of production to be withdrawn from their current uses and put into *new* ventures. See also Moura (2018, pp. 115–16).

external economies meant that progress could be automatic, he rejected the concept.[4] "Marshall was well aware of the role of consciousness, but not to the point of ignoring the driving force of unconscious, automatic trends" (ibid., p. 120). In Marshall's theory of evolution routine (repetitive work) and creativity both play an important role. The division of labour in Smith and Marshall is routine and facilitated by the use of machinery. For Schumpeter, the Walrasian static equilibrium theory captures the repetitive side of the economy but for economic progress a separate theory of creative destruction is required.[5] According to Raffaelli, Marshall "would have denied assent to Schumpeter's drastically dichotomic economics" (ibid., p. 120).

In the "trustified" phase of the Schumpeterian competition, progress becomes automated and impersonal, and the role of leadership and individual initiative declines. For Schumpeter, this phase leads to subversion of competitive capitalism in which progress was the result of conscious efforts. "Schumpeter's scheme of the evolution of capitalism is much more discontinuous than Marshall's and the former's prediction of inexorable outcome of the new phase, doomed thoroughly to replace competitive capitalism, does not compare favourably, in historical perspective, with the more mobile and less deterministic Marshallian picture of economic progress, in which consciousness and automatisms go side by side and old types of creative competition always die and spring up again (Langlois 2001)" (ibid., p. 120).

Allyn Young (1990, p. 54) emphasized on "large production" (total market size) in place of "large-scale production" (in large firms and industries) as the basis of increasing returns. He also stated that industrial differentiation, where industries continuously split up into specialized units, was a more dominant feature of industrial growth as compared

[4] Schumpeter (1928, p. 369, n.2; quoted from Clemence 1951, p. 55) was of the view "that economies before becoming 'external' must generally be internal ones in some firm or firms of the same *or some other* industry".

[5] Schumpeterian competition is not price competition as noted by Rosenberg (2000, p. 10). It takes the form of new product, new technology, new source of supply, and new type of organization (e.g., large-scale units), and gives decisive cost or quality advantage. In *The Theory of Economic Development*, Schumpeter (1934, p. 66) defines development as carrying out of new combinations which covers five cases: (1) the introduction of a new good, (2) the introduction of a new method of production, (3) the opening of a new market, (4) the conquest of a new source of supply of raw materials, and (5) creation of new industrial organization like a monopoly position.

to industrial integration (Young 1928). As Raffaelli notes, this makes room for small and medium businesses instead of large-scale units. Thus, contrary to Schumpeter, monopoly capitalism is not inevitable. Young also criticized Schumpeter for overstressing the role of leadership or entrepreneurship. "Now genuine leadership is rare; there is a flock behind any successful leader, and the thing is overdone. But does not Schumpeter overemphasize 'originality'? It is not important that someone should go ahead" (Young 1990, p. 82). Further: "Real leadership is no more common in industrial than in other pursuits. New catch-words or slogans like mass-production and rationalization may operate as stimuli; they may rouse men from routine and lead them to scrutinize again the organization and processes of industry... There is a danger, however, that we shall expect too much from these 'rational' industrial reforms. Pressed beyond a point they become the reverse of rational" (Young 1928, p. 531). According to Young the most important factor in the effectiveness of a country's industry is the size of the market rather than industrial leadership, better management or the use of more capital-intensive methods. "Taking a country's economic endowment as given, the most important factor in determining the effectiveness of its industry appears to be the size of the market" (ibid., p. 532).

In short, Schumpeter's growth theory is different from the Smith–Marshall–Young view of growth. It is endogenous growth alright, and is also based on the idea of capitalism as an evolutionary system.[6] But it has no place for the division of labour and its link with the total market

[6] Schumpeter viewed capitalism as an evolutionary system rather than a system that reverts back to equilibrium after departures from it (Rosenberg 2000, p. 9). For him "capitalist reality is first and last a process of change" (Schumpeter 1942, p. 77). At another place Schumpeter stated: "Whereas a stationary feudal economy would still be a feudal economy, and a stationary socialist economy would still be a socialist economy, stationary capitalism is a contradiction in terms" (Clemence 1951, p. 174). Moreover, he strongly felt "that there was a source of energy within the economic system which would of itself disrupt any equilibrium that might be attained. If this is so, there must be a purely economic theory of economic change which does not merely rely on external factors propelling the economic system from one equilibrium to another" (ibid., p. 160). As is clear, he had an endogenous view of growth but he still viewed Walras's static general equilibrium theory as the backdrop against which his own theory of change should be seen as a contrast. "Thus, the model of Walrasian circular flow constitutes Schumpeter's starting-point in understanding the essential elements of capitalist reality precisely because it shows how the system would behave in the absence of its most distinctive feature – innovation" (Rosenberg 2000, p. 15).

size. It also has no place for Marshallian external economies,[7] which as Young (1928) pointed out, should be seen as a safeguard against assuming that wherever increasing returns operate, there is an effective tendency towards monopoly. It also has no explicit place for the process of cumulative causation which takes an economy further and further away from equilibrium. While in the Smith–Young view, growth is demand driven, in Schumpeter it is driven by innovations (and inventions in so far as they get adopted) and entrepreneur is seen as the kingpin of the capitalist system.[8] Rosenberg (2000, pp. 3–9) is of the view that Schumpeter shared a stripped-down version of Marx's economic interpretation of history. He had high regard for Marx and the first four chapters of his *Capitalism, Socialism and Democracy* are devoted entirely to an examination of Marx's work. Thus, Schumpeter's analysis of economic change under capitalism has the following features which are common with Marx[9]:

[7] Schumpeter (1928; Clemence 1951, p. 70) is of the view that the existing firms cannot create external economies; it is the new firms (embodying innovation) which can change "internal" economies into "external" ones; and in so far as it means disturbance, external economies become important in the negative sense of destroying the old. "The new processes do not, and generally cannot, evolve out of the old firms, but place themselves side by side with them and attack them" (ibid., p. 70).

[8] Even his business cycle explanation is linked with "swarms" of innovations. This leads to the idea of development occurring in waves. "The swarm of projects explains the economic upswing, whereas the downswing occurs when the projects are no longer able to carry the increased economic activity. This idea of waveform economic evolution was an important part of Schumpeter's vision of the essence of capitalism..." (Andersen 2011, p. 115). Schumpeter was also of the opinion that the cycle is the form which growth takes. "The recurring periods of prosperity of the cyclical movement are the form progress takes in capitalistic society" (Schumpeter 1927; Clemence 1951, p. 30). He disagreed with Hawtrey (1919, 1923) that a cycle is a purely monetary phenomenon. "Booms and consequently depressions are not the work of banks: their 'cause' is a non-monetary one and the entrepreneur's demand is the initiating cause... But booms and depressions would not without banks be what they are..." (Schumpeter 1927; Clemence 1951, pp. 41–42). He also opined that cycles cannot be regarded as merely "evil"; they serve a purpose in capitalist evolution. It is possible to control them through credit management, but "this does not imply that it is in any sense desirable" (ibid., p. 43).

[9] Anderson (2011, p. 68) points out that though Schumpeter's vision of the role of the entrepreneur in social and economic evolution was unique, it had more similarities with Marx than with other economists or social scientists.

1. the inevitability of growth in the size of the firm and in industrial concentration, a central theme of *Capitalism, Socialism and Democracy*;
2. the inherent instability of capitalism and the inevitability of "crises," Schumpeter's major concern, as embodied in his most ambitious work, *Business Cycles*;
3. the eventual destruction of capitalist institutions, and the arrival of a socialist form of economic organization, as a result of the working out of the internal logic of capitalist evolution, a theme intimately connected with the growth of industrial bigness, spelled out in detail in *Capitalism, Socialism and Democracy* (ibid., p. 8).

Thus in both Marx and Schumpeter, capitalism would be destroyed and be ultimately replaced by socialism.[10] But it would happen because of different reasons. For Marx, capitalism would be destroyed because of its inner contradictions, for Schumpeter it would be destroyed because of its successes.[11] For Marx, the inner contradictions of the system would result in a class struggle to sound the death knell of capitalism, for Schumpeter

[10] In this regard Schumpeter (1928) writes: "Capitalism, whilst economically stable, and even gaining in stability, creates, by rationalizing the human mind, a mentality and a style of life incompatible with its own fundamental conditions, motives and social institutions, and will be changed, although not by economic necessity and probably even at some sacrifice of economic welfare, into an order of things which it will be merely matter of taste and terminology to call socialism or not" (as in Clemence 1951, pp. 71–72).

[11] Schumpeter does not see depressions as a failure of the capitalist system as development itself occurs through the cyclical process. As Elliot (1983, p. xxvii) puts it "the fundamental cause of depression is prosperity itself". Similarly, Schumpeter sees monopoly in a dynamic process of capitalist evolution, and does not regard it as a flaw, a contradiction or a failure of the system (ibid., p. xxxvi). In static conception, monopoly may lead to lower output and higher prices; in the dynamic world "Schumpeter's hero is not competitive market but the creative, daring entrepreneur, the 'captain of industry,' who makes the innovations that introduce new products, embodies resource discoveries and technological improvements, opens new markets, and, in the process, builds new industrial empires" (ibid., p. xxxvii). Further: "The 'perennial gale of creative destruction,' whereby new products and processes displace old ones, is vastly more important than price competition among existing firms and products" (ibid., xxxvii).

the emergence of monopoly capitalism[12] and its consequent bureaucratic nature would destroy the creativity and the habit of thriftiness (or saving) earlier associated with the small entrepreneurs and family-based businesses.[13]

Different Conceptions of Endogenous Growth

Unlike Marx and Schumpeter, where the capitalist system is destroyed and replaced by socialism, the Smith–Young approach views the capitalist system continuing and prospering as it contains the seeds of its own growth. Both Smith and Young had an evolutionary perspective towards society where the forces inherent in the system produce growth. In Smith the motive power of self-interest is such a powerful principle, that it alone is capable of taking not only an individual but the whole society to wealth and riches. This motive prompts an individual to save, accumulate and become rich. The desire for saving as Smith tells us is inborn, it comes to us from the womb and never leaves us till we die. Thus, an individual should be allowed to follow his own interest his own way provided he does not violate the laws of justice. Nothing should be done to create obstacles in the pursuit of self-interest; the rulers were advised to watch over their own economy rather than watching over the economy of private people. If their own spendthrift ways had not ruined the country, those of private people will never will. Thus the state should ensure two things—liberty and security. Smith, after analysing various systems of political economy based on extraordinary restraints or extraordinary encouragements such as slavery, agricultural systems, and mercantilism, concluded that liberty and security are best provided in the system of natural liberty.

[12] In trustified capitalism, innovation is not embodied in new firms but takes place in big units as a matter of course on the advice of specialists and loses its connection with individual persons. It becomes possible to have a conscious policy towards demand (in the sense of creating new wants) and long-term view towards investment. The fear of failure loses its grip. Progress becomes more automatized and impersonal, and depends less on leadership or individual initiative. See Clemence (1951), pp. 70–71.

[13] In this regard Steven Pressman (1999) points out that families are important for capitalism because they are the main reason for saving. "Families save so that if anything happens to the main breadwinner, other family members will be provided for. By undermining the motivation to save, capitalism destroys its own foundation – the capital needed for future growth" (ibid., p. 108).

For Marshall, evolution is continuous and slow; the growth resulting from this process can be described as organic growth. For him evolution was based on routine and creativity. He introduced organization as the fourth factor of production. Marshall then compares the economic organization with the biological organism of a higher animal. A living organism is divided into various organs each of which performs various specialized functions. At the same time coordination of those functions takes place from the central level. The same development of differentiation and integration is observed in an economic organization as it evolves. Differentiation of activity is achieved by the division of labour and specialization. Once tasks have been reduced to routine, they are soon taken over by machinery. Integration is achieved by the development of transport and communication and through increased security of commercial credit.

Organic growth can be achieved through the development of the division of labour which in turn is limited by the size of the market. For Marshall, growth achieved by the division of labour by itself is not enough. For him improving the working and living conditions of workers, providing them with clean air and water, investment in education and culture also mattered. The society has to consciously work towards developing moral and mental faculties of man. Ultimately progress lies in developing man's character, his fuller human potential, and his emergence as a responsible citizen of society. Thus while the operation of routine (through the division of labour and use of machinery) can give man his material progress, the development of higher human faculties and fuller human potential has to be consciously planned for.

The notion of growth in Marshall is essentially microeconomic as he tried to study change through the device of a representative firm. A representative firm is an average firm confining itself to a given range of activities, and to which innovation is available but not invention. Marshall makes the representative firm a vehicle for change; as it grows, both internal economies of scale as well as external economies (associated with the growth of the industry as a whole) become available to it. In short, the representative firm is a fictitious firm but serves as an expository device. The notion was criticized by Robbins (1928) as not being very sound. Sraffa (1926) criticized his notion of increasing returns as incompatible with perfect competition. In his opinion, one needed the theory of monopoly for modelling increasing returns.

For Young growth is not negated by its costs. Those who generally thought in terms of equilibrium of costs and advantages were prone to view growth as being negated by its costs. Young warned that such a conclusion would be repugnant to common sense as the historical fact of growth testified. For him economic progress was inherent in the very forces of the competitive economic system. Young (1928, p. 533) pointed out that growth was more due to the "permanent characteristics" of the system (or "the ways in which goods are produced") than due to "new or adventitious elements" coming from outside. Young did not deny the existence of equilibrating forces, but thought that they were continuously being overcome by more powerful counter forces so that the dominant paradigm was that of disequilibrium rather than equilibrium. Growth follows the law of cumulative causation so that change is progressive and propagates itself in a cumulative way. Therefore nothing is to be gained by looking for increasing returns under equilibrium conditions or at the level of a firm or industry even if they are large. Just as the dominant tendency of the system was that of disequilibrium, the dominant tendency of an industrial system was that of differentiation rather than integration. That is, increasing returns manifest themselves dominantly and increasingly in the form of industrial specialization (i.e., splitting up of an industry into a number of smaller specialized firms and industries) than in the form of integration or consolidation of industry. Thus monopoly capitalism is not inevitable; increasing returns are more commonly seen in the emergence of a large number of smaller specialized firms and industries. Young stated that evolution does not follow a single principle. Big size may be important where the products are standardized and operations routinized as in steel. But in most other branches of business small size had its advantages. He also compared an economic system to a living organism and stated that an economic system grows and evolves like a living organism through successive adjustments and adaptations where "change breeds change, and every new adjustment paves the way for another" (Young 1929; Mehrling and Sandilands 1999, p. 411).

Like Marshall, Young viewed economics as an instrument in solving communal problems of economic life. For Marshall economics had an ethical value in solving the problem of poverty. Young saw economics as having an instrumental value, and for that reason he disliked a sharp distinction between theoretical and applied economics. Theory was useless unless it was helpful in solving practical problems. Young was aware that the unchecked growth of credit had an inherently destabilizing effect, and the capitalist system was prone to frequent bouts of booms and busts. Thus a central bank was required for credit control as well as for the proper conduct of monetary policy based on discretion rather than preconceived rules. Similarly, monopoly capital had emerged in a few areas, and therefore appropriate legal–institutional framework to deal with this was required. Another area of public interest was utility regulation. Railways and other public utilities were natural monopolies, so there was no point in making them conform to competition. The best way forward in public service regulation was to follow the cost of service principle, any divergence from which should be justified by the special circumstances of the case. Thus Young was a great believer in institutions which acting in public interest would help solve economic problems. But legal–institutional framework appropriate to dealing with various problems had to be consciously planned for. Indeed, Young saw institutions as the saviours of capitalism; capitalism will neither be destroyed because of its contradictions, nor because of its successes, but would be reformed by conscious institutional interventions in a more humane direction.

The Smith–Young view of endogenous growth is important because of the fact that before intelligent policies can be designed to promote growth it is necessary to understand how growth takes place on its own "through the operation of forces engendered within the economic system" (Young 1928, p. 535). In Smith and Young growth largely takes place on its own, and as we noted, capitalism contains the seeds of its own growth. To understand it, the relationship between the division of labour and market size is of utmost important which Young cast in terms of cumulative causation to suggest that "the division of labour in large part depends on the division of labour" (ibid., p. 533). Smith and Young both had a macroeconomic (or generalized) notion of increasing returns. Different sectors or industries are seen in a reciprocal exchange relationship. If policy seeks to promote one sector (for example, manufacturing) at the cost of another (for example, agriculture), this reciprocal relationship is likely to be upset and results in retarding growth instead of accelerating it. In Smith's terminology, any policy based on artificial encouragements or restraints cannot facilitate growth as such a policy goes against his concept of natural liberty. Thus competition plays a crucial role where the field is levelled for everyone and winners and losers emerge from the competitive race itself rather than being picked and promoted. This book adopts this view of endogenous growth and judges other contributions in terms of how far they conform or deviate from this view.

This is not to suggest that policy is unimportant. For example, Smith had advocated public investment in transport and communication to integrate the market internally. He also advocated opening up to international trade to widen the narrow domestic market and to keep the domestic monopolies in check. Young interpreted Smith as a champion of competition rather than a champion of laissez faire. Therefore he recommended a proper institutional–legal framework to check the growth of monopoly power. Similarly he recommended central banking for the proper conduct of monetary policy as he recognized the inherent instability of credit. If capitalism itself is seriously destabilized through business cycles, growth can be jeopardized. Thus policy is crucial first to ensure the stability of the system, and then to ensure equality of opportunity (which is compromised in monopoly capitalism) and fair play. In the Smith–Young framework competition is seen as the best tonic for growth, and any policy framework which seeks to promote growth has to keep this in mind.

Two of Young's students, Lauchlin Currie at Harvard and Nicholas Kaldor at the London School of Economics, sought to extend his growth framework in different directions. Nicholas Kaldor[14] interpreted Smith and Young in sectoral terms to suggest that manufacturing was the increasing returns sector and therefore should be promoted through policies of protection, subsidies, dual exchange rates, and selective employment tax. He was also convinced of the empirical validity of Verdoorn's Law which postulated a strong causal relationship between output growth (as the dependent variable) and productivity growth in manufacturing (as the independent variable). He drew heavily on Young's 1928 paper on increasing returns and economic progress to criticize equilibrium economics and its assumptions. He was also influenced by Keynes (1936) and sought to supplement Young's insights with the Keynesian aggregated demand. Young had stated that given elastic demand, "an increase in the supply of one commodity is an increase in the demand for other commodities, and it must be supposed that every increase in demand will evoke an increase in supply" (Young 1928, p. 534). Kaldor (1972) agreed that an increase in demand will lead to an increase in supply but the reverse may not be necessarily true. He reasoned that increased expenditure on an elastically produced good diverts purchasing power from other goods, and this will have to be made good by an increase in bank

[14] For an appraisal of Kaldor's sectoral view of increasing returns, see Chandra (2019) and Chandra and Sandilands (2021).

credit. Otherwise aggregate demand will fall short of aggregate supply, and growth would be affected. Clearly, here Kaldor slips into the neoclassical opportunity cost reasoning forgetting that the real purchasing power is itself growing in a growing economy.

Lauchlin Currie (1974), on the other hand, was more faithful to the Smith–Young framework.[15] Young had cast Smith's theorem in terms of cumulative causation, as noted above, to suggest that the division of labour depends on the division of labour itself. From this Currie concluded that the cause of growth is growth itself. Given the institutional and policy framework, the same rate of growth tends to perpetuate itself. A low initial rate of growth would perpetuate low growth rate and a high initial rate would perpetuate high growth rate. To achieve a high rate of growth, he advocated a leading-sector strategy of growth with construction acting as the internal leading sector and exports as the external leading sector. This strategy is based on the logic of handicap removal rather than on the logic of granting selective favours. This strategy is consistent with the Smith–Young framework as it does not call for favoured treatment to the chosen leading sectors. It only calls for the removal of institutional barriers which handicap these sectors. For example, construction is handicapped by the absence of suitable financial products in a high inflation Latin-American economy such as Colombia, so making available suitable mortgage products which spread the instalments paid over a long enough period instead of bunching them upfront, can kick-start housing and other construction activities. Similarly, exports are handicapped because of overvalued exchange rate, therefore if a policy of realistic exchange rate is adopted either through devaluation or through market-determined exchange rates, then the institutional constraint facing exports can be overcome. In short, no favourable treatment to construction or exports is required; only a policy of handicap removal will do.

Post-war development economists such as Rosenstein-Rodan (1943, 1961) and Ragnar Nurkse (1953, 1962) quoted Smith and Young with approval but largely reached a supply-based view of growth. Rosenstein-Rodan talked of the vicious circle of poverty on the demand side which could be broken through the strategy of the "big push". If an isolated investment is undertaken, say in a shoe factory, then overall market would

[15] For an appraisal of Currie's leading-sector strategy, see Chandra (2006, 2020).

not expand as the workers are not expected to spend their entire incomes on shoes alone. If, however, investment in a number of complementary wage goods is undertaken, the difficulty on the demand side regarding the size of the market could be overcome. What was not true of a single isolated investment becomes true for a range of complementary investments. Rosenstein-Rodan (1961) later expanded the size of the big push to include social overhead capital (or infrastructure) without which even wage goods sectors cannot take off. Nurkse also talked of the vicious circles of poverty both on the demand and supply side, but for him the supply side of capital formation was more important. To break the vicious circle of poverty on the demand side, he advocated "synchronized application of capital to a wide range of different industries" or what he termed as "balanced growth" (Nurkse 1953, p. 11). Further: "People working with more and better tools in a number of complementary projects become each others' customers. Most industries catering for mass consumption are complementary in the sense that they provide a market support to each other. This basic complementarity stems, in the last analysis, from the diversity of human wants. The case for 'balanced growth' rests on the need for 'balanced diet'" (ibid., p. 11). In short, though the diagnosis of the problem of underdevelopment is largely on the demand side, the offered solution is "big push" or "capital formation". To make the big push a reality, market intervention in the form of protectionism and centralized investment board (or programming) to optimize the size and composition of investment is advocated. Nurkse (1962) recognized that trade acted as an engine of growth in the earlier century, but this option was no longer available as the world trade had considerably slowed down. Thus, the only option available for developing countries was to industrialize behind high tariff and non-tariff walls.

The big push idea has been revived in more recent years by Murphy et al. (1989) and Krugman (1993). The argument is that because of imperfect competition with large fixed costs, pecuniary external economies cause multiplicity of equilibria. Murphy et al. see big push industrialization as a move from bad equilibrium to a good equilibrium. They build on Rosenstein-Rodan's idea that simultaneous industrialization across sectors could be self-sustaining although no single sector could break even industrializing alone. Krugman observes that certain core of ideas called the "high development theory" got lost because they were not presented rigorously or mathematically. In his streamlined presentation of the big push idea, based on Murphy et al. (1989), Krugman (1993) points out that two conditions are necessary—that the modern sector has imperfect competition and unlimited supplies of labour are available to it from the traditional sector. Invoking Hirschman's (1958) linkages, Krugman (1993) argued that economies of scale at the plant level translated into increasing returns in the aggregate through the vehicle of pecuniary external economies. Although he was against interventionist trade and industrial policies or return to import substitution, he maintained that there was an intellectually solid case for some governmental promotion of industries.

New trade theory emerged from the pioneering work of Krugman (1979, 1980, 1981, 1990), Helpman and Krugman (1985, 1989) among others. In this theory, trade arises because increasing returns or economies of scale lead to specialization in a few product varieties. The traditional explanation of trade is in terms of comparative advantage where country differences arise due to differences in relative labour costs (Ricardian theory) or due to differences in relative factor endowment (Heckscher–Ohlin theory). But this explains only inter-industry trade, for example, trade between food and manufactures. New trade theory, on the other hand, explains intra-industry trade, for example, trade between manufactures and manufactures or between similar countries where each country specializes in a few product varieties and gets the rest through trade. But the pattern of intra-industry trade is itself left unexplained (i.e., which country will produce what product). Krugman pointed out that although Smith's explanation of trade was in terms increasing returns arising out of the division of labour (or differences in absolute costs) but this got lost because of the predominance of the comparative advantage theory. Since comparative advantage assumes perfect competition, and prices equal marginal costs of production, such models are mathematically more tractable. With the development of industrial organization theory, it became possible to deal with models of imperfect competition and economies of scale. These new models made it possible to deal with both economies of scale as well as external economies (where increasing returns arise in the production of intermediate goods). However, Smith had talked of the division of labour (increasing returns) arising from international trade but new trade theorists reversed the sequence from increasing returns to international trade. It can be argued that increasing returns result as much (or more) from international trade as being the cause of international trade. Besides, Smith and Young had a generalized conception of increasing returns whereas intra-industry trade in the new trade theory equates increasing returns with economies of scale at the firm or industry level. Finally, the new trade theory may itself be becoming outdated. Empirical evidence suggests that trade between similar countries may be giving way to trade between low-wage poorer countries and high-wage rich countries (for example, between Mexico and the US or China and the US).

The modern endogenous growth theory defines endogenous growth in relation to exogenous growth of the neoclassical theory. In the neoclassical theory, most of the growth results from exogenous technical change which is obtained as a residual after deducting the growth resulting from inputs such as labour and capital. According to the modern endogenous theory, growth "is an endogenous outcome of an economic system" and does not "impinge from outside" (Romer 1994, p. 3). It tries to study the private as well as public sector choices that result in the differences in the rate of growth of the residual across countries. The focus remains macroeconomic as in the neoclassical theory. As Fine (2000, p. 248) observes, what was earlier treated as exogenous is now explained. Within the neoclassical aggregate production function, the modern growth theory introduces new inputs like R&D expenditures and human capital so that the production function now yields increasing returns to scale rather than the neoclassical constant returns to scale. Thus, it basically remains a supply-side view of growth as opposed to the Smith–Young demand-side explanation.

Imperfect competition is not only the assumption of modern growth theory but also one of its policy implications. To recoup the costs of new research, it advocates anti-market prescriptions such as patents, protection, subsidies, and monopoly profits. Otherwise adequate investment by the private sector in research and development would not be forthcoming. It advocates greater integration with the international market only because it would give a greater impetus to new research. Young was aware that competition in the real world had imperfect elements, but imperfect competition for him was a part of a broader process of competition. For him imperfect competition meant imperfect working of competition as in the real world, not its absence. Thus, for example, the first innovator may reap supernormal profits, but as others enter the field or as some effective substitutes are found, these disappear and may reappear in some other area. So there is an effective lid on profits due to freedom of entry and availability of close substitutes. For Young, goodwill, differentiated products, selling costs, brand names, etc., were signs of imperfect working of competition, not its absence. Selling costs were not competitive wastes but competitive investments since each producer tried to distinguish his product from those of his competitors. Though competition took the form of non-price competition, for example, in after-sales service or better terms of payment, etc., but competition was still alive and kicking and kept an effective lid on the profits made. Therefore, he was against artificially created monopolies such as patents which, in his opinion, one could do away with without much retarding progress.[16]

Scheme of the Book

As is clear from above, different authors have differing perspectives on endogenous growth, and this book aims to bring all these perspectives together in a comprehensive volume. Young stated that there was no field in economics where there was so much loose thinking as in increasing returns. For example, authors such as Paul Romer and Paul Krugman link the genesis of increasing returns to the presence of fixed costs or economies of scale at the plant level. They often cite Adam Smith's pin-factory example to support the view that increasing returns arise due to economies of scale at the firm level. Young (1990, p. 54) had clearly stated that increasing returns arise not due to any relationship between supplementary (fixed) and prime (variable) costs but due to other causes. Young also discounted the Marshallian notion of consumer's surplus and stated that this was more a notional surplus summing up to exactly zero over all his purchases. A consumer did not benefit from consumer's surplus but from the lowering of costs (and prices) resulting from increasing returns. For him increasing returns were macroeconomic rather than microeconomic, generalized rather than sector-specific, arose from external economies rather than from internal economies of firms, and could be better studied from a disequilibrium perspective than from the equilibrium theory. Thus contributions of various authors who contributed to endogenous growth—Adam Smith, Allyn Young, Nicholas Kaldor,

[16] Young (1990, p. 52) stated that most patents (99%) are utterly useless because they depend on fundamental research or processes which are not patentable. For example, steam engines made use of Joule's laws of thermodynamics which were not patentable. The old process of inventing is probably less important than systematic scientific research. The system is so intricate that one patent is valueless without the other, so that the entire system can be done away with without affecting growth.

Lauchlin Currie, Paul Rosenstein-Rodan (and other post-war development economists), Paul Krugman (and other new trade theorists), and Paul Romer (and other new growth theorists)—will be discussed critically. An attempt will also be made to discuss how far the later authors were faithful to the original contributions of Adam Smith and Allyn Young.

There are several books either discussing individual authors or some aspect of the endogenous growth theory, but no book brings all these authors together in a comprehensive work. For example, Aghion and Howitt (1998) mainly discuss the modern version of the endogenous growth theory with the neoclassical model as the starting point. Similarly Barro and Sala-i-Martin (2004) discuss the theoretical and empirical literature on endogenous growth in relation to the neoclassical theory as the starting point. They regard the combination of theory and empirical work as the most exciting aspect of the ongoing research on economic growth. Krugman (1990) discusses new trade theory models based on increasing returns. But none of these authors discusses how the modern version of endogenous growth compares with the original authors such as Smith, Marshall, and Young. Although the modern growth theory claims to represent the earlier verbal ideas in a much more rigorous-mathematical fashion, it will emerge that they do not fully capture the earlier insights. They actually adopt the same neoclassical supply-side aggregate production function framework introducing new features such as R&D and human capital to explain the exogenous technical change left unexplained by the neoclassical theory. This is in sharp contrast to the essentially demand-based explanation of growth put forward by Adam Smith and Allyn Young. Allyn Young used demand not in the aggregate Keynesian sense but in the reciprocal sense of J. B. Say. The basic approach followed by modern growth theorists is largely innovation-based, and therefore closer to Schumpeterian approach of creative destruction as noted by Aghion and Howitt (1998, p. 1). Thus a critical evaluation of the modern endogenous growth authors in comparison with the original authors, who make the relationship between the division of labour and market size as the central pillar of their analysis, is an interesting and fruitful exercise and the task is attempted in the following chapters.

The chapter-wise scheme of the book is as follows. Chapter 2 discusses Smith's views on economic progress in which the analysis of the division of labour, motive power of self-interest, the role of saving, investment and capital accumulation, and institutions best suited to growth—all in an evolutionary framework—play a key role. Chapter 3 takes up Marshall's view of organic growth in which the emphasis is on the microeconomics of growth, and on the role of the representative firm which captures both the economies of scale and external economies as it grows. The representative firm is an expository device for deriving the long-run industry supply curve in an evolutionary framework in which statics is just a part of dynamics. In Chapter 4 we discuss Young's views on growth in terms of disequilibrium economics, cumulative causation, external economies and macroeconomic increasing returns—a vocabulary which did not exist in Smith's time. Thus, Young explained the process of endogenous growth more fully using modern vocabulary to which Smith did not have access. Chapter 5 takes up Nicholas Kaldor's interpretation of the Smith–Young growth framework in terms of sectoral increasing returns. He thought that increasing returns were confined to manufacturing—a belief which was reinforced by the empirical validity of Verdoorn's relation between output growth and productivity growth in manufacturing. In Chapter 6 we discuss Currie's leading-sector strategy of growth which is based on "no preferences, no restraints" policy framework arising from Smith–Young thinking. While Young emphasized how growth happens in an advanced economy, Currie's emphasis was to make it happen in a developing country which is caught in a low-growth equilibrium trap. His focus is to devise a strategy to move from a low rate of growth to a higher one. Chapter 7 takes up post-war development economists like Rosenstein-Rodan and Nurkse who analysed the problem of growth in terms of vicious circles of poverty. While diagnosing the problem on the demand side, they advocated largely supply-based prescriptions like the big push or balanced growth over a wide front. In fact, they (particularly Nurkse) regarded investment as "good" and consumption as "bad", for which they were taken to task by Lauchlin Currie. In Chapter 8, Krugman and other new trade theorists are taken up who regard increasing returns (or economies of scale) as the source of trade but forget that Adam Smith had regarded the reverse relationship of increasing returns (or the division of labour) as the outcome of trade as more important. Thus, increasing returns can be regarded at least as much an effect of trade as its cause. Chapter 9 discusses modern endogenous growth theory as pioneered by Paul Romer and Robert Lucas, among others. While the neoclassical growth accounting exercises by Abramovitz and Solow left technical progress as unexplained, the modern growth theorists endogenize technical change within the same neoclassical aggregate production function framework by introducing new inputs such as new knowledge and human capital. Chapter 10 concludes the book and summarizes the policy implications of the various approaches of endogenous growth taken up in this book.

References

Abramovitz, Moses. 1956. Resources and output trends in the United States since 1870. *American Economic Review, Papers and Proceedings* 46 (May): 5–23.

Aghion, Philippe, and Peter Howitt. 1998. *Endogenous Growth Theory*. Cambridge: MIT Press.

Andersen, Esben Sloth. 2011. *Joseph A. Schumpeter: A Theory of Social and Economic Evolution*. Basingstoke: Palgrave Macmillan.

Barro, Robert J., and Xavier Sala-i-Martin. 2004. *Economic Growth*, 2nd ed. Cambridge: MIT Press.

Chandra, Ramesh. 2006. Currie's 'leading sector' strategy of growth: An appraisal. *Journal of Development Studies* 42 (3): 490–508.

Chandra, Ramesh. 2019. Nicholas Kaldor on Adam Smith and Allyn Young. *Review of Political Economy* 31 (3): 445–463.

Chandra, Ramesh. 2020. *Allyn Abbott Young*. Cham: Palgrave Macmillan.

Chandra, Ramesh, and Roger J. Sandilands. 2021. Nicholas Kaldor, increasing returns and Verdoorn's law. *Journal of Post Keynesian Economics* 44 (2): 315–339.

Clemence, Richard V., ed. 1951. *Essays of J. A. Schumpeter*. Cambridge: Addison-Wesley Press.

Currie, Lauchlin. 1974. The leading sector model of growth in developing countries. *Journal of Economic Studies* 1 (1): 1–16.

Elliot, John E. 1983 (2017). Introduction to the transactions edition. In *The Theory of Economic Development*, ed. Joseph Schumpeter. London and New York: Routledge.

Fine, Ben. 2000. Endogenous growth theory: A critical assessment. *Cambridge Journal of Economics* 24 (2): 245–265.

Hawtrey, Ralph G. 1919. *Currency and Credit*, 1st ed. London: Longmans, Green and Co.

Hawtrey, Ralph G. 1923. *Currency and Credit*, 2nd ed. London: Longmans, Green and Co.

Helpman, Elhanan, and Paul Krugman. 1985. *Market Structure and Foreign Trade*. Cambridge: MIT Press.

Helpman, Elhanan, and Paul Krugman. 1989. *Trade Policy and Market Structure*. Cambridge: MIT Press.

Hirschman, Albert O. 1958. *The Strategy of Economic Development*. New Haven: Yale University Press.
Kaldor, Nicholas. 1972. The irrelevance of equilibrium economics. *Economic Journal* 82: 1237–1255.
Keynes, John M. 1936 (1964). *The General Theory of Employment, Interest and Money*. London: Macmillan.
Krugman, Paul. 1979. Increasing returns, monopolistic competition, and international trade. *Journal of International Economics* 9 (November): 469–479.
Krugman, Paul. 1980. Scale economies, product differentiation, and the pattern of trade. *American Economic Review* 70: 950–959.
Krugman, Paul. 1981. Intraindustry specialization and gains from trade. *Journal of Political Economy* 89: 959–973.
Krugman, Paul. 1990. *Rethinking International Trade*. Cambridge: MIT Press.
Krugman, Paul. 1993. Towards a counter-counterrevolution in development theory. *Proceedings of the World Bank Annual Conference on Development Economics 1992*, 15–38. Washington, DC: World Bank.
Langlois, R.N. 2001. The vanishing hand: The modular revolution in American business. DRUID Working Paper. http://www.business.auc.dk/druid.
Lucas, R.E. 1988. On the mechanics of economic development. *Journal of Monetary Economics* 22 (1): 3–42.
Marshall, Alfred. 1890 (1920). *Principles of Economics*, 8th ed. London: Macmillan.
Mehrling, Perry G., and Roger J. Sandilands. 1999. *Money and Growth: Selected Papers of Allyn Abbott Young*. London and New York: Routledge.
Moura, Mário Graça. 2018. Joseph Schumpeter. In *Great Economic Thinkers: From Adam Smith to Amartya Sen*, ed. Jonathan Conlin. New Delhi: Speaking Tiger.
Murphy, K.M., A. Schleifer, and R. Vishny. 1989. Industrialization and the big push. *Journal of Political Economy* 97 (5): 1003–1026.
Nurkse, Ragnar. 1953. *Problems of Capital Formation in Underdeveloped Countries*. Oxford: Basil Blackwell.
Nurkse, Ragnar. 1962. *Patterns of Trade and Development (Wicksell Lectures 1959)*. Oxford: Basil Blackwell.
Pressman, Steven. 1999. *Fifty Major Economists*. London and New York: Routledge.
Raffaelli, Tiziano. 2003. *Marshall's Evolutionary Economics*. London and New York: Routledge.
Robbins, Lionel. 1928. The representative firm. *Economic Journal* 38: 387–404.
Romer, Paul M. 1986. Increasing returns and long-run growth. *Journal of Political Economy* 94: 1002–1038.
Romer, Paul M. 1987. Growth based on increasing returns due to specialization. *American Economic Review* 77 (2): 56–62.

Romer, Paul M. 1989. Capital accumulation in the theory of long-run growth. In *Modern Business Cycle Theory*, ed. Robert J. Barro. Cambridge: Harvard University Press.
Romer, Paul M. 1990. Endogenous technological change. *Journal of Political Economy* 98 (5): S71–S102.
Romer, Paul M. 1994. The origins of endogenous growth. *Journal of Economic Perspectives* 8 (1): 3–22.
Rosenberg, Nathan. 2000. *Schumpeter and the Endogeneity of Technology*. London and New York: Routledge.
Rosenstein-Rodan, Paul. 1943. Problems of industrialization in eastern and south-eastern Europe. *Economic Journal* 53 (June–September): 202–211.
Rosenstein-Rodan, Paul. 1961. Notes on the theory of 'big push.' In *Economic Development of Latin America*, ed. H.S. Ellis and H.C. Wallich, 57–67. London: Macmillan.
Schumpeter, Joseph A. 1927. The explanation of the business cycle. *Economica*, December, 286–311. Reprinted in Clemence (1951, pp. 21–46).
Schumpeter, Joseph A. 1928 (1951). The instability of capitalism. *Economic Journal* 38: 361–386. Reprinted in Clemence (1951, pp. 47–72).
Schumpeter, Joseph A. 1934 (2017). *The Theory of Economic Development*, English trans. Redvers Opie. London and New York: Routledge.
Schumpeter, Joseph A. 1942. *Capitalism, Socialism and Democracy*. New York: Harper and Brothers.
Schumpeter, Joseph A. 1954 (1986). *History of Economic Analysis*, London: Allen and Unwin.
Shaw, G.K. 1992. Policy implications of endogenous growth theory. *Economic Journal* 102 (412): 611–621. Reprinted in Snowdon and Vane (1997, pp. 616–627).
Smith, Adam. 1776 (1976). *An Enquiry Into the Nature and Causes of the Wealth of Nations*, ed. Edwin Cannan. Chicago: University of Chicago Press.
Snowdon, Brian, and Howard R. Vane. 1997. *A Macroeconomics Reader*. London and New York: Routledge.
Solow, Robert M. 1956. A contribution to the theory of economic growth. *Quarterly Journal of Economics* 70 (February): 65–94.
Solow, Robert M. 1957. Technical change and aggregate production function. *Review of Economics and Statistics* 39 (August): 311–320.
Sraffa, Piero. 1926. The laws of return under competitive conditions. *Economic Journal* 6: 535–550.
Warsh, David. 2006. *Knowledge and the Wealth of Nations: A Story of Economic Discovery*. New York and London: W. W. Norton.
Young, Allyn A. 1928. Increasing returns and economic progress. *Economic Journal* 38 (152): 527–542.

Young, Allyn A. 1929. Big business: How the economic system grows and evolves like a living organism. In *The Book of Popular Science*, 5387–5394. New York: The Grolier Society. Reprinted in Mehrling and Sandilands (1999, pp. 411–420).
Young, Allyn A. 1990. Nicholas Kaldor's Notes on Allyn Young's LSE Lectures 1927–29. *Journal of Economic Studies* 17 (3/4): 18–114.

CHAPTER 2

Adam Smith and Economic Progress

In "Introduction and Plan of the Work" of the *Wealth of Nations*, Smith (1776) points out that a nation's annual supply of "necessaries and conveniences" of life is regulated by two factors: "first by the skill, dexterity, and judgment with which its labour is applied; and, secondly, by the proportion between the number of those who are employed in useful labour, and those who are not so employed" (ibid., I, p. 1). Further: "The abundance or scantiness of this supply too seems to depend more upon the former of those two circumstances than upon the latter" (ibid., I, pp. 1–2). A nation of hunters, where almost everyone is employed in useful labour, still suffers from want, disease, and poverty. In the civilized nation, on the contrary, a great number of people do not labour at all, yet it is abundantly supplied with all the conveniences and necessaries of life, so much so that even the poorest worker is able to enjoy a standard of life higher than a savage king.

Thus Smith places the theme of the division of labour right upfront in his book. His main concern, as the title of his book rightly suggests, is with the "wealth of nations" and economic progress rather than with the equilibrium notions of value and distribution. Yet, some influential authors such as Marshall (1890), Robbins (1932), Stigler (1976), Buchanan and Yoon (2000), Arrow and Hahn (1971), and Hahn (1981), to name a few, have argued that Smith's chief concern in the *Wealth of*

R. Chandra, *Endogenous Growth in Historical Perspective*, Palgrave Studies in Economic History,
https://doi.org/10.1007/978-3-030-83761-7_2

Nations is his equilibrium theory (or value and distribution). It is true that Smith has been subjected to varying interpretations over the years depending on the nature of the prevailing paradigm as well as the mood of the times. The problem also arises because the *Wealth of Nations* contains a wealth of ideas and doctrines, and successive generations have been able to find something in it which supports their own theories (Viner 1927).

This chapter takes the position that Smith's main contribution in the *Wealth of Nations* has to be understood in terms of his growth theory. It is true that Smith made many pronouncements which may resemble equilibrium economics in some loose sense. For example, he stated that the market price of a commodity has a tendency to gravitate towards its natural price in the long run. To take another example, the rate of profit tends towards equality in different employments. But Smith talked of them as tendencies and not as definite end results.[1] Smith's analysis of the division of labour, his analysis of the motive power of self-interest, the role of saving, investment and capital accumulation in growth, institutions best suited to promote growth, and his evolutionary perspective, all point to the fact that he was attempting a dynamic rather than a static analysis. We, therefore, start with Smith's growth theory in terms of these dynamic elements.[2]

Division of Labour

The division of labour is central to Smith's explanation of growth. Smith stated that the division of labour arises in the process of exchange and therefore becomes limited by the power which gives rise to it. In other words, the division of labour is limited by the size of the market. Exchange, in turn, arises because of the propensity in human beings to truck, barter, and exchange, which is found in humans and not in animals.

[1] Thorstein Veblen (1898) criticized the classical authors for studying economics in terms of tendencies towards static equilibrium and not in an evolutionary sense. But the classical authors did not present these tendencies as definite end results since they believed in a process view of competition. Mill (1844) talked of disturbing causes which implied that economic laws and generalizations had to be stated with due qualifications and allowances. Henry Sidgwick (1887) later commended Mill's approach of stating the classical doctrines in a guarded fashion.

[2] See Chandra (2004a) for an account of the institutional basis of the division of labour and Chandra (2004b) for the critical assessment of the view that Smith was an equilibrium theorist.

The full potential of the division of labour can be realized in an exchange economy. In a rude state of society or in a society of hunters, since the total exchange is quite limited, the division of labour also becomes circumscribed. On the other hand, in a commercial society in which Smith lived, the total exchange is quite large, so the division of labour is also extensive. The larger the market, the larger is the division of labour.

By division of labour, Smith largely meant specialization of jobs within a firm or the development of various arts and crafts in an economy as and when the opportunities for doing so arise. To explain the process, Smith gave an example of a pin factory. If each man performs all the tasks of pin-making, the total output as well as output per man (or productivity) would be limited. On the other hand, if each man specializes in a particular task, there is a dramatic increase in both total output as well as productivity.

For Smith the division of labour was not limited to manufacturing establishments (i.e., factories). There was a broader process of the social division of labour at work. For example, to manufacture even a simple product such as a woollen coat, a large number of arts and crafts had to join hands. "The shepherd, the sorter of the wool, the wool-comber or the carder, the dyer, the scribbler, the spinner, the weaver, the fuller, the dresser, with many others, must all join their different arts in order to complete even this homely production" (Smith 1776, I, p. 15). The development of these arts and crafts again depends on the market size (or the total exchange nexus).

Smith gives another example to illustrate his point. In the vicinity of a big city while many trades thrive, in remote countryside it is difficult to find any for miles. As Smith says: "In the lone houses and very small villages which are scattered about in so desert a country as the Highlands of Scotland, every farmer must be butcher, baker and brewer for his own family. In such situations we can scarce expect to find even a smith, a carpenter, or a mason, within less than twenty miles of another of the same trade" (ibid., I, p. 21).

Smith wanted man to live with dignity and make a living by working with his own hands. This can only happen if each man specializes in some trade and exchanges his surplus produce with the surplus produce of others. "Nobody but a beggar chuses to depend chiefly upon the benevolence of his fellow-citizens. Even a beggar does not depend on it entirely" (ibid., p. 18). So, self-interest is ultimately about self-respect and dignity. To live a dignified life, man has no alternative but to pursue the path of self-interest at least in his market dealings: "It is not from the benevolence of the butcher, the brewer, or the baker, that we expect our dinner, but from their regard to their own interest" (ibid., I, p. 18).[3]

The increase in the productivity arising from the division of labour, as Smith points out, is due to three circumstances: "first to the increase of dexterity in every particular workman; secondly, to the saving of the time which is commonly lost in passing from one species of work to another; and lastly, to the invention of a great number of machines which facilitate and abridge labour, and enable one man to do the work of many" (ibid., I, p. 11).[4]

Smith states that most improvements in machinery are inventions of workmen who had the occasion to use them. Each one involved in some simple operation turned his thoughts to find out easier and simpler ways of doing it. Smith then gives the example of a boy who brought about the greatest improvement in a machine because he wanted to divert himself to play with other companions. He had been employed to open and shut alternatively the communication between the boiler and the cylinder. He discovered that this could easily be done by tying a string between the valve and another part of the machine. Thus a great invention came about because of a boy who wanted to save his own labour.

Not all improvements are made by workmen. Some are made by men of philosophy and speculation:

> Many improvements have been made by the ingenuity of the makers of machines, when to make them became the business of a peculiar trade; and some by those who are called philosophers or men of speculation, whose trade it is not to do any thing, but to observe every thing; and who, upon that account, are often capable of combining together the powers of the most distant and dissimilar objects. In the progress of society, philosophy and speculation becomes, like every other employment, the principal or the sole trade and occupation of a particular class of citizens. (ibid., I, p. 14)

[3] Smith did not regard man as a "rational economic man" in the sense of utility (or profit) maximiser. The details of his broad approach to self-interest, which is based on a desire to better one's condition, is taken up below in the next section.

[4] Increase in skills of workers is akin to "learning by doing" which, in turn, is linked with the growth of employment opportunities resulting from capital accumulation, as noted by Eltis (1975, p. 427).

Smith stated that as the size of the market expands, different trades get subdivided, for example, different types of smiths or carpenters come into being. Likewise, speculation and philosophy also get subdivided which, in turn, improves dexterity and saves time. "Each individual becomes more expert in his own peculiar branch, more work is done on the whole, and the quantity of science is considerably increased by it" (ibid., I, p. 14).

In Smith's wages-fund theory, greater stock leads to higher employment. Greater employment, in turn, promotes the division of labour in two ways: first, by greater subdivision and distribution of tasks, and second, by encouraging the invention of better machinery. As Smith (ibid., I, pp. 96–97) says:

> The owner of the stock which employs a great number of labourers, necessarily endeavours, for his own advantage, to make such a proper division and distribution of employment, that they may be enabled to produce the greatest quantity of work possible. For the same reason, he endeavours to supply them with the best machinery which either he or they can think of. What takes place among the labourers in a particular workhouse, takes place, for the same reason, among those of a great society. The greater their number, the more they naturally divide themselves into different classes and subdivisions of employment. More heads are occupied in inventing the most proper machinery for executing the work of each, and it is, therefore, more likely to be invented.

Smith was of the view that the division of labour is better carried out in manufacturing than in agriculture. As he (ibid., I, pp. 7–8) explains:

> The nature of agriculture, indeed, does not admit of so many subdivisions of labour, nor of so complete a separation of one business from another, as manufactures. It is impossible to separate so entirely, the business of the grazier from that of the corn-farmer, as the trade of carpenter is commonly separated from that of the smith. The spinner is almost always a distinct person from the weaver; but the ploughman, the harrower, the sower of the seed, and the reaper of the corn, are often the same. The occasions for those different sorts of labour returning with the different seasons of the year, it is impossible that one man should constantly be employed in any one of them.

Smith stated that the impossibility of separating different kinds of labour in agriculture was responsible for it lagging behind in productivity in comparison with manufacturing. He also observed that most opulent nations excelled their neighbours in agriculture as well as manufacturing but their superiority in the latter was more than in the former. Comparing England with France and Poland, Smith further observed that there was not much variation in the price of corn (of the same quality) in the three countries. But manufactured goods like hardware and coarse woollens were cheaper and better in England than in France. In Poland there were hardly any manufactures of any kind except coarser household manufactures.

Smith's theory of international trade is also based on the concept of the division of labour.[5] International trade widens the market available to a nation and promotes the division of labour. It gives vent to surplus produce of a country and enables a country's superfluities to be exchanged for something valuable. The principal benefit of foreign trade is not gold and silver but the enhancement of the productive powers of a country through the process of the division of labour. A country produces those products in which its absolute costs are the lowest and exchanges its surplus produce with the surplus produce of other countries.[6] International trade is not only good for the consumer in terms of lower price and better quality of products, but also good for the country in terms of the most productive deployment of its capital. Any country which regulates its trade through tariffs and other import restrictions misdirects its capital from more productive employments to less. Thus in Smith, international trade and domestic growth can be viewed as two sides of the same coin as both are based on the concept of the division of labour. As Hla Myint (1977, p. 231) observes: "Smith's theory of foreign trade is so closely

[5] Buchanan and Yoon (2000, p. 43) argue that Ricardian explanation of trade in static terms (i.e., in terms of comparative advantage) led to Smith's insights regarding growth and international trade, and their link with increasing returns, being almost forgotten. "To Smith, mutually beneficial exchange emerges because of specialization, which, in its turn, implies the presence of increasing returns to the size of the exchange nexus. In the Ricardian logic, by contrast, trade presumably emerges because productive resources differ in their ability to create economic value... Comparative advantage ensures mutuality of gain. But, in this explanation, there is no direct linkage between the size of the exchange network and the degree of specialization that is viable. There is no need to introduce increasing returns. Comparative advantage may be present even if there are constant returns to scale, both for the economy and for its separate productive sectors".

[6] Smith's theory of international trade is also termed as "vent for surplus" theory.

intervowen with his theory of domestic economic development that the two have to be considered together".

Capital Accumulation

The role of self-interest is central in the Smithian marketplace. Self-interest, which prompts an individual to specialize in a trade and exchange his surplus produce with those of others, also prompts him to save. Man has an inborn desire to save to better his condition.[7] So self-interest in Smith takes the form of bettering one's condition rather than some hedonistic (or utilitarian) principle such as utility maximization or profit maximization. Moreover, man does not pursue his self-interest in a single-minded way; it is confined to only those aspects of his behaviour which involve market exchange.[8] Smith (1776, I, pp. 62–63) writes:

> [T]he principle which prompts to save, is the desire for bettering our condition, a desire which, though calm and dispassionate, comes with us from the womb, and never leaves us till we go into the grave. In the whole interval which separates those two moments, there is scarce perhaps a single instant in which any man is so perfectly satisfied with his situation, as to be without any wish of alteration or improvement of any kind. An augmentation of fortune is the means by which the greater part of men propose and wish to better their condition. It is the means the most vulgar and the most obvious; and the most likely way of augmenting their fortune, is to save and accumulate some part of what they acquire, either regularly and annually, or upon some extraordinary occasions.

This leads us to the theory of capital accumulation, for "Capitals are increased by parsimony, and diminished by prodigality and misconduct" (ibid., I, p. 358). Smith stated that it is parsimony, and not industry, which is the immediate cause of the increase in capital. "Industry, indeed,

[7] Smith believed that the desire to better one's condition does not arise to meet bodily needs which even an ordinary worker is able to satisfy. This desire in man arises to gain approval, admiration, and respect from his fellow men; by becoming economically successful he is able to rise in society.

[8] As Coase (1994, p. 116) points out: "It is wrong to believe as is commonly done, that Adam Smith had as his view of man an abstraction, an 'economic man', rationally pursuing his self-interest in a single minded way. Smith would not have thought it sensible to treat man as rational utility maximiser".

provides the subject which parsimony accumulates. But whatever industry might acquire, if parsimony did not save and store up, the capital would never be the greater" (ibid., I, p. 359).

Smith maintained that what is annually saved is as regularly consumed as what is annually spent. This happens nearly in the same time but by different sets of people. A rich man may spend his revenue on menial servants or idle guests leaving nothing behind in return for their consumption. A frugal man, on the other hand, uses his saving to employ not only productive hands for the current year, but as an owner of a public workhouse, establishes a perpetual fund to employ them in all future years. Therefore, "every prodigal appears to be a public enemy, and every frugal man a public benefactor" (ibid., I, p. 62).

In Smith, capital accumulation serves two purposes: it helps employ more productive labourers, and it helps equip them with better machines and instruments. In both cases, it promotes the division of labour. Smith also draws a strong association between total capital and total produce of a country. Over two periods of time, if the total produce of a country has increased we can be sure that its capital has also increased. Smith further states that "the accumulation of stock must, in the nature of things, be previous to the division of labour" (ibid., I, p. 291). But this does not imply that capital accumulation is an independent engine of growth. Capital is important because of its link with the division of labour. Since the division of labour is limited by the size of the market, the use of capital in production also becomes limited. Moreover, Smith did not say that saving and investment rates should be increased through government interference or by subverting the market.

Smith also made a distinction between productive and unproductive labour. He stated: "There is one sort of labour which adds the value of the subject upon which it is bestowed: there is another which has no such effect. The former which produces a value, may be called productive; the latter, unproductive labour" (ibid., I, p. 351).[9] The labour employed in manufacturing or agriculture adds value to the materials which are worked

[9] Physiocrats regarded agriculture to be the only productive sector and manufacturing as sterile. They thought that manufacturing only transformed the materials used as inputs without adding any value. Smith, though much influenced by physiocrats, regarded both agriculture and manufacturing to be productive. But he did state that in agriculture nature worked with man implying that in manufacturing it did not. His attitude towards rent as a "bounty of nature" also reflected a similar bias.

upon, and therefore can be regarded as productive; the labour of a menial servant, on the other hand, adds nothing to value, nor does it produce any vendible commodity, and is therefore unproductive. The services of a menial servant generally perish in the very act of their performance, and nothing of value is left behind.

That part of the total produce which replaces capital employs only productive hands. Part of the produce which constitutes rent and profit is called revenue, and unproductive hands (or those who do not labour at all) are maintained by this fund. In rich countries there is a greater proportion of funds for replacing capital; in poor countries a greater proportion consists of revenue. It is this proportion which determines the character of its people in terms of industry or idleness. Smith writes: "The proportion between capital and revenue, therefore, seems every-where to regulate the proportion between industry and idleness. Wherever capital predominates, industry prevails; wherever revenue, idleness. Every increase or diminution of capital, therefore naturally tends to increase or diminish the real quantity of industry, the number of productive hands, and consequently the exchangeable value of the annual produce of the land and labour of the country, the real wealth and revenue of all its inhabitants" (ibid., I, p. 358).

Smith observed that generally the misconduct of some private individuals was more than counterbalanced by the good conduct of others, particularly in a society where the annual produce has grown over time. While the principle of private frugality generally predominated, the same could not be said for public frugality. "Great nations are never impoverished by private, though they sometimes are by public prodigality and misconduct" (ibid., I, p. 363). Smith regarded sovereigns as unproductive spenders par excellence, who maintained splendid courts, great ecclesiastical establishments, and great fleets and armies, and advised them to look after their own economy rather than watching over the economy of the private people. While the frugality and good conduct of private people had taken England to opulence and improvement, the conduct of the rulers had the potential to ruin the countries they ruled:

> England, however, as it has never been blessed with a very parsimonious government, so parsimony has at no time been the characteristical virtue of its inhabitants. It is the highest impertinence and presumption, therefore, in kings and ministers, to pretend to watch over the economy of the private people, and to restrain their expence, either by sumptuary laws, or

> by prohibiting the importation of foreign luxuries. They are themselves always, and without any exception, the greatest spendthrifts in society. Let them look well after their own expence, and they may safely trust private people with theirs. If their own extravagance does not ruin the state, that of their subjects never will". (ibid., I, p. 367)

Smith also stated that if left free to find its own natural employments, a society's capital augments faster than when the government intervenes. The total industry of a country can never be out of proportion to its total capital, so any artificial direction to economic activity through regulations of commerce will make things worse. As Smith (ibid., I, p. 479) writes:

> The industry of a society can augment only in proportion as its capital augments, and its capital can augment only in proportion to what can be gradually saved out of its revenue. But the immediate effect of every such regulation is to diminish its revenue, and what diminishes its revenue is certainly not very likely to augment its capital faster than it would have augmented of its own accord, had both capital and industry been left to find out their natural employments.

Finally, self-interest, which prompts man to better his condition, to save and accumulate, also leads to the promotion of public welfare. Through specialization and exchange man is able to consume a great variety of goods which otherwise he will not be able to consume. In other words, the pursuit of self-interest leads to social cooperation through specialization and market exchange. The pursuit of self-interest also ensures growth, and brings prosperity and wealth to the society as a whole. "The natural effort of every individual to better his own condition, when suffered to exert itself with freedom and security, is so powerful a principle, that it alone, and without any assistance, not only capable of carrying on the society to wealth and prosperity, but of surmounting a hundred impertinent obstructions with which the folly of human laws too often incumbers its operations…" (ibid., II, p. 49–50).

But Smith did not favour unbridled pursuit of self-interest. He thought that businessmen suffered from monopoly spirit and therefore should be made to compete with each other. Domestic monopolies could be checked not only by more internal competition but also by subjecting them to international competition. He also thought that given a chance businessmen always conspired to subvert the public interest by raising prices.[10] So any proposal coming from this class should be examined with the greatest scepticism before being adopted as this class was too aware of its own interest.[11] While in the *Wealth of Nations* self-interest of man is kept in check by competition, in the *Theory of Moral Sentiments*, it is kept in check by the opposed motive of sympathy.

Institutional Arrangements

Smith devoted much energy and space in the *Wealth of Nations* for anlaysing and evaluating various systems of political economy from the point of view of growth.[12] According to Smith, institutional arrangements have to ensure two things. First, they have to provide liberty to each individual to pursue his own interest in his own way subject only to the laws

[10] "People of the same trade seldom meet together, even for merriment and diversion, but the conversation ends in a conspiracy against the public, or in some contrivance to raise prices" (Smith 1776, I, p. 144).

[11] "The proposal of any new law or regulation of commerce which comes from this order, ought always to be listened to with great precaution, and ought never to be adopted till after having been long and carefully examined, not only with the most scrupulous, but most suspicious attention. It comes from the order of men, whose interest is never exactly the same as the public, and who have generally an interest to deceive and even to oppress the public, and who accordingly have, upon many occasions, both deceived and oppressed it" (ibid., I, p. 278).

[12] Nathan Rosenberg (1960, p. 557) lamented that, as a result of increasing formalization of economics as a discipline, the institutional content and preoccupations of Adam Smith's *Wealth of Nations* had suffered a prolonged neglect. The widely held view that, if each individual is allowed to conduct his own affairs his own way it leads to a most rapid increase in the wealth of a nation, is not so much wrong as uninteresting. "By jumping directly from the conception of a man as a rational creature to the policy recommendation of laissez faire and all that, it completely short-circuits much of the substance of Smith's work. By visualizing the human agent as engaged in the effort to maximize a single, unambiguous magnitude, two aspects of Smith's book and the crucial importance of the interplay between them are ignored: (1) his much more elaborate conception of the *conflicting* forces which impel the human agent to action and, as a direct result, (2) his sustained enquiry into the ultimate impact, in terms of human action and its welfare consequences, of different kinds of institutional arrangements" (ibid., p. 557). Adolph Lowe (1975) also emphasizes the importance of institutions in the formation of which human choices play an important role: "Inexorable as the process of growth, the political and social conditions from which alone it can take off and by which it is sustained are not by themselves preordained. They are the product of history, but of history in which human choices in the form of political decisions play a decisive role" (ibid., p. 423).

of justice. Second, they have to provide a secure climate for the accumulation of private property. Once these are provided then the natural effort of each individual to better his condition is capable of taking not only him but the whole society to wealth and riches. Smith's conclusion was that the system of natural liberty, which ensured both liberty as well as security, was the best for growth.

The total industry of a country can never be out of proportion to its total capital. Thus, Smith (ibid., II, p. 208) argued that all systems based on preferences or restraints retarded the progress of society. "[E]very system which endeavours, either, by extraordinary encouragements, to draw towards a particular species of industry a greater share of the capital of the society than that would naturally go it; or, by extraordinary restraints, to force from a particular species of industry some share of the capital which would otherwise be employed in it; is in reality subversive of the great purpose which it means to promote. It retards, instead of accelerating, the progress of society towards real wealth and greatness; and diminishes, instead of increasing, the real value of the annual produce of its labour".

Smith regarded the system of slave labour to be very expensive. Ancient Greece and Rome, while emphasizing agriculture, tended to discourage manufactures and foreign trade. Employments of artificers and manufacturers were considered to make the human body unsuitable for rigours of war. Such occupations were considered fit only for slaves, who worked there for the benefit of their masters. The wealth, power, and protection of the rich made it almost impossible for the poor ranks of society to offer their labour as freemen while competing with the slaves of the rich. The slaves, apart from being expensive, also tended to be uninventive:

> Slaves, however, are very seldom inventive; and all the most important improvements, either in machinery, or in the arrangement and distribution of work, which facilitate and abridge labour, have been the discoveries of freemen. Should a slave propose any improvement of this kind, his master would be very apt to consider the proposal as the suggestion of laziness, and of a desire to save his own labour at the master's expence. The poor slave, instead of reward, would probably meet with much abuse, perhaps with some punishment. In the manufactures carried on by slaves, therefore, more labour must generally have been employed to execute the same quantity of work, than in those carried on by freemen. The work of the

> former must, upon that account, generally have been dearer than that of the latter. (ibid., II, p. 205)[13]

Finer products such as silk, which were generally very expensive in European countries such as Greece and Rome, were brought in from distant lands such as the East Indies. Fine linen was a European product but still tended to be extravagant because of the costly slave labour used. The same was the case for fine woollens, although the price was not as extravagant as linen. Comparing the use of slave labour in Turkish mines with free labour in Hungarian mines, Smith remarked that while the Hungarian mines made use of machinery to facilitate and abridge labour, Turkish mines only relied on the manual work of their slaves to work their mines.

In analysing the agricultural systems, Smith points out that the trade between the country and the townsmen consists of rude produce in exchange for manufactured produce. Whatever raises the price of manufactured produce tends to lower that of rude produce of land. This tends to discourage agriculture as it is sought to be promoted by restraining manufactures and foreign trade. Such systems, although meaning to promote agriculture, end up turning the internal terms of trade against agriculture. As Smith (ibid., II, pp. 207–8) writes:

> Those systems, therefore, which preferring agriculture to all other employments, in order to promote it, impose restraints upon manufactures and foreign trade, act contrary to the very end which they propose, and indirectly discourage the very species of industry which they mean to promote. They are so far, perhaps, more inconsistent than even the mercantile system. That system, by encouraging manufactures and foreign trade more than agriculture, turns a certain portion of the capital of society from supporting a more advantageous, to support a less advantageous species of industry. But still it really in the end encourages that species of industry which it means to promote. Those agricultural systems, on the contrary, really and in the end discourage their own favourite species of industry.

[13] At another place Smith (ibid., I, pp. 411–12) writes: "The experience of all ages and nations, I believe, demonstrates that the work done by slaves, though it appears to cost only their maintenance, is in the end dearest of any. A person who can acquire no property, can have no other interest but to eat as much, and to labour as little as possible. Whatever work he does beyond what is sufficient to purchase his own maintenance, can be squeezed out of him by violence only, and not by any interest of his own".

This brings us to the so-called mercantile system. Smith stated that the two principles of the mercantile system were: (1) wealth consisted of precious metals like gold and silver, and (2) the stock of precious metals could be enlarged through exporting more value than importing (ibid., I, p. 472).[14] Thus, the two engines of enriching a country were putting restraints on imports and giving encouragements to exports. The export of precious metals was discouraged as it amounted to drain of wealth. At the same time, consumption of luxuries was generally discouraged as they were thought to be largely imported. In the foreign trade sector, trading companies were granted monopolies and exclusive rights to trade in colonies. This system was based on a network of restrictions, patronage, and favouritism which was debilitating to growth.

In this system the interest of the producer predominated that of the consumer. The system considered production, and not consumption, as the ultimate objective:

> Consumption is the sole end and purpose of all production; and the interest of the producer ought to be attended to, only so far as it may be necessary for promoting that of the consumer. The maxim is so perfectly self-evident, that it would be absurd to attempt to prove it. But in the mercantile system, the interest of the consumer is almost constantly sacrificed to that of the producer; and it seems to consider production, and not consumption, as the ultimate end of all industry and commerce.
>
> In the restraints upon the importation of all foreign commodities which can come into competition with those of our own growth, or manufacture, the interest of the home-consumer is evidently sacrificed to that of the producer. It is altogether for the benefit of the latter, that the former is obliged to pay that enhancement of price which this monopoly almost always occasions.
>
> It is altogether to the benefit of the producer that bounties are granted upon the exportation of some of his productions. The home consumer is obliged to pay, first, the tax which is necessary for paying the bounty, and secondly, a still greater tax which necessarily arises from the enhancement of the price of the commodity in the home market. (ibid., II, p. 179)

[14] The balance of trade doctrine to enrich a country was advocated by an early mercantilist Thomas Mun (1664). According to Smith, nothing could be more absurd than this doctrine on which almost all regulations of commerce were founded.

Smith pointed out that the principal benefit of foreign trade was not the importation of gold and silver. A country without gold and silver mines is justified in importing them through foreign commerce but it constitutes an insignificant part. Two distinct benefits of foreign trade were (1) it enables the surplus produce of a country to be exchanged for something more valuable, i.e., gives value to its superfluities, and (2) by overcoming the narrowness of the domestic market it promotes the division of labour to the highest perfection (ibid., I, p. 469). It was not by cheapening of gold and silver that the discovery of America had enriched Europe but by opening up a new market which improved the productive powers of labour.

Smith, as we noted before, stated that the general industry of a country can never be out of proportion to its total capital (ibid., I, p. 475). Therefore any regulation of commerce is likely to divert a country's capital from more advantageous employments to less. As Smith (ibid., I, p. 475) points out: "No regulation of commerce can increase the quantity of industry in any society beyond what its capital can maintain. It can only divert a part of it into a direction into which it might not otherwise have gone; and it is by no means certain that this artificial direction is likely to be more advantageous to the society than that into which it would have gone of its own accord".

Further, each individual is the best judge of his own interest and therefore should be left free to pursue it. "Every individual is continually exerting himself to find out the most advantageous employment for whatever capital he can command. It is his own advantage, indeed, and not that of the society which he has in view. But the study of his own advantage naturally, or rather necessarily leads him to prefer that employment which is most advantageous to the society" (ibid., I, p. 475). This happens in two ways: first, he employs his capital as nearer home as possible so that it is constantly under his own "view and command". Secondly, an individual aims to produce the greatest possible value. In so doing the individual is led by an "invisible hand" to unintentionally promote the society's advantage. Further, the society is not worse off due to the lack of public mindedness of the self-seeking individuals. "I have never known much good done by those who affected to trade for the public good. It is an affectation, indeed, not very common among merchants, and very few words need be employed in dissuading them from it" (ibid., I, p. 478).

After analysing various systems of political economy based on restraints and preferences, Smith came to the conclusion that such systems retarded, instead of accelerating, the progress of society towards real wealth and greatness, and diminished, instead of increasing, the real value of its annual produce (ibid., II, p. 208). The "simple" system of natural liberty is the best from the point of view of growth. It naturally establishes itself on its own accord once all restraints and preferences are removed. Every man, provided he does not violate the laws of justice, is "perfectly free to pursue his own interest his own way" and bring his capital in competition with anyone else. The sovereign is completely discharged from the duty of superintending the industry of private people for the performance of which no human wisdom or knowledge can suffice. Outlining the role of the government in such a system Smith (ibid., II, pp. 208–9) writes:

> According to the system of natural liberty, the sovereign has only three duties to attend to; three duties of great importance, indeed, but plain and intelligible to common understandings: first, the duty of protecting the society from the violence and invasion of other independent societies; secondly, the duty of protecting, as far as possible, every member of the society from injustice or oppression of every other member of it, or the duty of establishing the exact administration of justice; and, thirdly, the duty of erecting and maintaining certain public works and certain public institutions, which it can never be for the interest of any individual, or small number of individuals, to erect and maintain; because the profit could never repay the expence to any individual or small number of individuals, though it may frequently do much more than repay it to a great society.

As the society evolves, accumulation of private property takes place, and the need to defend that property arises. In the society of hunters, there is hardly any private property, or at least none exceeding two or three days' labour, so there is no need felt for a civil magistrate or regular administration of justice. It is in the age of shepherds, when the inequality of fortune first begins to take place, a need arises for a civil government. "Civil government, so far as it is instituted for the security of property, is in reality instituted for the defence of the rich against the poor, or of those who have some property against those who have none at all" (ibid., II, p. 236).

The accumulation of private property reaches its culmination in the system of natural liberty, but a great inequality arises. "Wherever there is great property, there is great inequality. For one very rich man, there must be at least five hundred poor, and the affluence of the few supposes indigence of the many… It is only under the shelter of the civil magistrate that the owner of that valuable property, which is acquired by the labour of many years, or perhaps of many successive generations, can sleep a single night in security" (ibid., II, p. 231). The importance of security is clear from the fact that Smith regarded this, and not the bounty on corn, as the chief cause of Britain's prosperity. On the other hand, Spain and Portugal's relative poverty is accounted for by the fact that "Industry is there neither free nor secure" (ibid., II, pp. 49–50).

Despite the inequalities inherent in the system of natural liberty, Smith preferred this to any other system. First, it was the best from the point of view of growth. Second, the condition of the labouring poor is the best in a growing society where the real wages tend to rise. Third, this system ensured that even an ordinary worker enjoyed a standard of living higher than an African king.[15] Finally, although rents rose and profits fell with the progress of society, the stationary state was far away and profits were still positive. So Smith was optimistic that the system would promote "harmony of interests" instead of class conflict.

Theory of Evolution

The concept of equilibrium in Smith, although he did not use the term, is posed as a tendency and not as a definite end result. For example, Smith postulated that the market price of a commodity has a tendency to gravitate towards its natural price. He regarded the natural price as a "centre of repose" or the "central price" towards which all actual prices are tending.[16] Smith (1776, I, p. 65) wrote:

> The natural price…is, as it were, the central price, to which all commodities are continually gravitating. Different accidents may sometimes keep them suspended a good deal above it, and sometimes force them somewhat below it. But whatever may be the obstacles which hinder them

[15] Smith (ibid., I, p. 16) stated "that the accommodation of an European prince does not always so much exceed that of an industrious and frugal peasant, as the accommodation of the latter exceeds that of many an African king, the absolute master of the lives and liberties of ten thousand naked savages".

[16] See for example Milgate (1987, p. 105) who observes: "Equilibrium is, as Adam Smith might have put it (though he did not use the term), the centre of gravitation of the economic system – it is that configuration of values towards which all economic magnitudes are continually tending to conform".

> from settling in this center of repose and continuance, they are constantly tending towards it.

But the centre of gravity of an economic system has a tendency to shift in the long run.[17] Because of the productivity gains arising from the division of labour, the natural price of a commodity tends to fall. So an economic system can be seen as continuously adjusting to its shifting centre of gravity. Allyn Young (1928) used the term "moving equilibrium" to describe this phenomenon of endogenous change. In an evolutionary system endogenous change propels a system forward to its shifting centre of gravity, but the equilibrium outcome in a static sense is elusive.[18]

Smith had a process view of competition rather than a static view.[19] He viewed competition as a race in which the rules of the game and their enforcement cannot be left to the participants. A referee is required which can conduct the race in a free and fair manner. In the *Theory of Moral Sentiments*, he noted: "In a race for wealth, honours and preferments, [each participant] may run as hard as he can, and strain every nerve and muscle, in order to outstrip all his competitors. But if he should justle, or throw down any of them, the indulgence of the spectators is entirely at

[17] Smith (1776) observed that an increase in demand may raise prices in the short run, it never fails to lower them in the long run. "It encourages production, and thereby increase the competition of the producers, who, in order to undersell one another, have recourse to new divisions of labour and new improvements of art, which might never otherwise have been thought of" (ibid., II, pp. 271–72). Smith also stated that the natural effect of improvement was to lower gradually the price of almost all manufactures (ibid., I, p. 269).

[18] The neoclassical conception of equilibrium ignores (or displays ignorance of) Mill's "disturbing causes" and Young's (1928) "counterforces". The counterforces themselves may be so strong that the end result may not be equilibrium but disequilibrium. Even Marshall (1890) recognised this and placed his static analysis in an evolutionary framework which unfolds slowly.

[19] In Smith competition does not lead to Pareto optimality or some optimal end result. See, for example, Reid (1989) who points out that competition as a process needs to be distinguished from competition in terms of certain optimizing properties like all markets clear, prices are equated to marginal costs and factors of production are rewarded in line with their marginal productivity. See also Blaug (1999) who talks about competition as a "process of rivalry". He points out that it is this view of competition which the classical authors such as Smith, Marx, and Ricardo had in mind; it is only after Cournot's notion of perfect competition, an end-state conception, that competition went down a new road. Even then Marshall, as well as the Austrians, subscribed to the earlier classical view of competition.

an end. It is a violation of fair play, which they cannot admit of" (Smith 1759, p. 83).[20]

Young, who built on Smith, interpreted him as a champion of competition rather than a champion of laissez faire. But competition which produces a tendency towards "equilibrium", also brings about endogenous change. Now whether competition leads to equilibrium or cumulative change depends on the relative strength of both forces. Young stated that countertendencies are so powerful that an economic system is dominated by disequilibrium rather than equilibrium. Thus, change becomes progressive and propagates itself in a cumulative way.

Smith had an evolutionary perspective to society and viewed the system in a state of continuous dynamic motion. Unlike Marx, Smith thought that the system contained the seeds of its own growth. That is, growth is possible endogenously, by the very forces engendered within the system. For this to happen the system of natural liberty is the best where each individual unintentionally promotes public interest by pursuing his own interest through specialization and exchange. He was aware that with economic progress, the rate of profit has a tendency to fall, and a stationary state, where all growth and accumulation comes to a halt, was a possibility.[21] But for him a stationary state was far away as no European country, till Smith's time, had acquired its full complement of riches in accordance with its potential. The only exception was China, which had long become stationary before reaching its full potential, because its laws and institutions despised foreign commerce.[22]

[20] While some authors (e.g., Salter 1994) have suggested that Smith's notion of justice is confined to commutative justice in the sense of having one's body free from injury and liberty free from infringement in the tradition of natural law theories, others (e.g., Witzum 1997) argue that distributive justice cannot be divorced from Smith's conception of justice as "Smith does not have a theory of rights which can be easily distinguished from his general ethics" (ibid., p. 242).

[21] In Smith the tendency towards a falling rate of profit arises due to competition among capitalists and declining profitable opportunities as capitals increase. In contrast, Ricardo explained this tendency in terms of diminishing returns and land scarcity in agriculture. For Smith low profits were not a threat to growth as high profits not only destroyed parsimony of the business class but also signified a society going fastest to ruin. See also Winch (1997, pp. 396–97).

[22] "A country which neglects or despises foreign commerce, and which admits the vessels of foreign nations into one or two of its ports only, cannot transact the same quantity of business which it might do with different laws and institutions. In a country too, where, though the rich or the owners of large capital enjoy a good deal of security,

Again unlike Marx, Smith was aware that with economic progress, the share of profits declines and that of rents increases. So social conflict was a possibility, but he was not interested in developing a theory of class conflict or class struggle. He was confident that harmony of interests would prevail rather than any sharp social conflict. He was also confident that economic progress will benefit all classes. He was sympathetic to the cause of the poor and stated that real wages have a tendency to rise during periods of prosperity.[23] He also advocated education to the working classes to overcome the ill effects of the division of labour (or of repetitive tasks). He favoured publicly funded public health measures to eradicate offensive diseases like leprosy. He also advocated military training to inculcate martial spirit among the labouring classes. In his system of natural liberty owners of small as well as large capitals receive equal protection, and the system does not discriminate against small businesses.

In Smith the development process has been described in terms of different stages. There are elements of continuity from one stage to another but each stage also has its own distinct features. Change from one stage to another is both quantitative as well as qualitative. These different stages are hunting, pasturage, farming, and commercial society. Since the concept of private property first arises in the age of shepherds, so a civil government to protect private property is then needed. According to Raphael (1985), this historical picture is needed to explain the evolution of law and government.

The forward motion in an evolving society is given by the division of labour. As Richardson (1975, pp. 351–52) observes, it results from the fact that the division of labour has a two-way relationship with economic progress:

the poor or the owners of small capitals enjoy scarce any, but are liable, under the pretence of justice, to be pillaged and plundered at any time by the inferior mandarins, the quantity of stock employed in all the different branches of business transacted within it, can never be equal to what the nature and extent of that business might admit" (Smith 1776, I, pp. 106–7).

[23] "It deserves to be remarked, perhaps, that in the progressive state, while the society is advancing to the further acquisition, rather than when it has acquired the full complement of riches, that the condition of the laboring poor, of the greatest body of the people, seems to be the happiest. It is hard in the stationary, and miserable in the declining state. The progressive state is in reality the cheerful and the hearty state to all the different orders of the society. The stationary is dull; the declining melancholy" (ibid., I, pp. 90–91). Smith further stated that the liberal reward of labour, though results in an increase of population, also increases the industry of the people (ibid., I, p. 91).

> Perpetual motion results from the fact the division of labour is at once a cause and an effect of economic progress. In Chapter I [of the *Wealth of Nations*] we are told how the division of labour increases wealth and in Chapter III how a widening of the market, which increased wealth would bring about, enables the division of labour to be carried further forward... [W]hat we have here are the essentials of a theory of self sustaining growth, essentials that were to be more fully developed much later in Allyn Young's justly celebrated article entitled 'Increasing Returns and Economic Progress'.

Critical Assessment

We noted that Smith has been subjected to different interpretations. In this context four questions are briefly examined: (1) Was Smith an equilibrium theorist? (2) What is the relative role of capital accumulation vis-à-vis the division of labour in explaining growth? (3) Was he a laissez faire economist? (4) Does the motive of self-interest as portrayed in the *Wealth of Nations* conflict with the motive of sympathy in the *Theory of Moral Sentiments*?

Was Smith an Equilibrium Theorist?

Marshall (1890, p. 758) opined that Smith's main contribution was his value theory. "His highest claim to have made an epoch in thought is that he was the first to make a careful and scientific inquiry into the manner in which value measures human motive, on the one side measuring the desire of purchasers to obtain wealth, and on the other the efforts and sacrifices (or 'Real Cost of Production') undergone by its producers" (ibid., 758–59). Moreover: "[T]he best economic work which came after the *Wealth of Nations* is distinguished from that which went before, by a clearer insight into the balancing and weighting, by means of money, of the desire for the possession of a thing on the one hand, and on the other of all the various efforts and self-denials which directly and indirectly contribute towards making it. Important as had been the steps that others had taken in this direction, the advance made by [Smith] was so great that he really opened out this new point of view, and by so doing made an epoch" (ibid., p. 759).

Then came Schumpeter's (1954, p. 189) patronizing judgement on Smith: "The rudimentary equilibrium theory of Chapter 7, by far the best piece economic theory turned out by A. Smith, in fact points toward Say and, through the latter's work, to Walras. The purely theoretical developments of the nineteenth century consist to a considerable degree in improvements upon it". As against this view, Kaldor (1972) stated that economic theory went astray from the middle of Chapter 4 of the *Wealth of Nations*, the first three being devoted to the concept of the division of labour. However, as Winch (1997) notes, Schumpeter's judgement was more influential than that of Kaldor. "Thus began the business of assessing just how good a general equilibrium theorist Smith really was... Clearly, the underlying assumption is that the apparatus constructed upon the foundations laid by Walras and Pareto over the years provides the only language according to which Smith can be deemed to be speaking sense" (ibid., pp. 5–6).

According to Robbins (1932, p. 15), "Economics is the science which studies human behaviour as a relationship between ends and scarce means which have alternative uses". From this viewpoint, Smith's main contribution to economic theory is seen as value and distribution despite what the title of Smith's book *Wealth of Nations* suggests:

> Although Adam Smith's great work professed to deal with the wealth of nations, and did in fact make many remarks on the general question of the conditions of opulence which are of great importance in any history of applied Economics, yet, from the point of the history of theoretical Economics, the central achievement of his book was his demonstration of the mode in which the division of labour tended to be kept in equilibrium by the mechanism of relative prices – a demonstration which, as Allyn Young has shown, is in harmony with the most refined apparatus of the modern school of Lausanne. The theory of value and distribution was really the central core of the analysis of the Classics, try as they might to conceal their objects under other names... Thus, though the appearance of modern theory may be new, its substance is continuous with what was most essential in the old. (ibid., p. 68)

Similarly, Stigler (1976, p. 201) regarded the Smithian proposition—resources seek their most profitable uses so that in equilibrium rates of returns in various uses are equal—as the most substantive proposition in all of economics. In fact, Stigler considered this as the crown jewel of the *Wealth of Nations* and the foundation of the resource allocation theory. It is the logical outcome of individuals seeking self-interest under competition. More recently, Buchanan and Yoon (2000, p. 45) regard

Smithian proposition with respect to generalized increasing returns as compatible with competitive equilibrium, which is also Pareto optimal, as an end-state adjustment. Romer (1986, p. 1004) also thought that the Smith–Young theory of increasing returns "could be given a consistent, general equilibrium interpretation".

As we have seen, Smith's emphasis on the theme of the division of labour, capital accumulation, institutional arrangements best suited to promoting growth, and his evolutionary perspective all point to the fact that he was dealing with dynamic change rather than the static problem of resource allocation or value theory. It is true that Smith ventured into value theory but, as Barber (1967) observes, that was because he was searching for an invariant standard of value to measure aggregate economic change over time. Also, his foray into value was subordinate to his main programme of growth. Doubts were cast by Schumpeter and others as to how good an equilibrium theorist Smith was. But the simple answer is that Smith was not trying to be a general equilibrium theorist.[24] As Douglas (1928, p. 77), in a commemorative volume of the *Wealth of Nations*, suggested:

> The contributions of Adam Smith to the theory of value and distribution were not great, and in commemorating the publication of the Wealth of Nations it might seem the path of wisdom to pass these topics by in discrete silence and to reserve discussion instead for those subjects, such as the division of labour, where his realistic talents enabled him to appear at a better advantage.

Capital Accumulation vs the Division of Labour

Adam Smith (1776, I, p. 364) stated:

> The annual produce of the land and labour of any nation can be increased in its value by no other means, but by increasing either the number of productive labourers, or the productive power of those labourers, or the

[24] See also Blaug (1997, p. 60) who points out that Smith's faith in the invisible hand had nothing to do with allocative efficiency à la Walras and Pareto. Effort to enlist Smith in support of the "fundamental theorems of welfare economics" is a "historical travesty of major proportions". Smith had a process conception of competition instead of an end-state conception. Moreover, a decentralized competitive price system had dynamic effects in enlarging markets and promoting the division of labour.

> productive powers of those labourers who had before been employed. The number of its productive labourers, it is evident, can never be much increased, but in consequence of an increase of capital, or of the funds destined for maintaining them. The productive powers of the same number of labourers cannot be increased, but in consequence either of some addition and improvement of those machines and instruments which facilitate and abridge labour; or of a more proper division and distribution of employment. In either case an additional capital is almost always required.

Does the forgoing quote imply that capital accumulation is the chief factor in growth? There is a difference of opinion among scholars as to the exact role of capital accumulation vis-à-vis the division of labour in economic progress. While some authors such as Lewis (1954) and Winch (1997) emphasize the role of capital accumulation as being dominant in growth, others such as Cannan (1976), Young (1928), Richardson (1975), Currie (1997), and Kaldor (1972, 1975) emphasize the role of the division of labour.[25]

Lewis (1954, p. 155) in his famous "classical" model of growth with unlimited supplies of labour posed the central problem of development as a process by which a community previously saving and investing 4–5% of national income is transformed into one that could save and invest 12–15% or more. He emphasized the key role played by the capitalist surplus. "In so far as it is reinvested in creating new capital, the capitalist sector expands, taking more people into capitalist employment out of the subsistence sector. The surplus is then larger still, capital formation is still greater, and so the process continues until the labour surplus disappears" (ibid., pp. 151–52).

Winch (1997), similarly emphasized the role of capital accumulation, along with the proportion of productive workers in the total workforce, as central to Smith's explanation of growth. Later, in a letter (of September

[25] Schumpeter (1954, p. 187), in fact, indirectly criticised Smith for placing too much emphasis on the division of labour. As is well known, Schumpeter's (1911, 1942) theory of growth is based on the central role of the entrepreneur as an innovator and adaptor of inventions. In his theory of creative destruction or economic change, demand factors like the size of the market or the resulting specialization (or the division of labour) do not find any mention. His emphasis is mainly on supply factors such as new technology, new methods, new products, new sources of supply, and new organization (large-scale units). Thus the competition that matters is not price competition, and agency making for economic change, as noted by Rosenberg (2002, p. 10), is innovation defined broadly to include more than technological innovation.

2004) to the present author, he admitted that it depended on the stage of society. In some historical circumstances capital accumulation could be the dominant factor in growth, at others it could be the division of labour. In a cumulative process one can begin with one factor or another. So his stress on capital accumulation in the 1997 paper should not be seen as categorical.

Also, Walter Eltis (2000) in *The Classical Theory of Economic Growth*, emphasizes the positive association between capital accumulation and productivity growth in Smith's theory. Pointing out that while in the neoclassical theory (as well as in much of the twentieth-century growth theory), the rate of investment is predicted to have no effect on the long-term rate of growth and living standards, in Smith capital accumulation leads to increased population and employment. "In modern growth theory, Arrow comes nearest to Smith's results with his 'learning by doing' model, where the rate of growth of labour productivity and wages per head depend on the rate of growth of employment opportunities provided by new machines. Very few modern theorists have arrived at Smith's results. Thus, if a strong interconnection between investment and growth is central to the development process, Smith's theory of growth must stand high, for it is one of the very few where investment has highly favourable long-term effects" (ibid., p. 69).

Other authors such as Cannan emphasize the importance of the division of labour in Smith's theory of growth. Cannan (1976, p. xxxii) wrote that "Book I begins by showing that the greatest improvement in the productive powers of industry is due to the division of labour". It can further be inferred that the theme of capital accumulation contained in Book II was not essential to Smith's theory of growth. "[I]f Book II were altogether omitted the other Books could stand perfectly well by themselves" (ibid., p. xxxv). So dominant is the role of the division of labour in Smith's explanation of growth that Schumpeter (1954, p. 187) commented:

> [N]obody, either before or after A. Smith, thought of putting such a burden on the division of labor. With A. Smith it is practically the only factor in economic progress. Alone it accounts 'for the superior affluence and abundance commonly possessed by lowest and most despised member of the Civilized society, compared with what the most respected

> and active savage can attain to' in spite of so much 'oppressive inequality'... Technological progress, 'invention of all those machines' – and even investments – is induced by it and is, in fact, just an incident of it.[26]

Smith gave central importance to enlarging the size of the market to further the division of labour. He advocated several measures such as investment in transport and communication to integrate the market internally and free trade to open it up externally. Foreign trade opens up the narrow domestic market to the world market, and provides an opportunity for the division of labour to be carried to the highest perfection. As Myint (1977) pointed out, Smith's theory of international trade is closely tied up with his theory of growth. "The essential virtue of Smith's approach is that it attempts a unified analysis of foreign trade and the domestic economy, oriented towards the problem of long-run growth" (ibid., p. 246).

Currie (1997), who built on the Smith–Young framework, stated that if growth begets growth, it even begets the financing of growth. Growth in the market system is largely self-financing, financed by retained earnings and business profits of the firms themselves. "The higher the rate of growth, the larger the saving and investment... The dynamic element is not saving, but the increase in real demand, which in the longer term is dependent on improvements that reduce real cost and improve quality" (Currie 1997, p. 435).

Some authors such as Romer (1986, 1989) and Krugman (1993) have highlighted the role of *fixed costs* (or fixed capital) in growth and *imperfect competition* as its natural concomitant. For example, Smith's pin-factory example is misinterpreted to suggest that increasing returns are confined to industry, and that they depend on the reaping of economies of scale. Smith had used the pin-factory example for illustration purposes only

[26] However Schumpeter (1954, pp. 184–87) also stated that there was nothing original about Smith's treatment of the division of labour or indeed any other idea contained in the *Wealth of Nations*. Smith, being a methodical professor, performed the role of "co-ordination" extremely well. He never went beyond "plain common sense" and "never moved above the heads of even the dullest readers". He was full of "trivialities and homely observations" and never taxed the "reasoning power" of his readers. Further: "His very limitations made for success. Had he been more brilliant, he would not have been taken so seriously" (ibid., p. 185). Cannan (1929, p. 96) also noted that Smith's treatment of the division of labour is neither original nor complete. See also Groenewegen (1977, 1987), who points out that Smith's account of the division of labour contains a number of weaknesses.

as all aspects of pin-making can be observed under one roof. It was an example to illustrate specialization within a firm. As already noted, he was aware of the broader social division of labour which leads to emergence of specialized arts and crafts as the market expands. He also talked about the splitting up of trades even within the same specialism if the market size was large enough to support it. It is this idea which Young applied to firm and industry level specialization as the economy advances. In Young it is industrial differentiation, not industrial integration, which is more dominant. Pin manufacture, or emergence of new specialisms within the same trade, were small scale operations rather than examples of economies of scale (or economies of consolidation). Thus economies of specialization (or the division of labour) should not be confused with the economies of scale at the level of a firm.[27] Moreover, Smith favoured competition—both internal as well as external—as the surest way to keep the excessive greed of businessmen in check. Also, for Smith competition and growth were mutually reinforcing.

To sum up, had capital accumulation been the chief factor in growth there was no need for Smith to attack mercantilism which interfered in the efficient functioning of the competitive market; or to discuss the various systems of political economy to see which best promotes growth; or to portray the division of labour (as constrained by the size of the market) as the chief cause of opulence; or to discuss measures to expand the market such as transport and communication for internal market expansion and international trade for external expansion; or to expound the proper duties of the state in a system of natural liberty. Indeed, capital accumulation in Smith is important in so far as it promotes the division of labour. Since the division of labour is constrained by the size of the market, use of capital in production also becomes constrained by the same market.

[27] See, for example, Buchanan (2008, pp. 23–24) who notes that the "division of labour" may more inclusively translate as "specialization". He also noted that Adam Smith's pin-factory example has created confusion among economists who have come to associate specialization with economies of scale. This close association need not be present at all, and introduces ambiguity in the distinction between economic and engineering aspects of relationships.

Was Smith a Laissez Faire Economist?

Smith stated that since the individual was the best judge of his own interest he should be left free to pursue it. He also posited that the motive to better one's condition was such a powerful principle that it alone was capable of taking not only an individual but the whole society to opulence. He further observed that the "obvious and simple" system of natural liberty establishes itself once all preferences and restraints are removed. Smith not only criticized mercantilist restrictions but also all systems of political economy based on preferences and restraints. He generally disliked interference in economic activity, as it would make the economy worse off. He favoured competition as the best tonic for growth, and argued for free trade. Does all this make Smith a laissez faire economist?

Laissez faire is a French term not coined by Smith. The favourite phrase used by Physiocrats, as Marshall (1890, p. 757, f.n. 1) notes was "laissez faire, laissez alter": "*Laissez faire* means that anyone should be allowed to make what things he likes, and as he likes; that all trades should be open to everybody; that Government should not, as the Colbertists insisted, prescribe to manufacturers the fashions of their cloth. *Laissez alter* (or *passer*) means that persons and goods should be allowed to travel freely from one place to another, and especially from one district of France to another, without being subject to tolls and taxes and vexatious regulations". Marshall also noted that the phrase was commonly misapplied in his time.

Smith was however critical of the Physiocratic system, as noted by Cannan (1976): "The proper system is that of natural liberty, which discharges the sovereign from 'the duty of superintending the industry of private people and directing it towards the employments most suitable for the interest of society'" (ibid., p. xxxiii). As we noted earlier, Physiocrats regarded agriculture as the only productive sector whereas Smith regarded both agriculture and industry as productive. Smith believed in the natural progress of opulence, which is first to agriculture, then to manufactures, and lastly to foreign commerce.[28] But, as Cannan (ibid., p. xxxii) again points out, this order had been inverted by the modern European states.

[28] This apparent priority to agriculture does not arise as result of favours to that sector but as a result of market-determined higher rates of return, as noted by Reid (1989) and Hollander (1971).

Smith favoured natural liberty, which is not exactly laissez faire, because it provided two things. It provided liberty to individuals to pursue their self-interest in their own manner within the framework of justice. The system also provided security without which private property cannot accumulate. As Cannan (1976, pp. xxix–xxx) notes: "At first the governments were so feeble that they could not offer their subjects that security without which no man has any motive to be industrious... This led at first to cultivation by slaves, who had no motive to industry... Progress in arts and commerce was also hindered by slavery, as well as by the ancient contempt for industry and commerce, by want of enforcement of contracts, by the various difficulties and dangers of transport, by the establishment of fairs, markets and staple towns, by duties on imports and exports, and by monopolies, corporation privileges, the statutes of apprenticeship and bounties". Natural liberty also delineated the role of the government as justice, defence, and public works.[29] Public works included roads, bridges, canals, and other infrastructure which are in the nature of public goods, and where private investment is likely to be deficient.[30]

Allyn Young stated that the main lesson from Smith is not laissez faire but competition. "Despite some sweeping phrases which invite a different interpretation, Smith's real concern was for the establishing and maintaining of competitive conditions rather than for a vigorous observance by governments of a hands-off policy in respect of economic matters... What his attitude would have been under the later conditions of the nineteenth and twentieth centuries towards the factory acts, social insurance, and measures intended to help onward equality of competitive opportunity, we cannot tell. But there is very little in these newer types of legislation which runs counter to his principal contentions or is inconsistent with his general economic philosophy" (Young 1929; Mehrling and Sandilands 1999, p. 119).

[29] Cannan (1976) quoting from *Lectures* (Cannan 1896) which Smith read at Edinburgh during the winter of 1750–1751, and which according to Dugald Stewart contained "many of the most important opinions of the Wealth of Nations", points out that "Little else is requisite to carry a state to the highest degree of opulence from the lowest barbarism, but peace, easy taxes, and a tolerable administration of justice; all the rest being brought about by the natural course of things" (ibid., p. xI).

[30] For the view that Smith was a "market-failure pioneer", see Hollander (2013). Hollander also approvingly refers to J.S. Mill who had depicted Robert Lowe as "an enemy of political economy" for attributing a simplistic version Laissez faire to Smith.

In a letter (dated 9 September 1926) to his friend Frank Knight, Young stated that the economist of the second half of the eighteenth century got two kinds of natural orders—Newtonian which would prevail despite what men might do, and "natural law" order which had to be discovered and attained—badly mixed up.[31] He also stated that Quesnay or Smith did not base their case for laissez faire because it was natural, but that is how they dressed it up. Smith did not like favours to businessmen, thought that they were monopolists in spirit, and so should be made to compete. "[I]f Smith had been writing in the middle of nineteenth century, I am pretty sure he would not have advocated laissez-faire... Ricardo, Mill and the rest argued for laissez faire in respect of international trade and in some other specific fields, but here they based their conclusions on what they thought were the positive advantages laissez-faire gave. Practically all of these so-called laissez faire economists were, as you know, favorable to labor legislation".[32]

Smith was a complex economist who favoured self-interest as long as it promoted public interest. When self-interest ceased to be the vehicle for the promotion of public interest, or when public interest was not adequately promoted, he favoured intervention. Apart from public spending on market-enhancing infrastructure, Smith favoured public spending on education and public health measures, which Amartya Sen (1983) has more recently called "entitlements'.[33] In fact, Viner (1927) has compiled a long list of functions which a state can legitimately perform in the Smithian system.

Das Adam Smith Problem

In the *Theory of Moral Sentiments* Smith emphasized the motive of sympathy, and in the *Wealth of Nations* he was focused on self-interest. Thus the German critics in the second half of the nineteenth century saw

[31] See also Chandra (2020), pp. 47–48.

[32] At another place Young stated: "[N]o first rate economist ever was an upholder of laissez faire – though some second rate economists were: e.g., Bastiat" (Young 1990, p. 26).

[33] Smith was clearly aware that the provision of public goods cannot be left to the market. See, for example, Musgrave (1976, p. 298) for the view that Chapter I of Book V could be treated "as a fore-runner of the modern theory of social goods".

a contradiction in Smith's two works and characterized it as "Das Adam Smith Problem".

In a survey of German writing on Smith, August Oncken (1897) asked: "Are the two principal works of Adam Smith, the *Theory of Moral Sentiments* (1759) on the one hand, and the *Inquiry into the Nature and Causes of the Wealth of Nations* (1776) on the other, two entirely independent works, contradicting each other in their fundamental principles, or are we to regard the latter simply as a continuation of the former, though published at a later date, and both as presenting, when taken together, a comprehensive exposition of his moral philosophy?" (ibid., p. 444).

The so-called "Das Adam Smith problem" is however more apparent than real. As Keith Tribe (2008) points out the consensus now is that there is no incompatibility between the *Wealth of Nations* and the *Theory of Moral Sentiments*. Tribe suggests that the effort of the German critics was to understand the importance of Smith's work, an effort which lacked any parallel in England. Thus it contributed to the scholarship on Smith. This international attention on Smith played a major role in Smith emerging "from a simple partisan of free trade to a theorist of commercial society and human action" (ibid., p. 514).

Leondas Montes (2003) notes that the "problem" arises because of the misunderstanding of the term "sympathy". Sympathy does not "entail a simple means to end perspective...but also a sense of moral autonomy" (ibid., p. 64). It can be argued that sympathy of TMS does not imply charity or benevolence. As an individual virtue charity and benevolence may be commendable but it cannot be the organising principle of society in pursuit of wealth or economic progress. Indeed, self-interest at the individual level is converted into cooperation at the social level through the process of specialization and exchange. In Smith the process of exchange is not seen as a zero-sum game but as mutually beneficial which leads to a "win–win" situation for the concerned parties.[34] Thus self-interest leads to "mutual sympathy" at the societal level. Secondly, while in the TMS self-love of man is balanced by sympathy, in the *Wealth of Nations* self-interest is balanced by competition conducted in a free and fair manner in accordance with the laws of justice. Moreover, Smith favoured not only

[34] See, for example, Thomas Wilson (1976) who observes: "Smith's concern with results and motives led him to recognize that all may gain from activities in which the various participants are guided only by self-interest" (p. 77).

domestic competition but also international competition so that domestic monopolies do not emerge.

Smith (1776, I, p. 18) observed that man can gain cooperation from others by appealing not to their humanity but to their own advantages. "In a civilized society [man] stands at all times in need of co-operation and assistance of great multitudes, while his whole life is scarce sufficient to gain the friendship of a few persons… [M]an has almost constant occasion for the help of his brethren, and it is in vain for him to expect it from their benevolence only. He will be more likely to prevail if he can interest their self-love in his favour, and show them that it is for their own advantage to do for him what he requires of them… We address ourselves, not to their humanity but to their self-love, and never talk to them of our own necessities but of their advantages".

Therefore, as Ronald Coase (1976) points out, the cooperation of multitudes scattered all over the world cannot be secured by the exercise of benevolence. "Benevolence, or love, may be the dominant or, at any rate, an important factor within the family or in our relations with colleagues or friends, but as Adam Smith indicates, it operates weakly or not at all when we deal with strangers. Benevolence is highly personal and most of those who benefit from the economic activities in which we engage are unknown to us. Even if they were, they would not necessarily in our eyes be lovable. For strangers to have to rely on our benevolence for what they received from us would mean, in most cases, that they would not be supplied" (ibid., p. 544).

Coase notes that although the market exchange based on self-interest supplies everyone, the role of benevolence in the market system is still important. For example, if the young are cared and trained not by their families but by institutions run by people with their own self-interest, the task would be worse performed. Secondly, the observance of moral codes facilitates business and reduces transaction costs. Society cannot subsist if all members are at all times ready to hurt and injure each other.[35] Thus a minimum moral code is a prerequisite for the market system to function.

In the *Theory of Moral Sentiments*, Smith stated that any man showing the virtues of prudence, justice and benevolence is perfectly virtuous.

[35] Smith stated that when commerce is introduced in any country probity and punctuality always accompany it. The traders deal so often that they find honesty is the best policy (See Cannan 1776, p. xxx).

According to Campbell (1967), the two major restraints of prudence and justice are also important in the *Wealth of Nations*. Prudence in the *Wealth of Nations* takes the form of bettering one's condition, and becomes the engine of saving, capital accumulation, and growth. Justice takes the narrow form of abstaining from doing harm to our neighbours or their right to "life, liberty and property". "Justice is the limit or boundary beyond which no individual's pursuit of self-interest can extend" (ibid., pp. 573–74). It implies impartial treatment and equality before the law so that "no individual or group is to be awarded special privileges or forced to endure special restraints" (ibid., p. 576). The third characteristic, namely beneficence, figures only marginally in the *Wealth of Nations*. This is because "beneficence for Smith is the result rather than the cause of economic growth and development" (ibid., p. 571). In the *Theory of Moral Sentiments*, Smith had made it clear that before we feel for others, we must be at ease ourselves.

References

Arrow, K. J., and F. H. Hahn. 1971. *General Competitive Equilibrium*. Edinburgh: Oliver and Boyd.

Barber, William J. 1967. *A History of Economic Thought*. Harmondsworth: Penguin Books.

Blaug, Mark. 1997. *Economic Theory in Retrospect*, 5th ed. Cambridge: Cambridge University Press.

Blaug, Mark. 1999. The formalist revolution or what happened to orthodox economics after World War II? In *From the Classical Economics to the Theory of the Firm: Essays in Honour of D.P. O'Brien*, ed. R.E. Backhouse and C. John, pp. 257–280. Edward Elgar: Cheltenham and Northampton.

Buchanan, James M. 2008. Let us understand Adam Smith. *Journal of the History of Economic Thought* 30 (1): 21–28.

Buchanan, James M., and Yong J. Yoon. 2000. A Smithian perspective on increasing returns. *Journal of the History of Economic Thought* 22 (1): 43–48.

Campbell, William F. 1967. Adam Smith's theory of justice, prudence, and beneficence. *American Economic Review* 57: 571–577.

Cannan, Edwin, ed. 1896. *Lectures on Justice, Police, Revenue and Arms*. Oxford: Clarendon Press.

Cannan, Edwin. 1929. *Review of Economic Theory*. London: P.S. King & Son.

Cannan, Edwin. 1976. Editor's introduction. In *An Enquiry into the Nature and Causes of the Wealth of Nations*, ed. Edwin Cannan, xix–Iiv. Chicago: University of Chicago Press.

Chandra, Ramesh. 2004. Adam Smith, Allyn Young and the Division of Labour. *Journal of Economic Issues* 38 (3): 787–805.
Chandra, Ramesh. 2004. Adam Smith and competitive equilibrium. *Evolutionary and Institutional Economic Review* 1 (1): 57–83.
Chandra, Ramesh. 2020. *Allyn Abbott Young*. Cham: Palgrave Macmillan.
Coase, Ronald H. 1994. *Essays on Economics and Economists*. Chicago: University of Chicago Press.
Coase, Ronald W. 1976. Adam Smith's view of man. *Journal of Law and Economics* 19: 529–546.
Currie, Lauchlin. 1997. Implications of an endogenous theory of growth in Allyn Young's macroeconomic concept of increasing returns. *History of Political Economy* 29: 413–443.
Douglas, Paul. 1928. Smith's theory of value and distribution. In *Adam Smith 1776–1926*, 77–115. Chicago: University of Chicago Press.
Eltis, Walter A. 1975. Adam Smith's theory of economic growth. In *Essays on Adam Smith*, ed. A.S. Skinner and T. Wilson. Oxford: Clarendon Press.
Eltis, Walter A. 2000. *The Classical Theory of Economic Growth*. Basingstoke: Palgrave Macmillan.
Groenewegen, Peter. 1977. Adam Smith and the division of labour: A bicentenary estimate. *Australian Economic Papers* 16: 161–174.
Groenewegen, Peter. 1987. Division of labour. In *The New Palgrave Dictionary of Economics*, ed. John Eatwell, Murray Miligate and Peter Newman. London: Macmillan.
Hahn, F. 1981. Reflections on the invisible hand. *Lloyd's Bank Review* 144 (April): 1–21.
Hollander, Samuel. 1971. Some implications of Adam Smith's analysis of investment priorities. *History of Political Economy* 3: 238–264.
Hollander, Samuel. 2013. Adam Smith: Market failure pioneer and champion of natural liberty (Chapter 1). In *Essays in Classical and Marxian Political Economy*. London: Routledge.
Kaldor, Nicholas. 1972. The irrelevance of equilibrium economics. *Economic Journal* 82: 1237–1255.
Kaldor, Nicholas. 1975. What is wrong with economic theory. *Quarterly Journal of Economics* 89 (3): 347–357.
Krugman, Paul. 1993. Toward a counter-counterrevolution in development theory. In *Annual Conference on Development Economics 1992*, 15–38. Washington DC: The World Bank.
Lewis, W. Arthur. 1954. Economic development with unlimited supplies of labour. *Manchester School of Economics and Social Studies* xxii: 139–191.
Lowe, Adolph. 1975. Adam Smith's system of equilibrium growth. In *Essays on Adam Smith*, ed. A.S. Skinner and T. Wilson. Oxford: Clarendon Press.

Marshall, Alfred. 1890. *Principles of Economics*, 8th ed. (1920). London: Macmillan.
Mehrling, Perry G., and Roger J. Sandilands. 1999. *Money and Growth: Selected Papers of Allyn Abbott Young*. London and New York: Routledge.
Milgate, M. 1987. Equilibrium: Development of the concept. In *The Invisible Hand*, ed. J. Eatwell, M. Milgate, and P. Newman, 105–113. London: Macmillan.
Mill, John Stuart. 1844 (2009). *Essays on Some Unsettled Questions of Political Economy*. Rockville: Serenity Publishers.
Montes, Leondas. 2003. *Das Adam Smith Problem*: Its origins, the stages of the current debate, and one implication for our understanding of sympathy. *Journal of the History of Economic Thought* 25 (1): 63–90.
Mun, Thomas. 1664 (1959). *England's Treasure by Forraign Trade*. Oxford: Basil Blackwell.
Musgrave, R.A. 1976. Adam Smith on public finance and distribution. In *The Market and the State: Essays in Honour of Adam Smith*, ed. T. Wilson and A.S. Skinner, 296–329. Oxford: Clarendon Press.
Myint, Hla. 1977. Adam Smith's theory of international trade in the perspective of economic development. *Economica* 44: 231–248.
Oncken, August. 1897. The consistency of Adam Smith. *Economic Journal* 7 (3): 443–450.
Reid, Gavin. 1989. *Classical Economic Growth*. Oxford: Basil Blackwell.
Raphael, D.D. 1985. *Adam Smith*. Oxford and New York: Oxford University Press.
Richardson, G.B. 1975. Adam Smith on competition and increasing returns. In *Essays on Adam Smith*, ed. A.S. Skinner and T. Wilson, 350–360. Oxford: Clarendon Press.
Robbins, Lionel. 1932. *An Essay on the Nature and Significance of Economic Science*. London: Macmillan.
Romer, Paul. 1986. Increasing returns and long-run growth. *Journal of Political Economy* 94: 1002–1038.
Romer, Paul. 1989. Capital accumulation in the theory of long run growth. In *Modern Business Cycle Theory*, ed. R.J. Barro, 52–127. Cambridge: Harvard University Press.
Rosenberg, Nathan. 1960. Some institutional aspects of the Wealth of Nations. *Journal of Political Economy* 68: 557–570.
Rosenberg, Nathan. 2002. *Schumpeter and the Endogeneity of Technology*. London and New York: Routledge.
Salter, John. 1994. Adam Smith on justice and distribution in commercial societies. *Scottish Journal of Political Economy* 41 (3): 299–313.
Schumpeter, Joseph A. 1911 (2017). *The Theory of Economic Development*. London and New York: Routledge.

Schumpeter, Joseph A. 1942 (2003). *Capitalism, Socialism and Democracy*. London and New York: Routledge.

Schumpeter, Joseph A. 1954 (1982). *History of Economic Analysis*. London: Allen and Unwin.

Sen, Amartya. 1983. Development: Which way now? *Economic Journal* 93 (December): 745–762.

Sidgwick, Henry. 1887. *Principles of Political Economy*. London: Macmillan.

Smith, Adam. 1759 (1976). *The Theory of Moral Sentiments*. Oxford: Clarendon Press.

Smith, Adam. 1776 (1976). *An Inquiry into the Nature and Causes of the Wealth of Nations*, ed. Edwin Cannan. Chicago: University of Chicago Press.

Stigler, George. 1976. The successes and failures of professor Smith. *Journal of Political Economy* 84 (6): 1199–1213.

Tribe, Keith. 2008. Das Adam Smith problem and the origins of modern Smith scholarship. *History of European Ideas* 34: 514–525.

Veblen, Thorstein. 1898. Why is economics not an evolutionary science? *Quarterly Journal of Economics* 12 (4): 373–397.

Viner, Jacob. 1927. Adam Smith and laissez faire. *Journal of Political Economy* 35 (2): 198–232.

Wilson, Thomas. 1976. Sympathy and self-interest. In *The Market and the State: Essays in Honour of Adam Smith*, ed. T. Wilson and A.S. Skinner. Oxford: Clarendon Press.

Winch, Donald. 1997. Adam Smith's problems and ours. *Scottish Journal of Political Economy* 44 (4): 384–402.

Witzum, Amos. 1997. Distributive considerations in Smith's conception of economic justice. *Economics and Philosophy* 13: 241–259.

Young, Allyn. 1928. Increasing returns and economic progress. *Economic Journal* 38 (152): 527–542.

Young, Allyn. 1990. Nicholas Kaldor's notes on Allyn Young's LSE lectures 1927–29. *Journal of Economic Studies* 17 (3/4): 18–114.

CHAPTER 3

Alfred Marshall on Organic Growth

Peter Groenewegen (2007), Marshall's biographer, has listed his several achievements but growth is not one of them. However, it is important to reconstruct his growth ideas as the later authors including Allyn Young, Paul Krugman, and Paul Romer drew on them.[1] One of Marshall's (1890) main contributions to economic theory in the *Principles of Economics* was his supply–demand apparatus which was a useful tool in the analysis of value and distribution.[2] The classical authors such as Adam Smith and David Ricardo had a cost of production theory of value neglecting marginal utility (or demand). The later authors such as Léon Walras, William Stanley Jevons, and Carl Menger, all of whom independently discovered the concept of marginal utility, emphasized the role of demand in the determination of an equilibrium price. It was left to Marshall to complete the picture by presenting an analysis of the forces of

[1] See, for example, Marchionatti (1992) and Lavezzi (2003) for a reconstruction of Marshall's growth ideas. Lavezzi describes some aspects of Marshall's growth ideas as a "bridge" between Smith and Young.

[2] Marshall (1890, p. 758) stated that Smith's "chief work was to combine and develop the speculations of his French and English contemporaries and predecessors as to value". Marshall is also reported to have said: "It's all in A. Smith" (Schumpeter 1954, p. 835).

R. Chandra, *Endogenous Growth in Historical Perspective*, Palgrave Studies in Economic History,
https://doi.org/10.1007/978-3-030-83761-7_3

supply and demand.[3] Although the microeconomics texts today are full of supply–demand diagrams, Marshall adopted a verbal approach relegating the diagrams (and mathematics) to footnotes and appendices.

Marshall, who is thought to have led the neoclassical (marginalist) *revolution* at Cambridge, would not have himself characterized it as a revolution. For he believed in the dictum *natura non facit saltum* (or nature does not make jumps), and likewise regarded the progress of economic science to be "slow and continuous". The new is not antagonistic to the old, nor have new doctrines subverted the older ones. Marshall (1890, p. v) in "Preface" to the first edition of the *Principles* writes:

> Some of the best work of the present generation has indeed appeared to be antagonistic to that of earlier writers; but when it has had time to settle down into its proper place, and its rough edges have been worn away, it has been found to involve no real breach of continuity in the development of the science. The new doctrines have supplemented the older, have extended, developed, and sometimes corrected them, and often have given them a different tone by a new distribution of emphasis; but very seldom have subverted them.

Marshall noted that the principle of continuity was common to all modern schools of economic thought whether they were influenced by biology, history or mathematics. In his *Principles*, Marshall made liberal use of biological analogies and inductive knowledge. In this regard, he cited writings of Herbert Spencer on biology, Hegel on history and philosophy, and ethico-historical studies of the continental writers. Although the substance of the views in his book reflected these influences, their form reflected the mathematical conceptions of Cournot and to a lesser extent von Thünen. Marshall (ibid., p. x) stated:

[3] Perhaps Marshall was unaware of Jevons's and Walras's works, given his reading habits, before he wrote his *Principles* in 1890, as noted by Schumpeter (1952, p. 96). Further: "This seems to account for Marshall's tendency to impute to Mill and Ricardo practically all that the reformers of economic theory had to say" (ibid., p. 96). As Marshall, in a letter to J.B. Clark dated 24 March 1905, himself admitted: "[M]y main position as to the theory of value and distribution was practically completed in the years 1867 to 1870; when I translated Mill's version of Ricardo's or Smith's doctrines into mathematics" (See Pigou 1925, p. 416).

> Under the guidance of Cournot, and in a less degree of von Thünen, I was led to attach great importance to the fact that our observations of nature, in the moral as in the physical world, relate not so much to aggregate quantities, as to increment of quantities, and that in particular the demand for a thing is a continuous function, of which the 'marginal' increment is, in stable equilibrium, balanced against the corresponding increment of its cost of production. It is not easy to get a clear full view of continuity in this aspect without the aid of either of mathematical symbols or of diagrams.

Marshall extended the principle of continuity to economic evolution.[4] He was of the view that progress is gradual as a matter of habit whether conscious or unconscious. Most scientific and economic work represents orderly and frequent manifestations of nature rather than those which are spasmodic or infrequent or difficult of observation. In his "Preface" to the definitive eighth edition of the *Principles*, Marshall (ibid., p. xiii) wrote:

> Economic evolution is gradual. Its progress is sometimes arrested or reversed by political catastrophes: but its forward movements are never sudden; for even in the Western world and in Japan it is based on habit, partly conscious, partly unconscious. And though an inventor, or an organizer, or a financier of genius may seem to have modified the economic structure of a people almost at a stroke; yet that part of his influence, which has not been merely superficial and transitory, is found on inquiry to have done little more than bring to a head a broad constructive movement which had long been in preparation.

Marshall employed the device of a "representative firm" to characterize "normal" behaviour. Industry is subject to continuous and gradual evolution. New firms are coming up and competing with the more established ones, and may first rise to the first rank and then perhaps decay after a time. In such a scenario "the normal cost of production in it can be estimated with reference to 'a representative firm,' which enjoys a fair share of both those internal economies which belong to a well-organized individual businesses and of those general or external economies which arise out of the collective organization of the district as a whole" (ibid., p. xiii). Marshall further stated that when large firms or trusts try to dominate the

[4] See Niman (1998) for the view that Marshall, though classified as a neoclassical economist, was attempting "to create a framework suitable for capturing the characteristics of an 'evolutionary economics'" (ibid., p. 190).

market or indulge in large stock-exchange manoeuvres, normal action falls into the background.

Marshall cautioned that his emphasis on the normal behaviour or the use of the term "equilibrium" in the *Principles* may suggest something of a "statical analogy" rather than "dynamical" analysis. This however is not the case as the *Principles* "is concerned more with the forces that cause movement: and its key-note is that of dynamics, rather than statics" (ibid., p. xiv). Since the forces to be dealt with are so numerous, it is best to take a few at a time. A number of partial solutions are then worked out as "auxiliaries" while the main study remains "dynamics". "Thus we begin by isolating the primary relations of demand and supply, demand and price in regard to a particular commodity. We reduce to inaction all other forces by the phrase 'other things being equal': we do not suppose that they are inert, but for the time being we ignore their activity… In the second stage more forces are released from the hypothetical slumber that had been imposed on them: changes in the conditions of demand and supply of particular groups of commodities come into play; and their complex mutual interactions begin to be observed. Gradually the area of the dynamical problem becomes larger; the area covered by provisional statical assumptions becomes smaller…" (ibid., pp. xiv-xv). Further:

> The main concern of economics is thus with human beings who are impelled, for good and evil, to change and progress. Fragmentary statical hypotheses are used as temporary auxiliaries to dynamical – or rather biological – conceptions: but the central idea of economics, even when its foundations alone are under discussion, must be that of living force and movement. (ibid., p. xv)

It is therefore clear that partial analysis was a temporary device to be used as a stepping stone to change and progress. Even while talking of the partial analysis, Marshall (ibid., p. x) was well aware of the togetherness of the economic phenomenon, and referred to Cournot's *Principes Mathématiques de la Théorie des Richesses* with approval:

> He [Cournot] taught that it is necessary to face the difficulty of regarding the various elements of an economic problem, – not as determining one another in a chain of causation, A determining B, B determining C, and so on – but as all mutually determining one another. Nature's action is complex; and nothing is gained in the long run by pretending that it is simple, and trying to describe it in a series of elementary propositions.

Marshall was well versed with practical facts and inductive findings, and blended them in his theoretical analysis. He was well aware that the tendency to diminishing returns as understood by Ricardo and Malthus had been almost suspended by "low transport charges on land and sea". Marshall also stated that in every branch of production and trade there was a margin up to which an increase of any agent is profitable under the given conditions but beyond which further application yields diminishing returns "unless there be some increase in demand accompanied by an appropriate increase in other agents of production to co-operate with it" (ibid., p. xvi). Marshall further stated that this notion of margin was not uniform or absolute, and varied with the conditions of the problem in hand and the time period involved:

> The rules are universal that, (1) marginal costs do not govern price; (2) it is only at the margin that the action of those forces which do govern price can be made to stand in clear light; and (3) the margin, which must be studied in reference to long periods and enduring results, differs in character as well as in extent from that which must be studied in reference to short periods and to passing fluctuations. (ibid., p. xvi)

It is obvious from the foregoing that Marshall had an evolutionary perspective. His partial equilibrium analysis was a step to the togetherness of the economic phenomenon. He was aware that the long-term concern of economics was not equilibrium but change and progress.[5] He thought of growth as "organic growth" keeping the biological analogy in mind. He carefully gathered historical facts and blended them with abstract theory. For him economics was not divorced from practical concerns of poverty removal and rise in real wages and living standards. But he thought of economic evolution and growth in gradual (or incremental) terms, and not in terms of abrupt changes. Keeping these considerations in mind an attempt has been made in the following pages of the chapter to

[5] The high theme of progress, as Caldari (2018, p. 104) points out, is a very broad concept and underlies almost all of Marshall's writings. It encompasses "the growth of mankind in numbers, in health and strength, in knowledge, ability, and in richness of character" and constitutes "the end of all our studies" (Marshall 1920, p. 139). For Marshall "the Mecca of the economist lies in economic biology" as the inner nature and outer form are constantly changing. Therefore, mechanical analogies may be suited as a general introduction; in the later stages of economics when we approach the real conditions of life, biological analogies are to be preferred.

outline Marshall's theory of growth which has the following elements: (1) the role of the division of labour, (2) the distinction between internal and external economies, (3) the role of the representative firm, (4) the theory of economic evolution, and (5) the role saving, investment, and capital accumulation. After outlining his theory of growth, a critical assessment of Marshall, particularly with respect to his growth ideas, will be made.

The Division of Labour

Brian Loasby (1989, p. 48) observed that Marshall's view of the economic process is far more clearly revealed if we approach him from Adam Smith's perspective than from modern microeconomics. "Marshall, like Smith, was primarily concerned with a topic alien to modern microeconomics, namely the nature and causes of the wealth of nations" (ibid., p. 48). For him economics was a moral science which could be used to improve the condition of the people.[6] One of the important ways in which it could be done was through the division of labour—a problem not dealing with efficient resource allocation in a competitive economy. Marshall (1890, p. 240) in Chapter VIII of Book IV linked the increased efficiency of the division of labour with organization,[7] praising Smith[8] in this regard:

> [I]n this, as in other cases, Adam Smith gave new and larger significance to an old doctrine by the philosophic thoroughness with which he explained it, and the practical knowledge with which he illustrated it. After insisting on the advantages of the division of labour, and pointing out how they render it possible for increased numbers to live in comfort on a limited

[6] His student and successor at Cambridge, A. C. Pigou (1925), pointed out that he came to economics through ethics. "Economics for him was a handmaid to ethics, not an end in itself, but a means to a further end: an instrument, by the perfecting of which it might be possible to better the conditions of human life" (Pigou 1925, p. 82).

[7] For Marshall organization was the fourth agent (or factor) of production, the other three being land, labour and capital.

[8] Marshall (1890, p. 757) in the *Principles* is full of praise for Smith and noted that because of his wide travels both in Scotland and abroad (France), and also because of his close association with Scottish businessmen, he got to know the world practically and had "unsurpassed powers of observation, judgment and reasoning". Whenever he differed from his predecessors, "he was more right than they; while there is scarcely any economic truth now known of which he did not get the first glimpse". Further: "since he was the first to write a treatise on wealth in all its chief social respects, he might on that ground alone have a claim to be regarded as the founder of modern economics".

> territory, he argued that the pressure of population on the means of subsistence tends to weed out those races who through want of organization or for any other cause are unable to turn to the best account the advantages of the place in which they live. (ibid., p. 240)

He then draws a parallel between an industrial organization and physical organization of higher animals (which are more complex). In Marshall's opinion, the development of an organism, whether social or physical, involves an increasing subdivision of functions between its separate parts on the one hand and a more intimate connection between them on the other. Each part gets less self-sufficient, depends more and more on other parts, and disorder in one part affects the others. The key to understanding this lies in the concepts of "differentiation" and "integration":

> The increased subdivision of functions, or 'differentiation,' as it is called, manifests itself with regard to industry in such forms as the division of labour, and the development of specialized skill, knowledge and machinery: while 'integration,' that is, a growing intimacy and the firmness of the connections between the separate parts of the industrial organism, shows itself in such forms as the increase of security of commercial credit, and of means and habits of communication by sea and road, by railway and telegraph, by post and printing press. (ibid., p. 241)

Adam Smith, as Marshall points out, was careful in noting that while the division of labour resulting from the industrial organization had general advantages, there were many points where the system failed and involved many incidental evils. However, many of his followers were not so careful and argued too boldly in favour of the benefits of the division of labour. Moreover, the progress of industrial organization is by nature slow. It can be hastened a little by the principles of eugenics and appropriate education but, howsoever hastened, it has to be gradual and slow because it must wait on the development of man. If the institutions change too fast in comparison to man they cannot retain their stability; if they are to endure they must be appropriate to man. Changes which add only a little to immediate productive efficiency may be worth having if they make mankind ready and fit for an organization.

Chapter IX of Book IV is devoted to the role of machinery in furthering the division of labour. Marshall first points out that "practice makes perfect", and change is due to the gradual growth of new habits of reflex or automatic action rather than due to deliberate action.

In this context, Marshall refers to Smith who pointed out that a lad who made nothing but nails all his life could do so twice as fast as a first rate smith who took to nail-making occasionally. Further: "Anyone who has to perform exactly the same set of operations day after day on things of exactly the same shape, gradually learns to move his fingers exactly as they are wanted, by almost automatic action and with greater rapidity than would be possible if every movement had to wait for a deliberate instruction of will" (ibid., p. 252).

Once the action has been reduced to routine, it can then be taken over by machinery. The general rule is "that any manufacturing operation that can be reduced to uniformity, so that exactly the same thing has to be done over and over again in the same way, is sure to be taken over sooner or later by machinery" (ibid., p. 255). Thus the improvement of machinery and the growing subdivision of labour generally go together. But Marshall is quick to caution that this connection is not as close as generally supposed. The division of labour is intimately linked with the size of the market as Smith had explained. Marshall writes:

> It is the largeness of markets, the increased demand for great numbers of things of the same kind, and in some cases of things made with great accuracy, that leads to subdivision of labour; the chief effect of the improvement of machinery is to cheapen and make more accurate the work which would anyhow have been subdivided. (ibid., p. 255)[9]

Further, with the use of machinery there is a tendency for the scale of manufactures to rise. As Marshall notes: "Thus machinery constantly supplants and renders unnecessary that purely manual skill, the attainment of which was, even up to Adam Smith's time, the chief advantage of division of labour. But this influence is more than countervailed by its tendency to increase the scale of manufactures and to make them more complex; and therefore to increase the opportunities for division of labour of all kinds, and especially in the matter of business management" (ibid., p. 256).[10]

[9] "The framework of progress, for Marshall as for Smith, is provided by the division of labour, continually extended by the growth of the market, to which its results contribute in turn" (Loasby 1989, p. 52).

[10] Loasby (1989, pp. 52–53) notes that increasing returns have to be worked for and cannot be selected from a previously defined production set as an increase in labour and

While man-made parts of a machine required much care, labour, and cost, machine-made parts could easily replace the broken down parts of a machine. So the machine-made machinery had brought in a new era of "interchangeable parts". Earlier, while highly skilled craftsmen made Swiss watches, now the American system of making watches by machinery was becoming popular which required very little specialized manual skill. "In fact the machinery is becoming every year more and more automatic, and is getting to require less and less assistance from the human hand" (ibid., p. 257). Marshall cited another example from printing trades where improvement of machinery and increase in the volume of production leads to an elaborate subdivision of labour. When the printing trade was new, the printer (or the editor) had to set up the types, print off the sheets, and distribute the newspaper to his neighbours in addition to making all his appliances. But now appliances can be got from subsidiary trades, and there are different classes of workers within the walls of a large printing establishment apart from those who organize and superintend the business, do its office work, and keep its stores.

The Role of External and Internal Economies

Marshall stated that many of the economies of a large establishment employing specialized skill and machinery do not depend on the size of the individual establishment but on the aggregate volume of production in the neighbourhood; while still others, especially those connected with the growth of knowledge and arts, depend mainly on the aggregate volume of production in the whole civilized world. This leads to the distinction between internal and external economies. In Marshall's words:

> We may divide the economies arising from an increase in scale of production of any kind of goods, into two classes – firstly, those dependent on the general development of the industry; and secondly, those dependent on the resources of the individual houses of business engaged in it, on their

capital generally leads to improved organization which in turn improves their efficiency. Further, increasing returns are not returns to scale in the sense of an output resulting from an equi-proportional increase of all inputs. Changing methods of production call for machinery, unskilled and skilled labour to be combined in new proportions. "Thus, increasing returns result from the exploitation of possibilities of substitution which are opened up by production on a larger scale" (ibid., p. 53).

> organization and efficiency of their management. We may call the former *external economies*, and the latter *internal economies*. (ibid., p. 266)

Marshall (1890, pp. 284–85) believed that the importance of external economies had increased for the small producer in terms of diffusion of knowledge. Though a small producer is at a disadvantage in many ways, for example, in getting information or making experiments, yet the general course of life is on his side. "For External economies are constantly growing in importance relative to Internal in all matters of Trade-knowledge: newspapers, and trade and technical publications of all kinds are perpetually scouting for him and bringing him much of the knowledge he wants – knowledge which a little while ago would have been beyond the reach of anyone who could not afford to have well-paid agents in many distant places. Again, it is to his interest also that the secrecy of business is on the whole diminishing, and that the most important improvements in method seldom remain secret for long after they have passed from the experimental stage. It is to his advantage that changes in manufacture depend less on mere rules of thumb and more on broad developments of scientific principle; and many of these are made by students in the pursuit of knowledge for its own sake, and are promptly published in the general interest" (ibid., pp. 284–85).

Moreover:

> Although therefore the small manufacturer can seldom be in the front of the race of progress, he need not be far from it, if he has the time and the ability for availing himself of the modern facilities for obtaining knowledge. But it is true that he must be exceptionally strong if he can do this without neglecting the minor but necessary details of the business. (ibid., p. 285)

Marshall also believed that external economies are achieved by concentration of many small businesses of a similar character in particular localities, i.e., by "localization of industry". Once an industry locates in a particular place, it is likely to stay there for long as people following the same skilled trade get advantages from one another in the same neighbourhood. Marshall discussed several advantages in this regard: (1) the mysteries of the trade are known to everyone as if they are in the air, (2) good ideas relating to improvement of machinery, processes, and organization spread to others, (3) subsidiary trades grow up in the neighbourhood supplying it with implements and materials, (4) increased use of specialized machinery in a district where there is large aggregate production of the kind even though individual firms are small, (5) subsidiary industries concentrating on a process of production are able to keep in constant use highly specialized machinery since they supply to a number of small producers in the neighbourhood, and (6) localized industry offers a constant market for special skill. There are not only advantages in localization of production but also in localization of shops selling special goods. Such shops congregate together while those supplying ordinary domestic needs do not.

Marshall then discusses the advantages of large-scale production in terms of (1) economy of skill, (2) economy of machinery, and (3) economy of materials (ibid., p. 278). Marshall stated that the last of these is fast losing importance in relation to the other two. "It is true that an isolated workman often throws away a number of small things which would have been collected and turned to good account in a factory; but waste of this kind can scarcely occur in a localized manufacture even if it is in the hands of small men; and there is not very much of it in any branch of industry in modern England except in agriculture and domestic cooking" (ibid., p. 278–79).

A large establishment is also economical in the use of specialized machinery as it can afford the space with good light as well as the rent and general expenses of the factory. Besides, a large manufacturer can buy the best machinery in the market and can therefore benefit from the invention of new machinery. While a small manufacturer cannot afford to experiment, a large establishment making machines may devise improvements in it exclusively on its own and make it available to all on the payment of royalty or as a patent right as in agriculture and cotton industries. A large business also reaps the economies of large-scale buying and selling. Further:

> The economies of highly organized buying and selling are among the chief causes of the present tendency towards the fusion of many businesses in the same industry or trade into single huge aggregates; and also of trading federations of various kinds, including German cartels and central co-operative associations. They have also always promoted the concentration of business risks in the hands of large capitalists who put out the work to be done by smaller men. (ibid., p. 282)

Just as a large establishment can afford highly specialized machinery, it can also afford to employ highly specialized skill. A large manufacturer has a much better chance for getting hold of men of exceptional abilities who can be trusted in the most difficult of tasks crucial to the reputation of the establishment. Such people can be placed in leadership positions as foremen or heads of departments, and contribute towards the economies from the subdivision of work in business management. The head of a large business can concentrate on the broadest and the most fundamental problems of his trade and leave the operational work to others.

It is clear that a large firm can reap certain advantages over a smaller firm but its continued growth depends on two factors: internal economies of large-scale production and the ability to market its increased output. Marshall points out that there are many trades in which internal economies can be enjoyed, and there are many in which a large output could be marketed, but there are few in which both could be done. The firms producing raw materials or standardized products such as steel or calico, and where production can be reduced to routine, the economies of large-scale production are important. But many commodities, where there is a strong tendency to increasing returns, are specialized businesses either creating a new want or meeting an old want in a new way. Some may also be adapted to special tastes while some become acceptable slowly. While in such commodities production can be increased economically at a fast pace, sales cannot, for each such commodity is confined to a particular market which it has slowly and expensively acquired.

In retail trade, large establishments have an advantage as they can buy on better terms, can get their goods transported more cheaply, and can offer a large variety to meet the tastes of the consumer, and reap economy of skill requiring the use of judgement. As a result, there is a strong tendency for large establishments to drive out small ones, and "the small shopkeeper is losing ground daily". Although the small shopkeeper has the advantage of knowing his customers personally, can give them goods on credit, offer the convenience of bringing goods to their door, and use his personal relations to keep them in good humour, but such advantages are fast disappearing. Decline in the personal relations between the shopkeeper and his customers, the habit of buying on credit as well as the variety of goods catering to the latest fashions available in big stores have added to the woes of the small shopkeeper.

Large-scale manufactures require the use of new appliances and new methods, so they can be easily supplanted by younger and more dynamic firms using yet newer methods. A firm which has lost the exceptional energy which enabled it to rise is likely to quickly decay. Thus the full life of a large firm is seldom long.

The Role of the Representative Firm

We saw that the growth of scale brings economies of specialized machinery as well as skills, but after a time the energy and enterprise of this business may decline which may then be taken over by younger businesses with more energy, dynamism and better technology. Here Marshall (ibid., pp. 315–16) gives the example of trees in the forest:

> [H]ere we may read a lesson from the young trees of the forest as they struggle upwards through the benumbing shade of their older rivals. Many succumb on the way, and a few only survive; those few becoming stronger with every year, they get a larger share of light and air with every increase of their height, and at last in their turn they tower above their neighbours, and seem as though they would grow on for ever, and for ever become stronger as they grow. But they do not. One tree will last longer in full vigour and attain a greater size than another; but sooner or later age tells on them all. Though the taller ones have a better access to light and air than their rivals, they gradually lose vitality; and one after another they give place to others, which, though of less material strength, have on their side the vigour of youth.

What is true of trees is also true of businesses. In almost every trade there is a constant rise and fall of large businesses, and at any moment of time some firms are in ascending phase while others are in descending phase. In the meantime, there are external economies which do not depend on the size of the individual firms but result from the growth of correlated branches of industry which mutually assist one another, and tend to get concentrated in the same locality. But these have the effect of increasing the aggregate scale of production. Given the presence of internal and external economies, the analysis of the supply price of a commodity requires one to carefully analyse the normal cost of producing a commodity relative to a given aggregate volume of production. This can be done by studying the expenses of a representative producer for that aggregate volume.[11] This firm is neither new nor old but an average firm which allows us to study how far the economies, internal and external, of large-scale production to which it has access have extended to the industry and country in question. Marshall (ibid., p. 318) writes:

> The general argument of the present Book [Book IV] shows that an increase in the aggregate volume of production of anything will generally increase the size, and therefore the internal economies possessed by such a representative firm; that it will always increase the external economies to which the firm has access; and thus will enable it to manufacture at a less proportionate cost of labour and sacrifice than before.
> In other words, we say broadly that while the part which nature plays in production shows a tendency to diminishing return, the part which man plays shows a tendency to increasing return. The *law of increasing return* may be worded thus:- An increase of labour and capital leads generally to improved organization, which increases the efficiency of the work of labour and capital.

Under normal conditions, an industry is in a stable equilibrium where the upward sloping supply curve intersects the downward sloping demand curve from below. But in the presence of increasing returns, the supply curve is downward sloping in the long run as depicted by Marshall in his Appendix H (ibid., p. 806, f.n. 1). There may not be any unique equilibrium: at point A (at a small level of output) where the industry supply curve cuts the demand curve from below, there is stable equilibrium; at point B (at an intermediate level of output) where the supply curve cuts the demand curve from above, there is unstable equilibrium; and at point C (at a very large level of output) where the supply curve again cuts the demand curve from below, there is stable equilibrium.

[11] As noted by Katia Caldari (2018, p. 98), device of the representative firm was used by Marshall to introduce "time" in his analysis that "would allow [him to deal] with a long-period equilibrium without foregoing the several individual firms in disequilibrium, which belong to the industry in question". Neil Hart (2012, p. 86) regarded the representative firm as representing the supply curve of the industry in miniature. Further, through this device, Marshall was able to visualize the industry supply schedule which was different from the cost functions of heterogeneous firms comprising the industry (ibid., p. 90). This however prevented "time irreversibility" which arises when change is analysed in an equilibrium framework. Due to this difficulty Marshall (1920, p. 807), again as Caldari notes, had to admit that his theory was out of touch with reality.

Marshall stated that a fall in the price of a commodity always acted in one direction on demand, that is, demand curve is downward sloping. But the same cannot be said of the supply curve. In the short period, the supply curve may be upward sloping, but as the gradual increases in demand lead to greater efficiency due to internal and external economies of the representative firm, the supply curve becomes downward sloping in the long run. As Marshall (ibid., p. 460) says:

> [W]hen making lists of supply prices (supply schedules) for long periods in these industries, we set down a diminished supply price against an increased amount of the flow of goods; meaning thereby that a flow of that increased amount will in the course of time be supplied profitably at that lower price, to meet a fairly steady corresponding demand.

The notion of the representative firm, broadly speaking, excludes substantive new inventions but includes adaptations of existing ideas. Marshall (ibid., pp. 460–61) explains:

> We exclude from view any economies that may result from substantive new inventions; but we include those which may be expected to arise naturally out of the adaptations of existing ideas; and we may look towards a position of a balance between the forces of progress and decay, which would be attained if the conditions under view were supposed to act uniformly for a long time. But such notions should be taken broadly. The attempt to make them precise over-reaches our strength. If we include in our account nearly all the conditions of real life, the problem is too heavy to be handled; if we select a few then long-drawn-out and subtle reasonings with regard to them become scientific toys rather than engines of practical work.

In his Appendix H to the *Principles*, Marshall stated that the use of the term "margin of production" should be avoided for long periods where the cost of production diminishes with an increase in output. It is alright if the law of diminishing returns operates. "But in problems in which the tendency to increasing return is in effective force, there is no clearly defined marginal product. In such problems our units have to be larger; we have to consider the representative firm rather than a given individual firm: and above all we have to consider the cost of a whole process of production, without any attempt to isolate that of a single commodity, such as a single rifle or yard of cloth" (ibid., p. 805).

Lionel Robbins (1928) in an *Economic Journal* article criticized Marshall's notion of the representative firm. He stated: "The Marshallian conception of a Representative Firm has always been a somewhat unsubstantial notion. Conceived as an afterthought – so far as I am able to discover it does not figure at all in the first edition of the Principles – it lurks in the obscurer corners of Book V like some pale visitant from the world of the unborn waiting in vain for the comforts of complete tangibility" (ibid., p. 387). According to Robbins, the notion is superfluous to the hypotheses of either "equilibrium" or "stationariness". He opined that there is no problem in the whole range of value theory which cannot be treated more satisfactorily without it. The notion is also misleading:

> I have suggested already, in passing, certain ways in which, incautiously handled, the conception may give rise to misapprehension, the way in which it may mislead with regard to the construction of the supply curves, and the way in which, in discussions of the stationary state, it may lead us to imagine that the average is the condition rather than the result of equilibrium. But it is possible, I think, to condemn it on grounds more general than this. The whole conception, it may be suggested, is open to the general criticism that it cloaks the essential heterogeneity of productive factors – in particular the heterogeneity of managerial ability – just at that point at which it is most desirable to exhibit it most vividly. (ibid., p. 399)

Allyn Young (1990, p. 45), while analysing the long-run falling supply curve of a commodity (say M), asked: "would you take this curve to mean average costs or marginal costs of production?" Using the device of the representative firm, Young stated that Marshall, in effect took the average costs of production. He distinguished between average and marginal costs but believed that the distinction became blurred in the long run. "The Representative Firm is merely an expository device to aid in understanding this curve; it is the vehicle through which external economies – those outside a particular industry but to which the representative firm has access – affect supply… Robbins' article is 'overcritical'; he does not appreciate it as an expository device; the question is perhaps one 'hardly worth wasting an article in the *Economic Journal*'" (ibid., p. 45).

Young observed that if the long-run supply curve cuts the demand curve from below there is no difficulty. But it is a highly abstract situation. The demand curve is closely connected with the supply curve of other industries. If the demand for these other supplies is elastic, the demand curve of M shifts to the right indefinitely. But there may be equilibrium at any given point not only on the production of M but of other goods. But if the long-run supply curve cuts the demand curve from above, there is an increasing difference between demand and supply prices, giving a chance for profits. It is an important problem in the history of modern industry especially in times of rapid expansion. The "sellers' market" creates conditions for the middlemen to insert themselves into the situation. In times of industrial prosperity these people abound trying to sell branded goods (or goods with special characteristics) at high prices. The producers themselves may try to take advantage of the situation by expanding their supply rapidly given adequate time for the reorganization of industry. "But that is exactly the problem: how much time? The Marshallian statement is really meaningless. The period of time is relative to costs, and costs are relative to the period of time" (ibid., p. 47).

The supply curve may not remain falling for long, and may well turn upwards, as the changes made are costly involving huge capital costs, cutting on the supply of present goods. Further, a long-period supply curve is meaningless apart from the particular length of time considered. The curve is relative to the rate at which increasing returns exist. On the other side, one cannot postulate a constant demand curve for a good over a long period. According to Young (ibid., p. 47), it would shift as a result of the very forces which are shifting the supply curve.[12]

Under such circumstances (i.e., under conditions of increasing returns), looking for equilibrium conditions is as good as looking for a mare's nest (ibid., p. 45). Further, we need a theory of an equilibrium rate of progress or the optimum rate of progress which will keep the supply curve close up to the demand curve (ibid., pp. 47–48).

[12] Marshall postulates a constant demand curve in his theory of long-period equilibrium as noted by Dasgupta (1990, pp. 254–55). It is only the condition of supply which changes. Comparing Ricardo and Marshall, both of whom use a 'corn' model, he points out that in both the processes lead up to a stationary state; while in Ricardo land is held constant, in Marshall it is demand. "The process in both is irreversible and hence, as I would judge, 'dynamic'" (ibid., p. 255). Therefore he finds it intriguing that Harrod (1948, p. 15), who has done much towards clarifying the concept of dynamics, judges Marshall's system as static and Ricardo's system as dynamic.

Economic Evolution and Competition

We noted that Marshall believed in the principles of continuity and slow economic evolution. He recognized the interdependence of the economic phenomenon and his partial equilibrium analysis in the *Principles* was a step in that direction.[13] He also believed that the long-term goal of economics was not static analysis but change and progress. But change, in his opinion, is generally incremental and gradual rather than disruptive. All these taken together and combined with his biological analogies constitute his theory of evolution.[14] In *Industry and Trade*, which was meant to be a companion volume to *Principles*, Marshall (1919, p. v) wrote:

> Its motto is:- *The many in one, and the one in many.* Many tendencies have gone to making of each industry and each economic institution: therefore a thorough realistic study of any part of the economic field, calls for some reference to the interaction of many diverse tendencies, and gives some occasion to some care in analysis. And conversely, almost every important tendency is so far modified by the conditions under which it operates, that an exhaustive study of it may need to range over many fields of work. This motto supplements the motto of my *Principles* which is:- *Natura non facit saltum*: *i.e.* economic evolution is gradual and continuous on each of its many routes. (italics in original)

In *Principles*, Marshall (1890, p. 461) outlined the limitations of stable equilibrium and propounded his concept of "organic growth":

> The theory of stable equilibrium of normal demand and supply helps indeed to give definiteness to our ideas; and in its elementary stages it does not diverge from the actual facts of life, so far as to prevent its giving a fairly trustworthy picture of the chief methods of action of the strongest and the most persistent group of economic forces. But when pushed to its more remote and intricate logical consequences, it slips away from the conditions of real life. In fact we are here verging on the high

[13] Dardi (2003), for example, holds the view that Marshall's partial equilibrium analysis is "dynamics in disguise". See also Raffaelli (2003, p. 45).

[14] See Hodgson (1993) for the view that although Marshall recognized the value of biological analogies, he did not fully incorporate an evolutionary theory (or an adequate evolutionary analysis), with the result that his followers were easily able to replace the biological elements of his system with notions similar to Newtonian mechanics.

> theme of economic progress; and here therefore it is especially needful to remember that economic problems are imperfectly presented when they are treated as problems of statical equilibrium, and not of *organic growth*. For though the statical treatment alone can give a necessary introduction to a more philosophic treatment of society as an *organism*; it is yet only an introduction.
> The Statical theory of equilibrium is only an introduction to economic studies; and it is barely even an introduction to the study of the progress and development of industries which show a tendency to increasing returns. Its limitations are so constantly overlooked, especially by those who approach it from an abstract point of view, that there is a danger of throwing it into definite form at all. (italics added)

Marchionatti (1992, p. 557) has pointed out the Smith had two views of competition, one based on the division of labour and structural change (as in Chapters I–III of Vol. I on the division of labour) and the other based on his theory of value (as in Chapter VIII on the natural and market price of commodities) of the *Wealth of Nations* (Smith 1776).[15] He further notes that the same dichotomy appears in Marshall's *Principles* in Book IV and Book V. While book IV has a dynamic view of competition as producing "organic growth", Book V has a static view of competition in terms of "mechanical equilibrium".[16] As we noted,

[15] See also Richardson (1975, p. 351), who wrote: "Smith offers us in effect both a theory of economic equilibrium and a theory of economic evolution: and in each of these competition has a key role to play. Within *The Wealth of Nations* no obvious tension exists between the two theories, partly no doubt because they are sketched out in a manner loose enough to make it difficult to establish inconsistency. Later writers, however, in striving for greater analytical rigour, developed the theory of equilibrium in terms of a model of reality that is clearly very different indeed from that implicit in Smith's theory of evolution".

[16] Most authors generally agree, as Loasby (1989, p. 48) notes, that Book V is the "core" of Marshall's *Principles*. If one interprets Marshall from this perspective, "Marshall's contribution must appear hesitant, fumbling, and sometimes even willfully perverse. He fails to pursue the logic of his analysis, seems not to understand the formal requirements of perfect completion which nowadays are listed in elementary textbooks, wanders into imperfect competition without realizing it, and by his insistence on the prevalence of increasing returns exposes his whole scheme to destruction by Sraffa (1926)" (Loasby 1989, p. 48). However his theory of value in Book V appears in a very different light when read in its proper sequence after Book IV, which deals with economic change and the division of labour, and in conjunction with *Industry and Trade* (ibid., p. 49). Loasby points out that Marshall's motivation for studying economics was to improve the condition of the people, and for this division of labour was one of the chief means. So it would

for Marshall marginal analysis (or static equilibrium analysis) is a stepping stone for long-term change and growth.[17] Therefore competition produces evolutionary change in the long run, though it is change which is gradual rather than disruptive. And change is described mostly at the level of a firm than at the macroeconomic level.[18]

In Marshall the presence of increasing returns under competition does not produce monopoly. The dilemma is an old one. Cournot had stated that a firm cannot be in equilibrium in pure competition if its marginal costs are falling. As a solution he advocated adopting the hypothesis of some degree of monopoly. Later, Sraffa (1926, p. 542), in his contribution to the cost controversy published in the *Economic Journal*, also took a similar line suggesting that increasing returns make it necessary "to abandon the path of free competition and turn in the opposite direction, namely towards monopoly". Sraffa also criticized Marshall for postulating a falling long-run supply curve, or even a rising one, as in the long-run the costs of production must be regarded as constant for commodities produced competitively in line with Ricardo (ibid., p. 541).

A firm, which is energetic and shows vitality, can expand its operations but cannot grow indefinitely. Even if there were no marketing or transportation difficulties, the process of expansion cannot go on forever, though at first it may appear that "no point is marked out at which he [the entrepreneur] need stop" (Marshall 1890, p. 285). At best it can hope to reach a stage of what Marshall called 'limited monopoly'. He defined it as "a monopoly limited by the consideration that a very high price would

appear that Book IV should take precedence over Book V in Marshall's scheme although he himself did not help clarify matters by showing aversion to controversy, by displaying non-committal attitude to economic policy except free trade, and by his determination to build consensus which had unintended consequences (ibid., pp. 47–48).

[17] In an *Economic Journal* article, Marshall (1898, p. 44) stated that "economic problems are not mechanical but are concerned with organic life and growth". See also Groenewegen (1991, f.n. 1).

[18] In this regard Dasgupta (1990, pp. 256–57) notes: "I do not believe Marshall would ever go in for an over-all growth theory. Substitution between goods and factors which, like his marginalist contemporaries, he recognized as basic in economic theory would present a formidable obstacle to process analysis in the context of the economy as a whole. As it is, Marshall assumes stationariness for the whole economy, as he does for his chosen commodity; a single commodity could obviously not be in stationary equilibrium unless the rest of the economy which feeds it remained stationary also… He would much rather confine himself to his one-commodity world where he could enunciate propositions which were free from ambiguity".

bring rival producers into the field" (p. 286). Further: "[L]ong before this end is reached, his progress is likely to be arrested by decay, if not of his faculties, yet of his liking for energetic work" (ibid., p. 286).

In Marshall, several factors are at work thwarting the tendency towards monopolization. First, Marshall had what has been termed as the "life cycle" theory of firms. Energetic and vigorous firms grow in size but after a point lose vitality and are overtaken by younger firms. We noted the analogy of the trees in the forest where a constant struggle for air and sunshine leads to some trees looming over others while many others decaying and dying in the process. Similarly: "[I]n almost every trade there is a constant rise and fall of large businesses, at any one moment some firms being in the ascending phase and others in the descending. For in times of average prosperity decay in one direction is sure to be more than balanced by growth in another" (ibid., pp. 316–17).[19] Secondly, there are external economies which are not dependent on the size of a firm but on the growth of a group of correlated industries. Their presence acts in a way to ensure compatibility between increasing returns and competition.[20]

For Marshall barriers to entry, as also noted by Marchionatti (1992, p. 567), are limited. So in the actual market structure, elements of monopoly and free competition shade into one another. As Marshall (1919, p. 397) in *Industry and Trade* notes:

> [T]hough monopoly and free competition are ideally wide apart, yet in practice they shade into one another by imperceptible degrees: that there is an element of monopoly in nearly all competitive businesses: and that nearly all the monopolies, that are of any practical importance in the present age, hold much of their power by an uncertain tenure; so that they would lose it ere long, if they ignored the possibilities of competition, direct and indirect.

[19] While individual firms may rise and fall frequently, the industry on the whole may be moving forward. Marshall (1890, p. 457) again gives an analogy of leaves of a tree: "[A]s the leaves of a tree…grow to maturity, reach equilibrium, and decay many times, while the tree is steadily growing upwards year by year".

[20] Marchionatti (1992, p. 562) provides a list of four factors (including those noted above): "[F]irst, the rise of diminishing returns in the life of the firm so reducing the capability to adopt technological changes; second, the external economies stimulating the diffusion of technological change; third, the difficulties of marketing; and finally, the technical constraints on the exploitation of internal economies".

Raffaelli (2003) considers Marshall's earlier philosophical writings and their link with later economic writings. These philosophical writings were edited by him in a volume (Raffaelli 1994) of which "Ye machine", in his opinion, is the most important paper. "What emerges from these Marshallian papers is a powerful evolutionary device, formed of the complementary and conflicting relationship between innovation, change, creativity or contrivance on the one side and repetition, automation, routine or instinct on the other" (Raffaelli 2004, p. ix). Mind is a system which consists of specialized sub-units that help the upper level of the mind by dispensing it from routine or repetitive work. Where routine prevails little contrivance (or innovation) is required. Creativity comes into play if a new problem has to be solved which defies existing routines. When the problem has been successfully solved, and if repeatedly faced, becomes a foundation for new routine (or instinct). Thus mental evolution happens by contrivance and standardization. Economic evolution also follows the same process. In Book IV of the *Principles*, as we saw, Marshall pointed out that when actions are reduced to routine, they are taken over by machinery, which results in dispensing with repetitive and degrading aspects of human labour. Raffaelli further notes that though Marshall was fascinated by cumulative routinization, he feared that it could be at the cost of choice and freedom with the processes becoming more capitalistic. So the right mix of orderly behaviour and freedom is required. "The conclusion is that to increase the productivity of human beings is not the aim in itself, unless it also leads to developing their faculties" (ibid., p. 60). It is in this context that Marshall stressed on education as investment in human beings and, after Smith and Mill, can be regarded as among the forerunners of the theory of human capital formation (ibid., p. 61).

Marshall applied a mix of standardization and creativity in the growth of knowledge. "Being the product of human mind, which is an evolutionary system, science is also compelled to follow its rules and patterns" (ibid., p. 48). Marshall stated that the part which systematic scientific reasoning plays in the production of knowledge resembles that which machine plays in the production of goods. As in the production of a good repeated action is taken over by machinery, similarly the general propositions serve as machinery for working on facts. Nature is not simple but complex, so is economics. According to Marshall, complex problems must be broken up into simpler parts so that one is enabled to apply systematic reasoning. The complexity and intricacy of the problem increase the necessity of the economic organon in its proper place. "The growth of knowledge is a never-ending process requiring creativity and standardization. Imagination performs the same function as contrivance does in 'Ye machine' while the economic organon and previously tested experience provide ready-made ways of dealing with routine elements of reality, as instinct does in 'Ye machine', once it gets established. Since science relies on *ceteris paribus* pound, in which disturbing phenomenon are provisionally sunk, its achievements are always provisional and 'care and forethought and self-restraint are needed at every step' (Marshall 1920: 739 n.). This humble attitude towards the evolution of science bars any search for completeness and perfection" (Raffaelli 2003, p. 49–50).

Marshall also rejected the notion of rational economic man in favour of "a man of flesh and blood". In Raffaelli's (2003, p. 50) opinion, this is not because of his ethical concerns or his excessive preoccupation with realism but is related to "how the human mind – like any other evolving system – works" constituting "a model which is far from that embodied in the economic man". In any single moment human mind has certain stable and routine features, provisionally tested by evolution, which characterize a man of flesh and blood. The economic man is deprived of them as well as their endowments of instincts, motives and passions. "More than a question of realism and values, Marshall's criticisms are a question of different ideas about the human mind" (ibid., p. 50). According to Raffaelli, this conception is supported by advance studies in psychology and cognitive science, and has devastating consequences for general equilibrium theory as well as strong versions of methodological individualism. Marshall's conception is closer to American institutionalists like Thorstein Veblen who saw man as a "coherent structure of propensities and habits" and who rejected the notion of man as "a lightening calculator of pleasure and pain". However, while Marshall gave no list of instincts, Veblen hoped to discover the building blocks of human mind and enumerated the instincts which direct its evolution. While Marshall made the device of economic analysis at the centre of the forces of change in different ages that promote social evolution, Veblen saw economic reasoning relative to the historical context. But Marshall was also quick to see that the results of economic analysis are conditional, piecemeal, and partial seen against the pretensions of "pure economics".

Saving, Investment, and Capital Accumulation

In Chapter VII of Book IV on "The Growth of Wealth" Marshall (1890, p. 222) distinguishes between wealth as an agent of production and wealth as an object of consumption. While studying this subject, he is concerned with growth of wealth "simply" without emphasizing one or the other. Marshall then links the progress of society "to the adoption of new processes and new machinery which economize human effort on condition that some of the effort is spent a good while before the attainment of the ultimate ends to which it is directed" (ibid., p. 222). As civilization progresses, new wants are developed, vast amounts of capital are required to gratify them. "There seems to be no good reason for believing that we are anywhere near a stationary state in which there will be no new important wants to be satisfied; in which there will be no more room for profitably investing present effort in providing for the future, and in which the accumulation of wealth will cease to have any reward. The whole history of man shows that his wants expand with the growth of his wealth and knowledge" (ibid., p. 223).

With ever increasing opportunities for investment of capital, the "surplus of production over necessaries of life" constantly increases, and this gives rise to the "power to save". Further: "When the arts of production were rude, there was very little production... But every increase in the arts of production, and in capital accumulated to assist and support labour in future production, increased the surplus out of which more wealth could be accumulated... Thus from step to step wealth and knowledge have grown, and with every step the power of saving wealth and extending knowledge has increased" (ibid., p. 224).

The causes which govern the accumulation of wealth differ across races, countries, and ages. For example, in Indians and to a lesser extent in Irishmen, there is a general habit of self-denial but they spend all their savings on "lavish festivities at funerals and marriages". The increase in their productive resources by the great engineering works was accomplished by "the capital of the less self-denying race of Englishmen" (ibid., p 225). To take another example, thriftiness in earlier times was due to lack of security so that those who made a provision for the future could be better off. But in the border areas between England and Scotland, constant forays meant that it was better to enjoy one's wealth while there was a chance for this, and this led to little progress. With the spread of civilization, insecurity of this kind has nearly disappeared. The advent of the benefits of the "poor law" and "poor relief", which are distributed in inverse proportion to the industry, thrift and forethought of the people, making it look foolish to make provision for the future, has led to another kind of insecurity. For the earlier habits of hard work, thriftiness and providing for the future have declined hindering the progress of working classes.

While the growth of the money economy has increased the temptations to which extravagant people are prone, it has increased the variety of uses available to a person to distribute his future expenditure. In a primitive state a person may store up things which he may not need as much as others which he has not stored up. Besides, there are many future wants which cannot be met by storing up goods. "But he who has stored up capital from which he derives a money income can buy what he will to meet his needs as they arise" (ibid., p. 227).

Modern methods of business have increased opportunities for a safe investment of capital which earns a revenue for people who themselves do not engage in business. These opportunities have allowed people to put by something for their old age which otherwise they may not have done. And, what is more, a man can leave behind a secure income for his wife and children after he dies. Marshall points out that family affection is the main motive for saving. "A man can have no stronger stimulus to energy and enterprise than the hope of rising in life, and leaving his family to start from a higher round of the social ladder than that on which he began" (ibid., p. 228).

Now we turn to the sources of accumulation. In the nineteenth-century England, commercial classes saved much more than either the country gentlemen or the working classes. So savings, in the opinion of English economists, came largely from the profits of capital. But in modern England, earnings of professionals and hired workers constitute an important source of accumulation. Middle classes including professionals deny themselves to educate their children; and working classes invest in the health and physical strength of their children. Marshall underlines the importance of human capital in the production of material wealth:

> The older economists took too little account of the fact that human faculties are as a means of production as any other kind of capital; and we may conclude, in opposition to them, that any change in the distribution

> of wealth which gives more to the wage receivers and less to the capitalists is likely, other things being equal, to hasten the increase of material production, and that it will not perceptibly retard the storing-up of material wealth. Of course, other things would not be equal if the change were brought about by violent methods which gave a shock to public security. (ibid., pp. 229-30)

Coming back to providing for the future, Marshall talks about the interest on capital as a reward for the sacrifice involved in *waiting* for the enjoyment of material resources. Some economists have termed this as *abstinence*, while others have objected that rich persons who live in luxury do not practise any abstinence in trying to save or accumulate wealth. Marshall (ibid., p. 233) points out that Marx and his followers were amused that Baron Rothschild practised any abstinence while trying to accumulate wealth, and a poor person living on seven shillings a week, in trying to feed his family, shows extravagance, and practices no economic abstinence at all. Since, in Marshall's opinion, the term is liable to be misunderstood, we may avoid using it "and say that accumulation of wealth is generally the result of a postponement of enjoyment or of *waiting* for it. Or, in other words again, it is dependent on man's *prospectiveness*; that is his faculty of realizing the future" (ibid. p. 233).

Böhm-Bawerk stressed that the methods of production which take more time are more productive, and every lengthening of a "roundabout process" is accompanied by an increase in its technical result. So, a higher interest is paid for more roundabout methods as they are more productive. In Marshall's view, he seems to have inverted cause and effect. "The true doctrine appears to be that, because interest has to be paid for, and can be gained by the use of capital; therefore those long and roundabout methods, which involve much locking up of capital, are avoided unless they are more productive than others. The fact that many roundabout methods are in various degrees productive is one of the causes that affect the rate of interest; and the rate of interest and the extent to which roundabout methods are employed are two of the elements of the central problem of distribution and exchange that mutually determine one another" (ibid., pp. 583–84, f.n. 1).

Marshall pointed out that there is no universal rule that the use of roundabout methods is more efficient than direct methods. "[T]here are some conditions under which the investment of effort in obtaining machinery and in making costly provision against future wants is economical in the long run, and others in which it is not; and that capital is accumulated in proportion to the prospectiveness of man on the one hand, and on the other to the absorption of capital by those roundabout methods, which are sufficiently productive to remunerate their adoption" (ibid., p. 82, f.n. 1).

Marshall stated that though an alert businessman pushes his capital investment in several directions until his marginal gains in all directions balance, but he adopts roundabout methods only if they are more effective in relation to their costs. "He never assumes that roundabout methods will be remunerative in the long run. But he is always on the lookout for roundabout methods that promise to be more effective in proportion to their cost than direct methods: and he adopts the best of them, if it lies within his means" (ibid., p. 359).

Critical Assessment

Marshall is regarded as a great economist who left behind a school of thought which included such names as A.C. Pigou, D. H. Robertson, John M. Keynes, and Joan Robinson. In the words of Schumpeter (1954, p. 833) it was a "genuine school" whose members thought in terms of a "well-defined scientific organon" fortified with "strong personal cohesion". Keynes (1925, p.12) wrote: "As a scientist he [Marshall] was, within his own field, the greatest in the world for a hundred years". Schumpeter (1952) in his *Ten Great Economists: From Marx to Keynes* included him as one of the great ten.[21] But as Loasby (1989, p. 48) noted, his scheme of increasing returns within the competitive framework was destroyed by Sraffa (1926), so that "much of the work from 1920 to 1933 was merely the negative task of getting Marshall out of the way" (Samuelson 1967, p. 24). The task was so effectively done that Joan Robinson (1951) realized that what was got out of the way included a richly detailed theory of economic development.

[21] Schumpeter (1951, p. 93) notes that Marshall was one of the first economists to realize the evolutionary nature of economic science. For him, human nature was malleable and changed with environment. Like Mill, he did not say that in political economy some problem or the other was completely settled. "On the contrary, he was fully aware that he was building an essentially temporary structure" (ibid., p. 93).

Marshall understood the working of the capitalist system well. As Schumpeter (1954, p. 836) notes: "In particular, he understood business, business problems, and businessmen better than most other scientific economists, not excluding those who were businessmen themselves. He sensed the intimate organic necessities of economic life even more intensively than he formulated them, and he spoke therefore as one who has power and not like the scribes – or like the theorists who are nothing but theorists. I am afraid that this achievement – so remarkable in one who moved primarily within academic circles and largely shared their prejudices – together with his Olympian repose, which his attitudes to hotly debated practical problems display, accounts in part for the unpopularity that surrounds his name today".[22]

According to Caldari and Masini (2008), Marshall broke from the classical tradition on limits to growth in three important respects. First, Marshall regarded growth of population as an important source of economic growth. He regarded production of wealth as a means to the sustenance of man. At the same time man is regarded as a chief means of the production of that wealth. Therefore man is at the centre of economic growth provided he is well educated, has good health and is strong in character. Hence he emphasized human capital as a means to increase efficiency and productivity of British industry which had started to face competition from newly industrialized Germany and USA. Second, Marshall regarded the law of diminishing returns could be overcome by the development of the means of transport and communication, gains from free trade, opening up of new countries and new sources of supply and technical change in agriculture. He maintained that the wording of the law of diminishing returns by Ricardo was inexact for he could not have anticipated these changes. Malthus and Ricardo did not pay attention to knowledge (the essence of progress) and its applications. In

[22] Comparing Marshall with Smith, Schumpeter (1954, pp. 834–35) points out that both had a similarity of general conceptions particularly with respect to economic evolution. Both combined "theory" and "facts" in approximately equal measure. Marshall's work not only followed from Smith's but he also recognized his kinship with Smith. Both the *Wealth of Nations* and *Principles*, were the works of fully matured minds taking decades of thought to mature. While Marshall was more well received than Smith in Britain, Smith was more successful abroad. "The reason is not far to seek. Marshall's message – howsoever much he liked the idea of being 'read by businessmen' – was after all a message to the economics profession" (ibid., p. 834).

Industry and Trade Marshall (1919, p. 189) emphasized: "In agriculture, improved knowledge and methods are always contending against Nature's resistance to the demands made on her by an increasing population". Finally, Marshall (1890, p. 366) regarded the stationary state as "a fiction". For Ricardo a stationary state was gloomy and dismal, for Mill it was a privileged state where people could have recourse to all pleasures of life. For Marshall there were two relative limits to growth: social and natural. Social limits arise because man is a social animal who lives in particular cultural and institutional setting which is evolving over time. Economic institutions cannot change much faster than human nature, so change is slow and gradual. While progress increases man's command over Nature, its correct use requires the development of higher human faculties, and this takes time.

Following Stigler (1990), Groenewegen (2007) listed four major and several minor contributions made by Marshall to economics. One of the major contributions is that he "gave prominence to the theory of the firm and may be said to have formally initiated that research programme both in his Principles of Economics and in the subsequent Industry and Trade. His emphasis on the firm also enhanced the meaning of an industry without which the economic notion of the firm would be relatively meaningless" (ibid., 2007, p. 3). As we have seen, Marshall had a "life cycle" theory of firms where their rise and fall is frequent, but the industry as a whole can grow (or oscillate) in the long run. One can detect elements of evolution and endogeneity in the growth of a business, but nevertheless it remains a microeconomic theory of growth. In Marshall's (1890, p. 315) words:

> An able man, assisted perhaps by some strokes of good fortune, gets a firm footing in the trade, he works hard and lives sparely, his own capital grows fast, and the credit that enabled him more capital still grows faster; he collects around him subordinates of more than ordinary zeal and ability; as his business increases they rise with him, they trust him and he trusts them, each of them devotes with energy to just that work for which he is specially fitted, so that no high ability is wasted on easy work, and no difficult work is entrusted to unskillful hands. Corresponding to his steadily increasing economy of skill, the growth of his business brings with it similar economies of specialized machines and plant of all kinds; every improved process is quickly adopted and made the basis for further improvements; success brings credit and credit brings success; credit and success help to retain old customers and to bring new ones; the increase of his trade

> gives him great advantages in buying; his goods advertise one another, and thus diminish his difficulty in finding a vent for them. The increase in the scale of his business increases rapidly the advantages which he has over his competitors, and lowers the price at which he can afford to sell. This process may go on as long as his energy and enterprise, his inventive and organizing power retain their full strength and freshness, and so long as the risks which are inseparable from business do not cause him exceptional losses...[23]

Adam Smith pointed out that the division of labour depends on the extent of the market. Marshall placed a great deal of emphasis on the use of capital in promoting the division of labour, as he noted that anything which has to be done over and over again in the same way is sure to be taken over by machinery sooner or later. But he does well to note that it is the "largeness of markets" or "increased demand for great number of things" that leads to the subdivision of labour. Again he notes that indirect or roundabout methods are more productive, but only those will be used which are more remunerative relative to cost. Capital is accumulated in proportion to prospectiveness of man as well as its adoption through those roundabout methods which are remunerative. Thus, like Smith, the use of capital depends on the "largeness" of markets, and capital accumulation by itself is not an independent engine of growth. Smith had suggested a number of measures to increase the size of the market including international trade, but Marshall (1890, p. 270) apart from noting that the "causes which determine the economic progress of nations belong to the study of international trade", does not dwell much on the issue in the *Principles*.

Marshall (1890) also talked about the advantages of large-scale production by firms. He made a distinction between prime (variable) and supplementary (fixed) costs. He stated that while supplementary costs have to be covered to a considerable extent even in the short run, they must be completely covered in the long run (ibid., p. 360). Again: "It is of course just as essential in the long run that the price obtained should

[23] See also Loasby (1982, p. 112) who stated: "A fairly casual reading of Book IV of A. Marshall's *Principles* is sufficient to indicate that Marshall had an entrepreneurial theory of the firm and an entrepreneurial theory of competition...". After Marshall the theory of the firm broadly developed along two lines: Coase (1937)–Williamson (1981) transactions-cost analysis which has implication for the *size* of the firm, and Penrose's (1959) theory of the *growth* of the firm.

cover general or supplementary costs as that it should cover prime costs" (ibid., p.420). Allyn Young pointed out that increasing returns do not depend on any relationship between prime and supplementary costs but due to other causes. It is large production, and not large-scale production, that permits increasing returns (Young 1990, p. 54). Here Young is emphasizing the macroeconomic phenomenon of increasing returns.

Young (1928), who made Marshall's distinction between internal and external economies as one of the main pillars of his growth theory, stated that this distinction is useful in two ways. First, it is a safeguard against the common error of assuming that increasing returns necessarily lead to monopoly. Secondly, it simplifies the analysis of price determination under increasing returns. A representative firm, which maintains its identity and confines itself to a given range of activities, becomes the vehicle through which the economies achieved by the industry as a whole are transmitted to the market and show themselves in product prices. But this is a partial view of the matter as internal economies of firms, which may figure as external economies of other firms, when added up do not account for all available external economies. A representative firm manufacturing a product (or a group of products) works under conditions of comparative stability, but in the external field change is quantitative as well as qualitative. New products, processes, and industries come into being making the analysis of equilibrium an unfruitful task. "Not much is to be gained by probing into it to see how increasing returns show themselves in the costs of individual firms and in the prices at which they offer their products" (Young 1928, p. 528).

The supply–demand curve apparatus, being a partial equilibrium tool, is unsuitable for the analysis of the field which is dominated by disequilibrium and increasing returns. As Young (1990, p. 45) points out: "Certainly the matter cannot be explained by the curve apparatus which does not see things 'in their togetherness'". Moreover, under the influence of external economies the representative firms may sooner or later lose its identity. So its costs and prices may not be relevant to draw up the long-run supply curve (or even the demand curve) of the industry. The supply and demand curves are reciprocal in nature and shift as a result of the very forces shifting one of the curves.

Similarly, Schumpeter (1954, pp. 836–37) also notes that although Marshall talks about the evolutionary phenomena of economic life, "his theoretical apparatus is strictly static". Although he made many wise and penetrating remarks about dynamical problems,[24] his theory in the *Principles* "is itself impaired by the strain to which it is subject, especially in the neighborhood of the phenomena of decreasing average cost".[25] However, part of the problem arises because Marshall situated his statics as a part of dynamics. To Marshall's credit it may be stated that statics and dynamics for him were not watertight compartments. Since economic evolution happened slowly and incrementally, the same incremental approach could be applied to short-term problems where the disturbing causes are suppressed through the pound of ceteris paribus. The recent upsurge of interest in Marshall's evolutionary thought testifies to the wisdom and substance of his approach.

References

Blaug, Mark. 1996. *Economic Theory in Retrospect*, 5th ed. Cambridge: Cambridge University Press.

Caldari, Katia. 2018. Alfred Marshall. In *Great Economic Thinkers: From Adam Smith to Amartya Sen*, ed. Jonathan Conlin. New Delhi: Speaking Tiger.

Caldari, Katia, and Fabio Masini. 2008. The limits to growth: Alfred Marshall and the British economic tradition. In *Marshall and Schumpeter on Evolution: Economic Sociology of Capitalist Development*, ed. Y. Shionoya and T. Nishizawa, 166–187. Cheltenham and Northampton: Edward Elagar.

Coase, Ronald H. 1937. The nature of the firm. *Economica*, November: 386–405.

Dardi, Marco. 2003. Alfred Marshall's partial equilibrium: Dynamics in disguise. In *The Economics of Alfred Marshall: Revisiting Marshall's Legacy*, ed. Richard Arena and Michel Quéré, 84–112. Basingstoke and New York: Palgrave Macmillan.

Dasgupta, A.K. 1990. An aspect of Marshall's period analysis. In *Centenary Essays on Alfred Marshall*, ed. John K. Whitaker. Cambridge: Cambridge University Press.

Groenewegen, Peter D. 2007. *Alfred Marshall: Economist 1842–1924*. Basingstoke: Palgrave Macmillan.

Groenewegen, Peter D. 1991. Alfred Marshall and the history of economic thought. *Quaderni Di Storia Dell'economica Politica* 9 (2/3): 59–87.

[24] Schumpeter quotes John M. Keynes's (1930, II, p. 406) *Treatise on Money* here.

[25] See also Blaug (1996, p. 375) who points out that the device of the representative firm allowed Marshall to state the conditions of equilibrium for an industry without requiring the individual firms to be in equilibrium.

Harrod, Roy F. 1948. *Towards a Dynamic Economics*. London: Macmillan.
Hart, Neil. 2012. *Equilibrium and Evolution: Alfred Marshall and the Marshallians*. Basingstoke: Palgrave Macmillan.
Hodgson, Geoffrey M. 1993. The Mecca of Alfred Marshall. *Economic Journal* 103 (417): 406–415.
Keynes, John M. 1925. Alfred Marshall, 1842–1924. In *Memorials of Alfred Marshall*, ed. A.C. Pigou, 1–65. London: Macmillan.
Keynes, John M. 1930. *A Treatise on Money*, vol. II. London: Macmillan.
Lavezzi, Andrea. 2003. Smith, Marshall and Young on division of labour and economic growth. *European Journal of the History of Economic Thought* 10 (1): 81–108.
Loasby, Brian. 1982. Economics of dispersed and incomplete information. In *Method, Process and Austrian Economics: Essays in Honour of Ludwig von Mises*, ed. Israel M. Kirzner, 111–130. Toronto: Lexington Books.
Loasby, Brian. 1989. *The Mind and Method of the Economist*. Cheltenham: Edward Elgar.
Marchionatti, Roberto. 1992. Marshall on increasing returns and competition. *Quaderni Di Storia Dell'economica Politica* 10: 553–583.
Marshall, Alfred. 1890 (1920). *Principles of Economics*, 8th ed. London: Macmillan.
Marshall, Alfred. 1898. Distribution and exchange. *Economic Journal* 8 (29): 37–59.
Marshall, Alfred. 1919 (1920). *Industry and Trade*, 3rd ed. London: Macmillan.
Niman, Neil B. 1998. Marshall, Veblen, and the search for an evolutionary economics. In *The Economic Mind of America*, ed. Malcolm Rutherford. Abingdon: Routledge.
Penrose, Edith. 1959 (2009). *The Theory of the Growth of the Firm*, 4th ed. Oxford: Oxford University Press.
Pigou, Arthur C. 1925. In memoriam: Alfred Marshall. In *Memorials of Alfred Marshall*, ed. A.C. Pigou, 81–90. London: Macmillan.
Raffaelli, Tiziano. 1994. Marshall's early philosophical writings. *Research in the History of Economic Thought and Methodology, Archival Supplement* 4: 51–158.
Raffaelli, Tiziano. 2003. *Marshall's Evolutionary Economics*. London and New York: Routledge.
Raffaelli, Tiziano. 2004. *Marshall's Evolutionary Economics*. London and New York: Routledge.
Richardson, G.B. 1975. Adam Smith on competition and increasing returns. In *Essays on Adam Smith*, ed. A.S. Skinner and T. Wilson. Oxford: Oxford University Press.
Robbins, Lionel. 1928. The representative firm. *Economic Journal* 38 (151): 387–404.

Robinson, Joan. 1951. *Collected Economic Papers*, vol. I. Oxford: Basil Blackwell.
Samuelson, Paul. 1967. The monopolistic competition revolution. In *Monopolistic Competition Theory: Studies in Impact*, ed. R.E. Kuenne. New York: Wiley.
Schumpeter, Joseph A. 1951 (2003). *Ten Great Economists: From Marx to Keynes*. San Diego: Simon Publications.
Schumpeter, Joseph A. 1952 (1997). *Ten Great Economists: From Marx to Keynes*. London: Routledge.
Schumpeter, Joseph A. 1954 (1986). *History of Economic Analysis*. London: Allen and Unwin.
Smith, Adam. 1776 (1976). *An Enquiry into the Nature and Causes of the Wealth of Nations*, ed. Edwin Cannan. Chicago: Chicago University Press.
Sraffa, Piero. 1926. The laws of return under competitive conditions. *Economic Journal* 36: 535–550.
Stigler, George. 1990. The place of Marshall's *Principles* in the development of economics. In *Centenary Essays on Alfred Marshall*, ed. J.K. Whitaker. Cambridge: Cambridge University Press.
Williamson, Oliver E. 1981. The economics of organization: The transaction cost approach. *American Journal of Sociology* 87 (3): 548–577.
Young, Allyn A. 1928. Increasing returns and economic progress. *Economic Journal* 38 (152): 527–542.
Young, Allyn A. 1990. Nicholas Kaldor's Notes on Allyn Young's LSE Lectures 1927–29. *Journal of Economic Studies* 17 (3/4): 18–114.

CHAPTER 4

Allyn Young on Increasing Returns

Allyn Young, a Harvard economist, shot into international fame for his contribution to Paris peace conference after WWI. It was during his tenure at the London School of Economics, when on a three year leave from Harvard, that he wrote his most famous paper "Increasing returns and economic progress" (Young, 1928a). That paper was first presented as a presidential address in Glasgow on 10 September 1928 at Section F of the British Association for the Advancement of Science and subsequently appeared in the *Economic Journal* in December. In this paper Young postulated a new paradigm for economics, one which was based on disequilibrium rather than equilibrium. Young, for some years, had been criticizing the equilibrium paradigm in both its versions—general as well as partial. In a letter to his friend Frank Knight, dated 6 October, 1928, he stated that the purely static view did not interest him very much "because if it is *rigorously* adhered to, almost everything worth saying about it can be put into a very few pages". Further: "We *have* to depart from it somehow. The only question is just how".

Young's paper can be seen in the context of the cost controversy appearing in the *Economic Journal* in the 1920s. It started with J. M. Clapham's (1922) paper "Of empty economic boxes" in which he stated that any empirical attempt to classify industries into increasing, diminishing, and constant returns would end in failure. Another participant

R. Chandra, *Endogenous Growth in Historical Perspective*, Palgrave Studies in Economic History,
https://doi.org/10.1007/978-3-030-83761-7_4

in the controversy, Piero Sraffa (1926), criticized Marshall's concept of external economies which are attached to a group of correlated industries. He was of the view that they are incompatible with Marshall's partial equilibrium theory of taking a single firm or an industry at a time. Sraffa further thought that increasing returns are practically nonexistent; if at all they are present they are incompatible with competition and point in the direction of monopoly. Young (1928a), of course, did not agree with Sraffa that monopoly theory was the solution to the problem of increasing returns. Young, in line with Smith, thought that increasing returns and competition were mutually reinforcing.

As noted by Blitch (1995, p. 170), Young's paper was partly an answer to Sraffa's contention that increasing returns can only be reconciled with monopoly, and partly a refutation to D.H. MacGregor's presidential address to the British Association in 1927 entitled "Rationalisation of industry". MacGregor thought that the British industry, recovering from WWI, needed cartelization to overcome its problems. Young, on the other hand, was of the opinion that British industry, seen against its own problems and possibilities, was not less efficiently organized than the American industry. The higher productivity achieved by the American industry was not as much due to superior intelligence, or greater use of power and machinery, as due to its much larger market. Because of the largeness of its market, the use of highly capital-intensive production methods, which are economical in America, would not be profitable elsewhere. "Taking a country's endowment as given…the most important single factor in determining the effectiveness of its industry appears to be the size of the market" (Young 1928a, p. 532).[1]

Young was against the equilibrium method in economics both in its general as well as partial forms. He disliked the partial equilibrium method of Marshall because it was based on ceteris paribus or one-thing-at-a-time theorizing. Young liked to study the economic phenomenon in its togetherness. But Young recognized that this method was useful for the

[1] The use of capital-intensive methods (or roundabout methods) in Young does not depend on the rate of interest but on the size of the market. "[T]he actual industrialists (and bankers) deny that variations in the rate of interest influence the extent of their operations, providing their competitors pay the same. It is the 'market' on which they count" (Young 1990, p. 82). This point was also noted by Kaldor (1972, p. 1242) who wrote: "[Young] argued that the extent to which capital is used in relation to labour is predominantly a matter of the scale of operations – the capital/labour ratio in production is a function of the extent of the market rather than of relative factor prices".

beginner and easier to understand. Moreover, it also had relevance to practical economic problems. The general equilibrium method, on the other hand, was highly abstract. Although it had the benefit of bringing out the interdependence of factors which determine prices, costs, supply, demand, and distributive shares, it was far removed from the practical problems of economic life. In a letter to Frank Knight, dated 9 December 1922, he wrote: "The two variable method lends itself to analysis of practical problems. I have yet to see that the method of general equilibrium gives us anything at all that gets us anywhere. Perhaps we cannot get anywhere. It is extremely hard to frame a statement of the economic system of many variables that does not seem to be just truism".

For Young, economics was an eminently practical subject and had an instrumental value in solving practical economic problems. Although mathematical economics is useful in bringing out hidden assumptions and logical flaws which are likely to remain concealed in ordinary reasoning, it makes for highly abstract economics limiting its practical value. In his article "English political economy", Young (1928b; Mehrling and Sandilands 1999, p. 25) argued: "A perfectly abstract economics is impracticable. A system concerned merely with the relations of variables which are defined only by their mathematical attributes is not economics, any more than pure mathematics is mechanics". Young further stated that the final terms of every chain of economic inferences reach out into other systems of relations often non-economic in character. It is from these other relations that the final terms get their meaning and significance, and by treating them as mere algebraic symbols, neither all possible meanings get exhausted nor does economics remain a practically useful subject.

Having discarded the equilibrium method, Young (1928a) turned his attention to disequilibrium approach to economics. In his paper on increasing returns and economic progress, he built on Smith's famous aphorism that the division of labour is limited by the size of the market. In doing so, he described himself as a "minor composer" and Smith as "one of the masters". He wrote:

> That theorem, I have always thought, is one of the most illuminating and fruitful generalizations which can be found anywhere in the whole literature of economics. In fact, as I am bound to confess, I am taking it as the text of this paper, in much the way that some minor composer borrows a theme from one of the masters and adds certain developments or variations of his own. (Young 1928a, p. 529)

This chapter takes the position that Young's contribution was not that of a minor composer. As noted by Schumpeter (1954, p. 876, f.n. 23), Young was a modest man and had the habit of hiding rather than highlighting his best ideas.[2] Young cast his explanation of growth in terms of macroeconomic increasing returns, disequilibrium economics, cumulative causation, and external economies instead of internal economies of scale. Such vocabulary did not exist in Smith's time, so he could not have been expected to cast his explanation in these terms. Such ideas, when present, are implicit rather than explicit in Smith.

The rest of this chapter is organized as follows. First, we trace the origin of increasing returns in Youngian thinking as brought out in his contributions to *Outlines of Economics* and Young-Knight exchange on increasing returns. Then we reconstruct Young's theory of increasing returns which is based on the following elements: the role of the market size, the role of disequilibrium paradigm, the role of external economies, the role of roundabout methods and industrial specialization, and the role of competition. Next, we compare Young's theory with those of Smith and Marshall. Both played an important part in Young's thinking on growth. Finally, we make a critical assessment of Young's theory.

Tracing the Origins of Increasing Returns in Youngian Thinking

Contributions to Outlines of Economics

Young's thinking on increasing returns can be traced back to his contributions to the best-selling American economics textbook *Outlines of Economics* (Ely et al. various editions) as well as his exchange with Frank Knight (to be discussed below). Young was one of the four coauthors along with Richard Ely, Thomas Adams and Max Lorenz in the 1908, 1916, 1923, and 1930 editions. Following Marshall (1890), Young

[2] Young's modesty has been noted by several students and colleagues in letters and obituaries written after his death. In a letter of condolence (dated 17 March 1929) to Mrs. Young after Young's premature death, John M. Keynes wrote: "His was an outstanding personality in the economics world and the most lovable. His influence as a teacher and a critic and as one who would always share with others all his best ideas was far greater than anyone would suppose who only knew his printed words; for it was his own work – unfortunately perhaps – which always came last". Schumpeter (1954, p. 876, f.n.) also wrote of his habit hiding rather than highlighting his best ideas.

made a distinction between internal and external economies (see, for example, Ely et al. 1916, pp. 171–74). He noted that economies of large-scale production by themselves cannot bring any competitive industry to decreasing expenses. "Wherever the advantages of large-scale production are increasing, the principle effect must be merely to divide the aggregate operations of the industry among a somewhat smaller number of establishments than would otherwise be found. But the growth of the size of the business establishment has no direct bearing upon the existence of the condition of decreasing expenses in the industry at large, except in so far as an increase in the size of the individual establishment is found to be one of the ways of utilizing to best advantage the various economies made possible by the increased industrial product. Large-scale production does not create the condition of decreasing expenses, but it may be an indication, a manifestation of the presence of that condition" (ibid., pp. 173–74).

Young (Ely et al. 1923) stated that internal economies, associated with the increase in the size of an individual business establishment, are important. But their importance should not be exaggerated as average size of individual undertakings in agriculture and many special fields of manufacture was not increasing (or increasing very slowly) despite a rapid increase in total output. On the other hand, external economies, associated with the general organization of an entire industry when its output increases, are vastly more important:

> These economies take the form, for the most part, of a greater specialization or division of labor within the industry as a whole. It becomes profitable to separate the different processes in the operation of the industry. Opportunity is thus given for a more thoroughgoing and more efficient specialization of labor and for the use of highly specialized machinery. Plants themselves become specialized – devoted only to certain steps in production – and these specialized plants may be located at particularly advantageous points. Subordinate industries may be developed, supplying machinery, other equipment, and accessory products. Improved transportation may be developed. In short, a large output makes it possible for an industry to utilize the best and the most economical methods of production and to keep pace with the advance of technical knowledge.
>
> Indirect, roundabout ways of doing things, involving a thoroughgoing subdivision of processes and the use of large amounts of fixed capital in the form of elaborate plants and expensive machinery are advantageous only

> when the industrial output is large. All these things have played an important part in the progress of most of the great manufacturing industries, and in making their products cheaper. (ibid., p. 165)

Young, in the 1930 edition of *Outlines* (Ely et al. 1930, p. 203), maintained that while over the short period increasing expense was the normal condition of industry, in the long run the tendency to decreasing expense is to be found in increasing specialization of industries as a whole. He wrote:

> The principal cause of the tendency to decreasing expense is found in the 'progressive division and specialization of industries.' It is a phenomenon not so much of the typical unit of industry or of any one industry, as of increasing specialization of industries taken together. It is assisted of course by invention and new knowledge; and also retarded by the exhaustion of some natural resources; but it would probably go on even without invention, because of the economies resulting from the use of roundabout and indirect processes of production, manifesting themselves particularly in newer and more specialized industries. 'Decreasing expense,' as a resultant of many partly conflicting factors and forces, represents the long run tendency in a large and important group of industries under competitive conditions. (Ely et al. 1930, p. 203)

Young-Knight Exchange on Increasing Returns

Frank Knight wrote his thesis "The theory of business profits" under Young at Cornell (which was submitted in 1916) and published it as *Risk, Uncertainty and Profit* (Knight, 1921). The book broke new ground in the theory of profits and, as Young had predicted, established Knight's reputation as an economist. In the book, Knight made a distinction between risk and uncertainty. While the former could be handled by insurance markets, it is the latter which gave rise to profits. However, Knight had a static view of competition and on page 36 of his thesis wrote: "cost must always increase as supply increases". Young disagreed and on the margins of the same page noted:

> Not if the increase in supply is a response to an *increased* demand. External economies of certain sorts *will* be realized... The point is that certain

> economies are *possible only with large demand*. Take for example the installation of *automatic tools* in a machine industry. The case of 'tooling up' is too large to be distributed profitably over a small output.

In his thesis, on the same page, Knight also wrote: "New supply will then come through an increase in the number of similar establishments, not through an increase in the size of any one of them and no economies of any large scale production will be realized". Young commented that this was incorrect because the increase in supply will come from an increase in specialized undertakings, not similar undertakings. Young continued: "But I admit that economies of 'large-scale production' are really economies of large-scale demand".

In a letter to Knight dated 11 August 1928, Young maintained that increasing returns do not manifest themselves adequately from the point of view of equilibrium theory:

> Where I don't follow you, of course, is in respect of increasing returns. The reason may be that increasing returns do not exhibit themselves adequately when approached from the point of view of *equilibrium* price theory. To me it seems *obvious* that when larger output (i.e., larger *markets*) makes roundabout methods economical – or a degree of roundaboutness economical – which would be uneconomical otherwise, *potential* increasing returns exist, in the sense indicated by *your* definition of costs. That is, production can be increased while displacing a *progressively smaller* (proportionately) amount of other commodities,– quite apart from the question of whether this leads to large-scale firms or 'industries.' The economies which show themselves in increasing returns are the economies of *large* production, not large-scale production.

Young showed his 1928 presidential address to Knight and sought his opinion on it. Knight believed in making a sharp distinction between static and dynamic aspects of theory which Young had not done in his paper. In a letter to Young, dated 24 September 1928, he wrote: "Your discussion puzzles me especially because you admit the accumulation of capital into an otherwise static situation". In reply Young (dated 6 October 1928) wrote:

> I enjoyed your comments on my paper, The whole issue appears to be one of *exposition*... I can't see why to begin with static assumptions & *then* to inquire the effects of changing *any* particular variable should be

> taboo, & consequently I don't get the point of your objections of my introducing capital accumulation. Further, I should hold that the conditions of an equilibrium *rate* of change afford just as appropriate a hunting ground for 'pure theory' as the conditions of *static* equilibrium do.[3]

Reconstruction of Young's Growth Theory

The Role of Markets or Commerce

Like Smith, Young (1928a) placed great importance on the expansion of markets in economic progress. According to him technical change during the industrial revolution was driven by prior market expansion. It was dangerous, in Young's opinion, to assign a leading role to any single factor for the economic revolution of the eighteenth century. "But is there any other factor which has a better claim to that role than the persisting search for markets? No other hypothesis so well unites economic history and economic theory. The industrial revolution of the eighteenth century has come to be generally regarded, not as a cataclysm brought about by certain inspired improvements in industrial technique, but as a series of changes related in an orderly way to prior changes in industrial organization and to enlargement of markets" (ibid., p. 536).

In his 1929 article on "The creator of Wealth", Young (1929a; Mehrling and Sandilands 1999, p. 151) mentioned that in the growth of economic civilization it was commerce that has led the way. Moreover, the great inventions of Watt, Kay, Hargreaves, etc. were called into being by the growth of markets especially the Indian one:

> Quite in keeping with what we have seen to be the general character of free commercial activity is the fact that in the growth of our economic civilization it has been commerce, rather than agriculture or industry, that has led the way. Production is limited by the market. It can advance only as markets are increased. Commerce creates markets. The industrial revolution at the end of the eighteenth century, when the factory system came into being and when the use of power was first successfully applied to manufactures, cannot be ascribed merely to the great inventions of Watt,

[3] The theme of equilibrium rate of growth also appears in his LSE Lectures (See Young 1990, p. 45). Demand curve is not constant, as in Marshall, but shifts as a result of the very forces shifting the supply curve. It was therefore more appropriate to have a theory or equilibrium or optimum rate of progress which would keep the supply curve close up to the demand curve. See also Chandra (2020, p. 165).

> Kay, Hargreaves, Arkwright, and Crompton. These mechanical improvements were, from one point of view, really called into being by the fact that the growth of English commerce, and especially the development of the Indian market, had, for the first time, made the factory system and large-scale production possible.

It was sometimes said that in the earlier ages industry was the servant of commerce, but now since the rise of "industrial capitalism" the relation had been reversed, with commerce merely being the agent of industry. "If this means that finding markets is one of the tasks of modern industry it is true. If it means that industry imposes its will upon the market, that whereas formerly the things which were produced were the things which could be sold, now the things which have to be sold are the things that are produced, it is not true" (Young 1928a, p. 536).

Young emphasized the role of the "potential market" in this regard. The cost per unit of a firm producing a given volume of output varies substantially from the cost per unit of an undertaking where the output is five times as large. Reduction in cost is not merely due to economies of scale as the firm expands its operations, but also due to the economies resulting from the expansion of industrial operations as a whole. The search for markets is not a matter of disposing of a "surplus product", in the Marxian sense, but of finding an outlet for a "potential product". It is not entirely a matter of multiplying profits by multiplying sales; it is partly a matter of augmenting profits by reducing costs (ibid., p. 537).

While Smith was dismissive about mercantilism, Young praised the mercantilist instinct of businessmen. Schumpeter had emphasized the role of an innovative entrepreneur in economic progress but Young stated that this was exaggerated. "Now genuine leadership is rare; there is a flock behind any successful leader, and the thing is overdone. But does not Schumpeter overemphasise 'originality'? It is not so important that someone should go ahead" (Young 1990, p. 82). Young also pointed out that the normal state of industry was not depression but something closer to the statistical average. Moreover, the role of "adventitious" elements in starting an industry is not sufficient. Thus, the role of the entrepreneur is perhaps more in terms of his continuous search for markets rather than in his innovative ability. As Young (ibid., p. 537) writes:

> The business man's mercantilistic emphasis upon markets may have a sounder basis than the economist who thinks mostly in terms of economic

> statics is prone to admit. How far 'selling expenses,' for example, are to be counted sheer economic waste depends on their effect upon the aggregate product of industry, as distinguished from their effects upon the fortunes of particular undertakings.

Young (1929a; Mehrling and Sandilands 1999, p. 151) also stated:

> Men do not produce or manufacture goods in the blind hope that in some way buyers will be found. In manufacturing and agriculture alike production increases only when larger markets are available. The history of commerce has been the history of the growth of markets.

The Disequilibrium Paradigm

Young built on Smith's dictum regarding the relationship between the division of labour and the market size and cast it in terms of cumulative causation. If the division of labour depends on the size of the market, the size of the market also depends on the division of labour. The two-way relationship between the division of labour and market size leads to a theory of growth as a process of cumulative causation, and as something endogenous to the competitive economic system.[4]

Young defined market, not in terms of population or geographical area alone, but in terms of purchasing power or the capacity to absorb a large annual output of goods. This leads to the observation that capacity to buy depends on the capacity to produce. Thus:

> In an inclusive view, considering the market not as an outlet for the products of a particular industry, and therefore external to that industry, but as the outlet for goods in general, the size of the market is determined and defined by the volume of production. If this statement needs any qualification, it is that the conception of a market in this inclusive sense – an aggregate of productive activities, tied together by trade – carries with it the notion that there must be some sort of balance, that different productive activities must be proportioned one to another. (Young 1928a, p. 533)

[4] "Seeking equilibrium conditions under increasing returns is as good as looking for a mare's nest" (Young 1990, p. 45).

In the light of this broader definition of the market, Young posited that Adam Smith's dictum amounts to the theorem that "the division of labour depends in large part upon the division of labour" (ibid., p. 533). This was more than a tautology, and implied that the counterforces which were continuously defeating those making for equilibrium were more pervasive and deeply rooted in the modern economic system than what one commonly realizes. Young (ibid., p. 533) continued:

> Not only new or adventitious elements, coming in from the outside, but elements which are permanent characteristics of the ways in which goods are produced make continuously for change. Every important advance in the organization of production, regardless of whether it is based upon anything which, in a narrow or technical sense, would be called new 'invention,' or involves a fresh application of the fruits of scientific progress to industry, alters the conditions of industrial activity and initiates responses elsewhere in the industrial structure which in turn have a further unsettling effect. Thus change becomes progressive and propagates itself in a cumulative way.

Young was skeptical of traditional supply–demand formulas in explaining these broader aspects of increasing returns.[5] If, however, one insisted on using them it was better to use them in reciprocal sense. Young made use of Marshall-Edgeworth idea of offer curves or reciprocal demand to explain the endogenous growth process. If one assumes elastic demand for each commodity in the sense that a small increase in its supply is attended by an increase in the amounts of other commodities exchanged for it (or that goods are produced competitively under conditions of increasing returns):

> Under such conditions an increase in the supply of one commodity is an increase in the demand for other commodities, and it must be supposed that every increase in demand will evoke an increase in supply. The rate at which one industry grows is conditioned by the rate at which other industries grow, but since the elasticities of demand and of supply will differ for different products, some industries will grow faster than others. Even with a stationary population and in the absence of new discoveries in pure and applied science there are no limits to the process of expansion

[5] Young (ibid., p. 26) felt that Marshall's supply and demand curves hold ceteris paribus and cannot be integrated to give the whole economic structure or the social picture.

> except the limits beyond which demand is not elastic or returns do not increase. (ibid., p. 534)

Young (1929b; Mehrling and Sandilands 1999, p. 145) in his article "supply and demand" stated that Say's law or the theorem that "supply creates its own demand" has proved to be misleading. It is significantly true only if the demand for commodities is elastic. Given elastic demand, general overproduction is impossible. There may be maladjustments of supply and demand in individual industries or the overall production may exceed expansion of incomes. But these will be attended to by changes in relative prices or the general price level. Thus, given elastic demand, supply and demand in the aggregate are merely different aspects of a single situation. In other words, Say's law would work only if demand is elastic, not otherwise.

Young maintained that increasing returns are not negated by their costs. Increasing returns are not spread through time in such a way as to secure an equilibrium of costs and advantages. Arguing otherwise would amount to saying that no real economic progress was possible by the operation of forces engendered within the economic system. This would be a conclusion at variance with common sense as the fact of economic growth testifies. "I shall merely observe, first, that the appropriate conception is that of moving equilibrium, and second, that the costs which (under increasing returns) grow less rapidly than the product are not the 'costs' which figure in an 'equilibrium of costs and advantages'" (Young 1928a, p. 535).

Young listed two main obstacles to this virtually unending process of endogenous growth. First, human material may be resistant to change as new trades have to be learnt and new habits have to be acquired. Moreover, geographical distribution may need to be changed by breaking up existing communal groups. Second, accumulation of necessary capital may take time, even though the process of accumulation is largely one of turning incremental product into further increase of product. Accelerating the rate of accumulation may encounter increasing costs in terms of technical and psychological factors. Other factors may include natural scarcities or supply limitations and the fact that progress in most fields cannot be continuous. Next important step may not be taken unless certain critical mass of prospective advantages has accumulated. In other words, Young was talking about indivisibilities of capital and technology.

The Role of External Economies

As we have seen from his contribution in the *Outlines*, Young followed Marshall in making a distinction between internal and external economies. He recognized that external economies were far more important to growth than internal. But his position on external economies evolved over the years. In his review of Pigou's *Wealth and Welfare*, Young (1913) criticized Pigou for stating that provided certain external economies are common to all the suppliers in the agriculture sector, the presence of diminishing returns to each individually was compatible with increasing returns in respect of all taken together. Young (ibid.; Mehrling and Sandilands 1999, p. 95, n. 10) wrote: "I cannot imagine 'external economies' adequate to bring about this result". However, in 1928, (pecuniary) external economies formed the main pillar in his growth theory.

Young (1928a) stated that Marshall's distinction between external and internal economies had been useful in at least two ways: Firstly, it was a safeguard against the common error of assuming that the operation of increasing returns necessarily led to monopoly. Secondly, it simplified the analysis of price determination under increasing returns. A representative firm, which was able to maintain its identity by devoting itself to a given range of activities, was made the vehicle through which economies achieved by the entire industry are transmitted in the market affecting the product price. However this was a partial view of the matter:

> Certain aspects of those processes are illuminated, while, for that very reason, certain other aspects, important in relation to other problems, are obscured. This will be clear, I think, if we observe that, although internal economies of some firms producing, let us say, materials or appliances may figure as external economies of other firms, not all of the economies which are properly to be called external can be accounted for by adding up the internal economies of all the separate firms. (ibid., p. 528)

When we discuss internal economies of a firm we have in mind a condition of comparative stability in which a firm confines itself to a particular product or to a particular stage in its production. Although the firm expands its operations, they are kept within circumscribed bounds. But in the external field, changes of another order are happening. New products, new firms, and new industries are appearing. The older firms are assuming new tasks. The change is quantitative as well as qualitative. "No analysis of the forces making for economic equilibrium, forces which we might say are tangential at any moment of time, will serve to illuminate this field, for movements away from equilibrium, departures from previous trends, are characteristic of it" (ibid., p. 528).

Scitovsky (1954) in his famous paper "Two concepts of external economies" made a distinction between technological and pecuniary external economies. While the former operate directly through the production function, the latter operate indirectly through the price system within the market. Scitovsky pointed out that from the point of view of development it was the pecuniary external economies which were of relevance. While pecuniary external economies were all pervasive, examples of technological external economies were rare in industry. The literature on pecuniary external economies links their presence to some kind of market failure as it leads to a divergence between private and social benefit. To overcome this market failure Scitovsky recommended complete integration of all industries. Rosenstein-Rodan (1943, 1961), likewise, recommended that the entire industrial sector needed to be planned like one big firm or trust. Thus government intervention is seen as the logical step to overcome the market failure caused by pecuniary external economies.

In Young, however, pecuniary external economies are a sign of well-functioning market system rather than its failure.[6] These economies manifest themselves in the form of reduced costs and prices and are more effectively transmitted in a competitive market system. The more competitive the system, the more effective is their transmission. Reduced costs and prices, in turn increase the size of the market reinforcing the cumulative growth process. While for Krugman (1993) internal economies of scale at the firm level are indispensable for causing pecuniary external economies at the economy level, for Young it is the specialization (or the industrial division of labour) at firm or industry level which is the main source of pecuniary external economies. Thus increasing returns arise when more and more specialist firms and industries emerge in response to increasing market size.

Young discounted the notion of internal economies of scale or large-scale production at the firm level. He stated that if we look for increasing returns at the firm or industry level, we are likely to miss them. Increasing returns arise not due to any relationship between fixed and variable costs

[6] For a discussion of the role of pecuniary external economies vis-a-vis economies of scale in the theory of increasing returns, see Chandra and Sandilands (2006).

but due to pecuniary external economies. "In fact, these economies lie under our eyes, but we may miss them if we try to make of *large-scale* production (in the sense of production by large firms or industries), as contrasted with large production, any more than an incident in the general process by which increasing returns are secured and if accordingly we look too much at individual firm or even, as I shall suggest presently, at the individual industry" (Young 1928a, p. 531).

The economies of large-scale production or of "mass production" are often referred to as if they are available for the taking by means of "rational" reorganization of industry. Young stated that such reforms have their limits. New catch words such as "mass production" or "rationalization" can rouse men from routine and can act as stimuli. Economies can also be achieved by "simplification and standardization" or by saving on deeply rooted competitive wastes. "There is a danger, however, that we shall expect too much from these 'rational' industrial reforms. Pressed beyond a point they become the reverse of rational" (ibid., p. 531). The main point is that the scale of a firm or an industry is very rarely a matter for the firm (or industry) to decide. The scale of a firm at the micro level merely reflects the size of the overall market for the products of the industry (or industries) to which its own operations are ancillary.

The Role of Roundabout Methods and Industrial Specialization

In his 1928 paper, Young stated that he did not wish to enumerate all the different aspects of the division of labour, but wanted to confine himself to two related aspects only: the growth of indirect or roundabout methods of production and the division of labour among industries.

When Smith talked about the division of labour (or specialization) what he mostly had in mind was "splitting up of occupations and development of specialized crafts". As the market expands, not only job-specialization takes place within a firm but there is also a broader process at work, namely the development of arts and crafts at the societal level. Young went a step further and extended the concept of the division of labour to cover a situation when specialist firms and industries emerge. As the market expands, increasing returns take the form of industrial differentiation rather than industrial integration. As Young (ibid., p. 537) says:

> Much has been said about industrial integration as a concomitant or a natural result of an increasing industrial output. It obviously is, under particular conditions, though I know of no satisfactory statement of just what those particular conditions are. But the opposed process, industrial differentiation, has been and remains the type of change characteristically associated with the growth of production. Notable as has been the increase in the complexity of the apparatus of living, as shown by the increase in the variety of goods offered in the consumers' markets, the increase in the diversification of intermediate products and of industries manufacturing special products or groups of products has gone even further.

Young gave the example of printing trades in this regard. As the market expands, printing trade splits up into a number of specialized producers of wood pulp, of different kinds of paper, of inks and their ingredients, of type metal and of type, and of industries producing specialized tools and machines for use in printing. Young stated that printing trades were not exceptional, but were fairly representative of the entire industrial system. Thus: "It is sufficiently obvious, anyhow, that over a large part of the field of industry an increasingly intricate nexus of specialized undertakings has inserted itself between the producer of raw materials and the consumer of the final product" (ibid., p. 538).

In another illuminating article "Big business: how the economic system grows and evolves like a living organism" Young (1929c) maintained that no one dominating principle shapes the course of economic evolution. Large-scale production and unified managements can succeed when the product can be standardized and the complex processes can be reduced to a succession of routine operations. Typical examples of standardized products would be those producing "semi finished" and "intermediate" goods (or "heavy" industries). Out of these products a bewildering variety of specialized products are produced. In general, a typical establishment producing a specialized product is not as large as those producing "semi-finished" and "intermediate" products. There is no magic formula for business success. The small and the big businesses both coexist. Thus, to suggest that an increase in the size of a business undertaking is inevitable, that the small businesses are going to become extinct, that monopoly capitalism is inevitable, or that the competitive system is headed towards its doom, is incorrect.[7]

Young also observed that the economies which manifest themselves in increasing returns are basically the economies of capitalistic or roundabout methods of production but they are limited by the size of the market. With the division of labour a group of complex processes is transformed into a succession of simpler processes some of which lend themselves to the use of machinery. With the increased use of machinery and adoption of roundabout processes there is a further division of labour. "It would be wasteful to make a hammer to drive a single nail; it would be better to use whatever awkward implement lies conveniently at hand. It would be wasteful to furnish a factory with an elaborate equipment of specially constructed jigs, gauges, lathes, drills, presses and conveyors to build a hundred automobiles; it would be better to rely mostly upon tools and machines of standard types, so as to make relatively larger use of directly-applied and relatively smaller use of indirectly-applied labour. Mr. Ford's methods would be absurdly uneconomical if his output were what many other manufacturers of automobiles would call large" (ibid., p. 530).

Then there are economies of secondary order. How far it pays to equip factories with special appliances for making hammers or specialized equipment to make automobiles depends on how many nails are to be driven and how many automobiles can be sold. The derived demands for such specialized production appliances are inelastic over a large range. If the costs and benefits of using such appliances can be spread over a large final output, their technical effectiveness is more important in deciding to use them than whether they are produced on a small or a large scale. Again, it is large production of the final output rather than large-scale production in undertakings producing specialized appliances which leads to their economical adoption.

[7] "If consolidation always meant economy, there would be no effective limit to consolidation. That means that competition would inevitably everywhere end in monopoly. But, as we all know, in most fields of economic life competition maintains its health and vigor. This proves that supposed benefits of consolidation are often illusory" (Young 1929d; Mehrling and Sandilands 1999, p. 222). At another place Young (1990, pp. 53–54) writes: "Most of the advantages of increasing returns can be had in an industry not consolidated – such, in fact, is the typical modern industry… The advantages of consolidation are not, generally speaking, those of increasing returns. Rather they are those of increased specialization, those of reorganization, not mere increase of size of operating units".

The Role of Competition

Like Smith, competition plays a key role in Young's theory of increasing returns. Smith thought that the businessmen were monopolists in spirit and often subverted the public interest by conspiring to raise prices. Therefore they needed to be compelled to compete with each other through greater domestic as well as international competition. In Young we noted that increasing returns take the form of pecuniary external economies which are transmitted more effectively in a competitive system. By competition Young did not mean perfect competition or a competition producing some end result such as Pareto optimality. By competition he meant a process of competition as it existed in real life.

In real life competition had many imperfections. So imperfect competition did not mean absence of competition but rather imperfect working of competition. Young had gathered together various building blocks of imperfect competition theory such as product differentiation, selling costs, advertising expenses, trademarks, brand names, goodwill, and non-price competition, availability of close substitutes, and the threat of entry. As early as 1908, he regarded trademarks as a feature of competitive businesses. He also stated that goodwill profits should not be confused with monopoly profits. While monopoly implies absence of competition, goodwill profits result from imperfect working of competition—a competition which is characterized by inertia, friction and the fact that consumers are more guided by habits and customs rather than conscious choice (Ely et al. 1908, pp. 447–48). Trademarks, like patents, are legal monopolies in the sense that no one else can use them, but unlike patents, they do not lead to monopoly in the economic sense. They are largely used by competitive businesses to establish and maintain goodwill. The producer aims to lift himself a little above the "dead level of competition". So he may charge a price which is a little higher than a purely competitive price to gain extra profits. But there is a limit to the price he can charge as the availability of close substitutes and threat of entry puts an effective lid on his profits (Ely et al. 1916, p 196). Similarly, Young regarded selling costs as competitive investments. They are not production costs but are incurred to induce demand for the products which a producer has for sale.

Young linked the process of industrial differentiation, alluded to in the preceding section, with his theory of imperfect competition. In imperfect competition each producer tries to differentiate his product from others and competition mostly takes the form of non-price competition. Although a producer may have some control over price, but underneath the surface the forces of supply–demand still work relentlessly and competition still rules the roost. As Young (Ely et al. 1930, pp. 216–18) writes:

> The laws of normal price and monopoly price...represent two extreme norms. In case of consumption goods, an increasing number of price transactions fall somewhere between the two... We live today under a regime in which competition has to be shifted, by the 'differentiation of products and sale effort,' away from price. The average producer today dreads the acid test of exact price comparison. He multiplies styles, grades, brands, and terms. He spends millions in advertising to convince purchasers that he has something that cannot be supplied by other producers... Price determination becomes a question of individual business policy in which the principal object is to keep the customer's loyalty and divert his attention from price considerations.
>
> But the monopoly is more apparent than real. Underneath the surface the old law of supply and demand exercises just as much control as in the past; not with as much precision but with quite as much power... It is only in electric power, gas, telephone, water and street-car service that the average consumer is conscious of monopoly in any important degree... Competition is just as powerful as ever, but it works out through substitutes, through the offer of supplementary service or better terms of payment. Monopolistic control is probably less widespread and important than it was in the last quarter of the nineteenth century.

Thus product differentiation, industrial specialization, and fragmentation of processes and industries are all an inevitable result of the forces of competition and growth. Young had all the elements of the imperfect competition theory in unassembled form but he never put them together in a coherent analysis as was done by his PhD student Edward Chamberlin (1933) at Harvard. But Chamberlin had a static view of competition and was more interested in equilibrium analysis than dynamic theory.[8]

[8] See Machovec (1995, Chapter 10) who points out that both Knight and Chamberlin had a static view of competition while Young subscribed to a process view.

Comparing Young with Smith and Marshall

Young and Smith

Chandra (2004) has argued that Smith painted on a much wider canvass as compared to Young for he not only explained growth mechanics but also the role of institutions, motive power of self interest, and the role of saving and capital accumulation in growth. His larger contribution was in analyzing various systems and arrangements best suited to growth. His conclusion was that all systems based on preferences or restraints retard rather than facilitate the progress of society. The best system to incentivize growth was the system of natural liberty. The "simple and obvious" system of natural liberty establishes itself once all preferences and restraints are removed. This leads to a "no preferences, no restraints" policy framework in which all sectors are treated equally, and winners and losers emerge from the competitive race itself. Competition is regarded as the best tonic for growth. Smith lived at a time when mercantilist institutions were widespread and the system of natural liberty had to be deliberately created through conscious state efforts.

Given natural liberty, Young's main contribution was to explain the growth process (or growth mechanics) more fully. Young's explanation of increasing returns was in terms of pecuniary external economies, disequilibrium and cumulative causation, and generalized (or macroeconomic) increasing returns rather than microeconomic (and equilibrium) notion of economies of scale. Such vocabulary, as noted before, did not exist in Smith's time though some of these notions may have been implicit in Smith.

While Smith's pin-factory example gave the misleading notion that increasing returns are microeconomic, Young emphasized the need to view the industrial operations as an integrated whole. Young maintained that if we focus too much on a firm or industry we are likely to miss increasing returns although they may lie under our very eyes. They are generalized rather than sector-specific, transmitted in the form of external economies rather than internal economies of scale, are a result of a disequilibrium (cumulative) process rather than arising from any tendency towards economic equilibrium.

Both Smith and Young emphasized the role of competition in increasing returns. Both had a process view of competition rather than an end-state conception. Both viewed growth as endogenous in the sense that it occurs as a result of the very forces engendered within a competitive economic system. Both viewed capitalism as containing the seeds of its own growth rather than the seeds of its own destruction (as in Marx). While for Smith the stationary state was far away as no country had yet acquired the full complement of riches, for Young there was virtually no limit to increasing returns even in the absence of new scientific knowledge both theoretical and applied. Both emphasized the prior expansion of markets before growth could take off. While Smith emphasized the role of international trade in widening the market, Young regarded commercial revolution as a precondition of industrial revolution. In both capital accumulation and the division of labour are two sides of the same coin. In Smith more capital helps promote the division of labour by helping employ more productive hands as well as by equipping them with better tools and equipment. In Young increasing returns are the economies of indirect and roundabout methods of production but they are limited by the size of the market. So capital accumulation (or the use of machinery in production) by itself could not be regarded as an independent engine of growth.

Young and Marshall

As we noted in Chapter 2, Marshall did not have an explicit growth theory. It was pieced together from fragments scattered in *Principles of Economics* and *Industry and Trade*. Young borrowed many elements of Marshall's analysis such as the distinction between internal and external economies, Marshall-Edgeworth idea of offer curves[9] and the principle of reciprocal demand inherent in them, and biological analogies in the explanation of growth. But Marshall's approach was essentially microeconomic whereas Young talked about generalized (or macroeconomic) increasing returns, and stressed the need to view the industrial operations as an integrated whole.

[9] It is interesting to note that Young employed offer curves (or the principle of reciprocal demand) to analyse the growth process though he held money to be central to an economic system. As noted by Blitch (1995, pp. 173–74), perhaps the idea of reciprocal demand (or barter exchange) comes closest to explaining the cumulative process of growth. In offer curves demand and supply are interdependent; along such curves cost of production and marginal utility are released from the pound of ceteris paribus.

Marshall had an evolutionary perspective and carried out his partial equilibrium analysis making the oneness of the whole thing clear. For him ceteris paribus (or one-thing-at-a-time approach) was a stepping stone to the longer-term analysis of change and growth. But change in Marshall is slow and gradual rather than disruptive. He also emphasized the principle of continuity in his theory of evolution. Young, however, thought that change follows the law of cumulative causation in which change is seen as progressive which propagates itself in a cumulative way (Young 1928a, p. 533).

Young pointed out that one needs to be very careful while using the ceteris paribus method. It is very easy to forget what one is doing as Marshall does when talking about the consumers' surplus. Young stated that the concept is a general equilibrium one and cannot be analysed by partial equilibrium tools. The concept is not additive and over a consumer's entire purchases exactly sums up to zero. Young stated that a consumer does not gain from the demand side but from the supply side, by falling costs and prices as a result of the division of labour. Thus, the nature of gains to the consumer cannot be sought in the analysis of demand schedules.

Marshall was aware that while in the market period and the short term demand factors are important, in the long-run supply or cost factors become dominant. So in the long run he drew downward sloping supply curves as one of the possibilities. Young stated that the period of time is relative to costs and costs are relative to a period of time. "A long period supply curve is meaningless apart from the particular length of time considered: the curve is relative to the rate at which increasing returns exist. On the other hand you cannot postulate a constant demand curve for a good over a long period. It would shift as a result of the very forces which shift a supply curve. We need a theory of equilibrium rate of progress. Probably, the optimum rate of progress which will keep the supply curve close up to the demand curve" (Young 1990, pp. 47–48). Given the reciprocal nature of exchange, Young appeared to be suggesting that the forces shifting the supply curve shift the demand curve as well. In the long-run there is no constancy of either the supply or demand schedules. The forces endogenous to the system constantly shift both.

Marshall made use of the device of a representative firm to show the growth of a firm which has access to both internal and external economies. But the firm taken is an average firm which maintains its identity by devoting itself to a given range of activities or products. In

Young the external economies are such that the firm loses its identity sooner or later and becomes a specialized firm. To take an example, a firm manufacturing a hundred automobiles (which is a small output) may turn into a firm manufacturing some component. To put it another way, the whole industry splits up into a number of component manufacturers through the process of industrial differentiation. One or two firms may then assemble the final product by buying components from a large number of producers. As Young (1928a, p. 539) points out, "the mechanism of increasing returns is not to be discerned adequately by observing the effects of variations in the size of an individual firm or of a particular industry, for the progressive division and specialisation of industries is essential part of the process by which increasing returns are realized. What is required is that industrial operations are seen as an interrelated whole".

Moreover, the Marshallian representative firm by maintaining its identity is able to capture all available external economies which are available through the overall growth of a group of related industries. It is therefore able to internalize all such economies. Thus increasing returns, in this way of thinking, result from the relationship between a firm's prime (variable) and supplementary (fixed) costs.[10] But Young was of the view that all external economies cannot be obtained by adding up individual internal economies of all firms. The process was simply not additive, as the total picture was bigger than the summation of its parts. Moreover, as Young maintained, change was both quantitative as well as qualitative.

Marshall used the analogy of "trees in a forest" to characterize the evolution of firms, which when full of vigour and vitality, have an ascending phase, and after exhausting their vigour may enter a declining phase. This has been termed as "life cycle" theory of a firm. But Young's emphasis was macroeconomic as he wanted to study the economic phenomenon in its togetherness. He therefore gave the analogy of an economic system and how it grows like a living organism. As Young (1929c; Mehrling and Sandilands 1999, p. 411, emphasis added) says:

> The vast and intricate system of economic organization, by means of which the varied needs of modern life are met, is mostly a product of a continuous process of evolution. In only very small part is it a result of conscious

[10] "Large production, not large-scale production, permits increasing returns" (Young 1990, p. 54).

> collective planning or devising. It grows and changes unceasingly as men, in their work as producers and money-makers, try to find new and more economical ways of providing consumers with goods which they are willing to buy. Every innovation, whether in the technique of production or in the organization of business, affects in some degree the conditions which govern the activities of other producers. *The economic system grows and evolves, like a living organism, by means successive adjustments and adaptations. But change breeds change, and every new adjustment paves the way for another.*

As noted earlier, Marshall spoke of increasing returns becoming available with the growth of a group of related industries. Like Smith, he thought that increasing returns are confined to manufacturing and agriculture was a diminishing returns sector. But more recent research suggests that Smithian proposition relating to the division of labour and market size leads to a generalized conception of increasing returns, and this conception does not require any artificial distinction between agriculture and industry (See, for example, Buchanan and Yoon 2000). A larger exchange nexus is more efficient in securing increasing returns than a smaller one. Young, likewise, did not regard the law of diminishing returns operational in agriculture as something immutable. It could be overcome by powerful counterforces such as improvement in agricultural technique and revolution in the means of transportation bringing new fertile lands closer to Britain's doorsteps. Moreover, reciprocal nature of exchange in Young meant that different industries will grow at different rates depending on the demand and supply elasticities, so any artificial restraint on the diminishing returns sector (agriculture) and any artificial encouragement to the increasing returns sector (manufacturing) would upset this reciprocal exchange, distort internal terms of trade, and therefore retard growth instead of facilitating it.

In Marshall's life cycle theory of firms, while older firms may lose vitality and decline, younger and more vigorous firms may rise. How the picture will look at the macroeconomic level is difficult to tell. But one can guess that since evolution in Marshall is a slow process (of both standardization and creativity), it only leads to incremental growth rather than disruptive change. Institutions also evolve slowly as man evolves. In Young the process of growth is limitless even with a stationary population and with no new advances in scientific knowledge and discoveries. Growth is based more on existing knowledge, as Sandilands (2000, p. 325) observes. The growth of technology and knowledge are themselves demand (or market) driven. Young held that progress need not always be continuous or incremental. Sometimes the next step may be costly and cannot be taken unless certain quantum of prospective advantages has accumulated. At other times, when conditions are more favourable, the process of growth may accelerate looking virtually unstoppable. Therefore the horse of growth can trot at certain times, canter at some others, and break into a gallop at still others.

However, the high theme of progress in Marshall is much broader. It not only includes a rise in the material standard of living of the mass of people but also wholesome development of man which includes his living conditions, his access to clean air and water, his bodily health, his educational opportunities, his abilities and knowledge, and ultimately his character. For Young, the democratic process involved a constant tension between money interest and public interest, led to institutional development geared towards public interest, and produced reforms to save capitalism from its excesses like unemployment, business cycles, and economic concentration (Chandra 2020, pp. 320–23). While for Marshall economics arose out of ethics, for Young it had an instrumental value in solving communal problems of economic life. Marshall was inclined towards socialism as an ideal but disliked administrative and bureaucratic controls it involved stifling initiative and economic progress (see Raffaelli 2003, p. 78). For him socialist movement was the greatest danger to human wellbeing. Young thought that class struggle was an ugly and repellent doctrine. Socialism would realize itself better through the democratic process involving social reforms rather than through revolution (see Chandra 2020, p. 172).

Critical Assessment

Young's (1928a) paper on "increasing returns and economic progress" was the most famous paper he ever wrote. About this paper, Schumpeter (1954, p. 875, f.n. 23) wrote that one can form an idea about a lion from this single claw. It is a much quoted paper and forms the starting point of both modern endogenous growth theory as well as the post-war development theory. Kaldor (1972, 1975) based his attack on the neoclassical orthodoxy largely based on this paper. It needed to be sustained by more work in the area, but unfortunately Young died unexpectedly at the age of 52 from the influenza epidemic in London in 1929 before he could do so. At the time of his death Young was working on two treatises, one on theory and the other on money. But the unfinished manuscripts were lost when his family hastily departed from London after his death, and no trace of either was ever found subsequently. Moreover, Young was survived by a wife who was completely blind. What happened to these unfinished manuscripts remains a mystery even to this day.

Young's presidential address was well received by the British press as noted by Blitch (1995, pp. 175–76). The *Financial Express* (London) headline on the front page read "British industry praised". The paper wrote: "There is a danger in relying mainly on non-British trumpeters, but when the note is sounded by an authority of eminence and repute of Professor Allyn Young, the room for misinterpretation is reduced to a minimum". Young had compared British and American industries and pointed out that the British industry, seen against its own problems and prospects, was not less ably organized than the American one, the crucial difference being the size of the market. The methods which are economical in America cannot be applied to British industry because of the smallness of its market. This was typical of the newspaper comments about Young's paper. None of the papers, however, dealt with the technical aspects of increasing returns and growth.

Young's work on increasing returns came on the eve of the Great Depression of the 1930s which started with the stock market crash of 1929. Soon attention turned to problems of cyclical fluctuations rather than secular growth.[11] Young's paper remained forgotten till it was discovered by post-war development economists including Rosenstein-Rodan, Nurkse and Lauchlin Currie. Modern growth theorists (e.g. Romer 1986, 1989) as well as modern trade theorists (e.g., Krugman 1990) also drew on this paper. In between, Kaldor's (1972) attack on the neoclassical equilibrium theory liberally draws on it. In recent decades there has been a revival of interest in Young with the publication of Kaldor's lecture notes (Young 1990), biography by Blitch (1995), collection of papers on money and growth by Mehrling and Sandilands (1999), and an intellectual biography by Chandra (2020). His monetary thought was pieced together by Mehrling (1996, 1997) and Laidler (1993, 1999). As Mehrling and Sandilands (1999, p. xii) note, the grand themes in

[11] Kaldor (1972, p. 1243) thought that Young's 1928 paper was "so many years ahead of its time that the progress of economic thought passed it by".

Young's writings are money and growth and both are inextricably intertwined. They also dispel the widely-held notion that Young published little by compiling a bibliography of about a hundred items.[12] But most of these writings were in encyclopedia articles or obscure journals such as *The Book of Popular Science*. Chandra (2020) adopts a thematic approach to Young and finds that there is much more to him than merely money and growth. He had clear-cut views on other topics such as the nature, scope, and method of economics, business cycles, imperfect competition, value and distribution, socialism and Marxism. He was also deeply interested in applied economic problems such as railway rate making, old-age pension, enumeration of children, anti-trust laws, Germany's reparation damages during WWI, and MacNary-Haugen Bill on farm relief.[13] Moreover, he was a great critic and commented on famous authors, both his contemporaries as well as earlier economists.

Despite Young's seminal contribution to growth theory, some authors have interpreted his achievement in terms of equilibrium.[14] For example, Robbins (1932) opined that central achievement of Young (and indeed Smith) was "the mode in which the division of labour tended to be kept in equilibrium by the mechanism of relative prices". Similarly, Romer (1986) held that the most prominent attempt to give a competitive equilibrium interpretation to Smith's depiction of increasing returns through his pin-factory example or Marshall's distinction between internal and external economies was made by Allyn Young. More recently, Buchanan and Yoon (1999, 2000) have interpreted Smithian proposition regarding the relationship between the division of labour and market size as leading to competitive equilibrium as an end-state of adjustment. Young did talk

[12] Schumpeter (1937, p. 154), for example, writing after his death, stated: "Rarely if ever has fame such as his been acquired on the basis of so little published work".

[13] Young (1928b), in fact, considered any distinction between theoretical and applied economics as largely artificial. He wrote: "Economic theory, divorced from its functional relations to economic problems, or with those relations obscured, is no better than an interesting intellectual game. It gives endless opportunities for dialectical ingenuity. But it cannot advance knowledge, for it leads up a blind alley" (also in Mehrling and Sandilands 1999, p. 20).

[14] Young (1929e) related the concept of equilibrium with time, and was of the opinion that all economic equilibria are unstable. "Market price is the price which will be found in a given market at a given time. It may be regarded as the limiting form of the short-time or temporary equilibrium price" (also in Young 1990, p. 154).

about competition but his economics cannot be characterized as "equilibrium". In fact he was clear that the forces of disequilibrium were continuously defeating those of equilibrium so that change follows the law of cumulative causation. The only concession he gave to equilibrium theorists was to characterize change as a "moving equilibrium", a conception where the centre of gravity of an economic system continuously shifts in response to forces endogenous to the system.

Nicholas Kaldor (1972, p. 1243) characterized Young's diagrammatic appendix to his 1928 paper as "obscure". In this appendix, Young makes an attempt to trace the path of a "moving" equilibrium" from a lower tangential point P between the production possibility curve (which Young calls the curve of equal costs) and the community indifference curve (of two commodities x and y) to a higher point of tangency between the two curves P_1. This path can be conceived in two ways. Either it is an equilibrium rate of growth where the movement between P and P_1 is constant and undeviating, and where an acceleration or a deceleration would be costly or disadvantageous. Young then alludes to a mountain climber who adjusts his pace to the ascent and his own physical strength. Or alternatively, the movement between P and P_1 can be seen as a series of small steps where the next step depends on the last step already taken. As Mehrling and Sandilands (1999, p. xxv, n. 4) note, Young's (1990) "particular expenses and supply curves" help explain this famously puzzling mathematical and diagrammatical note.[15]

Kaldor (1972) also thought that Youngian mechanism of reciprocal demand needed to be supplemented by Keynesian insights of induced investment. Young had highlighted the role of elasticity of demand (or that goods are produced under competitive conditions) in the transmission of increasing returns. Kaldor felt that diversion of purchasing power to elastically demanded goods would mean that less is spent on other goods, and this would need to be made good by creating additional credit to hold these inventories of other goods. Thus Kaldor wanted to

[15] Young (1990, pp. 41–43) noted that Marshall's particular expenses curve should not be confused with the supply curve. It was not a true supply curve, but since not all the producers have the same costs, it was upward sloping. Everyone, including those producing at the lowest costs, sell at the equilibrium price, and the area under the curve gives the producers' total expenses. See also Chandra (2020, p. 164).

marry the Smith-Young conception of increasing returns with the Keynesian effective demand.[16] Kaldor, of course, assumed that total purchasing power remains static, and does not grow with economic progress. He also assumed that the size of the market remains static whereas division of labour leads to reduction of costs and prices and thereby increasing the size of the real market. It should also be noted that the decline in the relative share of inelastically produced goods is consistent with an absolute increase in their total output. Currie also criticized Kaldor on this point and his critique of Kaldor will be discussed later in Chapter 6.[17]

As noted by Blitch (1995, p. 173), Young presented a model of growth for an advanced economy. Young's approach to dynamic external economies was later applied to developing countries by early development economists such as Paul Rosenstein-Rodan and Ragnar Nurkse in their theories of the "big push" and "balanced growth", respectively (Perala 2006, p. 462). These later theories greatly influenced Myrdal's "cumulative causation" and Hirschman's "backward and forward linkages". Again as noted by Perala, Young's approach has a balance between demand and supply side factors in growth. By concentrating on the supply side, these early development theorist applied Young's vision only partially. Colacchio (2005), on the other hand, interprets Young's logic in terms of a "multisectoral model" which results in "the rupture of correct proportionality among various branches of the economic system" (p. 334). Thus, "disproportionality crisis must have been continually in Young's mind" (p. 334). This is a characterization of disequilibrium and appears valid in Young's growth theory in so far as different industries grow at different rates depending on the elasticities of demand and supply. It also appears valid in his theory of business cycles where these result not from mismatches in aggregate demand and aggregate supply but from mismatches of individual demands and supplies. An expansion of money supply increases the price level but its more important effect is to change the structure of relative prices. So business cycles result from distortions of relative prices. It is in this context that Young talked about an "equilibrium rate of growth",

[16] For Kaldor's interpretation of Smith and Young see Chandra (2019).

[17] For Currie-Kaldor exchange on increasing returns see Sandilands (1990), and for Sandilands-Currie-Kaldor exchange see Chandra and Sandilands (2020, 2021).

that is, the need to keep the demand curve close up to the downward sloping supply curve in each sector.

References

Blitch, C. (1995). *Allyn Young: The Peripatetic Economist*. Basingstoke and London: Macmillan Press Ltd.

Buchanan, James M., and Yong J. Yoon. 1999. Generalised increasing returns, Euler's theorem, and competitive equilibrium. *History of Political Economy* 31 (3): 511–523.

Buchanan, James M., and Yong J. Yoon. 2000. A Smithian perspective on increasing returns. *Journal of the History of Economic Thought* 22 (1): 43–48.

Chamberlin, Edward H. 1933. *The Theory of Monopolistic Competition*. Cambridge: Harvard University Press.

Chandra, Ramesh. 2004. Adam Smith, Allyn Young and the division of labour. *Journal of Economic Issues* 38: 787–805.

Chandra, Ramesh. 2019. Nicholas Kaldor on Adam Smith and Allyn Young. *Review of Political Economy* 31 (3): 445–463.

Chandra, Ramesh. 2020. *Allyn Abbott Young*. Cham: Palgrave Macmillan.

Chandra, Ramesh, and Roger J. Sandilands. 2006. The role of pecuniary external economies and economies of scale in the theory of increasing returns. *Review of Political Economy* 18 (2): 193–208.

Chandra, Ramesh, and Roger J. Sandilands. 2020. Nicholas Kaldor, Increasing returns and Verdoorn's law. *Strathclyde Discussion Papers in Economics*, No. 20-02. Glasgow: University of Strathclyde.

Chandra, Ramesh, and Roger J. Sandilands. 2021. Nicholas Kaldor, increasing returns and Verdoorn's law. *Journal of Post Keynesian Economics* 44 (2): 315–339.

Clapham, J.M. 1922. On empty economic boxes. *Economic Journal* 32: 305–314.

Colacchio, Georgio. 2005. Reconstructing Allyn A. Young's theory of increasing returns. *Journal of the History of Economic Thought* 27 (3): 321–344.

Ely, Richard T., Thomas S. Adams, Max O. Lorenz, and Allyn A. Young. 1908. *Outlines of Economics*. New York: The Macmillan Company.

Ely, Richard T., Thomas S. Adams, Max O. Lorenz, and Allyn A. Young. 1916. *Outlines of Economics*. New York: The Macmillan Company.

Ely, Richard T., Thomas S. Adams, Max O. Lorenz, and Allyn A. Young. 1923. *Outlines of Economics*. New York: The Macmillan Company.

Ely, Richard T., Thomas S. Adams, Max O. Lorenz, and Allyn A. Young. 1930. *Outlines of Economics*. New York: The Macmillan Company.

Kaldor, Nicholas. 1972. The irrelevance of equilibrium economics. *Economic Journal* 82: 1237–1255.

Kaldor, Nicholas. 1975. What is wrong with economic theory. *Quarterly Journal of Economics* 89 (3): 347–357.

Knight, Frank H. 1921. *Risk, Uncertainty and Profit*. Boston: Houghton Mifflin Co.

Krugman, Paul. 1990. *Rethinking International Trade*. Cambridge and London: MIT Press.

Krugman, Paul. 1993. Toward a counter-counterrevolution in development theory. *Annual Conference on Development Economics 1992*, 15–38. Washington, DC: World Bank.

Laidler, David. 1993. Hawtrey, Harvard, and the origins of the Chicago tradition. *Journal of Political Economy* 101 (6): 1068–1103.

Laidler, David. 1999. *Fabricating the Keynesian Revolution*. Cambridge: Cambridge University Press.

Machovec, Frank H. 1995. *Perfect Competition and the Transformation of Economics*. London and New York: Routledge.

Marshall, Alfred. 1890 (1938). *Principles of Economics*, 8th ed. London: Macmillan.

Mehrling, Perry G. 1996. The monetary thought of Allyn Abbott Young. *History of Political Economy* 28 (4): 607–632.

Mehrling, Perry G. 1997. *The Money Interest and the Public Interest*. Cambridge and London: Harvard University Press.

Mehrling, Perry G., and Roger J. Sandilands. 1999. *Money and Growth: Selected Papers of Allyn Abbott Young*. London and New York: Routledge.

Perala, Maiju. 2006. Looking at the other side of the coin: Allyn Young and the early development theory. *Journal of the History of Economic Thought* 28 (4): 461–488.

Raffaelli, Tiziano. 2003. *Marshall's Evolutionary Economics*. Abingdon and New York: Routledge.

Robbins, Lionel. 1932. *An Essay on the Nature and Significance of Economic Science*. London: Macmillan.

Romer, Paul M. 1986. Increasing returns and long-run growth. *Journal of Political Economy* 94: 1002–1038.

Romer, Paul M. 1989. Capital accumulation in the theory of long-run growth. In *Modern Business Cycle Theory*, ed. Robert J. Barro. Cambridge: Harvard University Press.

Rosenstein-Rodan, Paul. 1943. Problems of industrialisation in eastern and south-eastern Europe. *Economic Journal* 53: 202–211.

Rosenstein-Rodan, Paul. 1961. Notes on the theory of the big push. In *Economic Development of Latin America*, ed. H.S. Ellis and H.C. Wallaich. London: Macmillan.

Sandilands, Roger J. 1990. *The Life and Political Economy of Lauchlin Currie*. Durham and London: Duke University Press.
Sandilands, Roger J. 2000. Perspectives on Allyn Young in theories of endogenous growth. *Journal of the History of Economic Thought* 22 (3): 309–328.
Schumpeter, Joseph A. 1937. Allyn A. Young. In *Encyclopedia of Social Sciences*, 514–515.New York: Macmillan.
Schumpeter, Joseph A. 1954 (1982). *History of Economic Analysis*. London: Allen and Unwin.
Scitovsky, Tibor. 1954. Two concepts of external economies. *Journal of Political Economy* 62: 143–151.
Sraffa, Piero. 1926. The laws of return under competitive conditions. *Economic Journal* 6: 535–550.
Young, Allyn. 1913. Pigou's wealth and welfare. *Quarterly Journal of Economics* 27 (4): 672–686. Reprinted in Mehrling and Sandilands (1999, pp. 86–96).
Young, Allyn. 1928a. Increasing returns and economic progress. *Economic Journal* 38 (152): 527–542. Reprinted in Mehrling and Sandilands (1999, pp. 49–61).
Young, Allyn. 1928b. English political economy. *Economica* 8 (22): 1–15. Reprinted in Mehrling and Sandilands (1999, pp. 15–28).
Young, Allyn. 1929a. The creator of wealth. In *The Book of Popular Science*, 110–116. New York: The Grolier Society. Reprinted in Mehrling and Sandilands (1999, pp. 149–152).
Young, Allyn. 1929b. Supply and demand. In *Encyclopaedia Britannica 1928*, 579–580. London: The Encyclopaedia Britannica Company. Reprinted in Mehrling and Sandilands (1999, pp. 143–146).
Young, Allyn. 1929c. Big business: How the economic system grows and evolves like a living organism. In *The Book of Popular Science*, 5387–5394. New York: The Grolier Society. Reprinted in Mehrling and Sandilands (1999, pp. 411–420).
Young, Allyn. 1929d. The making of wealth. In *The Book of Popular Science*, 3377–3385. New York: The Grolier Society. Reprinted in Mehrling and Sandilands (1999, pp. 220–230).
Young, Allyn. 1929e. Price. In *Encyclopedia Britannica 1928*. London: The Encyclopedia Britannica Company.
Young, Allyn. 1990. Nicholas Kaldor's notes on Allyn Young's LSE lectures 1927–29. *Journal of Economic Studies* 17 (3/4): 18–114.

CHAPTER 5

Nicholas Kaldor on Equilibrium Economics and Economic Growth

Nicholas Kaldor was Hungarian by birth, and like so many other European emigrants, was more English than the English themselves, and revelled in her institutions (Thirlwall 1987a, p. 519). He was an undergraduate student of Allyn Young at the London School of Economics during 1927–1929, and later made important contributions in the areas of growth, distribution, capital theory, welfare economics, and trade cycles.[1] *The Economist* (dated 20 January 1979) termed him as the best known economist not to have received the Nobel Prize.[2] Luigi Pasinetti (1981, p. 59) described him as one of the most original and provocative theoretical economists of the twentieth century. Hahn and Matthews (1994, p. 901) noted that his range was wider than almost any other economist of his time. In the post-war years, he emerged as an influential policy adviser, not only advising Britain, the country of his adoption, but also many developing countries such as India, Sri Lanka, Ghana, and

[1] As an undergraduate student at the London School of Economics during 1927–1929, he took Young's lecture notes which were published much later (See Young 1990). See also Chandra (2020) for a recent biography of Young.

[2] Douglas Wass (1987, p. xiv) noted that it remained a mystery to him as well as to his other admirers as to why his achievements were not crowned by a Nobel Prize. "Perhaps he offended the economic establishment too much. Perhaps his progressive politics were not to the liking of the Committee of Award. We shall probably never know."

R. Chandra, *Endogenous Growth in Historical Perspective*, Palgrave Studies in Economic History,
https://doi.org/10.1007/978-3-030-83761-7_5

Guiana particularly on taxation matters (see Targetti 1992, p. 220). As John King (2007, p. 3) points out, his thinking in the post-war years underwent a change from theoretical problems to practical policy issues such as post-war reconstruction and applied problems (such as applied economics of growth, and other applied issues such as trade, exports, balance of payments, inflation, etc.).

Kaldor (1972, 1975a) was highly critical of the neoclassical equilibrium theory and the assumptions on which it was based.[3] He believed that neoclassical theory was largely irrelevant in explaining the manner of the operation of economic forces or predicting the effect of economic changes. He was of the opinion that theory should be more concerned with cumulative causation rather than optimum allocation of scarce resources among alternative uses. He maintained that the more proper role of the market was resource creation rather than resource allocation. The basic assumptions of equilibrium theory are either unverifiable (e.g., profit maximization or utility maximization) or directly contradicted by experience (e.g., perfect competition, perfect knowledge, etc.). Besides, this theory assumes constant costs, ignoring the role that increasing returns play in real life. Also, it elevates the principle of substitution (in response to changing relative prices) to the forefront neglecting complementarity of factors in the production process.

Kaldor stated that economic theory went astray from the middle of Chapter 4 of the *Wealth of Nations*, the first three being devoted to the analysis of the division of labour. While in the first part of Chapter 4 the role of money in a social economy is discussed, Smith then gets diverted to the determination of product and factor prices. For the rest of the book, in Kaldor's opinion, Smith (and Ricardo) assumed constant costs as is implicit in the notion of natural price. In his analysis of increasing returns, Kaldor drew on the first three chapters of the *Wealth of Nations* assuming that Smith had nothing much to contribute towards increasing returns in the rest of the book.

Kaldor was also influenced by Allyn Young (1928) in his theory of increasing returns as well as his attack on the neoclassical equilibrium theory. But his understanding of increasing returns, as noted by Thirlwall (1987b, p. 545), was based on a sharp distinction between agriculture

[3] As noted by Thirlwall (1987a, p. 317), Kaldor was not alone in critiquing the equilibrium theory. A major assault on the general equilibrium methodology was launched by Janos Kornai (1971), a fellow Hungarian, in his *Anti-Equilibrium*.

and manufacturing. Since increasing returns are confined to industry only special measures are required to promote it. Kaldor also had an empirical bent of mind and was influenced by Verdoorn's Law (Verdoorn, 1949) which stated that the relationship between productivity growth and output growth was stronger in manufacturing than in other sectors. Although later Verdoorn (1980) himself diluted the validity of his own law, stating that it was less generally applicable than what he was led to believe in 1949, Kaldor continued to show strong allegiance to it.

Anthony Thirlwall (1987b, pp. 545–46) in his article "Nicholas Kaldor 1908–1986" writes about Kaldor's contribution to "applied economics of growth". Two things particularly interested Kaldor: (1) the search for empirical regularities associated with interregional growth rate differences; and (2) the limits to growth in a closed economy. He took a sectoral approach to increasing returns; for him while manufacturing was the increasing returns sector, services and agriculture were diminishing returns activities. His name is also associated with three laws one of which, depicting the relationship between productivity growth and output growth in manufacturing through static and dynamic economies of scale, is known as Verdoorn's Law. Growth of manufacturing itself depends on growth of demand which comes from agriculture in the initial stages, and exports from the later stages of development. Kaldor initially thought that labour shortages posed a constraint on Britain's growth rate, but soon changed his mind to Harrod trade multiplier hypothesis of slow rate of export growth in relation to income elasticity of imports, the ratio of which determined the balance of payments constrained growth rate.[4] Kaldor believed that growth follows Myrdal's principle of "circular cumulative causation" in which success breeds success and failure breeds failure.

This chapter first discusses Kaldor's attack on equilibrium economics, and then examines his views on increasing returns and Verdoorn's Law. These are followed by his contribution in terms of policy advice to Britain as well as other countries. Finally, a critical assessment of Kaldor, particularly concerning his growth and related policy ideas, is also made.

[4] Kaldor never specified the dynamic form of the Harrod trade multiplier which was done by Thrilwall (1979).

Irrelevance of Equilibrium Economics

In his *Economic Journal* article "The irrelevance of equilibrium economics", Kaldor (1972) launched a scathing attack on the neoclassical theory. He believed that equilibrium economics was irrelevant and barren as an apparatus to study the economic phenomenon and to predict the effects of economic change. In fact equilibrium economics had become an obstacle to the development of economics as a science in which its theorems as well as assumptions cannot be subjected to tests. Although Gerard Debreu (1959), a French economist, stated that the subject matter of his book related to "the explanation of the price of commodities", it is put forward not as an explanation of actual prices in the real world but as a set of theorems logically deducible from precisely formulated assumptions. "[T]he purpose of the exercise is to find the minimum 'basic assumptions' necessary for establishing the existence of an 'equilibrium' set of prices (and output/input matrixes) that is (a) unique, (b) stable, (c) satisfies the conditions of Pareto optimality. The whole progress of mathematical economics in the last thirty to fifty years lay in clarifying the minimum requirements in terms of 'basic assumptions' more precisely: without any attempt at verifying the realism of those assumptions, and without any investigation of whether the resulting theory of 'equilibrium prices' has any explanatory power or relevance in relation to actual prices" (Kaldor 1972, pp. 1237–38).

Kaldor maintained that in any scientific theory the assumptions are chosen on the basis of empirical observations. But in equilibrium economics the assumptions are either unverifiable or contradicted by observation.[5] As Kaldor (ibid., p. 1238) writes:

> [T]he basic assumptions of economic theory are either of a kind that are unverifiable – such as producers 'maximise' their profits and consumers 'maximise' their utility – or of a kind which are directly contradicted by observation – for example, perfect competition, perfect divisibility, linear-homogenous and continuously differentiable production functions, wholly impersonal market relations, exclusive role of prices in information flows

[5] In this regard Thirlwall (1987b, p. 555) writes: "At the methodological level, Kaldor was strongly against the deductive method of building models on a priori assumptions without any firm empirical basis. For models to be useful, the assumptions must be verifiable, not axiomatic which makes theories tautological."

> and perfect knowledge of all relevant prices by all agents and perfect foresight. There is also the requirement of a constant and unchanging set of *products* (goods) and constant and unchanging set of *processes of production* (or production functions) over time – though neither category, goods nor processes, is *operationally* defined: in other words, no attempt is made to show how these axiomatic concepts are to be defined or recognized in relation to empirical material.

Kaldor observed that this theory is not designed for the real world; it is put forward as a conceptual framework to explain how a decentralized system works. Individuals, guided entirely by the market, are able to attain maximum satisfaction not only for themselves but for the society as a whole in the Pareto-sense. However, the "intellectual experiment" of equilibrium economics had not been converted into a "scientific theory" which can be tested with observable phenomena. As Kaldor (ibid., p. 1239) writes:

> [T]he ship appears to be much further away from the shore now than it appeared to its originators in the nineteenth century. The latest theoretical models, which attempt to construct an equilibrium path through time with all prices for all periods fully determined at the start under the assumption that everyone foresees future prices correctly to eternity, require far more fundamental 'relaxations' for their applicability than was thought to be involved in the original Walrasian scheme. The process of removing the 'scaffolding', as the saying goes,- in other words of *relaxing* the unreal basic assumptions – has not yet started. Indeed, the scaffolding gets thicker and more impenetrable with every successive reformulation of the theory, with growing uncertainty as to whether there is a solid building underneath.

Kaldor stated that the propositions of this theory—the economy always approaches or approximates a state of equilibrium, there is maximum possible production of goods and services consistent with the available resources, there is full and efficient utilization of all resources, wages reflect the net contribution of labour, rate of profit reflects the net advantage of substituting capital for labour, etc.—can be shown to be valid only on assumptions which are manifestly unreal. The equilibrium theory had reached a stage where its main implications cannot possibly hold in reality. Referring to the presidential addresses (to Royal Economic Society and Section F of the British Association) of E.H. Phelps Brown and G.D.S.

Worswick, published in the *Economic Journal* (March, 1972), Kaldor pointed out that it was now increasingly recognized that mathematical models lead nowhere. It was also recognized that econometrics and refined methods of statistical inference cannot substitute for the understanding of how real economies work. As Thirlwall (1987b, p. 555) notes, such mathematical models "for the sake of scientific precision, invariably [substitute] elegance for relevance".

According to Kaldor, economic theory went wrong when the theory of value took the centre stage focusing attention on the allocative function of markets as opposed to their creative function. This happened in the middle of Chapter 4 of the *Wealth of Nations*, the first three being devoted to the principle of the division of labour. These explain that larger production leads to lower real per unit cost as more efficient modes of production are employed leading to greater specialization and subdivision of processes. But in the fourth chapter, after discussing the need for money in a social economy, Smith suddenly gets interested in the distinction between money and real prices on the one hand and use and exchange values of commodities on the other. "[A]nd from then on, hey presto, his interest gets bogged down in the question of how values and prices for products and factors are determined. One can trace a more or less continuous development of price theory from the subsequent chapters of Smith through Ricardo, Walras, Marshall, right up to Debreu and the most sophisticated of the present-day Americans" (Kaldor 1972, p. 1241).

Kaldor stated that the basic assumption of this theory is constant costs, or constant returns to scale. With Smith and Ricardo, this was implicit in the very notion of "natural price" determined solely by costs of production (irrespective of demand). With neoclassical school, it was explicit in the assumption of homogenous and linear production functions. This is one of the required "axioms" necessary to make the assumptions of perfect competition and profit-maximization consistent with one another. Marshall thought that with the notion of "external economies" and the use of the partial equilibrium method he could accommodate both increasing and decreasing returns to scale within the same analytical framework. But Piero Sraffa (1926) showed that this attempt was logically faulty. The general equilibrium school, on the other hand, has always assumed the absence of increasing returns as one of the basic "axioms" of the system. Thus, according to Kaldor, the existence of increasing returns and its consequences for the whole framework of economic theory have been completely neglected (ibid., p. 1242).

Kaldor was also influenced by Young's (1928) disequilibrium economics in criticizing the neoclassical theory. Young cast Smith's dictum that the division of labour depends on the size of the market in terms of cumulative causation and came to the conclusion that the division of labour in large part depends on the division of labour. Young stated that this was more than a tautology as the counterforces of disequilibrium were so powerful that they were continuously defeating forces making for equilibrium. Any change leads to further changes so that growth becomes progressive and propagates itself in a cumulative way. In a similar vein Kaldor wrote: "When every change in the use of resources – every reoganisation of productive activities – creates the opportunity for further change *which would not have existed otherwise*, the notion of an optimum 'allocation' of resources – when every particular resource makes as great or greater contribution to output in its actual use as in any alternative use – becomes meaningless and contradictory notion: the pattern of the use of resources at any given time can be no more than a link in the chain of an unending sequence and the very distinction, vital to equilibrium economics, between resource-creation and resource-allocation loses its validity. The whole view of the economic process as a medium for the 'allocation of scarce means between alternative uses' falls apart – except perhaps for the consideration of short-run problems..." (ibid., p. 1245).

About Young's 1928 paper on increasing returns and economic progress, Kaldor (ibid., p. 1243) observed:

> On re-reading this paper after a lapse of many years, I feel convinced that it was so many years ahead of its time that the progress of economic thought had passed it by despite the attention it received at the time of its original publication. Economists ceased to take any notice of it long before they were able to grasp its full revolutionary implications. This was partly because Young was a man of exceptional modesty who underplayed, rather than emphasized, the full implication of what he was saying; his manner of exposition is suggestive, rather than compelling, and at times (as for example in the Appendix attached to the paper) obscure. It was partly also because its importance as a basic criticism of general equilibrium theory could not be appreciated at a time when the theory itself was not properly understood.

Increasing Returns

Kaldor maintained that once one abandons the assumption of linearity (or constant returns to scale) and assumes increasing returns to scale, the consequences are far reaching. The most important casualty is the notion of general equilibrium which carries the implication that economic forces are constrained by a set of exogenous variables (given from outside). It further assumes that economic forces operate in an environment which is almost independent of history. These exogenous features of the environment include Pareto's "tastes and obstacles" (or the preferences of individuals as consumers, the transformation functions of factors into products and the supply of resources). The nature of social institutions and markets is such as to make the system converge to a unique equilibrium point or a state of rest characterized by unchanging prices and production patterns over time. Continuous economic change under these assumptions can be conceived as some kind of "moving equilibrium" consistent with exogenous shift of production functions per unit of time.

Once we allow for increasing returns, the forces making for change are endogenous in the sense that they are engendered from within the economic system. The actual state of an economy at any period of time cannot be predicted except by the events of the previous period which led up to it. Under such circumstances Kaldor, quoting Young (1928) with approval, pointed out that change becomes progressive and propagates itself in a cumulative way. Further, no analysis of forces making for equilibrium can illuminate this field for movements away from equilibrium and departures from past trends are characteristic of it. Kaldor (1972, pp. 1244–45) further writes:

> The basic consideration underlying Young's analysis is surprisingly the same as that underlying Say's Law. If one takes an all-inclusive view of the economic process, economic activity ultimately consists of the exchange of goods against goods; this means that every increase in the supply of commodities enlarges, at least potentially, the market for other commodities. (The qualification 'potentially,' as we shall see is very important and distinguishes Young's views from that of Say or Mill.) Hence the 'extent of the market' depends on the division of labour almost as much, according to Young, as the division of labour depends on the extent of the market...

Young had stated that Smith's dictum if modified in the light of the broader conception of the market (i.e., an aggregation of economic activities tied together by trade) amounted to the theorem that the division of labour in large part depends on the division of labour. This was more than a tautology, as the counter forces of disequilibrium are more pervasive and deeply rooted in the constitution of an economic system than we commonly realize. This was the principle of circular cumulative causation which was restated by Myrdal (1957) writing more than twenty-five years later. As noted by Hicks (1939), unless we are able to assume that marginal costs increase with output at the point of equilibrium the very basis of economic laws is shorn away. Thus, "an equilibrium of costs and advantages" ceases to be meaningful notion in the presence of increasing returns (or diminishing costs).

According to Kaldor, Young was able to see that a combination of Adam Smith's theorem and Say's Law was not enough to ensure a self-sustaining growth process. Something more was required which he supplied in the form of elastic demand (or that commodities be produced competitively under increasing returns). According to Young, given elastic demand, there were no limits to increasing returns even with a stationary population and in the absence of new discoveries in pure and applied sciences. But, in Kaldor's opinion, elastic demand was not enough as Young lacked a theory of income generation which was later propounded by Keynes (1936) in his *General Theory*. Moreover, there was some obscurity surrounding the meaning of "elasticity of demand" as a result of which Young did not receive the attention he deserved. As Kaldor (1972, p. 1247) writes:

> Clearly what Young intuitively perceived was that the pre-condition of cumulative change is that a rise in the production of any one commodity *a*, should be associated with an increase in demand for all other commodities. He thought that this condition will be satisfied when the elasticity of demand for commodity *a* is greater than unity, since in that case, the sales-receipts (or income) of the producers of *a* will be the greater the larger the production.
>
> A little reflection will show however that if by 'elasticity of demand' we mean something that is a reflection of the elasticity of substitution of consumers—in other words, of elasticity of 'flow' demand...—the increase in purchasing power of the producers of commodity *a* following upon the rise in the production of *a* must have been the result of a *diversion* of expenditure in favour of *a* and against other commodities. The rise in

> incomes of *a* producers must therefore be offset by reduced incomes of the producers of some other commodities. It is possible that if the elasticities of substitution are high, and income elasticities are all positive, the elasticities of demand for all commodities, *taken individually*, should be greater than unity. But this is not enough to produce a chain reaction of rising demand followed by rising production, followed by rising demand, and so on, unless *total income* measured in terms of money is rising as well, which in turn presupposes that *total* expenditure, and not just the expenditure on a particular commodity, rises in response to a rise in production.

Kaldor then distinguishes between "flow" and "stock" demand (and supply). While the former refers to demand and supply of the "outsiders", i.e., consumers and producers, the latter refers to demand and supply originating inside the market. While in the world of pure theory "flow" demand and supply may be in continuous equilibrium, in the real world there are persistent differences in production and consumption which are reflected in increment and decrement in stocks. Therefore, competitive markets are inconceivable without dealers (or merchants) who are both buyers and sellers at the same time. The dealers' job is to absorb stocks in the event of excess supplies and release stocks in the event of excess demand. The difference between buying and selling price is known as the "dealer's margin" depending on the degree of perfection of the market and the amount of processing or transformation gone through by the dealers. These merchants may exercise a stabilizing influence on the market if they release stocks when prices are rising and accumulate them when they are falling. According to Kaldor, the very notion of "merchanting" or "commercial" activities may involve the notion of some elasticity of demand for holding stocks by traders, an elasticity which ultimately depends on their expectations of future prices and selling opportunities in their bid to make profits. Kaldor (ibid., p. 1249–50) adds:

> The essential element missing from Young's presentation, and which can only be supplied on the basis of Keynesian economics, is the addition to income resulting from the accumulation of capital (in other words, from investment expenditure) combined with the induced character of such investment which arises more or less as a by-product of changes in the organization of production. It operates moreover in two different ways. In really 'competitive' markets, such as those of primary products, which approximate the economist's notion of perfect competition…the stocks which are essential for the functioning of the market are carried

> by merchants who are independent both from the producers and the consumers... In the markets for commodities in which increasing returns are important, and which, for that very reason, are only 'imperfectly' competitive – as is the case with manufactures – the producers carry their *own* stocks and adjust the rate of their production in response to changes in their sales (or in the state of their 'order book') and there will be 'induced investment' in response to an *increase* in demand and the associated depletion of stocks.

Kaldor maintained that a monetary and banking system was required to enable the capital investment to increase in response to inducements, so as to generate additional investment out of additional income. Paper money and credit creation through the banking system provide the pre-condition for self-sustaining growth. Under metallic money, on the other hand, the supply of money is given and does not respond elastically to increase in profit opportunities. Kaldor also outlined three main consequences of the marriage between Smith-Young theory of increasing returns and Keynesian doctrine of effective demand. First, the distinction between full employment situation where real income is limited by resource-endowment, and unemployment situation where it is limited by effective demand, disappears. Total output can never be confined by resources except in a short-term sense. Second, the coexistence of increasing returns and competition is a very prominent feature of decentralized economic systems. Third, self-sustaining growth in such systems is due to endogenous causes such as demand, but tends to be fragile unless a number of favourable factors are present such as merchants, who have a stabilizing influence on prices, and "passive" monetary and banking policies where money supply grows in automatic response to an increased demand for credit.

Young (1928, p. 534) had stated if commodities are produced competitively, under conditions of increasing returns, "an increase in supply of one commodity is an increase in demand for other commodities, and it must be supposed that every increase in demand will evoke an increase in supply". Kaldor agreed that while an increase in demand may evoke an increase in supply, the reverse proposition that an increase in supply evokes an increase in demand may not necessarily hold. It is in this context that Kaldor felt the need to supplement the Youngian growth mechanism with Keynesian effective demand. Lauchlin Currie criticized this position. In a letter (dated 16 January 1978) to Kaldor, Currie expressed the view that an increase in investment in the Keynesian sense was not necessary. Kaldor's argument that there was a substitution of purchasing power in favour of elastically demanded goods assumed that there was no slack in the system. This was contrary to observed facts in developing countries where an increase in supply could come from previously underutilized factors. As Currie writes:

> Is there not, in your observation, an implicit assumption that there is no slack in the system – a useful expository assumption but hardly in accordance with reality, especially in LDCs? If the increased supply came from the work of previously underutilized factors, there need be no diminution in the aggregate production of goods and hence, in the Sayian sense, in aggregate demand nor a shift in demand… If there is no slack in the system, even an increase in 'investment' in one sector will not result in a substitution of demand and production, as in the case also of an increase in consumption; but if the financing comes from outside the system, through the mechanism of a rise in prices, the only increase in aggregate supply (and demand in real sense) would come from the presumed greater yield or productivity. So it is not an increase in investment in the Keynesian sense that is the key but the increase in output arising from (a) economies of scale induced by actual growth (b) the taking up of slack (unemployed labour) or (c) the possible economies of more roundabout production (a special Harrod Domar case of increased productivity from division of labour and specialization).[6]

Currie (1997) also thought that Kaldor had slipped into one-thing-at-a-time thinking. While Young thought of barter exchange, Kaldor brought money into the picture. In Currie's opinion, additional money may help the barter system to work more smoothly, but the barter system was always working under the money economy to stimulate demand and supply. Even in a recession, improvements and cost reductions continuously took place. This boosts real demand which in turn boosts production. In every recovery, while money flows are important, what was lost in the explanations was improvements, diffusions of knowledge and economies of scale of the thousands of producers. Currie (1974, p. 4) made an important distinction between Keynesian monetary demand and Sayian intersectoral demand. While the former may stimulate an economy

[6] Letter from Currie to Kaldor dated 16 January 1978 (quoted in Sandilands 1990, pp. 298–99).

facing depression, it may not be effective in a situation where the slack is due to low mobility or low utilization of equipment. In such circumstances, an increase in monetary demand may be inflationary but measures to boost mobility and better factor combinations may result in increased output even if aggregate money demand falls. Thus while additional money helps to lubricate the barter system, the Keynesian mechanism diverts attention from the endogenous forces of demand to exogenous elements.

Verdoorn's Law

Kaldor was influenced by the Smith-Young approach to increasing returns, but his emphasis on manufacturing as an engine of growth as well as the consequent interventionist policies owed much to his empirical bent of mind, particularly to the empirical relationship postulated by Verdoorn's Law. As noted by Thrilwall (1987a, pp. 188–89), Kaldor was the first to use the term "Verdoorn's Law" in print although he had heard Kenneth Arrow use it in conversations on models of "learning-by-doing".[7] Verdoorn (1949) wrote his paper in Italian, and perhaps for that very reason it was largely unfamiliar to a broader audience.

Taking a cross-section of twelve developing countries over the period 1952–1954 to 1963–1964, Kaldor estimated a strong correlation between GDP growth and manufacturing growth. This brings us to Kaldor's first growth law which states that there exists a strong relationship between the growth of manufacturing output and the growth of total output. Kaldor also tested the relationship between the growth of manufacturing output as the independent variable and growth of manufacturing productivity as a dependent variable.[8] This is Kaldor's second law (also known as Verdoorn's Law), and again a strong causal relationship was found. Kaldor's third law states that the growth of overall productivity is positively related to output and employment growth in

[7] At another place, Thirlwall (2002, p. ix) mentions that two economist had made reference to Verdoorn's Law before Kaldor: Colin Clark (1957) and Kenneth Arrow (1962).

[8] This is equivalent to testing employment growth (e) on manufacturing growth (q) since $q = p + e$.

manufacturing and negatively associated with the growth of employment outside manufacturing.[9]

Returning to the strong relationship between productivity growth and output growth in manufacturing (Verdoorn's Law), one may ask as to what is the cause and what is the effect? Thirlwall (1987a, pp. 189–90) answers:

> It could be argued that causation is from fast productivity growth to fast output growth because faster productivity growth causes demand to expand faster than through relative price movement. On this view, all productivity growth would be autonomous. But if this were so, how can large differences in productivity growth in the same industry over the same period in different countries be explained? The reverse causation argument would also be a denial of the existence of dynamic scale economies and increasing returns. Kaldor later conceded, however, that there is an interaction process at work through cost and price changes, and this indeed is an integral part of his circular and cumulative causation model of regional growth rate differences. It also means that a well determined estimate of the Verdoorn's coefficient requires a simultaneous equation estimation.

Later Kaldor converted to the view that the rate of growth of industrial output and GDP is determined by the rate of growth of exports in relation to income elasticity of demand for imports. Faster manufacturing growth leads to faster export growth, and in the framework of circular cumulative causation leads to international growth disparities.[10] While there is relative improvement of some countries and decline of others, faster growing countries are able to sustain their advantage in export activities (which gave fast growth in the first place), and slower growing countries find it difficult to break out of the vicious circle working against them. In his fifth annual lecture to the Scottish Economic Society in February 1970, Kaldor (1970) propounded a verbal presentation of a regional model of export-led growth. This was based on Hicks's (1950) view that in the long run the growth of output in open economies is governed by the growth of autonomous demand (exports) to which other components of demand (consumption and investment) adjust via the "super multiplier"

[9] This happens because of the faster labour transference to manufacturing from non-manufacturing activities, as noted by Thirlwall (1987a, p. 192).

[10] See Thirlwall (2014) "A new interpretation of Kaldor's first growth law for an open developing economy".

(Thirlwall 1987a, p. 196).[11] Thirlwall (1987a, pp. 196–99) then derives a dynamic Harrod trade multiplier result that the growth of income is equal to the growth of export volume divided by income elasticity of demand for imports assuming the real terms of trade to be constant (an assumption also made by Harrod).[12]

Rowthorn (1975) criticized Kaldor (1966) for implicitly regressing the growth of labour productivity (p) on the growth of employment (e) instead of on the growth of output (q). He termed the regression of p on e as "Kaldor's Law". Rowthorn pointed out that this procedure may be justified when one is trying to understand the role of labour supply as a constraint on labour productivity. He wrote:

> Taking his law as established, Kaldor went on to argue that Britain's slow growth of industrial productivity has been caused by a chronic shortage of labour in this sector. Since Britain, unlike its rivals, does not possess a large surplus of agricultural labour available for employment in industry, he concluded that, if potential economies of scale are to be realized, labour must be found elsewhere. One potential source of labour is the service sector and to force labour out of this sector into industry Kaldor devised the Selective Empolyment Tax (SET). More recently he has argued for export led growth on the grounds that this will concentrate labour in export industries, where substantial economies of scale can be realized. Thus, where SET was based upon the application of Kaldor's Law to the entire industrial sector, the drive for export-led growth is based upon its application to the export subsector alone. (Rowthorn 1975, p. 11)

Kaldor did not regress p on e but rather it was e on q (Thirlwall 1987a, p. 191). Kaldor preferred to regress e on q because he thought this was useful in a situation where e was either zero or constant, leading to a perfect correlation between p and q (i.e., output and productivity grow at the same rate). Secondly, Kaldor (1975b), in his reply to Rowthorn, pointed out that for agriculture and commerce, the Verdoorn's coefficient

[11] Hicks was not concerned with open economy, and his autonomous demand component was investment, but his model was adapted by McCombie (1985) where exports replace investment.

[12] As noted by King (2009, pp. 77–78), most economic historians like Crafts (1991) rejected the Kaldorian hypothesis that growth in Britain was balance of payments constrained as the relevant elasticities (as formalized by Thirlwall) were less favourable to Britain than to her major competitors like Germany and the US, and a real devaluation was more difficult in Britain because of real-wage resistance.

of p on q was around 1, not a meaningful result. For manufacturing, the results were meaningful irrespective of whether Japan was included or not (for reasons discussed below). The regression coefficients of p on q and e on q were both around 0.5. Thirdly, Kaldor mentioned that he had abandoned his earlier view of labour shortages being responsible for the slow growth rate in the UK. New statistical evidence since 1966 showed this might be true in the short term, but from the long run point of view low growth trend was constrained by demand.

Before Rowthorn wrote, Cripps and Tarling (1973) interpreted Kaldor as believing that manufacturing output growth (q) is dependent on employment growth (e). So they set up Verdoorn's relation with productivity growth in manufacturing as a function of employment growth in manufacturing in a sample of 12 advanced countries. This version of the law held during 1951–1965 but broke down during 1965–1970. Cripps and Tarling maintained that Kaldor's results were dependent on the inclusion of Japan (which was not an advanced country in 1950, the starting point of their study). Kaldor (1968) had retracted from his view on the UK economy in 1968 after criticisms from Wolfe (1968). Rowthorn, without any reference to Kaldor's (1968) reply to Wolfe, continued to interpret Kaldor in the same way as Cripps and Tarling. As noted by Thirlwall (1987a, p. 192), Rowthorn believed that Kaldor's results (as well as those of Cripps and Tarling) were heavily dependent on the inclusion of Japan in the sample of advanced countries.

Verdoorn (1980, p. 385), who wrote his original paper in Italian in 1949 but now writing in English in the *Economic Journal*, clarified that "The 'law' which has been given my name appears...to be much less generally valid than I was led to believe in 1949". He stated that in 1949 he had overlooked the requirement of steady state which requires the model to be solved for asymptotic growth rates (when time tends to infinity) as, for example, was done by Domar (1946). "As a consequence, my final formula for productivity output elasticity is burdened by quite a few terms that vanish in the asymptotic case" (ibid., p. 382). Despite the dilution of the "law" by Verdoorn himself, Kaldor (1981) continued to declare his loyalty to Verdoorn's Law (See Turner 1993, p. 141).

Thirlwall (1987a, p. 192) points out that even if Verdoorn's Law is invalid, it is not an indispensable element of the complete Kaldor model:

> Whether or not Verdoorn's Law holds, however, it is not, contrary to the popular view, an indispensable element of the complete Kaldor model

> by which it stands and falls. Even in the absence of increasing returns in manufacturing the growth of industry would still be the governing factor determining overall output growth as long as resources used by industry represent a net addition to the use of resources (a) because they would otherwise have been unused, (b) because of diminishing returns elsewhere, and/or (c) because industry generates its own resources.[13]

In Thirlwall's (2002) view, Verdoorn's Law naturally follows from the principle of the division of labour postulated by Adam Smith. A priori one can expect a correlation between labour productivity (or the division of labour) and scale of output as this creates possibilities akin to mechanization. As the division of labour improves the dexterity of workers, the relation was akin to a learning function. Thus Verdoorn's Law was a lynchpin of the models of circular cumulative causation, for example, of the type put forward by Myrdal (1957). Further, there were strong affinities between Verdoorn's Law and Kaldor's technical progress function and new endogenous growth theory. In the concept of the technical progress function technical progress is embodied in capital rather than resulting from exogenous changes in the production function. Erkin Bairam (1987) endorsed Thirlwall in his conclusion that Verdoorn's Law forms the basis of cumulative causation model of economic growth. This along with the balance of payments constraint can be used to explain growth rate disparities among advanced countries. However, according to Bairam, Verdoorn's Law as estimated by Kaldor may have been misspecified as it does not include the rate of growth of capital stock explicitly as an explanatory variable. Moreover, there is a "static-dynamic Verdoorn's Law paradox" involved as the static relationship between productivity and scale of output may be significantly different from the dynamic relationship between growth of productivity and growth of output.

Although Kaldor emphasized Verdoorn's Law and special favours to manufacturing (which are discussed below), he recognized that agriculture could pose a constraint on the growth of industry. He favoured the creation of an agricultural surplus ahead of demand as this, apart from overcoming the overall demand constraint, would also supply foodstuffs and raw materials for industrialization. He advocated price support

[13] See also Thirlwall (1983) in the symposium on Kaldor's growth laws published by the *Journal of Post Keynesian Economics*. McCombie (1983), writing in the same symposium, also endorsed Thirlwall's conclusions.

and creation of agricultural marketing boards to overcome the problem of depressed incomes for the agriculture sector. He was of the view that it was food shortages, and not excessive creation of money, which explained inflation. Sandilands and Currie, in a trilateral exchange, criticized Kaldor for favouring the creation of agricultural surplus ahead of demand (See Chandra and Sandilands 2021). In their opinion agriculture was not so much supply constrained as demand constrained. It is ironic that Kaldor wanted to promote industry by giving it special favours, and when this tilted the internal terms of trade against agriculture, he wanted to compensate agriculture by price support and marketing boards. But the basic question is: why favour industry in the first place?

In the Currie-Sandilands view, the objective should be to boost growth with price stability. For this, creation of an agricultural surplus ahead of demand is not required as it is likely to depress agricultural incomes. Moreover, because of its low income and price elasticities, agriculture cannot act as a leading sector but would benefit if the chosen leading sectors (construction and exports) expand first. Both agriculture and manufacturing then follow in response to construction and exports. Therefore, this view discounts Verdoorn's Law as it does not consider manufacturing as the leading sector, nor does it advocate subsidies, protection and other special favours involved in promoting it.[14]

Policy Advice

As already noted, Kaldor shifted his attention from theoretical problems to policy issues in the post-war years. Many of his policies sprang from the belief that manufacturing was special and had to be promoted through special policy measures. Kaldor believed that manufacturing was an engine of growth. In his study of the differences in the cross-country growth rates, it was manufacturing that made the difference. Manufacturing moreover was subject to increasing returns while other sectors like services and agriculture were not. Further, it was also a sector where major advances in labour-saving technology took place. Thus there was a strong observed relationship between productivity growth and output growth in manufacturing (Verdoorn's Law), a relation not generally present in other sectors. Kaldor, therefore, wanted to promote manufacturing through a

[14] For the theoretical underpinnings of Currie's leading-sector strategy see Chandra (2006, 2020), and Chandra and Sandilands (2021) for policy implications.

policy of subsidies and protection. He was opposed to Britain's entry into European Economic Community because he felt that if a country started weak in the growth race, it will be disadvantaged by the application of the principle of circular cumulative causation. He cautioned that Britain might become the Northern Ireland of Europe if it entered the community on the wrong terms. Kaldor (1978a), in his paper "The nemesis of free trade" felt that free trade may be a good policy under constant costs, but under increasing returns it benefits some regions or countries at the cost of the impoverishment of others. His conclusions were similar to those reached by Myrdal (1957) that international free trade accentuated international and interregional inequalities, and that developing countries would be better off if they followed an import-substitution model of growth under tariff and non-tariff barriers. Further, protectionism was not only good for underdeveloped countries but even for an advanced country like Britain which faced competition from Germany, France, Japan, and the US, with the spectacle of British exports being chased from pillar to post, as market after market became closed. Free trade may have suited Britain initially when she embarked on the path of industrial revolution, but now different policies were required. Kaldor pointed out that living standards would have been much higher had Britain not been wedded to free trade ideologically.

Kaldor (1964) recommended a system of dual exchange rates to give a boost to manufacturing and exports for developing countries. A uniform devaluation could be dangerous given the inelastic world demand for developing country exports as well as imports. Under the dual exchange rate system a free market rate would apply to exports of manufactured goods as well as non-essential manufactured imports; a fixed official rate would apply to agricultural exports as well as all essential imports. In order to ensure that receipts of primary exports are surrendered at the official rate, state-owned marketing boards would have to be constituted. Clearly, in order to promote manufacturing exports, discrimination against agriculture is involved. Subsequently, however, as noted by Thirlwall (1987a), the dual exchange argument was never repeated again.

Kaldor was a tax adviser to Britain and many developing countries. He advocated an expenditure tax on the ground that income was not a true guide to "ability to pay" since property owners also spent from accumulated property. Thus the ability to pay was better measured by spending power. The expenditure tax proposal was put forward in his book *An Expenditure Tax* (Kaldor 1955), but went back to his earlier work on the Royal Commision on the Taxation of Profits and Income constituted in 1951. Kaldor was a member of this Commission but since expenditure tax was outside its terms of reference, the proposal was not implemented in Britain.[15] It was however introduced among the upper income groups in India and Ceylon (now Sri Lanka) when Kaldor was a tax adviser to these countries during 1956–1958. Later Kaldor (1978b), as also noted by Thirlwall (1987a, p. 127), admitted that he had underestimated the problems relating to avoidance, evasion as well as political objections. Moreover, the tax favours saving and penalizes consumption, jeopardizing the chances of consumption-led growth. Thus, apart from the administrative feasibility, the wisdom of treating consumption and saving differentially for taxation purposes is also doubtful.

Kaldor (1966), in his famous essay on the "Causes of the slow rate of economic growth in the United Kingdom", identified labour shortage as a major constraint in industry. Perhaps he thought that Britain had reached a stage of maturity where there were no labour surplus sectors outside the industry that could be tapped for manufacturing. Therefore, to transfer labour to manufacturing (which was an increasing returns sector) from services (which was not) Kaldor recommended Selective Employment Tax (SET) on services.[16] This amounted to subsidizing manufacturing and putting a handicap on services, and was similar to the Pigovian idea of subsidizing increasing returns industries and taxing decreasing returns industries in order to maximize the social dividend. However, as Clapham (1922) showed, any empirical attempt to identify industries in this way results in "empty economic boxes". This went against the Smith–Young idea of competition where winners and losers emerge from the competitive race but cannot be identified a priori for policy purposes. The diagnosis of a labour constraint in industry was considered wrong even

[15] Although Kaldor may have wanted an expenditure tax for Britain, he never expressed this publicly and it was never a part of Labour Party policy when Kaldor was an adviser.

[16] As Targetti (1992, p. 22) notes, SET was adopted in a modified form. As part of regional policy, differentiated subsidies for regions were recommended which were called regional employment premiums (REP) and "had the same effect on the regional economy as a devaluation on the national economy".

by Thirlwall (1987a, p. xv), Kaldor's biographer.[17] To Kaldor's credit, he quickly retracted from this view in 1967.

Both Smith and Young had a generalized notion of increasing returns. For Smith, a larger exchange nexus was more efficient than a smaller one to facilitate specialization and the division of labour. He did say that the division of labour is better carried out in industry (than in agriculture) but he did not want to give any priority to it. In fact, he was vehemently ranged against mercantilist policies of favouring industry at the cost of agriculture. As for Young, he did say that elasticity of demand and supply are different in different sectors, therefore the rates of growth are likely to differ among them, but he did not say that winners should be picked and promoted on an a priori basis. Any policy of sectoral favours and handicaps, in his opinion, would distort intersectoral trade relationships, distort the internal terms of trade, and retard rather than facilitate growth. He regarded productive activities as an "interrelated whole", and defined the market in an inclusive sense as a totality of productive activities tied together by trade.

The Smith–Young framework on increasing returns leads to a policy of "no favours, no handicaps". By contrast, Kaldor had an interventionist bent of mind and, as noted by Thirlwall (1987a, p. 11), had a more dirigiste approach to policy than even Keynes. A number of reasons can be cited for Kaldor's statist approach. First, Kaldor was empirically inclined particularly in respect of policy formulation. Although he was influenced by Smith and Young on increasing returns, when it came to policymaking he was guided more by empirical relationships such as Verdoorn's Law. Second, Kaldor was deeply influenced by the Keynesian revolution and the policy of intervention it implied. In his initial years as an academic, Kaldor was influenced by Robbins and Hayek but gradually discarded the narrow Austrian view and the implied libertarian philosophy. Third, Kaldor was also influenced by the principle of "circular cumulative causation" as propounded by Myrdal (1957). Here, trade is viewed with scepticism because of its role in promoting international and interregional inequalities rather than growth. Fourth, Kaldor was attracted to Fabian Socialism and its philosophy of change through democratic means. This attracted him to the Labour Party where, when it came to power, he occupied

[17] However, Thirlwall (1987a, p. xv) did not question his stress on manufacturing as an engine of growth or the causal impact of output growth on productivity growth working through scale economies, induced capital accumulation and embodied technical progress.

important policy positions. He was appointed as a Special Advisor Chancellor of the Exchequer during 1964–1970 and again during 1974–1976. As noted by Thrilwall (1987a, pp. 230–31), his appointment along with that of Thomas Balogh[18] was typically depicted in the national press as the "Hugarian mafia", "Terrible Twins", and "Bulgarin and Kruschev" about to launch a sinister East European economic experiment on the British people by squeezing out the capitalist class. Finally, Kaldor appeared to have gone overboard with his criticism of the neoclassical theory and its assumptions. By discarding their focus on the static resource allocation problem, he appeared to have discarded their stress on the markets as well. Although their stress on markets arose from the wrong premises it was however not entirely incorrect. He forgot that Smith and Young had emphasized markets (and competition), not as allocative devices, but for better realization of increasing returns.

Critical Assessment

To Kaldor's credit, he discarded equilibrium economics as unsuitable for explaining the nature and manner of the working of economic forces. He was also influenced by the Smith–Young approach to increasing returns and thought that disequilibrium was the mainstay of an economic system. He emphasized the creative function of markets as opposed to their allocative role. He had an empirical bent of mind and did not follow any existing theoretical framework blindly if it came in conflict with empirical findings or observations. He disliked the so-called "axiomatic" theory where assumptions are not verifiable. He also retracted from his earlier views if new evidence came to light as in the case of labour shortage constraints for Britain. He was a much sought after policy adviser and offered advice not only to Britain but also to many developing countries.

This section however critically assesses Kaldor's contribution in terms of three questions. (1) Did Smith have nothing much to contribute after Chapter 3 of the *Wealth of Nations* in terms of increasing returns? (2) Are increasing returns confined to manufacturing, and therefore

[18] Thirlwall (1987a, p. 24) writes that Balogh and Kaldor had attended the same school in Hungary, and continued as life-long friends although they often disagreed. Kaldor also shared a flat with Balogh (along with Rosenstein-Rodan) in Gordon Square in Bloomsbury. Balogh came to England via America with a letter of recommendation from Schumpeter to Keynes who secured for him a job in the City.

special favours are required to promote it? (3) What are the important differences between Smith-Young and Kaldor as far as policy is concerned?

1. Thirlwall (1987a, p. 188) wrote: "Kaldor used to bemoan that it was from Chapter 4, Book One of *The Wealth of Nations* that economics went wrong, when Smith abandoned the assumption of increasing returns.".[19] Did Smith abandon increasing returns and assume constant costs for the rest of the book? We argue that this is not the case for a number of reasons. First, Smith's interest in value and price theory after the middle of Chapter 4 partly arose because he was trying to tackle the problem of interspatial and intertemporal aggregate economic change, or what is now known as the index number problem. Schumpeter (1954, p. 188) observed that Smith was unaware of the index number method which had been invented by then, and went in for labour as a numeraire. Second, as a result of progress and improvements, the price of manufactures falls (Smith 1776, I, p. 269). Also, as a result of the productivity gains due to the division of labour, the natural price of a commodity falls in the long run (ibid., II, pp. 271–72). Thus Smith talked of long-term falling costs rather than constant costs. Third, Smith had an evolutionary perspective of society. He regarded the system in a state of internally generated change. For example, the idea that capitalism contains the seeds of its own growth is inherent in Smith. Fourth, Smith studied various systems of political economy to arrive at the best one suited for growth. His conclusion was that the system of natural liberty, which ensured security as well as liberty, was the best for this purpose.[20] This system naturally establishes itself once all preferences and restraints are removed, and each individual is left free to pursue his own interest in his own way provided he does not violate

[19] At another place, Thirlwall (1987b) uses the word "joke" instead of "bemoan". Whether Kaldor really meant that economic theory went wrong from Smith's Chapter 4 or not, the fact remains that he made no references to the rest of the book which deals with important matters such as motive power of self interest, the role of saving and capital accumulation, analysis of various systems and institutions, institutions best suited to growth, the proper role of government in the system of natural liberty, and his evolutionary thinking.

[20] See also Chandra (2019) who, inter alia, argues that it is doubtful whether Kaldor fully understood Smith's institutional context of growth.

the laws of justice. Despite the inequalities inherent in the system, it was fair to the poor because in it even an ordinary worker was able to enjoy a standard of living higher than any savage king. Fifth, Smith also made a study of the motive power of self-interest which does not manifest itself in some hedonistic principle but in bettering one's condition. Smith tells us that self-interest is such a powerful principle that it alone is capable of taking not only an individual but the whole society to wealth and opulence. Governments were therefore advised not to put "a hundred impertinent obstructions" in its operation; they should look after their own economy rather than watching over the economy of the private people. Finally, the institution of private property was crucial as an incentive to growth. In this regard, a secure climate for its accumulation as well as the institution of a civil magistrate to protect it were emphasized by Smith.

2. Coming to the second question of whether increasing returns are sectoral or generalized, it is true that Smith regarded manufacturing to be better suited from the point of view of the division of labour. His pin-factory example, where Smith demonstrates how the division of labour leads to a dramatic increase in output as well as per worker productivity, is also taken from manufacturing. The nature of agriculture is different from manufacturing as there cannot be as complete a specialization or subdivision of tasks. The same person, at different times in the year, is engaged in different activities such as ploughing, sowing, weeding, reaping, thrashing etc. However, Smith did not say that industry should be promoted at the cost of agriculture as mercantilism sought to do. In fact, Smith was against all favours and handicaps or any artificial direction to any kind of industry. Such artificial directions are likely to diminish a country's revenue, and consequently its saving, investment, and growth rates (ibid., I, p. 479). Moreover, in Smith's view mercantilist favours to industry upset the "natural progress of opulence" where capital is first employed in agriculture, then in manufacturing and lastly in foreign commerce (ibid., I, p. 405).

Buchanan and Yoon (1999, 2000) argued that the Smithian proposition regarding the division of labour and the size of the market is best understood in terms of the generalized notion of increasing returns. In its minimalist formulation, the Smithian proposition does not imply a distinction between separate industries or sectors, only that a larger economic nexus is more efficient than a smaller one as specialization is more fully exploited. Kaldor's understanding of increasing returns, as we noted, depended on a sharp distinction between agriculture and manufacturing.[21] He thought that manufacturing was an engine of growth, therefore special efforts should be made to promote it. The agriculture sector, on the other hand, is a diminishing returns sector but was important because it supplies foodstuffs and raw materials to industry. Also, depressed agricultural incomes can pose a constraint on the industry itself. Therefore Kaldor recommended price support to farmers through agricultural marketing boards that are expected to hold stocks. But the depressed incomes in agriculture arise because the terms of trade tilt against the sector when favours are granted to promote the industry. So the original mistake lies in providing protection and subsidies to industry. Studies in effective protection rates reveal that protection to manufacturing necessarily implies deprotection (or negative effective protection) to agriculture and exports. The picture gets murkier if one throws in dual exchange rates, selective employment tax and expenditure tax into the mix with seriously adverse implications for growth and efficiency.

Allyn Young emphasized the togetherness of the economic phenomenon and viewed various sectors of the economy as an "integrated whole". He defined market in an inclusive sense not as an outlet for goods of a particular industry, and therefore external to that industry, but as an outlet for goods in general. He also emphasized the reciprocal nature of exchange. A policy of favouring one sector at the cost of another upsets the exchange relationships, and is likely to retard growth rather than facilitating it. All this leads to a macroeconomic notion of increasing returns where pecuniary external economies rule the roost rather than economies of scale at the firm level. Young stated that we are likely to miss increasing returns if we look for them under a firm or even an industry. It is large production at the macroeconomic level rather than large-scale production at the firm level which leads to increasing returns.

[21] Kaldor's two-sector model referred to the world economy which was generalized to apply to individual countries by Thirlwall (1986).

Young viewed the operation of diminishing returns in agriculture just as a "tendency" but not as a definite "outcome". The law of diminishing returns was operative but was overcome by powerful counterforces such as technological improvements in agriculture and revolution in the means of transport. Rents in the older parts of the world had not risen and the wheat fields of the newer world had been brought to the doorstep of Britain. Young's conclusion was that the law of diminishing returns was true as a tendency but not as a prophecy regarding growth prospects of the agricultural sector. The law of diminishing returns operated in an extremely elastic manner and did not constitute a formidable constraint on growth contrary to what Ricardo and Malthus believed.

3. Finally, we come to the question about the policy differences between Kaldor and Smith-Young approaches. Although Kaldor was influenced by the Smith–Young framework, his policy approach was interventionist and out of line with this framework. To start with, Kaldor favoured the continuance of wartime controls such as rationing, price controls, import controls, and restrictions on capital outflows in the post-war period. He also favoured public ownership of key industries. In his letters to *The Times*, he advocated planning and criticized the Labour government for running a planned economy without a plan. As already noted, he advocated several measures to boost manufacturing (which he thought was the increasing returns sector) such as protection,[22] subsidies, dual exchange rates, selective employment tax on services to transfer labour to industry and expenditure tax. To overcome the problem of depressed incomes in agriculture, which might pose a constraint on the industrial sector, he advocated price support to the farmers and agricultural market boards. All this creates a needless policy maze which can be avoided by not favouring industry in the first place.

Kaldor deviated substantially from the premises of both natural liberty and competition. In stating that economic theory went astray

[22] To be fair to Kaldor, his advocacy of import-substitution under protection was in line with the mainstream development thinking in the post-war years. First stage import substitution can always be justified on infant industry grounds. As Balassa (1980) has shown, it is not import substitution per se, but the more difficult second stage which takes a developing country too far away from its comparative advantage, that leads to poor economic performance.

from chapter 4 of the *Wealth of Nations*, it appears doubtful whether he properly understood Smith's institutional context underpinning growth. Smith had devoted much space and effort in that book for analysing various systems of political economy from the point of view of growth. While for Smith domestic economic growth and international trade are two sides of the same coin, Kaldor viewed international trade with suspicion as it, in his opinion, promoted international inequalities because of circular cumulative causation. In Smith–Young the objective is to facilitate market exchange; Kaldor's approach of favouring manufacturing, on the other hand, upsets the intersectoral trade relationships. Kaldor's empirical bent of mind, his dirigiste approach to policymaking, and his moral imperative to make things happen appear to have overridden all theoretical considerations arising from the Smith–Young framework.

References

Arrow, Kenneth. 1962. The economic implications of learning by doing. *Review of Economic Studies* 29 (3): 155–173.

Bairam, Erkin I. 1987. The Verdoorn Law, returns to scale and industrial growth: A review of the literature. *Australian Economic Papers* 26 (48): 20–42.

Balassa, B. 1980. The process of industrial development and alternative development strategies. *Essays in International Finance* 141 (December). International Finance Section, Princeton University.

Buchanan, James M., and Yong J. Yoon. 1999. Generalised increasing returns, Euler's theorem, and competitive equilibrium. *History of Political Economy* 31 (3): 511–523.

Buchanan, James M., and Yong J. Yoon. 2000. A Smithian perspective on increasing returns. *Journal of the History of Economic Thought* 22 (1): 43–48.

Chandra, Ramesh. 2006. Currie's leading sector strategy of growth: An appraisal. *Journal of Development Studies* 42: 490–508.

Chandra, Ramesh. 2019. Nicholas Kaldor on Adam Smith and Allyn Young. *Review of Political Economy* 31 (3): 445–463.

Chandra, Ramesh. 2020. *Allyn Abbott Young*. Cham: Palgrave Macmillan.

Chandra, Ramesh, and Roger J. Sandilands. 2021. Nicholas Kaldor, increasing returns and Verdoorn's law. *Journal of Post Keynesian Economics* 44 (2): 315–339.

Clapham, J.M. 1922. On empty economic boxes. *Economic Journal* 32: 305–314.

Clark, Colin. 1957. *The Conditions of Economic Progress*. London: Macmillan.
Crafts, Nicholas F.R. 1991. Economic growth. In *British Economy Since 1945*, ed. N.F.R. Crafts and Nicholas Woodward. Oxford: Clarendon Press.
Cripps, T.F., and R.J. Tarling. 1973. *Growth in Advanced Capitalist Economies 1950–70*. Cambridge University Press.
Currie, Lauchlin. 1974. The 'leading sector' model of growth in developing countries. *Journal of Economic Studies* 1: 1–16.
Currie, Lauchlin. 1997. Implications of an endogenous theory of growth in Allyn Young's macroeconomic concept of increasing returns. *History of Political Economy* 29: 413–443.
Debreu, Gerard. 1959. *Theory of Value: An Axiomatic Analysis of Economic Equilibrium*, Monograph No. 17. New York: Cowles Foundation.
Domar, E. 1946. Capital expansion, rate of growth and employment. *Econometrica* 14 (April): 137–147.
Hahn, F., and R. Matthews. 1994. Nicholas Kaldor (Lord Kaldor) 1908–1986. *Economic Journal* 104 (July): 901–902.
Hicks, John R. 1939. *Value and Capital*. Oxford: Clarendon Press.
Hicks, John R. 1950. *The Trade Cycle*. Oxford: Oxford University Press.
Kaldor, Nicholas. 1955. *An Expenditure Tax*. London: Allen and Unwin.
Kaldor, Nicholas. 1964. Dual exchange rates and economic development. In *Essays on Economic Policy II*. London: Duckworth.
Kaldor, Nicholas. 1966. *Causes of the Slow Rate of Economic Growth in the United Kingdom*. Cambridge: Cambridge University Press.
Kaldor, Nicholas. 1968. Productivity and growth in manufacturing industry: A reply. *Economica* 35 (November): 385.
Kaldor, Nicholas. 1970. The case for regional policies. *Scottish Journal of Political Economy* 82 (November): 1237.
Kaldor, Nicholas. 1972. The irrelevance of equilibrium economics. *Economic Journal* 82: 1237–1255.
Kaldor, Nicholas. 1975. What is wrong with economic theory. *Quarterly Journal of Economics* 89 (3): 347–357.
Kaldor, Nicholas. 1975. Economic growth and Verdoorn's law: A comment on Mr Rowthorn's article. *Economic Journal* 85 (December): 891–896.
Kaldor, Nicholas. 1978a. Nemesis of free trade. In *Further Essays in Applied Economics*. London: Duckworth.
Kaldor, Nicholas. 1978b. A new look at the expenditure tax. In *Collected Economic Essays 7*. New York: Holmes and Meier.
Kaldor, Nicholas. 1981. Discussion. In *Microeconomic Analysis*, ed. D. Currie, A.R. Nobay and D. Peel. London: Croom Helm.
Keynes, John M. 1936. *The General Theory of Employment*. Interest and Money, London: Macmillan.

King, John E. 2007. Kaldor's war. Discussion Paper 25/07. Department of Economics, Monash University, Australia.
King, John E. 2009. *Nicholas Kaldor*. Basingstoke: Palgrave Macmillan.
Kornai, Janos. 1971. *Anti-equilibrium: On Economic Systems Theory and the Tasks of Research*. Amsterdam: North-Holland.
McCombie, John S. L. 1983. Kaldor's laws in retrospect. *Journal of Post Keynesian Economics* 5 (3): 414–429.
McCombie, John S. L. 1985. Economic growth, the Harrod foreign trade multiplier and the Hicks' super-multiplier. *Applied Economics* 17 (1): 55–72.
Myrdal, Gunnar. 1957. *Economic Theory and Underdeveloped Regions*. Oxford: Gerald Duckworth.
Pasinetti, Luigi. 1981. Portrait: Nicholas Kaldor. *Challenge* 23 (6): 59–61.
Phelps Brown, E.H. 1972. The underdevelopment of economics. *Economic Journal* 82 (March): 1.
Rowthorn, R.E. 1975. What remains of Kaldor's Law? *Economic Journal*, March: 10–19.
Sandilands, Roger J. 1990. *The Life and Political Economy of Lauchlin Currie*. Durham and London: Duke University Press.
Schumpeter, Joseph A. 1954 (1982). *History of Economic Analysis*. London: Allen and Unwin.
Smith, Adam. 1776 (1976). *An Inquiry into the Nature and Causes of the Wealth of Nations*, ed. Edwin Cannan. Chicago: University of Chicago Press.
Sraffa, Piero. 1926. Laws of return under competitive conditions. *Economic Journal* 6 (December): 535–550.
Targetti, Ferdinendo. 1992. *Nicholas Kaldor: The Economics and Politics of Capitalism as a Dynamic System*. Oxford: Clarendon Press.
Thirlwall, Anthony P. 1979. The balance of payments constraint as an explanation of international growth rate differences. *Banca Nazionale Del Lavoro Quarterly Review* 32 (1): 45–53.
Thirlwall, Anthony P. 1983. A plain man's guide to Kaldor's growth laws. *Journal of Post Keynesian Economics* 5 (3): 345–358.
Thirlwall, Anthony P. 1986. A general model of growth and development on Kaldorian lines. *Oxford Economic Papers* 38 (2): 199–219.
Thirlwall, Anthony P. 1987. *Nicholas Kaldor*. Washington Square: New York University Press.
Thirlwall, Anthony P. 1987b. Nicholas Kaldor 1908–1986. *Proceedings of the British Academy* LXXIII: 517–566.
Thirlwall, Anthony P. 2002. Foreword. In *Productivity Growth and Economic Performance: Essays on Verdoorn's Law*, ed. John McCombie, M. Pugno and B. Soro. Basigstoke: Palgrave Macmillan.

Thirlwall, Anthony P., and P. Pacheco Lopez. 2014. A new interpretation of Kaldor's first growth law for an open developing economy. *Review of Keynesian Economics* 2 (3): 384–398.

Turner, Marjorie S. 1993. *Nicholas Kaldor and the Real World*. New York: M.E. Sharpe.

Verdoorn, P.J. 1949. Fattori che regolano lo sviluppo della produttivitá del lovoro. *L'industria* 1: 3–10.

Verdoorn, P.J. 1980. Verdoorn's Law in retrospect: A comment. *Economic Journal* 90 (358) (June): 382–385.

Wolfe, J.N. 1968. Productivity and growth in manufacturing industry: Some reflections on Professor Kaldor's inaugural lecture. *Economica*, May.

Wass, Douglas. 1987. Foreword. In *Nicholas Kaldor*, ed. Anthony P. Thirlwall. Washington Square: New York University Press.

Worswick, G.D.N. 1972. Is progress in economic science possible? *Economic Journal*, March.

Young, Allyn. 1928. Increasing returns and economic progress. *Economic Journal* 38 (152): 527–542.

Young, Allyn. 1990. Nicholas Kaldor's notes on Allyn Young's LSE lectures, 1927–29. *Journal of Economic Studies* 17 (3/4): 18–114.

CHAPTER 6

Lauchlin Currie and the Leading-Sector Model of Growth

Lauchlin Currie (1902–1993) was a student of Allyn Young at Harvard. He was initially interested in monetary economics and the problems emanating from the Great Depression but later headed a World Bank Mission to Colombia in 1949 and became a development economist. As a development theorist and a practitioner, he advised almost every Colombian president from 1950 till he died in 1993. He had a very varied career not only as a monetary economist, New Dealer, and presidential adviser in the US,[1] but also had interludes as a farmer (in Colombia) and a full-time academic. He was Canadian by birth but took up Colombian citizenship from 1958.

[1] As a Presidential Adviser, and lease-lend administrator, Currie was involved in the US policy in China and, after the communist takeover there, was subjected to a witch hunt in the hysteria arising out of the McCarthy trials in the early 1950s. Currie was also suspected of having links with the two alleged Soviet espionage rings headed by Victor Perlo and Nathan Gregory Silvermaster, both economists who worked in the government during the war (Sandilands 1990, p. 145). No charges were however either framed or pressed. But further employment in the American government ceased to be a live option (Barber 1991, p. 110).

R. Chandra, *Endogenous Growth in Historical Perspective*, Palgrave Studies in Economic History,
https://doi.org/10.1007/978-3-030-83761-7_6

As a development economist, he emphasized construction and exports as the leading sectors.[2] He recognized that the future of most people employed in agriculture lay in non-farm occupations particularly relating to urban housing. He did not like import-substituting industrialization behind high tariff and non-tariff barriers. He also did not like strategies of agricultural development aimed at creating an agricultural surplus ahead of demand. He also did not like technical aid programmes to agriculture which sought to divide land holdings[3] and to provide subsidized inputs as well as credit.[4] According to him the main problem in agriculture was not on the supply but on the demand side. He was not against manufacturing and agriculture sectors as such but thought that they could be better viewed as the following sectors once the leading sectors had been stimulated.

Currie's (1974) leading-sector strategy of growth is based on the Smith–Young approach to increasing returns which views the main constraint on growth not on the supply but on the demand side. Smith (1776) had stated that the division of labour, the main source of productivity gains, is limited by the size of the market. Young (1928), building on Smith, cast this relationship in terms of cumulative causation and came to the conclusion that the division of labour in large part depends on the division of labour. From this Currie drew the implication that the main cause of growth is growth itself. This approach sees growth not so much as constrained by savings, capital, skills, technology, and foreign exchange as by the size of the overall market or real demand.

[2] Currie believed that the vicious circle of poverty could not be attacked on all fronts simultaneously as that would diffuse and dissipate effort. It was better to concentrate effort at the strategic points (Sandilands 1990, pp. 243–44).

[3] Currie thought that the main problem was not excessively large landholdings in Colombia but rather small holdings and primitive technology. Thus the future of Colombian agriculture lay with plots of sufficient size to make mechanization and soil conservation practices more economical. See Sandilands (1990, p. 189).

[4] As noted by Sandilands (1990, p. 224), Currie's biographer, strategies of agricultural development aimed at building an agricultural surplus ahead of demand ignored the fact that agriculture was faced with low income and price elasticities of demand. Thus, increasing agricultural productivity may not translate into increased farm incomes. So farmers as a group would not like to increase agricultural surplus ahead of demand; even if they tried it with technical assistance, subsidized credit, land reforms, greater rural infrastructure, they would only increase dualism within the agriculture sector. Further: "The key to development was to create the conditions that would greatly expand the number of better paying nonagricultural jobs" (ibid., p. 225).

It should be noted that Currie's approach is based on the notion of intersectoral demand in the Sayian or Youngian sense rather than aggregate demand in the Keynesian sense. In the Youngian sense, the expansion of one sector constitutes the demand for the products of other sectors. The expansion of other sectors in turn fuels growth in the original sector. Since the economy is treated as an integrated whole where sectors are in reciprocal exchange relationships, the growth of the leading sector stimulates growth in the rest of the economy. Thus the growth of construction and exports leads to growth in the following sectors such as agriculture and manufacturing. The growth in the following sectors in turn leads to further growth of the leading sectors. This sets off a cumulative process of growth where "growth begets growth".

Based on these ideas Currie wanted to push up the pace of urbanization, and published *Operation Colombia* in 1961. Because of its controversial nature, the plan was refined and republished as an award-winning book *Accelerating Development: The Necessity and the Means* (Currie 1966). At the behest of President Misael Pastrana, it was republished as the famous *Plan of Four Strategies*.[5] Before working on this plan, Currie had been working as an academic in Canada and Britain during 1967–1971, and had been reading, thinking, teaching, and writing on how to accelerate development. In 1971 he was urged to return to Colombia and become the chief adviser in the National Planning Office headed by Roberto Arenas. The *Plan of Four Strategies* was adopted as the official national plan aimed at boosting urban housing and export diversification.[6] It also established supporting institutions for

[5] These four strategies included construction-led growth, export-led growth, measures to raise agricultural productivity and the new housing-finance system. As Sandilands (1990, p. 246) notes, the third and fourth strategies follow naturally from the first two. Measures to boost agricultural productivity were expected to be stimulated by the rise in real incomes from urbanization and export programmes. Similarly the new housing-finance system had to be index-linked to be self-sustaining.

[6] The plan of four strategies faced major opposition from the Banco de la Republica (the central bank) and the monopolistic Central Mortgage Bank (BCH). The BCH, which enjoyed a monopoly in private housing finance, was itself largely owned the Banco de la Republica. It was, inter alia, argued that it would be wrong to divert savings from other parts of the capital market and that monetary correction would perpetuate inflation. Currie explained to the Colombian President that the system would stimulate saving and this would be counter-inflationary as it was excessive monetary expansion, not excessive saving, that caused inflation. To rally further opposition to the plan, Professor Gustav Ranis from Yale was invited to a conference for the specific purpose of blasting the plan.

accelerating Colombia's urbanization.[7] Implemented in Colombia during 1971–1974, the *Plan of Four Strategies* built "a system too strong to dismantle" by the subsequent regimes (Sandilands 1990, p. 258).[8]

Some National Planning Department (DNP) officials were hostile to the emphasis on private housing finance for middle income and upper working class groups rather than the public sector housing for the very poor. As Sandilands (1990, p. 242) explains, these programmes would be inadequate from Currie's point of view: "Firstly, they would depend heavily on public subsidy. Secondly, even with heavy subsidies this kind of housing can be little better than slum buildings. Thirdly, in order to reduce costs these programs are usually located on the periphery of towns and cities where land costs are low. But land costs are low because access and public services are poor. These must later be provided with great

Ranis argued that the plan would be inflationary as his own model of development led him to believe that the main source of saving was agricultural surplus. Further, Ranis emphasized rural rather than urban housing as the latter would lead to migration to the cities with consequences in terms of increased unemployment and reduced agricultural surplus. This was the famous Harris-Todaro thesis fashionable with development theorists but at variance with the historical experience of every developed country. Currie, of course, was furious with Ranis for doubting the sincerity of his plan and his absurd logic that an increase in urban employment increased unemployment. See Sandilands (1990, pp. 247–49).

[7] Currie's aim was to make urbanisation as the main motor of development (Sandilands 1990, p. 242). He did not like North American style urban sprawl based on private automobile. He favoured "cities within cities" design (first proposed in 1967 to the Mayor of Bogota) based not on a mono city centre, but on multi centres. These in turn are based on the idea of largely self-contained centres within the existing city boundaries to prevent further encroachments of valuable agricultural lands (ibid., p. 260). Wilfred Owen, who authored the well-known book *The Accessible City*, in his report to the World Bank in 1971, endorsed Currie's misgivings on the existing pattern of urbanization based on rapid transit system. He advocated "a mixture residential and work places and associated community facilities" to reduce many transport trips. Further: "The existing pattern of development, based on outmoded zoning principles, separates housing in the suburbs from work places at the center, and misses the opportunities for providing good residential community development in the vicinity of industrial plants, and vice versa" (quoted in Sandialnds 1990, p. 261).

[8] When Alfonso Lopez won the presidential election in March 1974, the new regime was hostile to the scheme and launched a suit in the Council of the State against its constitutionality. This resulted in slackening off of savings growth, but to Currie's delight too many vested interests had developed by then (as he had hoped and planned). The President and his team developed cold feet, and decided to continue with the scheme in a diluted form after introducing several measures benefitting the powerful lobby of rich borrowers. See Sandilands (1990, pp. 258–59).

cost… Fourthly, the value of what is produced in such programs is low; and, since the potential size of such programs is small, both the quantity and the quality of employment will be relatively low. It is the economics of Robinson Crusoe".

Again, as noted by Sandilands (1990, p. 256), Currie had visited Singapore in March 1973 mainly to observe the nature of urban planning there. But he was equally impressed by Singapore's high growth rate, based on extraordinary expansions of housing and exports, which were achieved at the cost of a low-inflation rate of only 1%. This showed that it was possible to increase real intersectoral (or Sayian) demand with austere monetary policies. At the same time, high real growth rates permit greater monetary expansion without incurring inflation.

The term "leading sector" was first used by W.W. Rostow (1960) in the context of the historical process of "take off". He interpreted economic history in terms of stages such as the traditional society, the preconditions to take off, the take-off, the drive to maturity, and the age of mass consumption. The emergence of one or two leading sectors (such as textiles, heavy industry, railroads, dairy products, and timber) is essential for take-off. These sectors had played an important role in the past from a historical perspective. Currie's interest, on the other hand, was to engineer a take-off through appropriate policy. As Currie (1974, p. 14) writes:

> My interest is not to explain the historical growth process but rather to develop a strategy of accelerating growth. Most of the cases mentioned by Rostow happened 'once upon a time'. My interest rather lies in developing a strategy to make things happen, and for that purpose to identify large sectors where growth can be stimulated exogenously or independently of the overall rate of growth.

Once the potential leading sectors have been chosen (on the basis of large latent demand and their capability of being stimulated independently of the overall growth rate) and stimulated, the economy can take off given the reciprocal nature of exchange between the leading and following sectors. Currie identified housing as the internal leading sector and exports as the external leading sector. Both had large latent demand waiting to be actualized if the appropriate constraints or barriers could be removed. Both could be stimulated independently of the overall growth rate. Once the latent demand in these sectors gets an opportunity to be realized, it sets in motion what Currie described as the "Young multiplier". This multiplier is based on the notion of reciprocal demand and is different from the Keynesian multiplier based on autonomous demand.

Currie's leading-sector strategy is a market-friendly strategy that aims to make the market work better in the chosen sectors. It is consistent with the endogenous growth process as outlined by the Smith–Young approach. It does not advocate any favoured treatment to the chosen sectors, only removal of handicaps these sectors may face. It is not based on the logic of increasing returns in specific sectors, but on the notion of generalized increasing returns. In the rest of the chapter, we discuss the rationale of Currie's strategy, the criteria used for selecting a leading sector, whether it requires a favoured treatment vis-a-vis other sectors, and the contemporary relevance of Currie's approach in terms of the current development thinking. Finally, we also make a critical assessment of this strategy.

Rationale

Currie's leading-sector strategy is justified on a number of grounds. First, it can alleviate a country from a low-growth to a high growth equilibrium. Currie (1981a, 1983, 1997) was of the view that in a given institutional and policy framework the same rate of growth perpetuates itself. That is, a high rate of growth will perpetuate a high rate of growth, and a low growth rate will perpetuate a low growth rate. Because of the nature of its policies and institutions, if a country happens to be in a low-growth trap, this could be remedied through exogenous changes in institutions and policies. The endogenous growth process once kick-started has a tendency to perpetuate or sustain itself through what Currie described as "Youngian multiplier" (and what Sandilands (1990) described as "Currie-Young multiplier"). This happens because change is not confined to the original sector only but spreads throughout the economy in a cumulative way. As Currie (1981a, pp. 56–57) writes:

> Any increase in the market itself sets in motion forces to create economies, which increase output per capita not only in the original sector but in all other sectors (since, in Sayian terms, an increase in output is an increase in demand through barter terms of trade) which in turn creates further economies. As this concept of increasing returns was (and is) so novel it might be thought of as 'the Youngian Multiplier' – any increase in real

> demand in a period creates economies which tend to increase the rate of output correspondingly in the succeeding period. It not only makes technical change an integral element of the growth process, but provides what is now missing – a causal explanation of the growth of technical change itself.

Further, through the power of compounding, this growth rate has tremendous implications for GDP in absolute terms. Currie (1983, p. 45) stated that the Youngian multiplier is "more truly a multiplier than the multiplier of Keynes" because the constant rate of growth due to its compounding effect "leads to progressive increase in absolute figures". Moreover, the Keynesian multiplier may be useful in explaining the oscillations around the trend, it does not explain the trend itself. The Youngian multiplier, on the other hand, not only explains the trend but also provides a justification for making greater efforts to introduce exogenous policy and institutional changes so that the power of compounding is realized in terms of progressive increases in absolute incomes. As Currie (1983, p. 45) explains: "The tremendous gain resulting from high rates of growth sustained over a period justifies a great effort to attain a higher rate of growth, especially for countries in the process of development to capture the tremendous exponential gains from compound interest".

Secondly, a leading-sector strategy is justified because it enhances the mobility mechanism of society and shifts people from low-paid agricultural jobs to higher paid non-farm activities. Thus, it provides an opportunity for better factor utilization as well as better factor combinations. In a developing economy, the slack in the system results not from the shortage of monetary demand but from institutional barriers arising from low mobility, low utilization of equipment, and inappropriate factor proportions. Under such circumstances, an increase in Keynesian monetary demand may not produce growth but inflation. On the other hand, measures to ensure better mobility or better combination of factors may increase real output even if aggregate money demand may be falling (Currie 1974, p. 4).[9]

[9] As Sandilands (1990, p. 256) observes: "Though the theory of leading sectors emphasized a demand constraint this certainly did not involve inadequate monetary demand. The chronic persistence of inflation testified to that. Rather, institutional constraints reduced factor mobility and so kept output and, hence, real demand low. Real demand was particularly repressed by these institutional obstacles in the fields of housing and exports.

Currie's argument that endogenous growth once started has a tendency to perpetuate itself at the same rate unless influenced by extraneous events and policies also had an empirical basis. Currie (1997, p. 418) plotted the US real GNP per capita for a long period of 120 years (1869–1989). The plot showed a steady growth of 3.3% per annum which is disturbed by only two external events, namely, the Great Depression and WWII. Short-term fluctuations like booms, recessions, and recoveries appear as mere ripples on the graph without any significant impact on the secular growth rate.

Criteria

How did Currie select the leading sectors? They are not based on the logic of sectoral increasing returns as mentioned earlier. If sectoral increasing returns are the criterion then manufacturing would be the first candidate. But Currie regarded manufacturing as a following rather than a leading sector. Smith had stated that the division of labour was better carried out in manufacturing than in agriculture. But he did not say that manufacturing should be favoured at the cost of other sectors because it would have gone against his "no favours, no restraints" approach or the concept of natural liberty. Young thought that favouring one sector at the cost of another would upset intersectoral exchange relationships, and would therefore be inimical to growth. Kaldor, however, interpreted the Smith–Young approach in sectoral terms. He thought that since manufacturing was special it should be promoted through subsidies, protection, selective employment tax, and other policies discussed earlier in the preceding chapter.

Currie had a generalized concept of increasing returns and also thought that increasing returns could not be identified a priori for policy purposes. Pigou (1912), in his *Wealth and Welfare*, had suggested taxing increasing cost industries and subsidizing decreasing cost ones to maximize the social dividend. Young (1913) had criticized this position on the ground that increasing cost industries did not use up more resources but paid a higher price for their specialized inputs. So higher cost in these industries merely represented a transfer of purchasing power from the users of specialized inputs to their owners. Pigou's tax-cum-subsidy framework assumes that various industries can indeed be empirically identified into increasing, constant, and diminishing cost industries. Clapham (1922), on the other hand, differed from Pigou, and suggested that any such attempt would only yield "empty economic boxes". In Currie's (1981a, p. 54) opinion, Clapham's position was closest to Young who was reluctant to speak of an increasing returns sector even as a hypothetical example. The leading-sector strategy is closely tied up with the Smith–Young approach. As Currie (1981a, p. 56) explains: "This strategy is more consistent with Young's overall or reciprocal supply–demand approach than with those who operate on same sectors by filling Clapham's empty boxes and stressing the internal economies of those particular sectors. Also it provides a means of passing from a constant low to a constant high rate of growth".

Currie postulated two criteria for a leading sector. First, it should have a latent demand waiting to be actualized. This demand should be large enough to make a significant overall impact. For this reason, it may be preferable to have two or more leading sectors. Second, the increase in a sector's growth rate should be exogenous or independent of the overall growth rate. Currie examined several options such as food production, food processing, cotton textiles, transport, and other services, but all of them faced low price and income elasticities of demand. Thus, they are adjusted to supply growth in demand little in excess of population growth. Moreover, these sectors would need to grow very fast to have any overall impact. The intermediate sector cannot be stimulated independently of the final products to which they supply inputs. Consumer durables such as automobiles have a high income elasticity of demand but making them a leading sector becomes dubious in a developing economy with other unmet needs. Thus, we are left with exports and housing which have a hidden demand potential and can be stimulated independently of the overall growth rate.

Leading Sectors and Favoured Treatment

The notion of a leading sector normally conjures up notions of a favoured or privileged treatment to the chosen sector. For example, as we have seen, Pigou (1912) had advocated taxing increasing cost industries and subsidizing decreasing cost industries to maximize the social welfare. Kaldor, who thought that increasing returns are confined to manufacturing, not only favoured import-substituting industrialization behind high tariff and non-tariff barriers but also recommended Special Employment Tax (SET) on services to transfer labour from services to industry. Post-war development economists such as Rosenstein-Rodan

(1943, 1955, 1961) and Nurkse (1953), and more recently Krugman (1993) and Murphy et al. (1989), all recommended favoured treatment to promote industries. Currie's leading-sector strategy, as we noted, is not based on the logic of sector-specific increasing returns but Young's reciprocal supply–demand approach.

To be self-sustaining a leading-sector strategy does not require any special treatment such as subsidies, protection, or grant of monopolies; it only requires that any institutional barriers or handicaps facing the chosen sectors are removed so that the market is made to function better in these sectors. A government role is involved but the nature of the intervention is to facilitate the market process. Currie's leading-sector strategy is a market-friendly strategy that, by releasing latent demand in the chosen sectors, enlarges the size of the overall market. Smith had recommended a number of measures including free trade and public investment in transport and communication to enlarge the size of the market. Therefore Currie's strategy is perfectly consistent with Smith's approach of enlarging the market size.

Currie's strategy is also consistent with the Youngian approach of macroeconomic increasing returns. Young viewed the industrial operations as an integrated whole and eschewed the narrow view of looking at increasing returns under specific firms, sectors, or industries even if they were large. His definition of the market was all-inclusive—an aggregate of productive activities tied together by trade. Young (1913) in his review of Pigou (1912), while criticizing him, did not say that Pigou's policy of preferences and restraints (which Smith had also decried) goes against the macroeconomic notion of increasing returns. This notion was elaborated later in his famous 1928 paper on increasing returns and economic progress.

Currie's approach, being consistent with the Smith–Young framework, cannot be defended if it accords a favoured treatment to certain sectors. It can only be defended on the ground that some sectors face handicaps or discrimination vis-a-vis the rest of the economy which frustrates the operation of the market forces in these specific sectors. Thus the strategy is based on the logic of handicap removal than on granting favours to the chosen sectors. Once the repressed demand in these sectors is released through appropriate intervention, the entire economy gains because of the reciprocal nature of exchange.

Based on the criteria outlined earlier, Currie selected two leading sectors—housing and exports. Currie found that the housing sector suffered from a lack of suitable financial products. The current income of a typical household is much smaller than the value of the asset. So the down payment as well as the subsequent monthly payments have to be within the capacity of the households to bear. This can be done by institutional finance schemes which spread the monthly installments over long periods. Otherwise, there is what is known as the "front end loading problem" where the payments get bunched up in the initial periods. Also, in high inflation Latin American countries such as Colombia, index-linked saving schemes have to be devised so that the system is fair to both borrowers as well as savers. Once suitable financial products are devised in this manner, the large untapped housing demand in developing countries can be met and housing can take off. When this happens, there is a boost in demand for construction materials such as steel, cement, bricks, wood, tiles, glass, sanitary ware, electric cables and appliances, paints, pipes, etc., and some of these industries would then be able to reap the economies of scale. Increased incomes in housing would be spent on food, meat, poultry, consumer goods, etc. Thus an expansion of housing has repercussion on agriculture as well as industry; and growth in these sectors in turn fuels growth in housing. It is truly a "Currie-Young multiplier" at work boosting real incomes all round.

Initially, Colombia devised an index-linked saving system so that it was self-sustaining in character. The system worked well without major recourse to subsidies, as noted by Sandilands (1990, chapter 10). The Colombian growth rate also improved. But over the years a strong lobby of borrowers developed which compelled the government to loosen the link between savings and inflation. This made the system unfair to the savers and affected the competitiveness of housing finance in comparison with the other uses of finance. The government therefore became dependent on subsidized social housing to implement its housing policy with the result that fewer houses were constructed and the drain on the exchequer (because of the subsidy) increased. While the system was sustainable in the absence of subsidies, their injection made it unsustainable. Thus the Colombian experience suggests that a leading sector does not require a favoured status to make it sustainable.

The other leading sector selected by Currie was exports. Currie did not like import-substituting strategies and the protectionism they involved. He wanted to promote exports in an outward-oriented framework where both efficient import substitution and efficient export promotion find a place. Smith had highlighted the role of free international trade in furthering the division of labour. Trade not only keeps the domestic monopolies in check but is also beneficial to the consumer in the form of lower price and better quality. Young had also talked about the commercial revolution preceding the industrial revolution. He observed that it was not the technical change that had brought about the industrial revolution. Rather it was the prior enlargements of markets that had brought about the technical revolution. Currie's export-led growth is again consistent with this framework.

Currie pointed out that the export sector suffered from overvalued exchange rate making exports dearer and imports cheaper. Exports also suffered from export taxes or export controls designed to divert production to the home market. If these constraints are overcome through policy, exports can take off. Moreover, exports can be stimulated independently of the internal rate of growth. As Currie (1974, p. 7) writes: "The concept of the leading sector strategy permits us to see an export-led high growth not simply as a happy accident or as the result of policy to overcome the exchange constraint, but rather as the result of growth strategy that can be generalized. In essence, a growth in exports can take place exogenously and independently of the internal aggregate rate of growth by policies that permit the exploitation of a very small percentage of enormous world market without depressing prices". Further: "Exports owe their effectiveness in stimulating activity to the fact that they add to real demand outside the internal production-consumption circle. They may permit a perpetuation of a higher growth rate for a number of years, as in the case of some Far Eastern Countries" (Currie 1997, p. 438).

The export sector, like the construction sector, has a large element of latent demand waiting to be actualized. Here the constraint is the inward-oriented policy framework which favours home production but discriminates against both exports and agriculture. This policy framework, by making the exchange rate overvalued, encourages imports and discourages exports. Thus, to facilitate exports in a non-discriminatory way, protection to domestic industries including tariff as well as quantitative needs to be reduced. The exchange rate has to be made more competitive either by devaluation or by a policy of freeing up the exchange rate so that it is market-linked or market-determined.[10] Domestic inflation also needs to be kept in check through prudent monetary and fiscal policies,

[10] The exchange rate should be allowed to adjust to the inflation differential between the country in question and its major trading partners if exports are to remain competitive.

otherwise the exchange rate will become continuously overvalued. Again, no favoured treatment to the export sector is called for; neither subsidies nor trading monopolies are required. In fact, such policies would interfere with self-sustaining export-led growth.

Contemporary Relevance

In the post-war years, the newly independent developing countries adopted import-substituting industrialization. In doing so they were not only influenced by their colonial past in which trade was seen as exploitative, but also by trade pessimism philosophies of Raul Prebisch (1950), Hans Singer (1950), Ragnar Nurkse (1953), Rosenstein-Rodan (1943, 1961) and Gunnar Myrdal (1956, 1957). There was also the Singer (1950)-Prebisch (1950) hypothesis of declining terms of trade for primary goods exporting developing countries. Nurkse (1962) did not doubt the ability of trade to act as an engine of growth but doubted its availability to contemporary developing countries. So the only way, it was argued, open for these countries to industrialize was to follow an inward-looking strategy of growth behind high tariff and quantitative protection. While many East Asian countries such as Singapore, Taiwan, and South Korea, after completing the easy first-stage import substitution, switched over to export-led growth to take advantage of the fast-expanding world trade in the 1960s, countries of Latin America and South Asia persisted in their import-substitution strategy and, in fact, carried it to a deeper second stage. The destructiveness of the second stage import-substitution model is well analysed by Bela Balassa (1980).[11]

When the performance of developing economies was analysed it was discovered that those countries which had adopted outward orientation had done much better than those adopting import substitution. For example, a World Bank (1987) study found the economic performance of outward-oriented economies to be far better in almost all respects including GDP growth, industrial growth, agricultural growth, and overall productivity growth. Subsequent econometric studies by

[11] Second stage import-substitution takes a country far from its comparative advantage, and requires high-level skills and technology beyond the competence of most developing countries. Thus, the second-stage import substitution has been described as "travelling up the staircase", and can only be sustained in highly restrictive and protective frameworks involving quantitative restrictions and exchange controls.

Dollar (1992), Edwards (1992, 1997, 1998) confirmed that outward orientation leads to better economic performance. The earlier studies on effective rates of protection (ERPs) by Little et al. (1971) and Balassa (1971) showed that the actual protection to manufacturing was much greater than that indicated by nominal tariffs. Further, protection to manufacturing implied deprotection to exports and agriculture. There was also evidence of declining internal terms of trade for the agriculture sector. It was also found that different industrial sectors were protected at different rates leading to a wide dispersion of effective protection rates. This was particularly so when the final products are protected at a higher rate as compared to inputs or intermediates. Thus nominal protection had two distortionary effects—effective protection was much higher than the nominal protection, and there was a wide dispersion of effective rates as inputs and final products were taxed at different rates.

World Bank (1987) defined outward-oriented strategy as one where the system of incentives is neutral between production for exports and production for the home market.[12] Currie's leading-sector strategy is consistent with an outward-oriented framework in which exports are promoted not through subsidies but through an exchange rate policy which avoids overvaluation. Thus it recognizes the importance of neutrality of incentives and removal of distortions. Similarly, the construction sector is promoted not by granting it favours (or subsidies) but by a policy of handicap removal, i.e., by making available suitable financial products that can keep the down payment and the subsequent installments at reasonable levels. By emphasizing construction along with exports, the strategy strikes a balance between the export sector and the domestically orientated sectors such as construction materials and consumer goods. Construction also involves index-linked saving schemes (for high inflation Latin American countries) which are fair to both the savers as well as the borrowers. Currie's strategy also does not give a prominent role to a prior increase in saving and investment rates in growth. In fact, Currie criticized the capital formation approach for regarding investment as "good" and consumption as "bad".[13]

[12] Inward orientation, on the other hand, favours home production and discriminates against exports.

[13] The dilemma is expressed thus: "Why invest more when consumption is being restrained?" (Sandilands 2000, p. 319).

While the stress on markets and outward orientation is common to both Currie and the current development thinking, the underlying theoretical framework is very different. The current pro-trade and pro-market thinking owes much to the neoclassical revolution (which looks at markets in terms of their static resource-allocation function), while Currie's approach derives from the Smith–Young framework which looks at markets in terms of their dynamic role. The Smith–Young approach stresses disequilbrum rather than equilibrium, views competition as a process rather than an outcome (such as Pareto optimality), and emphasizes the creative function of markets (as in Kaldor) rather than their allocative role.

Critical Appraisal

To break the vicious circles of underdevelopment, to achieve the critical minimum effort for this purpose, and to put a developing economy on a self-sustaining non-inflationary high growth path, Currie advocated a leading-sector model of growth. Currie's approach is so novel that it dared think outside the then prevalent two-sector (agriculture–industry or rural–urban) framework of Arthur Lewis (1954), John Fei, and Gustav Ranis (1964), Michael Todaro (1971), and others and their tendency to identify increased agricultural productivity with higher agricultural incomes. Increased farm output ahead of demand may not translate into increased agricultural incomes because of low income and price elasticities of demand. Currie rejected the import-substitution model of industrialization behind high protective walls and instead opted for export-led growth in an outward-oriented framework. By making construction and exports[14] as the leading sectors, he thought that other sectors like agriculture and industry would then follow after sufficient demand had been created for their products through increased incomes in construction and export sectors. His approach aims not at granting sectoral favours but only at sectoral handicap removal. Construction sector lacks suitable financial products, and exports sector suffers from the overvalued exchange rate.

[14] Thirlwall (2003) and Thirlwall and Sanna (1996) have highlighted the role of export growth in promoting overall growth. Faster export growth, in their opinion, releases the balance of payments constraint on other components of demand. On the supply side, a faster export growth enables a faster import growth, and thus improves productivity of domestic resources.

If these handicaps or institutional barriers can be removed, these sectors can take off and the market can be made to work better in these areas.

Chandra (2006) has argued that the logic of handicap removal need not be confined to construction and exports but should be extended to the whole economy. The field should be levelled for all sectors so that winners and losers emerge from the competitive race itself. The policy should aim at neutrality between different sectors of the domestic economy on the one hand, and between production for the domestic and export markets on the other. Once this is achieved, it is for the market to throw up winners or losers. Indeed the winners and losers emerge from the competitive process itself and are difficult to identify on a priori grounds. Moreover, leading sectors do not remain the same over time. Thus, a policy framework must provide equal opportunity to all sectors or industries; and this can best be achieved in a framework of handicap removal than in that of selective favours (ibid., p. 504).[15]

In the rest of this section, we critically assess Currie's leading-sector strategy in terms of (a) the "big push"' idea to which it is often linked, and (b) Hirschman's "unbalanced growth" approach which he criticized.

Lauchlin Currie and the "big Push"

Currie was influenced by Rosenstein-Rodan's (1943, 1961) theory of the "pig push" and admitted that the idea of a leading-sector strategy or the breakthrough plan came to him from the idea of the big push. "The use of leading-sectors to achieve a Big Push (Rosenstein-Rodan's phrase) in developing countries occurred to me in 1960 and was published in *Operation Colombia* in the following year. It was further elaborated in *Accelerating Development*..." (Currie 1974, p. 14). The idea was that any piecemeal attempts to tackle the vicious circle of poverty on the demand side are bound to fail, a big push over a large number of consumer or wage goods is more likely to succeed. For example, if a single investment takes place in a shoe factory, it will not enlarge the size of the market as the workers are not going to spend all their incomes on shoes alone. But if a number of complementary investments are undertaken in clothing, bread, meat, poultry, beer, and other consumer goods, then the workers can act as each other's buyers and the demand problem can be solved.

[15] See also Chandra (2020, Chapter 4).

While a single act of investment may not solve the demand problem, a big push over a wide front may overcome the obstacles to development. That is why Currie loved such words as the "big push" or "critical minimum effort" to overcome the "vicious circles of underdevelopment" which kept an economy in a "low equilibrium trap".

Although the diagnosis of the problem was on the demand side, the offered solution by the post-war development economists was the supply of capital or capital formation. For example, Nurkse (1953) acknowledged that the problem of capital formation had a supply as well as a demand dimension, but he regarded the supply side to be more important. He stated that underdeveloped countries are underdeveloped in terms of capital in relation to their population or natural resources. Similarly, Rosenstein-Rodan maintained that the size of the big push (or total investment programme) had to be large enough to make any dent in the problem of underdevelopment. This would require large domestic resources as well as foreign aid (as in Marshall Plan). Arthur Lewis (1954), a Nobel Prize winning development economist, had stated that the key to development lies in how an economy is transformed from one saving 5% of its income or less to one saving 12–15% or more. Currie castigated development economists for their excessive preoccupation with capital formation approach where investment is seen with approval while consumption is frowned upon. He thought that Nurkse had overlooked the possibilities of increasing consumer goods by underemployed labour and capital resources. He also overlooked the possibility that labour is unproductive not due to lack of capital but due to lack of effective demand in relation to supply.

In Currie's opinion poverty in developing countries could be reduced if these countries concentrated on goods which the masses wanted such as housing, textiles, and other consumer and wage goods. Given the gross inequalities of income and expenditures, and also the existence of idle labour in developing countries, it made little sense to think of increasing saving by curbing consumption of the masses. The solution may not lie in holding back consumption but by providing more remunerative work, whether in consumption (textiles) or investment (housing). The sequence has to be from housing and exports as the leading sectors to industry and agriculture as followers. By getting the sequence right, Rosenstein-Rodan's big push automatically becomes a reality. There is no prior need to push up saving and investment rates; by getting the correct sequence, the economy is launched on the path of self-sustaining growth where inputs of capital, labour, and technology are seen more as an effect than a cause of growth.[16]

Currie stated that if growth begets growth, it even begets the financing of growth. Business growth is largely self-sustaining, financed largely out of the depreciation funds and retained earnings of the businesses themselves. Currie (1997, p. 435) was of the view that the dynamic element in growth is not saving but real demand. As he says:

> The higher the rate of growth, the larger the savings and investment… The dynamic element in growth is not saving, but the increase in real demand, which in the longer term is dependent on improvements that reduce real cost and improve quality… Thus, the discussion of the role of factors of production suggests that, in seeking contributions to growth, greater emphasis should be placed on the past role played by the growth in the market itself; and that underlying this growth, demand plays a more important role than the supply of factors.

Rosenstein-Rodan's (1943) big push requires large doses of foreign aid to make it a reality. In his famous *Economic Journal* article "Problems of industrialization of eastern and south-eastern Europe", he admitted that if the region is to be industrialized without much sacrifice of present consumption, a substantial foreign lending was required. He estimated that the total capital required would be £6 billion out of which £2.4 billion would have to come from outside. The size of the big push becomes even bigger if one adds social overhead capital to the consumer or wage goods sector as in Rosenstein-Rodan (1961). Some authors such

[16] "Growth is due not to inputs of capital, labour, and technology, but rather to conditions that determine the extent to which existing and new knowledge is used" (Currie, 1997, p. 437). Considerable evidence exists to suggest that growth is not caused by inputs of labour or capital. Currie (1997) summarized this evidence for the US. In his study of the relationship between GDP and non-residential business investment, he found that GDP preceded non-residential business investment during 1960–1992 fairly consistently. He also presented supporting evidence from Montenegro (1989) who, employing Granger-causality, found that it was GDP which caused non-residential business investment in the US, and not the other way round. (For a similar evidence on panel date see Blomström et al. (1996); for India see Chandra and Sandilands (2003); and for the UK see Chandra and Sandilands, 2002). Currie also found negative correlation between per capita income growth and population growth for a sample of 100 countries. This accords well with studies by Mankiw et al. (1992) and Knight et al. (1993) which suggest that population growth has a negative and statistically significant impact on both the level as well the growth of per capita income.

as Bauer (1966, 1971) take the view that aid is neither a necessary nor a sufficient condition for economic development. In Bauer's opinion, the major determinants of development are human qualities, attitudes, social and political institutions and market opportunities. Aid does nothing to affect these factors favourably. On the contrary, it perpetuates the government's hold over the economy and diverts them from their basic tasks of governance such as law and order, efficient management of fiscal and monetary systems, and the provision of basic transport and education. Currie's leading-sector strategy, in contrast to Rosenstein-Rodan's big push, does not involve a large foreign aid programme. It involves more trade rather than aid.

Rosenstein-Rodan's big push requires centralized investment planning to maximize the size and optimize the composition of investment.[17] He stated that the whole industry needs to be planned like a big firm or trust. Rosenstein-Rodan thought more in terms of market failure than in making use of the market to achieve growth. He thought that the pecuniary external economies caused a divergence between social and private marginal net products, so were a sign of market failure. He therefore favoured massive governmental intervention in an inward-looking framework to correct these market failures and to kick start development. Currie, on the other hand, had great faith in the silent workings of the market forces. "But intelligent policy can help these forces move more quickly along the desired paths" (Sandilands 1990, p. 378).

Thus, Currie's leading-sector strategy has nothing much in common with Rosenstein-Rodan's big push except the name. Currie was fascinated by the big push as an objective, but obviously had his own ideas to attain it. In fact, by getting the sequence right from the leading sectors (exports and construction) to the following sectors (agriculture and industry), he showed a better way of achieving it without much recourse to foreign aid or an anti-market statist framework. His was a market-friendly approach which made the market work in areas where it was frustrated by the prevalence of various institutional barriers.

[17] Rosenstein-Rodan (1955) viewed investment theory to be the weakest link of the liberal theory. Thus programming was required either directly through public investment or indirectly through commercial, monetary and fiscal policies and provision of information.

Currie and Hirschman's Unbalanced Growth

If Currie's leading-sector strategy has nothing much in common with Rosenstein-Rodan's theory, why was he sympathetic to the idea of the big push? First, as we have noted, he was sympathetic to the idea of the big push as an objective but obviously had his own plans to make it work in reality. Second, the idea of a big push was an integral part of the mainstream thinking on development. If Currie was to be successful in selling his own idea of a leading-sector strategy it had a better chance of success if couched in terms of the big push idea. Indeed the big push idea has proved to be so durable that it not only fascinated Currie but, more recently, attempts have been made to revive it (e.g., Krugman 1993; Murphy et al. 1989). Thirdly, the big push idea acted as a counterweight to Hirschman's (1958) "unbalanced growth" thesis which Currie disliked. Therefore, the big push came in handy in his criticisms of Hirschman.

Hirschman (1958) in his *The Strategy of Economic Development* had advocated the need to invest in those industries which had the maximum forward and backward linkages in terms of input–output coefficients such as steel. Steel had important backward linkages with iron ore and coal; it had forward linkages with railways and construction. Thus for him concentrating effort in industries with the greatest linkages made more sense than moving simultaneously on a wide front. He maintained that the process of economic growth had to be kept alive by the deliberate creation of shortages, bottlenecks, imbalances, and other forms of disequilibria. In his book *Development Projects Observed*, Hirschman (1967) emphasized the "principle of the hiding hand" where project planners exaggerate benefits and understate costs in order to induce risk-averse entrepreneurs into investing.

Currie (2017) in a posthumous paper (which was written in 1970) stated that the dichotomy between balanced and unbalanced growth was a false one.[18] Rosenstein-Rodan's (1943) was a specific policy proposal (and not a growth doctrine) to accelerate industrialization in post-war south-eastern Europe by utilizing abundant domestic labour and outside aid. The idea of balance was inherent in the complementarity of wage

[18] See also Amartya Sen (1960) who in his *Economic Journal* review of the *Strategy* wrote about the undesirability of making a sharp distinction between balanced and unbalanced growth. Both strategies differ with respect to the degree of interdependence they assume.

goods industries acting as each other's buyers. The so-called balanced growth writers such as Rosenstein-Rodan (1943, 1961), Nurkse (1953) and Scitovsky (1954) never had a "balanced growth" thesis in mind:

> It is interesting to note that none of the three writers commonly credited with holding or elaborating a 'theory of balanced growth' regarded themselves as doing so. They were all, in more or less degree, concerned with accelerating development (or with current inadequate rates of growth) and stressed the obstacle imposed by an initial small market in inducing investment. They all believed that success breeds success or that growth breeds growth, that the more widely based the development movement, the more likely is it to beget demand, employment, profit, investment and further growth. (Currie 2017, p. 14)

The idea of balance is inherent in a free market economy which strives to attain an equilibrium of demand and supply and equalization of returns in different lines of production. But, as Currie notes, since equilibrium is never actually attained, a disequilibrium is simultaneously implied. However, the idea of balance in this market sense does not imply that all sectors will grow simultaneously at the same rate. Young had very clearly stated that different sectors will grow at different rates depending the demand and supply elasticities. So, for Currie, it was hard to imagine that these theorists had balanced growth in mind or a theory where all sectors grew at the same rate.

Currie (2017, p. 11) further pointed out that the real issue was not balanced versus unbalanced growth but the need to make a massive effort to accelerate the growth process and to escape the vicious circles of poverty. He wrote:

> The need for a massive effort to activate or accelerate the growth process, to achieve the take off, to escape from the vicious circle of poverty or from the trap of underdevelopment, to make the critical minimum effort for sustained growth, to make a big push, to achieve the breakthrough or transition to the developed category, and the means by which this might be done, which should have been the main issues with which underdevelopment literature and policy are concerned, have never been given adequate consideration. Part, at least of the reason can be found in the creation of a false issue – that of balance vs unbalance – and the absorption of the real issue underlying the big push into this false issue, or the identification of the big push proposal with a particular theory of growth. (ibid., p. 11)

Currie criticized Hirschman's stress on backward and forward linkages particularly his support for Paz Del Rio steel plant based on these linkages. Currie (1981b) made a case study of this plant and found that it was a costly error that burdened the Colombian industry with high cost as well as inferior quality steel. It, moreover, relied on government support to be viable as there was neither a large home market for steel nor a domestic availability of good quality iron ore. It also hampered export effort because of poor-quality and high-priced steel inputs into production. As Currie noted: "The infant has remained an infant, dependent on government protection and support. Production has remained small, and as much must be spent on steel imports as formerly. It is one of the smallest integrated steel plants in the world" (ibid., p. 157).

Currie (2017, p. 21) also criticized the "principle of the hiding hand" which aims to exaggerate benefits and understate costs to induce investment decisions. He termed this way of action through error as "dubious economics and even more dubious morality". Hirschman did not link the inducement to invest with the size of the market but with the scarcity of "decision-making ability"—the only constraint identified by him in the context of development. In Hirschman's hands the hiding hand is useful in generating learning, but as Sandilands (2017, p. 4) points out it "ignores the adverse incentive effect of those losses on future investors".

To be fair to Hirschman, he clearly recognized the growth process to be one of disequilibrium (rather than equilibrium) much in line with Smith–Young–Kaldor–Currie thinking. Moreover, as noted by Bell (1987), the balanced growth strategy by eschewing detailed centralized planning economizes on the decision-making ability. Hirschman's approach appears more market friendly to the extent that its stress on the deliberate creation of scarcities and disequilibria to keep the growth process alive is attended to by the market process to eliminate them. The concept of linkages has proved enduring and is often referred to without the name of its original author. Even in Currie's leading-sector strategy, the concept of backward linkages is not totally missing. Once construction takes off, construction materials will be stimulated, which is an important backward linkage.[19] But the point remains that investing in a steel plant just on the basis of its linkages, irrespective of demand conditions or the quality of the ore available, is untenable. Moreover, the growth process

[19] Therefore, in practical terms there may not be a big gap between Currie and Hirschman, as Currie's criticisms implied.

is itself characterized by tensions, imbalances and shortages. Therefore, a policy of deliberately creating imbalances may not be a good way of promoting growth.

Jeremy Adelman (2013), Hirschman's biographer, thought that Currie was "ambitious" and given to "grandiose" plans. He talked of underdevelopment as if the poor countries suffered from a disease and therefore needed treatment as in pathology. Hirschman, on the other hand, thought of small interventions, had a micro orientation, emphasized the role of the entrepreneur, and wanted to concentrate on businesses and projects at the local level. To get a feel of the grassroots he liked chatting with bankers, businessmen, farmers, workers, and many others. Hirschman had also published "an uncharacteristically scabrous" review of Currie's (1966) *Accelerating Development*, which left Currie furious and fuming. Currie complained bitterly to the editor Moses Abramovitz who admitted "that it was poor judgment to let an adversary review another's work" (Adelman 2013, p. 306).

Sandilands (1990, p. 259), on the other hand, described the system Currie personally established and nurtured based on his *Plan of Four Strategies* "as one of Currie's most notable achievements". Currie was also not totally bereft of practical experience as he first worked as a consultant businessman in the export–import trade after leaving his White House post. Moreover, when the military junta seized control in Colombia in 1953, Currie bought a farm near Bogota to work as a farmer to await the return of a civilian rule in Colombia which happened in 1958. According to Sandilands, Currie's achievement was to help Colombia in attaining the benefits of better policy and, more importantly (and perhaps less tangibly), it was to elucidate the "togetherness" of the economic system for the benefit of the future generation of economists and policy makers (ibid., p. 378). Further, Currie was "always a very hard taskmaster", "very critical of demagogues" and with both opponents and friends alike he could "be rough and aggressive in debate, exposing fallacious reasoning and not letting his opponents easily off the hook" (ibid., p. 377).

References

Adelman, Jeremy. 2013. *Worldly Philosopher: Odyssey of Albert O Hirschman*. Princeton and Oxford: Princeton University Press.

Barber, William J. 1991. Review of *The Life and Political Economy of Lauchlin Currie: New Dealer, Presidential Adviser, and Development Economist*'. *Journal of the History of Economic Thought* 13 (1): 109–110.

Bauer, Peter. 1966. Foreign aid: An instrument of progress? In *Two Views on Aid in Developing Countries*. London: The Institute of Economic Affairs.

Bauer, Peter. 1971. *Dissent on Development*. Cambridge: Harvard University Press.

Balassa, Bela. 1971. *The Structure of Protection in Developing Countries*. Baltimore: John Hopkins University Press.

Balassa, Bela. 1980. The process of industrial development and alternative development strategies. *Essays in International Finance*, No. 141 (December). International Finance Section, Princeton University.

Bell, Clive. 1987. Development economics. In *The New Palgrave: Economic Development*, ed. J. Eatwell, M. Milgate, and P. Newman. London: Macmillan.

Blomström, M., R.E. Lipsey, and M. Zejan. 1996. Is fixed investment the key to economic growth? *Quarterly Journal of Economics* 111 (February): 269–273.

Chandra, Ramesh. 2006. Currie's 'leading sector' strategy of growth: An appraisal. *Journal of Development Studies* 42 (3): 490–508.

Chandra, Ramesh. 2020. *Allyn Abbott Young*. Cham: Palgrave Macmillan.

Chandra, Ramesh, and Roger J. Sandilands. 2002. Three variants of endogenous growth: as applied to the United Kingdom 1948-2000. A paper presented to *The Scottish Economic Society Annual Conference*, April 11–12. Dundee: University of Abertay.

Chandra, Ramesh, and Roger J. Sandilands. 2003. Does investment cause growth? A test of an endogenous demand-driven theory of growth applied to India 1950–96. In *Old and New Growth Theories: An Assessment*, ed. N. Salvador, 240–260. Cheltenham and Northampton: Edward Elgar.

Clapham, J.M. 1922. On empty economic boxes. *Economic Journal* 32: 305–314.

Currie, Lauchlin. 1966. *Accelerating Development: The Necessity and the Means*. New York: McGraw-Hill.

Currie, Lauchlin. 1974. The leading sector model of growth in developing countries. *Journal of Economic Studies* 1 (1): 1–16.

Currie, Lauchlin. 1981. Allyn Young and the development of growth theory. *Journal of Economic Studies* 8: 52–60.

Currie, Lauchlin. 1981. *The Role of Economic Advisers in Developing Countries*. Westport and London: Greenwood Press.

Currie, Lauchlin. 1983. The 'multiplier' in economic literature. *Journal of Economic Studies* 10 (3): 42–48.

Currie, Lauchlin. 1997. Implications of an endogenous theory of growth in Allyn Young's macroeconomic concept of increasing returns. *History of Political Economy* 29: 413–443.

Currie, Lauchlin. 2017. The big push and balanced and unbalanced growth. In Albert Hirschman, Lauchlin Currie, 'linkages' theory, and Paul Rosenstein-Rodan's 'big push', ed. Roger J. Sandilands. *Strathclyde Discussion Papers in Economics* 17: 17. Department of Economics, University of Strathclyde, Glasgow.

Dollar, David. 1992. Outward oriented developing economies really do grow more rapidly: Evidence from 95 LDCs, 1976–85. *Economic Development and Cultural Change* 4: 523–544.

Edwards, S. 1992. Trade orientation, distortion and growth in developing countries. *Journal of Development Economics* 39: 31–57.

Edwards, S. 1997. Trade policy, growth and income distribution. *American Economic Review: Papers and Proceedings* 87: 205–210.

Edwards, S. 1998. Openness, productivity and growth: What do we really know? *Economic Journal* 108: 383–398.

Fei, John C. H., and Gustav Ranis. 1964. *Development of Labour Surplus Economy: Theory and Policy*. Yale University (Homewood): Richard D. Irwin Inc.

Hirschman, Albert O. 1958. *The Strategy of Economic Development*. New Haven: Yale University Press.

Hirschman, Albert O. 1967. *Development Projects Observed*. Washington DC: The Brookings Institution.

Knight, M., N. Loayza, and D. Villanueva. 1993. Testing the neoclassical theory of economic growth. *IMF Staff Papers* 40 (3): 512–541.

Krugman, Paul. 1993. Toward a counter-counterrevolution in development theory. *Annual Conference on Development Economics* 1922: 15–38.

Lewis, W. Arthur. 1954. Economic development with unlimited supplies of labour. *The Manchester School of Economics and Social Studies* 22: 139–191.

Little, I.M.D., T. Scitovsky, and M. Scott. 1971. *Industry and Trade in Some Developing Countries*. London: Oxford University Press.

Mankiw, N.G., D. Romer, and D.N. Weil. 1992. A contribution to the empirics of economic growth. *Quarterly Journal of Economics* 107 (May): 407–437.

Meier, G.M. 1989. *Leading Issues in Economic Development*, 5th ed. Oxford and New York: Oxford University Press.

Montenegro, A. 1989. Inversión y PIB: relaciones de causalidad. *Desarrollo y Sociedad* (Bogota: CEDE) 24 (September): 53–61.

Murphy, K.M., A. Schleifer, and R. Vishny. 1989. Industrialisation and the big push. *Journal of Political Economy* 97 (5): 1003–1026.

Myrdal, Gunnar. 1956. *Development and Underdevelopment*, 47–51. Cairo: National Bank of Egypt Fiftieth Commoration Lectures. Reprinted in Meier (1989, pp. 385–387).

Myrdal, Gunnar. 1957. *Economic Theory and Underdeveloped Regions*. Oxford: Gerard Duckworth.

Nurkse, Ragnar. 1953. *Problems of Capital Formation in Underdeveloped Countries*. Oxford: Basil Blackwell.
Nurkse, Ragnar. 1962. *Patterns of Trade and Development (Wicksell Lectures 1959)*. Oxford: Basil Blackwell.
Pigou, A.C. 1912. *Wealth and Welfare*. London: Macmillan.
Prebisch, R. 1950. *Economic Development of Latin America and its Principal Problems*. New York: United Nations Economic Commission for Latin America.
Rosenstein-Rodan, Paul. 1943. Problems of industrialisation in eastern and south-eastern Europe. *Economic Journal* 53: 202–211.
Rosenstein-Rodan, Paul. 1955. Programming in economic theory and Italian practice. In *Investment Criteria and Economic Growth*. Cambridge: MIT Centre for International Studies.
Rosenstein-Rodan, Paul. 1961. Notes on the theory of the big push. In *Economic Development of Latin America*, ed. H.S. Ellis and H.C. Wallaich. London: Macmillan.
Rostow, W.W. 1960. *The Stages of Economic Growth*. Cambridge: Cambridge University Press.
Sandilands, Roger J. 1990. *The Life and Political Economy of Lauchlin Currie*. Durham and London: Duke University Press.
Sandilands, Roger J. 2000. Perspectives on Allyn Young in theories of endogenous growth. *Journal of the History of Economic Thought* 22 (3): 309–328.
Sandilands, Roger J. 2017. Albert Hirschman, Lauchlin Currie, 'linkages' theory, and Paul Rosenstein-Rodan's 'big push'. *Strathclyde Discussion Papers in Economics*, 17–17. Department of Economics, University of Strathclyde, Glasgow.
Scitovsky, Tibor. 1954. Two concepts of external economies. *Journal of Political Economy* 62: 143–151.
Sen, Amartya K. 1960. Review of *The Strategy of Economic Development* by A.O. Hirschman. *Economic Journal* 70 (279): 590–594.
Singer, H.W. 1950. The distribution of gains between investing and borrowing countries. *American Economic Review* 40 (May): 473–485.
Smith, Adam. 1776 (1976). *An Inquiry into the Nature and Causes of the Wealth of Nations*, ed. Edwin Cannan. Chicago: University of Chicago Press.
Thirlwall, Anthony P. 2003. Old thoughts on new growth theory. In *Old and New Growth Theories: An Assessment*, ed. N. Salvadori. Cheltenham and Northamton: Edward Elgar.
Thirlwall, Anthony P., and G. Sanna. 1996. The macrodeterminants of growth and new growth theory: An evaluation and further evidence. In *Employment, Economic Growth and the Tyranny of the Market: Essays in Honour of Paul Davidson*, Vol. II, ed. P. Arestis. Cheltenham and Brookfield: Edward Elgar.

Todaro, Michael P. 1971. Income expectations, rural-urban migration and employment in Africa. *International Labour Review* 104 (5): 391–413. Reprinted in Meier (1989, pp. 142–146).

World Bank. 1987. *World Development Report*. New York: Oxford University Press.

Young, Allyn. 1913. Pigou's Wealth and Welfare. *Quarterly Journal of Economics* 27: 672–686.

Young, Allyn. 1928. Increasing returns and economic progress. *Economic Journal* 38 (152): 527–542.

CHAPTER 7

Paul Rosenstein-Rodan and the Post-war Development Model

Development economics as a sub-discipline within economics started after WWII when many countries in Asia, Africa, the Caribbean, and Latin America gained political independence. If political independence of these countries was to be meaningful, it was argued, it had to be supplemented with economic development and rise in the living standards of the mass of the people. It was felt that the colonial powers had exploited their colonies extracting minerals, raw materials, and other primary goods from these countries and selling finished goods in exchange. It was further felt that this kind of exchange was an unequal exchange which developed the centre at the cost of the periphery.[1] The nationalist governments of these newly independent countries, by pursuing appropriate policies, could kick-start development and raise the living standards of the mass of the people. Thus state intervention was seen critical both in kick-starting economic development as well as in sustaining it.

Market failure was cited as the chief reason for governmental intervention. If left to its own devices the market was thought to be sub-optimal, and was not expected to overcome the obstacles to development in order to launch an economy into self-sustaining growth. Development

[1] For dependency theories, which talk about the development of the centre at the cost of the periphery, see Raul Prebisch (1950), Paul Baran (1957), and A.G. Frank (1967).

R. Chandra, *Endogenous Growth in Historical Perspective*, Palgrave Studies in Economic History,
https://doi.org/10.1007/978-3-030-83761-7_7

economics with an agenda for interventionism saw its heydays during the 1950s and 1960s with important contributions from Paul Rosenstein-Rodan (1943, 1955, 1961), Ragnar Nurkse (1953, 1962), Hans Singer (1950), Raul Prebisch (1950), Arthur Lewis (1954, 1955) and Gunnar Myrdal (1956, 1957). While some authors emphasized the need for a big push or balanced growth to overcome the barriers to development especially related to the smallness of internal markets, others emphasized the unfavourable world demand conditions for the primary products of underdeveloped countries. The mainstream model of development which emerged after the WWII was based on export pessimism; it was pointed out that because of elasticity pessimism and a secular decline in the terms of trade for primary goods, underdeveloped countries could not grow on the basis of export growth. The rapid expansion of world trade in the nineteenth century may have acted as an engine of growth, but the engine was no longer available because of a considerable slowdown in international trade (Nurkse 1962). An import-substitution model of industrialization behind high quantitative and tariff protection became the preferred option for development. This model also implied an interventionist role for the government both direct and indirect.[2]

However, the actual experience with government policies showed that governmental failure in ensuring adequate infrastructure, health and education, poverty eradication, and in other tasks of development was monumental. Although overly interventionist states did make some headway in their task of development, they had obviously taken on more than what they could handle. Thus during the 1970s and 1980s, the pendulum began to swing towards the neoclassical resurgence with the focus on markets. Some authors began to advocate the universality of neoclassical economics and dismissed the claim for development economics as a special sub-discipline within economics. For example Krueger (1986, pp. 62–63) wrote:

[2] The mainstream model of growth based on the ideas of big push (or balanced growth) evoked dissent from economists like Albert Hirschman (1958, 1984) and Peter Bauer (1966, 1971). Hirschman (1958) criticized the balanced growth strategy and put forward in its stead the unbalanced growth strategy where "the task of development policy is to maintain tensions, disproportions and disequilibria" (ibid., p. 66). Bauer argued that while foreign aid is neither a necessary nor a sufficient condition of development because it increases the dependency syndrome of the poor countries and strengthens the government's grip on the economy. The major determinants of development are human qualities, attitudes, social and political institutions and market opportunities.

> Once it is recognized that individuals respond to incentives, and market failure is the result of inappropriate incentives rather than of nonresponsiveness, the separateness of development economics as a field largely disappears. Instead it becomes an applied field in which the tools and insights of labour economics, agricultural economics, international economics, public finance and other fields are addressed to the special questions of policy issues that arise in the context of development.

Thus with the resurgence of neoclassical ideas, interest in development theory and policy began to wane, so much so that Albert Hirschman (1981, p. 1) wrote an obituary to development economics: "As an observer and long time participant I cannot help feeling that the old liveliness is no longer there, that new ideas are ever hard to come by and the field is not adequately reproducing itself". Further, "our subdiscipline had achieved its considerable luster and excitement through the implicit idea that it could slay the dragon of backwardness virtually by itself or, at least, that its contribution to this task was central. We now know that this is not so" (ibid., p. 23). Amartya Sen (1983, p. 745), however, put forward the counter-view that this obituary may be premature as "the original themes – while severely incomplete in coverage – did not point entirely in the wrong direction, and the discipline of development economics does have a crucial role to play in the field of economic growth in developing countries". The broad development themes emphasized by traditional development economics—industrialization, rapid capital accumulation, mobilization of underemployed manpower, and planning and economically active state—are still relevant.

More recently, attempts have been made to revive the big push idea and the other core of ideas termed as the "high development theory" (see, for example, Murphy et al. 1989a, b; Krugman 1993). It has been pointed out that the original authors did not express their ideas of big push or backward and forward linkages with sufficient mathematical rigour, as a result of which these ideas got lost. But these ideas are enduring, need to be expressed with analytical clarity, and there is still a role for governmental intervention to promote industries.

The Big Push and Balanced Growth

Paul Rosenstein-Rodan (1943) set the ball rolling in the context of the problem of industrialization in Eastern and South-Eastern Europe. These countries were characterized by surplus labour in agriculture and the question was how to put this labour to better productive use. There were two options available to these countries—emigration or industrialization. But the major part of the problem would have to be solved by industrialization as emigration is beset with difficulties of its own. As Rosenstein-Rodan (1943, p. 202) wrote:

> If the principles of the international division of labour are to be applied, labour must either be transported towards capital (emigration), or capital must be transported towards labour (industrialization). From the point of view of maximizing the world income, the difference between these two ways is one of transport costs only, and may be assumed to be negligible. Emigration and resettlement would, however, present so many difficulties in immigration areas (and in emigration areas) that it cannot be considered feasible on a large scale. A very considerable part of the task will have to be solved by industrialization.

Rosenstein-Rodan further observed that to optimize the size of units, the area of industrialization must be sufficiently large consisting of the whole area between Germany, Russia, and Italy. This area, though large in terms to square miles, would still be about 40% of Britain's national income. There were two ways to industrialize. One way was to follow the "Russian model" aiming at self-sufficiency without international investment. This would involve constructing all stages of industry including heavy, light, and machine industry built like a vertical industrial concern. This would imply unnecessary sacrifice of present consumption as the required capital would have to be internally generated, and so the process of industrialization could only proceed slowly. Besides, this would reduce the international division of labour and lead to a waste of world resources by adding to the world excess capacity of heavy industry. The alternative way was to fit Eastern and South-Eastern Europe into the world economy involving substantial international investment and capital lending. It would have several advantages over the first plan. It would proceed more quickly since it would involve less sacrifice of consumption; would be based on the sound principles of the international division of labour, and the existing heavy industries of the world would be in a position to supply all the needs of these internationally depressed areas.

This tremendous task, without any precedent of industrializing the region, would have to be properly planned largely on the basis of the existing technical knowledge. Since there had been an increase in fixed and overhead costs as compared to the earlier century, the average size of the firm would be considerably larger. Also, the political risks of international investments were higher, so the state would have to be actively involved in supervision and providing guarantees. Thus, an institutional arrangement different from what existed was necessary for implementing a plan of successful industrialization. East European Industrial Trust (E.E.I.T.) with 50% domestic participation would need to be created to carry out the job which could not be accomplished through the principles of laissez faire. The whole industry, in Rosenstein-Rodan's opinion, would need to be treated and planned like one huge firm or trust.[3]

Invoking external economies, Rosenstein-Rodan pointed out that the first task was to provide skills and training to workers if they were to carry out the task of industrialization. It was an area where the private initiative would not be forthcoming adequately because of the Pigovian divergence between private and social marginal net product. Although not a good investment for the private sector, it was the best investment for the state to undertake. However, external economies were not the most important reason for a large investment unit. "Complementarities of different industries provides the most important set of arguments in favour of a large-scale planned industrialization" (ibid., p. 205). Without using the terms "big push" or "balanced growth", Rosenstein-Rodan in his celebrated 1943 *Economic Journal* article was advocating a simultaneous investment in a number of complementary wage goods industries which use more labour and less capital and, therefore, are in accordance with the concept of the international division of labour particularly for a labour surplus economy.

[3] Rosenstein-Rodan (1943, pp. 206–7) stated that when the whole industrial structure has to be created, individual investment decisions in the market framework become distorted. "The main driving force of investment is the profit expectation of an individual entrepreneur which is based on experience of the past. Experience of the past is partly irrelevant, however, where the whole economic structure of a region is to be changed. An individual entrepreneur's knowledge of the market is bound to be insufficient in this case because he cannot have all the data that would be available to the planning board of an East European Investment Trust [E.E.I.T.]. His subjective risk estimate is bound to be higher than the objective risk. If industrialization of the internationally depressed areas were to rely entirely on the normal incentive of private entrepreneurs, the process would not only be very much slower, the rate of investment smaller and (consequently) national income lower, but the whole economic structure of the region would be different. Investment would be distributed in different proportions between different industries, the final equilibrium would be below the optimum which a large E.E.I.T. could achieve".

To illustrate the concept of complementarities in production, Rosenstein-Rodan gave the example of an investment in a large shoe factory employing 20,000 workers. If workers spent all their wages on shoes alone the problem is largely solved. "The trouble is that workers will not spend all their wages on shoes. If, instead, one million unemployed workers are taken from land and put, not into one industry, but a whole series of industries which produce the bulk of wage goods on which the workers would spend their wages, what was not true in the case of one factory would become true in case of a whole system of industries: it would create its own additional market, thus realizing an expansion of world output with minimum disturbance of the world markets. The industries producing the bulk of wage goods can therefore be said to be complementary. The planned creation of such a complementary system reduces the risk of not being able to sell, and, since risk can be considered as a cost, it reduces costs. It is in this sense a special case of 'external economies'" (ibid., pp. 205–6).[4] Here, Rosenstein-Rodan mentions two other types of external economies when a whole industrial system is planned and created: the strictly Marshallian external economy which is external to a firm within a growing industry, and economies external to one industry because of the growth of other industries.

External economies could also be invoked to advocate a different path of industrialization, i.e., to build "basic industries" and public utilities in the hope that the rest will follow in response to new opportunities. Rosenstein-Rodan cautioned that while this may be helpful in countries like China and parts of Latin America where transportation and other infrastructure were lacking, in Eastern and South-Eastern Europe the situation was different. There was no deficiency of railroads here, and the general vision of the future economic structure was necessary in order to build communications taking into account the needs of complementary wage goods industries to be set up. To some extent complementarity made all industries basic. The advocates of basic industries argue that once they are created, the normal multiplier process can naturally lead to further industrialization. Rosenstein-Rodan warned that in a structural disequilibrium situation, equilibrium mechanisms of

[4] Rosenstein-Rodan (1957, p. 9), invoking Say's Law, stated: "The new producers would be each other's customers and would verify Say's Law by creating an additional market. The complementarity of demand would reduce the risk of not finding a market. Reducing such interdependent risks increases naturally the incentive to invest".

balance of payments and capital movements cannot be expected. "Industrialisation of internationally depressed areas, once it is accomplished, may create an equilibrium, from which onwards normal private incentives may operate successfully. But it seems hopeless to rely on them before that point is reached" (ibid., p. 208).

Rosenstein-Rodan estimated the capital requirements of industrializing the region to be £4.8 billion out of which at least 50% would have to be generated internally. Another £1.2 billion would be required for improving agriculture (the bulk of which would have to be provided internally) making the total funds to be generated internally to the tune of £3.6 billion during 1946–1956. Assuming optimistically that national income would rise at 4% per annum and the average investment rate to be 12%, internal capital supply would only amount to £3 billion, so emigration consisting of 20–30% of the unemployed workers would still be necessary.[5]

After WWII, as the British interest in East Europe declined, "Rosenstein-Rodan made a point of underscoring how those early reflections transcended the borders of 1940s Eastern Europe" (Alacevich 2020, p. 12). In an interview in 1961, he stated that his 1943 paper had been mistitled and there was a "general development theory" involved there. Eastern Europe served as an example for a Third-World model "not because of any interest in Eastern Europe or Germany but only because representatives of Eastern European governments in exile were in London, and one could use them".

In his paper "Notes on the theory of the 'big push'" written at the Centre for International Studies (MIT), Rosenstein-Rodan (1957, p. 1) was more explicit in explaining the big push:

[5] A word about the political context of Rosenstein-Rodan's 1943 paper is also in order. Born in Poland, Rosenstein-Rodan became a British citizen in 1930, and taught at the University College, London. He was appointed as secretary of the Economic Group of the Royal Institute of International Affairs (also known as Chatham House) in 1941 which evolved into a prominent think-tank in international relations (see Alacevich 2020, p. 7). East Europe was considered to be crucial to the balance of power not only in Europe but also at the global level. There was a widely held opinion that whoever controlled Eastern Europe would eventually control Europe and the world. Thus the British government considered the development of Eastern Europe as "a necessary bulwark against German expansionism, and fundamental to a pacified, non-totalitarian Europe" (ibid., p. 9). The economic backwardness of the region had caught the attention of scholars in the face of Nazi aggression, but after World War II, cold war politics implied that the region was "no longer the target of UK development plans" (ibid., p. 12).

> 'There is a minimum level of resources that must be devoted to...a development program if it is to have any chance of success. Launching a country into self-sustaining growth is a little like getting an airplane off the ground. There is a critical ground speed which must be passed before the aircraft can become airborne...' Proceeding 'bit by bit' will not add up in its effects to the sum total of the single bits. A minimum quantum of investment is necessary (though not sufficient) condition of success. This is in the nutshell the contention of the theory of the big push.

The big push contradicted the equilibrium theory and its motto "natura non facit saltus" for three reasons. First, it was based on more realistic assumptions of indivisibilities and non-appropriabilities in the production process giving rise to increasing returns and external economies. Second, since it dealt with growth, it examined the path towards equilibrium rather than only the conditions at the point of equilibrium. "At the point of static equilibrium net investment is zero. The theory of growth is very largely a theory of investment" (ibid., p. 2). Since investment markets were notoriously imperfect, prices do not provide all the information, so additional signalling devices are required to arrive at optimal results. This can be achieved by programming. "Given the imperfect investment market, pecuniary external economies have the same effect in the theory of growth as technological external economies[6]; they are a cause of a possible divergence between the private and the social marginal net product. Since pecuniary (unlike technological) external economies are all-pervading and frequent, the price mechanism does not necessarily put the economy on an optimum path" (ibid., pp. 2–3). Third, markets in general in underdeveloped countries are more imperfect in comparison with those in developed countries, so the price mechanism does not lead the economy to an optimum position.

Rosenstein-Rodan distinguished three kinds of indivisibilities: (1) indivisibility of the production function particularly related to the supply of social overhead capital (or lumpiness of capital), (2) indivisibility (or

[6] "Technological external economies are rare in a static competitive economy with one important exception: training of labor and education. In the theory of growth, however, external economies abound because given the inherent imperfection of the investment market, imperfect knowledge of risks, pecuniary and technological external economies have a similarly disturbing effect on the path towards equilibrium" (Rosenstein-Rodan 1957, p. 4). Further, the distinction between technological and pecuniary external economies become practically irrelevant in the theory of growth (ibid., p. 4).

complementarity) of demand, and (3) indivisibility of the supply of savings (or kink in the supply curve). The first indivisibility is fundamental as the others arise because of it. While linear homogenous production functions are unrealistic and obscure the true nature of the economic process (and risks involved), indivisibilities in the production function are real and create not only non-constant returns but also investment risks and imperfect markets. While in his 1943 paper Rosenstein-Rodan concentrated on the complementarity of wage goods industries, in 1957 he enlarged the size of the big push to include social overhead capital.

Rosenstein-Rodan (1957) pointed out that the social overhead capital is the most important instance of indivisibility,[7] its services are indirectly productive, and become available after long gestation periods. Its most important effect is to create investment opportunities for other industries. Social overhead capital consists of basic industries like power, transport, and communications and cannot be imported. A high initial investment in this sector must precede more quick-yielding directly productive investments. Initially this investment is characterized by lumpiness but variable costs are low. Since their minimum size is large, excess capacity may be unavoidable in underdeveloped countries in the initial period. Normal market mechanisms cannot be relied upon to supply these industries optimally, so programming, based on an overall vision and a correct appraisal of future development, would be required.

In an open economy, the world market can be a substitute for the additional domestic market required in a closed economy. Does it then dispense with the need for the big push? Rosenstein-Rodan (1957) argued that the mobility of products in the real world is imperfect substitute for the mobility of factors. International trade undoubtedly reduces the range of wage goods produced at home, it does not altogether eliminate the need for the minimum push. In other words, while the size of the big push is reduced, its need is not eliminated in an open economy. The rapid increase in the international trade in the nineteenth century had neither equalized factor rewards nor reduced their inequality. This is

[7] Rosenstein-Rodan (1957, p. 7) stated that social overhead capital is characterized by four indivisibilities: First, it is indivisible (irreversible) in time. It must precede other "directly productive" investments. Second, its equipment has high minimum durability. Lesser durability is either technically impossible or much less efficient. For this and other reasons it is very lumpy. Third, it has long gestation periods. Fourth, an irreducible minimum social overhead capital industry mix is a condition (consisting of at least 30–40% of total investment) for getting off the dead-end.

because (1) transportation costs have impeded factor mobility; (2) since the English industrial revolution, which increased the share of complete specialization, subsequent industrial revolutions have led to a decline in the share of complete specialization in international trade; and (3) there are different production functions in different countries depending on effective knowledge. Effective knowledge cannot be acquired by "reading a book or editorial exhortation", but by being "on the job". Thus development leads to a cumulative increase in effective knowledge, and constitutes a major source of increasing returns when the industrial system as a whole grows. International trade has not been able to eliminate the inequality in this regard. Since the markets in underdeveloped countries are more imperfect than in developed countries, the conclusion reached is that international trade does not eliminate but reduces the indivisibility of demand; "it effectively reduces the size of the 'minimum quantum' of investment – but it does not dispense with the need for a 'big push'" (ibid., p. 13).

A high rate of savings would be required to achieve the big push. Since high savings are difficult in underdeveloped countries, the problem can be overcome by creating mechanisms to save more from additional income in the first round so that the marginal rate of saving is very much higher than the average rate. "Adam Smith's dictum that frugality is a virtue and prodigality a vice has to adapted to a situation of growing income. Economic history does not show that the English industrial revolution was preceded by a period of falling consumption; it only shows that the proportion saved from an increase in income was higher than the previous average savings" (ibid., pp. 13–14).[8]

Rosenstein-Rodan was of the view that the classical prescriptions of peace, order, and security as well as a reasonable policy of free trade during 1815–1914 did not attract much foreign capital in underdeveloped countries despite low wages. International income differences increased in the nineteenth century despite maximum international trade, technological progress, and very large factor movements of both labour and capital. The absence of a big push or social overhead capital in underdeveloped

[8] According to Rosenstein-Rodan (1957, p. 14), the economic factors constitute the necessary condition for the big push, to jump over the obstacles to development. Psychological factors remain important even though our knowledge regarding them may be deficient. "[Psychology] may well constitute the difference between the necessary and sufficient condition of success" (ibid., p. 14).

countries prevented them from having a rate of growth comparable to the western world. As he explains:

> The classical economists' forecast proved wrong because they neglected external economies. The deficiency of Social Overhead Capital caused diseconomies on capital account which more than compensated the economies on wage accounts. The Western industrialists were not induced to invest much in industries of underdeveloped countries. Take for example the Lancashire textile industrialists in the middle of the nineteenth century. India was firmly under the British Rule. There were neither insecurity nor balance of payments or transfer risks, and wages in India were very much lower than in Lancashire. Yet any textile mill project in India would have found an obstacle in the deficiency of Social overhead Capital which, for this single project alone, was insurmountable so that it could not avail itself of the advantage of lower wages. The lumpiness of Social Overhead Capital would, however, have made one hundred single project investments pay if there had been a sufficiently integrated force to organize it. An investment trust like the East India Company might have done it, but the single project approach of the City of London made this integration impossible. Had there been an integrating synchronizing 'big push' the course of the economic history of the world would have been different. (Rosenstein-Rodan 1957, p. 16)

Ragnar Nurkse (1953, p. 4), another advocate of balanced growth thesis, in his *Problems of Capital Formation in Underdeveloped Countries* stated that "a country is poor because it is poor". He identified vicious circles of poverty both on the supply side as well as the demand side as being responsible for keeping an underdeveloped country in a low equilibrium trap:

> On the supply side, there is a small capacity to save, resulting from the low level of real income. The low real income is a reflection of low productivity, which in its turn is due largely to the lack of capital. The lack of capital is the result of the small capacity to save, and so the circle is complete.
>
> On the demand side, the inducement to invest may be low because of small buying power of the people, which is due to their small real income, which again is due to low productivity. The low level of productivity, however, is a result of the small amount of capital used in production, which in turn may be caused at least partly by the small inducement to invest.

> The low level of real income, reflecting low productivity, is a point that is common to both circles. (Nurkse 1953, p. 5)

What is the way out of these vicious circles? Here Nurkse propounds his thesis of "balanced growth" (or synchronized application of capital to a wide range of industries) which is akin to Rosenstein-Rodan's big push. Referring to Schumpeter's innovation though originating in one particular industry but having "waves" of new applications over a range of industries creating permanent real income effects, Nurkse wrote: "[A] frontal attack of this sort – a wave of capital investments in a number of different industries – can economically succeed while any substantial application of capital by single entrepreneur in any particular industry may be blocked or discouraged by the limitations of the pre-existing market... Through the application of capital over a wide range of activities, the general level of economic activity is raised and size of the market enlarged" (ibid., pp. 13–14).

Nurkse regarded capital as the "missing component" which if provided in proper amounts could help break the vicious circles of poverty. He stated: "The so called underdeveloped areas, as compared to advanced, are underdeveloped with capital in relation to their population or natural resources" (ibid., p. 1). Though he talked about the problem of development both from the demand as well as the supply side, he considered the supply side of the problem to be more important. He maintained that "capital formation is not entirely a matter of capital supply, although this is no doubt the more important part of the problem" (ibid., p. 4).

The Post-war Model of Development

The mainstream model of growth (or industrialization) which emerged after the post-war years gave emphasis to physical capital accumulation to the neglect of human capital formation or technical change.[9] It therefore emphasized high rates of savings and investment and paid little attention to the efficiency of resource use or productivity aspects of capital employed. It also advocated an import-substitution model of growth behind high protectionist barriers both tariff and non-tariff. It

[9] The role of human capital or R&D in growth during the 1950s and 1960s was emphasized by scholars such as Griliches (1957), Schultz (1961), and Denison (1967). See Chapter 9.

was felt that underdeveloped countries would not be able to grow on the basis of exports, and an atmosphere of trade pessimism prevailed. Some authors (Myrdal 1956, 1957) invoked circular cumulative causation to point out that international trade perpetuated international inequalities rather than growth. The state, through its control and command mechanisms, was thought necessary to engineer an economic take-off into self-sustaining growth. It employed both direct instruments like industrial and import licencing, increase in the share of the public sector, exclusive areas reserved for the public sector, price controls and rationing, exchange controls, and indirect instruments like subsidies, taxation, and tariff policies which work through the market system. Thus, the mainstream model of industrialization in the post-war years had the following features: (1) primacy to capital accumulation, (2) import-substitution under protection, and (3) a large interventionist state often going well beyond infrastructure and public utilities.[10]

Primacy to Capital Accumulation

We noted that the "big push" or "balanced growth" required a synchronized application of capital on a wide front. Thus, post-war development economists like Rosenstein-Rodan and Nurkse who propounded these theories placed capital accumulation at the centre of development. Proceeding bit by bit will not add up to much, a minimum level of centrally coordinated investment programme was necessary to overcome the forces of inertia and to launch a developing country into self-sustaining growth. To achieve a high rate of capital accumulation, Rosenstein-Rodan placed emphasis on two factors—domestic resources as well as foreign aid. As we saw, Rosenstein-Rodan estimated that out of the total capital requirements of £4.8 billion during 1946–1956 for industrializing Eastern and South-Eastern Europe, 50% would have to come from internal sources. This would require an average saving rate of 12% (starting from a lower initial rate of 8 percent and then reaching

[10] Meier (2005, pp. 55–56) summarizes the early development thought thus: "In approaching development problems, the early development economists first thought of what 'obstacles' to development had to be overcome, and what 'missing components' of the development process had to be supplied... The emphasis was on planned investment in physical capital, utilizing reserves of surplus labor, adopting import-substitution industrialization policies, practicing centralized planning, and relying on foreign aid".

15 percent at the end of the ten year period). Even then industrialization would not employ all surplus labour; emigration of about 20–30% of the workforce would still be necessary.

W. Arthur Lewis (1954) in his famous article "Economic development with unlimited supplies of labour" pointed out that the central problem in development was the process by which a community previously saving and investing 4 or 5% of national income was transformed into onto one where the voluntary saving rate was 12–15% or more. Further: "The key to the process is the use which is made of capitalist surplus. In so far as it is reinvested in creating new capital, the capitalist sector expands, taking more people into capitalist employment out of the subsistence sector. The surplus is then larger still, capital formation is still greater, and so the process continues until the labour surplus disappears" (ibid., pp. 151–52).[11]

The Indian example is illustrative. Its development strategy did not diverge from the mainstream view which accorded primacy to physical capital accumulation in development. Since the second plan (1956–1961) onwards, India patterned its plans on the Soviet model of according primacy to heavy industries and capital goods sector. This strategy obviously involved larger sacrifice of present consumption than an alternative strategy of industrialization based on consumer goods such as textiles. It was thought that larger the sacrifice of present consumption, the higher would be the growth rate of future consumption, so that after a sufficient time lag this strategy would pay dividends in terms of higher future consumption. As a result of governmental efforts to push the rates of saving and investment, India succeeded in pushing these rates from about 10% in 1950 to about 22% in 1980, but there was no commensurate increase in the growth rate because of inefficient utilization of resources. Indian economy continued to grow at the same sluggish average growth rate of 3–4% per annum. Jagdish Bhagwati (1993) stated that the weak growth performance during the first three decades of Indian planning

[11] At the very outset, Lewis (1954) posed the problem of growth in terms of capital formation thus: "This essay is written in a classical tradition, making the classical assumption, and asking the classical question. The classics, from Smith to Marx, all assumed, or argued, that an unlimited supply of labour was available at subsistent wages. They then enquired how production grows through time. They found the answer in ***capital accumulation***, which they explained in terms of their analysis of the distribution of income" (p. 139, emphasis added).

reflected a weak productivity performance and not a weak savings performance.[12] It was only after liberalization reforms were initiated in the 1980s and 1990s that growth picked up.

Import-Substitution Under Protection

There are several arguments for import-substitution under protection—infant industry protection, export pessimism, and the principle of circular cumulative causation. Infant industry protection is the oldest argument for protection put forward by Alexander Hamilton in the US and Friedrich List in Germany. List argued that free trade may have been good for Britain whose industrial position was well established, but for a latecomer like Germany, whose industries were young and emerging, protection was required. The infant industry argument soon became widely acceptable, and many authors including J.S. Mill recognized its importance. At the heart of infant protection is the argument that a small firm, unless protected, cannot reap the economies of scale. Once the firm has grown up under protection, free trade can be allowed by dismantling the tariff. Thus the argument is for short-term protection in exchange for long-term welfare gains.

It may however be argued that economies of scale may not be a sufficient basis for infant protection. Infant protection can only be justified if the capital market does not function properly as in many developing countries. Even here it can be argued that it is better to deal with capital market imperfection directly rather than protecting industries. Underlying infant protection may be the existence of external economies (or external spillovers) which a firm may not be able to internalize. For example, a firm may train labour but may not be able to retain it. So training and educating the workforce has external spillover effects, which make these kinds of investments unprofitable for the firms undertaking them. The state can therefore help in subsidizing such investments rather than protecting industries with external spillovers.

Raul Prebisch (1950), the Latin American prophet of export pessimism, argued that primary exports of developing countries faced adverse market conditions and decline in their terms of trade. Since they could not rely on manufactured exports because of low competitiveness

[12] Indian five-year plans started from 1951. So the first three decades of planning would correspond to the period 1951–1981.

in comparison with manufactured exports from developed countries, the only available alternative was to produce for the home market behind high tariff and non-tariff barriers. Prebisch made an empirical analysis of the British terms of trade for the years 1873–1938, and from this analysis he derived the famous Prebisch-Singer hypothesis of secular decline in the terms of trade of the primary goods exporting countries. Hans Singer (1950) gave theoretical justification for the decline in the terms of trade of primary producing countries. First, with the rise in per capita income in advanced countries, proportionately less is spent on primary goods because of low-income elasticity for such goods. Secondly, due to technological advances, developed countries had developed substitutes for primary goods like synthetics. Thirdly, while the demand for primary goods produced by developing countries does not increase rapidly, manufactured goods produced by multinationals in developed countries had a price advantage as multinationals enjoyed monopoly power to set prices. The net result was the deterioration in the terms of trade of developing countries who mainly produced primary goods.

However, Prebisch's empirical analysis was questioned on a number of grounds. First, it was based on the UK's terms of trade, and not those of developing countries. If UK's terms of trade had improved, it did not imply that those of developing countries had declined. Second, a substantial part of the UK's primary imports came from Australia and New Zealand which were not exactly developing countries. Third, issues like improvement in the quality of British manufactures or fall in import prices due to decline in shipping costs were ignored. Grilli and Yang (1988), however, show that during 1900–1986 relative primary goods prices fell by 0.5% per annum and those of non-fuel primary commodities by 0.6% per annum. Thus, while the terms of trade of primary producers have fallen, but perhaps not by as much as was implicit in Prebisch (1950). Sapsford and Balasubramanyam (1994) confirmed this finding and, after taking account of new statistical refinements, concluded that the balance of evidence supported the hypothesis of secular decline in terms of trade of primary goods exporting countries. They suggest that "there can be few hypothesis in economics that have stood the test of time, and new statistical techniques so well" (ibid., p. 1743).

Even if the terms of trade of primary exporters have declined it does not warrant the conclusion that developing countries cannot grow on the basis of manufactured exports. The examples of South-East Asian countries, China, and more recently Vietnam and Bangladesh, show that it is possible to grow on the basis of labour intensive manufactured exports, even though such exports may employ simple technology of processing primary exports or may involve simple manufactures like footwear, toys, and garments.

Gunnar Myrdal (1956, 1957) and Nicholas Kaldor (1978), on the other hand, argued that because of the operation of circular cumulative causation free trade led to interregional and international inequalities. Myrdal (1956) maintained that "if left to its own course, economic development is a process of circular and cumulative causation which tends to award its favours to those who are already well endowed and even to thwart the effort of those who happen to live in regions that are lagging behind" (quoted from Meier 1989, p. 385). Further, "on the international as well as national level trade does not by itself necessarily work for equality. A widening of markets strengthens often on the first hand the progressive countries whose manufacturing industries have the lead and are already fortified in surroundings of external economies, while the underdeveloped countries are in continuous danger of seeing even what they have of industry and, in particular, their small scale industry and handicrafts outcompeted by cheap imports from industrial countries, if they do not protect them" (ibid., p. 385). International trade does promote primary exports from developing countries but here they face adverse demand conditions or inelastic demand in world markets. Any technological improvements which reduce primary goods prices benefit the importing countries. Thus, "forces in the markets will in a cumulative way tend to cause even greater international inequalities between countries as to their level of economic development and average national income per capita" (ibid., p. 385).

Likewise, Kaldor (1978), in his paper "Nemesis of free trade", thought that free trade may be good under constant costs but under increasing returns it benefitted some countries (or regions) at the cost impoverishment of others. He agreed with Myrdal that international trade perpetuated international inequalities, and developing countries would do well if they industrialized behind tariff and quantitative restrictions. Kaldor also stated that protectionism was good not only for developing countries but also for a developed country like Britain. In the initial stages of her growth, free trade suited Britain. But after Germany, France, USA, and Japan industrialized, Britain could not compete and one market after another became closed. Had Britain not been ideologically wedded to free trade, her living standards would have been much better.

The evidence, however, does not suggest that greater openness leads to greater inequalities or worsening of income distribution. World Bank (1987) study suggests that outward-oriented economies did better in almost all respects including reduction in income inequalities. Citing Fields (1984), it pointed out that outward orientation leads to improvement in income distribution as measured by the Gini Coefficient. Edwards (1997) in a study involving 44 countries finds that there is no evidence to suggest that greater openness (or trade liberalization) is linked to greater inequality.

Interventionism

The post-war mainstream view assigned a central role to government in the task of economic development. As the widespread market failure was seen as a hinderance in maximizing the size and optimizing the composition of investment, an interventionist state was thought necessary to coordinate the investment programme or the "big push" (Rosenstein-Rodan 1943, 1961). Rosenstein-Rodan (1955) points out that the price mechanism works reasonably well for allocation of a given stock of consumer goods, or allocation of production given the fixed stock of land, labour, and capital. But when it comes to allocation of investment or maintenance of aggregate monetary equilibrium (or Say's Law) the price system fails. In the investment market the price system fails (1) because of the presence of external economies and complementarities of industries, the individual investor maximizes the private rather than the social net marginal product, so external economies are not sufficiently exploited; (2) the lifetime of equipment is long, so an investor's foresight is likely to be more imperfect than that of a buyer or a producer; (3) lumpiness of investment implies large changes rather than marginal changes; and (4) capital markets are notoriously imperfect, more so in developing countries. Rosenstein-Rodan thus comes to the conclusion that the investment theory is the weakest link in the liberal theory. Also, to maintain an equilibrium between aggregate demand and aggregate supply, deliberate policy intervention is required. The task cannot be achieved by the automatic working of the market forces. Without this macro equilibrium, prices cease to be reliable guides in the economy. Thus the price mechanism does not lead to an optimum outcome in two out of four markets. Hence programming is required to ensure maximum national income over time, and to maximize the amount and to optimize the composition of investment. The means adopted may be indirect (monetary, fiscal and commercial policies or providing information on economic trends) or direct (public investment).

Scitovsky (1954), in his celebrated article "Two concepts of external economies", made a distinction between technological and pecuniary external economies. While the former work through direct interdependence through the production function (e.g., bees and orchards), the latter work indirectly through the market system. He identified pecuniary external economies as the ones more relevant for development. In Scitovsky's opinion, the presence of pecuniary external economies causes a divergence between private and social benefit and hence leads to market failure in the development context. Thus, there is a case for centralized investment planning. As he wrote:

> In an economy in which economic decisions are decentralized, a system of communications is needed to enable each person who makes economic decisions to learn about economic decisions of others and coordinate his decisions with theirs. In the market economy, prices are the signaling device that informs each person of other people's economic decisions; and the merit of perfect competition is that it would cause prices to transmit information reliably and people to respond to this information properly. Market prices, however, reflect the economic situation as it is and not as it will be. For this reason, they are more useful for co-ordinating current production decisions, which are immediately effective and are guided by short-run considerations, than they are for co-ordinating investment decisions, which have a delayed effect and – looking ahead for a long future period – should be governed not by what the present economic situation is but by what the future economic situation is expected to be. The proper co-ordination of investment decisions, therefore, would require a signaling device to transmit information about present plans and future conditions as they are determined by present plans; and the pricing system fails to provide this. Hence the belief that there is need either for centralized investment planning or for some additional communication system to supplement the pricing system as a signaling device. (ibid., p. 150)

While Rosenstein-Rodan argued for an industrial sector to be created and planned like a huge firm or trust, Scitovsky thought "that vertical integration alone would not be enough and complete integration of all industries would be necessary to eliminate all divergence between private profit and public benefit" (ibid., p. 149). In the revised versions of the big push models (e.g., Murphy et al. 1989b, Krugman 1993), the idea of a coordinated investment programme in developing countries characterized by demand spillovers, fixed costs, and imperfect competition is revisited. Because of pecuniary external economies, multiplicity of equilibria exist, and the big push or planned and comprehensive industrialization consists of switching "from cottage production equilibrium to industrial equilibrium" (Murphy et al. 1989b, p. 1004). Thus, an economy may get trapped in low-level equilibrium unless coordinated industrialization over a wide range is pursued. Krugman (1993, p. 32) comes to the conclusion that "there is an intellectually solid case for some government promotion of industry".

Meier (1989, p. 515) mentions four types of market failures: (1) the market does not function properly (market imperfections), (2) the market result is incorrect (externalities), (3) No market exists for some activities (public goods), and (4) the market results in undesirable outcomes like pollution or unequal distribution of income. "Although market failure may provide a rationale for public policy intervention, this is only a necessary – not a sufficient – condition for policy formulation. The realized inadequacies of market outcomes must be compared with potential inadequacies of nonmarket efforts to ameliorate them: market failure must be weighed against nonmarket failure" (ibid., p. 515).

In their enthusiasm to speed up development in post-war era, many developing country governments went overboard.[13] Krueger (1990) stated that many developing country governments by the 1970s and 1980s became mired down in policies that were manifestly unworkable, and government failures significantly outweighed market failures. Since government's resources are limited, it is better off concentrating in areas where it has comparative advantage like law and order, enforcement of contracts, provision of infrastructure such as roads and communications, and provision of information such as improved agricultural methods and extension services. Because the state did not play to its strengths, it ended up committing many failures of omission (such as costly and inefficient public sector enterprises engaged in manufacturing

[13] Bardhan (1984) describes the "all pervasive" nature of the Indian state well where it even occupied low-priority areas such as hotels, tourism, scooters, bicycles, cars and bread.

and other non-traditional activities) and commission (such as poor provision and maintenance of infrastructure or widespread corruption). To minimize rent-seeking, tariffs may be preferable to quantitative restrictions (such as import licensing) and uniform devaluation may be better than tariff-subsidy regime. Direct controls of private activities are often less efficacious than providing incentives through the market.

Revival of the Big Push

Despite the massive government failures of omission and commission, the government-sponsored big push argument for industrialization was revived in the late 1980s and early 1990s. Murphy et al. (1989a) discuss two conditions required for high enough domestic demand for the increasing returns technologies to break even: (1) a leading sector such as agriculture or exports should grow to provide autonomous demand for manufactures, and (2) the income generated by the leading sector should be broadly distributed so that a broad range of manufactures are demanded. In other words, boom in the leading sector by itself may not suffice; the composition of demand as determined by the distribution of income has to be broad enough to create a large market for domestic manufactures. Thus, income distribution is an important determinant of market size. In a companion paper, Murphy et al. (1989b) explore self-sustaining industrialization without autonomous demand. Here income from industrial production turns into demand for industrial goods, and leakages into agriculture are smaller. It is based on Rosenstein-Rodan's idea that simultaneous industrialization across many sectors of the economy can be profitable even when no sector can break even industrializing alone. An imperfectly competitive economy with aggregate demand spillovers is characterized by multiple equilibria,[14] and a big push industrialization is a move from bad to good equilibrium. As Murphy et al. (1989b, pp. 1003–4) explain:

> Of the many causes of lack of growth of underdeveloped countries, a particularly important and frequently discussed constraint on industrialization is the small size of domestic market. When domestic markets are

[14] Murphy et al. (1989b, p. 1004) point out that "the source of multiplicity of equilibria is pecuniary externalities generated by imperfect competition with large fixed costs".

> small and world trade is not free and costless, firms may not be able to generate enough sales to make adoption of increasing returns technologies profitable, and hence industrialization is stalled... According to Rosenstein-Rodan [1943], if various sectors of the economy adopted increasing returns technologies simultaneously, they could each create income that could become a source of demand for goods in other sectors, and so enlarge their markets and make industrialization profitable. In fact, simultaneous industrialization of many sectors can be self-sustaining even if *no* sector could break even industrializing alone. This insight has been developed by Nurkse (1953), Scitovsky (1954), and Fleming (1955) into a doctrine of balanced growth or the big push, with two important elements. First, the same economy must be capable of both the backward preindustrial and the modern industrialized state. No exogenous improvement in endowments or technological opportunities is needed to move to industrialization, only the simultaneous investment by all the sectors using the available technology. Second, industrialization is associated with a better state of affairs. The population of a country benefits from its leap into the industrial state.

In Krugman's (1993) opinion, the neoclassical counterrevolution that caused the demise of development economics went too far. Certain core of ideas regarding external economies, strategic complementarity, and economic development called "high development theory" are still valid and may have practical applications. He regarded Murphy et al.'s (1989b) formalization of the big push as close to the original spirit. Basing himself on this model, he offered a streamlined presentation of their model. Two conditions are necessary to generate pecuniary external economies (which are responsible for two equilibria in the model, one low and the other high): (1) there must be economies of scale in production implying that there is imperfect competition in the modern sector, (2) the modern sector must be able to draw labour out of the traditional sector where wages are lower, i.e., there must be elastic labour supply.[15] Invoking Hirschman's (1958) backward and forward linkages both of which allude to minimum economic scale (backward linkage more explicitly than forward linkage), Krugman (1993, p. 22) stated: "I would argue, then, that a central concept of high development theory circa 1958 was the

[15] Several development theorists made this assumption—Lewis (1954) talked of "unlimited supplies of labour" at subsistence wages, Rosenstein-Rodan (1943) of "agrarian excess population" and Nurkse (1953, 1957) of "surplus labour" and "disguided unemployment" in agriculture.

idea that economies of scale at the level of the individual plant translated into increasing returns at the aggregate level through pecuniary external economies".

Krugman also opined that high development theory was virtually buried because the founders of development economics failed to make their points with sufficient analytical clarity. Recent changes in economics made it possible to recover the invaluable insights that had been lost, so it is possible to launch a counter-counterrevolution in development theory. The high development theory had, in a number of ways, anticipated the insights of modern trade and growth theories. Did the latter theories reinvent the wheel then? Krugman's answer is in the negative as there are a number of essential differences. First, the latter theories tried to explain the persistence of growth whereas the high development theory was preoccupied with how to get it started. Second, the latter models assume only one sector or that all sectors are symmetric. The high development theory was preoccupied with the distinction between the modern sector which exhibited economies of scale and traditional sector which did not. The third and the most essential difference is that while the high development theory was intended as a guide to policy (and thought that it could change the world), the later theories only provided an explanation of the world.

Finally, a word about the policy implications of the revised version of the big push. Krugman stated that he was not advocating interventionist trade and industrial policies much less a return to import substitution. Properly interpreted, the insights from high development theory suggested that costs of fragmenting markets are high precisely because they are not characterized by constant returns to scale and perfect competition. Krugman offers two modest suggestions: (1) the free market orthodoxy should not be carried too far and there is an intellectually solid case of some government promotion of industry, and (2) there is a need to reorient research which was earlier preoccupied by horrors of import substitution and distortions of government policy. Time had come to focus on the market along with government failures.

Critical Appraisal

The temptation for interventionism is so strong indeed that in the initial stages of development theory it manifested in the balanced growth and big push doctrines of Rosenstein-Rodan, Nurkse, Scitovsky, and Fleming among others. More recently it manifested itself in the revised versions of the big push models of Murphy et al. (1989a; b) and Krugman (1993) despite the neoclassical counterrevolution in the late 1970s and 1980s against the widespread government failures in development. The idea that winners and losers emerge from the competitive race (Smith 1776; Young 1928), and any attempt to identify them on a priori grounds leads to "empty economic boxes" (Clapham 1922), has somehow got lost. This section will attempt a critical appraisal of the literature surveyed above in terms of (a) Currie's critique, (b) Hirschman's critique, and (c) empirical critique.

Currie's Critique

We saw that early development economists regarded capital formation as central to economic growth. Rosenstein-Rodan (1943) emphasized domestic saving as well as foreign aid (both in equal measure) in the theory of the big push. Nurkse (1953) emphasized synchronized application of capital on a wide front to overcome the vicious circles of poverty. Although he recognized the demand dimension of the problem of capital formation, for him the supply side was more important. Both quoted classical authors like Adam Smith (1776) and Young (1928) with approval but mainly came to a supply-based prescription for growth. Nurkse (1953) quoted Smith with approval when he stated that the inducement to invest is limited by the size of the market is a modern variant of Adam Smith's relationship between the division of labour and the size of the market. He further stated: "It was Allyn A. Young who suggested this reinterpretation in his well-known essay, 'Increasing Returns and Economic Progress,' Economic Journal, December 1928... It is easy to see, and Adam Smith recognized it himself, that the division of labour is closely connected with the use of capital in production" (ibid., p. 6). Therefore his remedy for growth was mainly a supply-based prescription that emphasizes capital formation. He forgot that capital accumulation, like the division of labour, is limited by the size of the market. So capital formation cannot be regarded as an independent engine of growth. Young was clear that the economies of the industrial division of labour are the economies of capital-intensive roundabout methods of production but they are limited by the size of the market.

Likewise, Rosenstein-Rodan (1957, 1961) referred to Young (1928) with approval when he wrote:

> Increasing returns accrue to a firm not only with the growth of its size but also with the growth of the industry and with the growth of the industrial system as a whole (Allyn A. Young). Greater specialization and better use of resources become possible when growth helps to overcome indivisibilities generating pecuniary external economies. The range of increasing returns seems to be very wide indeed. (Rosenstein-Rodan 1957, p. 6)

But his prescription was the "big push" not only covering a wide range of complementary consumer goods industries (Rosenstein-Rodan 1943) but also social overhead capital (Rosenstein-Rodan 1957, 1961). Although the inclusion of social overhead capital is a sensible idea as it integrates the domestic market and enlarges it, but it makes for a large big push requiring yet more resources. Lauchlin Currie (1966) criticized the capital formation view of growth in which investment is regarded as "good" and consumption as "bad". He took Nurkse and others to task for overlooking the use of chronically underemployed labour and capital so rampant in underdeveloped countries. In his opinion both consumer and investment goods will get a boost if proper incentives are provided to mobilize unemployed resources. Particularly, these economists overlooked the possibility that labour may be unproductive not because of lack of capital but because of lack of effective demand in relation to supply. For example, a girl's labour may be unproductive in agriculture, but may become productive as an urban domestic help while using no more capital.

Currie, who built on the Smith–Young growth framework, pointed out that given gross inequalities of income and expenditure in developing countries, and also the existence of underemployed labour, it made little sense to increase savings by curbing consumption of the masses. The proper solution is not to restrain the consumption of the poor masses but to provide more remunerative employment whether in consumption (textiles) or in investment (housing). This could be done by creating proper incentives. Saving and investment rates would then increase as derivative factors of growth rather than as initiating factors. According to Currie, if growth begets growth, it even begets the financing of growth. He stated that growth was very largely financed by depreciation accounts and retained earnings of the businesses themselves. Thus, if growth is to be regarded as endogenous in the sense that it results from the forces engendered within the system, the required resources for growth will also get generated from within the system.

Currie (1974) enunciated his leading-sector theory of growth in which he made an important distinction between "Keynesian" demand and "Sayian" (or intersectoral) demand. While the former may be useful for an economy experiencing depression, it may have little impact on the underlying trend growth rate or the intersectoral demand. In the Sayian sense an increase in the output of one sector (say housing or exports as the leading sectors) constitutes an increase in demand for the products of other sectors, which when met raises the overall growth rate through the operation of the principle of reciprocal demand (or exchange). Thus the overall growth rate is raised by weighting the average of "leading" and "following" sectors' growth rates. Currie did not regard manufacturing or agriculture as the leading sectors. For him a leading sector was one which was capable of being stimulated independently of the overall growth rate. For this purpose he chose housing as the internal leading sector and exports as the external leading sector. Once the leading sectors have been stimulated by appropriate incentives—a realistic exchange rate in case of exports instead of chronically overvalued exchange rate, and appropriate financial products which can spread the initial and subsequent instalments over a long period (otherwise there would be front-end loading problem)—manufacturing and agriculture would then follow in response. Currie did not believe in creating an agricultural surplus ahead of demand.

The Keynesian mechanism may not operate to stimulate an economy even in the presence of a slack if this slack consists of institutional barriers to mobility or better utilization of existing capital equipment. In that case a Keynesian boost to monetary demand may only fuel inflation with no incentives to better or fuller resource allocation. On the other hand, measures to ensure better mobility or better combination of factors will boost real output growth even if aggregate money demand may be falling (Currie 1974, p. 4). According to Currie, during depression a barter system is always working under the money system to boost intersectoral demand. Although money may facilitate exchange, what are lost in the recovery are the improvements to reduce costs and to better utilize resources and equipment.

Thus, while the early development economists emphasized the role of capital formation in growth, and an interventionist state to kick-start the big push, Currie's emphasis was to make the markets work better. By overcoming the institutional barriers to growth, the market is made to function better. So Currie's approach was not to institute control and command mechanisms designed to replace markets but to emphasize market-enhancing interventions. Although he was attracted to the big push as an objective, he obviously had his own ideas on how to achieve it (Chandra 2006). By getting the sequence right with housing and exports as the leading sectors, and with agriculture and manufacturing following in response, the big push automatically becomes a reality.

Hirschman's Critique

Hirschman (1984) saw himself as a dissenter to the development mainstream represented by Rosenstein-Rodan, Nurkse, Scitovsky, and others. He saw himself as not only an "insurgent" against the old orthodoxy called neoclassical economics, but also against the new one which developed in the 1950s and 1960s called development economics. His 1984 essay is titled "A dissenter's confession: 'The Strategy of Economic Development' revisited". He saw his main contribution as making the development debates more "lively", "attractive and exciting". As he wrote:

> Since my thoughts on development were largely dissents, critical of both old and new orthodoxies, they have led to lively debates, thus helping, together with the contributions of others, to make the new field of development economics attractive and exciting, back in the 1950s and 1960s. I think that this was the major positive contribution of my work as well as its principle impact. (Hirschman 1984, p. 110)

As against the ideas of "balanced growth" and "big push" put forward by the mainstream development economists he, in his *The Strategy of Economic Development* (1958), put forward his own "unbalanced growth" thesis. According to this thesis, effort should be concentrated on those industries where the forward and backward linkages are maximum in terms of input–output coefficients. For example, the steel industry has a backward linkage with coal (as coal is used as an input into steel) and a forward linkage with locomotives (as steel industry supplies its output to locomotive industry). The right strategy was to concentrate effort on those industries where such linkages were the greatest rather than moving simultaneously on all fronts as in the big push. In other words, he favoured a number of sequential solutions to the problem of industrialization rather than simultaneous solutions. Hirschman stated that a balanced growth strategy fails as a strategy of development, and the process of growth has to be kept alive by a deliberate creation of shortages, bottlenecks, tensions, disproportions and disequilibria.[16]

In another book *Development Projects Observed* (1967), he stressed the "principle of the hiding hand" in which the planners were advised to understate costs and exaggerate benefits so that risk averse entrepreneurs are induced into investing. Since projects had "side effects", it was not possible to plan beforehand for every detail or eventuality. Once projects are undertaken, the implementing managers discover "hidden rationalities" to overcome tensions and bottlenecks generated by the project.[17] For example, in Bangladesh a paper mill was set up using bamboo as the raw material. But this became suddenly unavailable due to flowering, and the managers had no alternative but to look for some other raw material. Hirschman thought that the only scarce resource in developing countries was the decision making ability and this can be economized by concentrating effort in a few strategic areas with maximum backward and forward linkages. He also preferred investment in directly productive activities rather than social overhead capital. As his biographer Adelman (2013, p. 346) writes: "Developing countries were not fragile infants at the risk of being choked in the cradle without expanded infrastructures. Better to invest in industries, agriculture, and trade directly; allow them to expand the obstacles and bottlenecks – and therefore create shortfalls in social overheads. Herein lay the idea of spawning pressure points".

For Hirschman capital formation was not central to growth. The only scarce resource in development was, as we noted, the ability to take decisions. Hirschman (1958, p. 5) stated: "development depends not so much on finding optimal combinations of given resources and factors of production as on calling forth and listing for development purposes resources and abilities that are hidden, scattered or badly utilized". In a similar vein, another unbalanced growth theorist Paul Streeten (1959, pp. 182–83) wrote: "One aspect of the case for unbalance is that it highlights the

[16] Hirschman (1984, p. 92), however, warned: "There is no doubt that the unbalanced growth strategy can be overdone, with dire consequences".

[17] Hirschman tried to look for hidden rationalities in the Colombian reality of shortages and bottlenecks, capital intensive production processes, inflation and balance of payments pressures on the decision makers. He stated that his approval of hidden rationalities was not an exercise in apology for the existing order as these were principally those changes which were already under way so that progressive economic and political forces that deserved recognition and help could be identified (ibid., 93–94).

spots where action is needed most urgently, and thus economizes in a resource often in a short supply, viz. the power to take decisions".

The unbalanced growth strategy yields a "structuralist" view of inflation and balance of payments. Shortages and bottlenecks in the unbalanced growth strategy lead to a rise in relative prices. If supply responses are elastic, these shortages and bottlenecks are overcome. If they are not, structuralist inflation, which is the side effect of a certain type of growth process, may result. Similarly, balance of payments difficulties result not because of saving constraint but due to some disproportionality arising in the growth process. A country needs foreign assistance not because it is poor but because some capital-intensive activities are under way. Foreign exchange shortages do not necessarily reflect profligate fiscal and monetary policies, but are a feature of unbalanced growth. However, this strategy is consistent with alternate periods of good and bad times in terms of foreign exchange.

The unbalanced growth strategy itself is not free from criticisms. Several authors (e.g., Alacevich 2007) have noted that in any practical strategy elements of both balance and imbalance are always present. Amartya Sen (1960) while reviewing Hirschman's *Strategy* pointed out that controversies on balanced vs. unbalanced leave readers puzzled as they "have a considerable amount of common ground" (p. 591). Further: "one cannot, however, help feeling that Professor Hirschman is overstating his case" (p. 592). Perhaps this is how economic thought progresses—through thesis, antithesis and finally synthesis. Currie (2017, p. 11) in a posthumous paper (originally written in 1970) pointed out that the issue of "balanced" vs. "unbalanced" growth was a false one as the real issue was to make "critical minimum effort" or the "big push" necessary to transition to the developed category. In his later writings, Hirschman (1984) recognized that the unbalanced growth strategy could be overdone, and the big push could be broken up into a series of smaller steps. Even Paul Steeten, another advocate of unbalanced growth strategy, as noted by Alacevich (2007, p. 18), regarded the controversy as "a sham dispute".

Empirical Critique

After the Second World War, most underdeveloped countries chose import-substitution under protection. In doing so they were not only guided by their colonial past but also by the prevailing mainstream thinking on the subject. However, the pendulum began to swing in the other direction during the 1980s towards freer trade (or trade liberlisation). One reason was that many empirical studies showed the destructiveness of protectionist policies under import-substitution strategies. As noted by Dornbusch (1992), major research projects under the World Bank and NBER documented the ill effects of inward orientation and also the lessons of successful export promotion strategies. Thus, trade vs. protection perspective gave way to more neutral regimes. Successful performance of outward-oriented economies prompted the World Bank to encourage trade liberalization and to make it a condition for lending.

Bela Balassa (1980, 1989) pointed out that it is not import substitution per se but the more difficult second stage which has major ill effects. The first stage is easy as production processes as well as the required technology are simple. The second stage is difficult as production processes are more complex and require sophisticated skills and technology. Second stage is like "travelling up the staircase" and requires high rates of protection both tariff and quantitative. It also implies financial repression and overvalued exchange rates. Therefore those countries which embarked on the second stage found themselves increasingly out of tune with their comparative advantage with high domestic resource cost (DRC) ratios for the products produced. While infant industry protection calls for temporary protection until industries become internationally competitive, in many countries of Latin America and Asia which followed second stage import substitution, protection was regarded as permanent and there was a tendency to indulge in import substitution at any cost. Uncritical acceptance of protection also implied considerable variations in explicit and implicit rates of protection.

Studies on effective rates of protection (see Little et al. 1970, Balassa 1971) suggested that while domestic industries enjoyed high effective protection, exports and agriculture suffered from negative effective protection. The discrimination against exports implied that manufactured exports could not develop; primary exports suffered because of low prices as this discouraged production and encouraged domestic consumption. This also tilted the internal terms of trade against agriculture and other primary activities, leading to a decline in export market shares. It was also revealed that high nominal protection translated into much higher effective protection to domestic industries particularly when inputs are taxed at a lower rate. Further, the practice of taxing different inputs and the final products at different rates implied wide variations in nominal and effective rates resulting in large distortions in the allocation of resources. The presence of quantitative restrictions like import licencing and exchange controls further added to the problem.

World Bank (1987) classified a sample of 41 developing countries in terms of their trade orientation using indicators such as effective rate of protection, use of direct controls, use of export incentives, and the degree of exchange rate overvaluation.[18] It was found that outward-oriented economies performed better "in almost all respects" be it growth rates of GDP, agriculture, manufacturing, or reduction in income inequalities. Evidence on total factor productivity further indicated that outward orientation is associated with rapid economic growth and efficient industrialization. In the design of trade reform World Bank (1987) suggested a move from non-tariff barriers to tariff barriers (as the former are more distortionary). It also suggested greater neutrality of trade regime by lowering the average level of protection as well as its dispersion (or variance). This could be done by simple schemes such as cutting tariffs above a certain level rather than case by case approaches. The ceiling itself can be lowered with the passage of time and in light of the experience gained in the previous round of trade liberalization. This approach would imply lower adjustment costs without a rise in effective protection rates. Thirdly, as long as average tariffs are not zero, discrimination against exports will remain, and this could be offset by subsidizing exports or making available inputs at international prices. Subsidizing exports could however be problematic leading to WTO disputes and countervailing duties in importing countries.

World Bank (1991) outlined a market-friendly strategy where the appropriate role of the government is to ensure adequate investment in people, provide competitive climate for private enterprise, keep the economy open to international trade, and maintain a stable macroeconomy. Beyond these functions, governments are likely to do more harm than good unless interventions are market friendly.

[18] Broadly two types of trade strategies were distinguished—inward orientation and outward orientation. An inward-oriented strategy is one where the system of incentives is biassed in favour of home production and discriminates against exports. An outward-oriented strategy, on the other hand, provides a neutral incentive structure between exports and import substitution.

The example of East Asian "miracle" economies (such as South Korea, Taiwan and Singapore) shows that it is possible to grow on the basis of export growth. World Bank (1993) report titled "The East Asian Miracle" pointed out that a key factor in the superior performance of high performing Asian economies (HPAEs) was the market-oriented policy framework:

> What are the main factors that contributed to the HPAEs superior allocation of physical and human capital to high-yielding investments and their ability to catch up technologically? Mainly the answers lie in fundamentally sound, market oriented policies. Labour markets were allowed to work. Financial markets, although subject to more selective interventions to allocate credit, generally had low distortions and limited subsidies as compared with other developing economies. The result was limited differences between international relative prices and domestic relative prices in the HPAEs. Market forces and competitive pressures guided resources into activities that were consistent with comparative advantage, and in the case of labour intensive exports, laid the foundation for learning international best practice and subsequent industrial upgrading. (ibid., p. 325)

Further, referring to Amsden (1989), the Report points out that governmental interventions were selective, took place in a disciplined environment and the cost of distortions was kept to a minimum. For example, when fiscal costs threatened the macroeconomic stability of Korea and Malaysia during their heavy and chemical industry phase, governments pulled back. When selective interventions threatened macroeconomic stability, these governments consistently came on the side of prudent macroeconomic management. Price distortions due to selective interventions were not as extreme as in many other developing countries.

References

Adelman, Jeremy. 2013. *Worldly Philosopher: Odyssey of Albert O Hirschman*. Princeton and Oxford: Princeton University Press.

Alacevich, Michele. 2007. Albert Hirschman, development economics, and the social sciences. A paper presented at the *First Conference on Albert Hirschman's Legacy: Theory and Practice*, October 6–7, 2017. Pardee School of Global Studies, Boston University.

Alacevich, Michele. 2020. Paul Rosenstein-Rodan and the birth of development economics. CHOPE Working Paper No. 2020-04. Center for the History of Political Economy, Duke University.

Amsden, A.H. 1989. *Asia's Next Giant: South Korea and Late Industrialization*. New York: Oxford University Press.

Balassa, Bela. 1971. *The Structure of Protection in Developing Countries*. Baltimore: John Hopkins University Press.

Balassa, Bela. 1980. The process of industrial development and alternative development strategies. *Essays in International Finance No. 141* (International Finance Section). Princeton: Princeton University.

Balassa, Bela. 1989. Outward orientation. In *Handbook of Development Economics*, Vol. II, ed. H. Chenery and T.N. Srinivasan. Amsterdam: North-Holland.

Baran, Paul A. 1957. *The Political Economy of Growth*. New York: Monthly Review Press.

Bardhan, Pranab. 1984. *The Political Economy of Development in India*. Oxford and New York: Oxford University Press.

Bauer, Peter. 1966. Foreign aid: An instrument of progress? In *Two Views of Trade in Developing Countries*. London: The Institute of Economic Affairs.

Bauer, Peter. 1971. *Dissent on Development*. Cambridge: Harvard University Press.

Bhagwati, Jagdish. 1993. *India in Transition: Freeing the Economy*. Oxford: Clarendon Press.

Chandra, Ramesh. 2006. Currie's 'leading sector' strategy of growth: An appraisal. *Journal of Development Studies* 42 (3): 490–508.

Clapham, J.M. 1922. On empty economic boxes. *Economic Journal* 32: 305–314.

Currie, Lauchlin. 1966. *Accelerating Development: The Necessity and the Means*. New York: McGraw Hill.

Currie, Lauchlin. 1974. The leading sector model of growth in developing countries. *Journal of Economic Studies* 1 (1): 1–16.

Currie, Lauchlin. 2017. The big push and balanced and unbalanced growth. In Albert Hirschman, Lauchlin Currie, 'linkages' theory, and Paul Rosenstein-Rodan's 'big push', ed. Roger J. Sandilands. *Strathclyde Discussion Papers in Economics* 17: 17. Department of Economics, University of Strathclyde, Glasgow.

Denison, E. 1967. *Why Growth Rates Differ: Post-war Experience in Nine Western Countries*. Washington DC: Brookings Institution.

Dornbusch, R. 1992. The case for trade liberalization in developing countries. *Journal of Economic Perspectives* 6 (1): 69–85.

Edwards, Sebastian. 1997. Trade policy, growth and income distribution. *American Economic Review: Papers and Proceedings* 87: 31–57.

Frank, Andre Gunder. 1967. *Capitalism and Underdevelopment in Latin America*. New York: Monthly Review Press.

Fields, Gary S. 1984. Employment, income distribution and economic growth in seven small open economies. *Economic Journal* 94 (373): 74–83.

Fleming, J. Marcus. 1955. External economies and the doctrine of balanced growth. *Economic Journal* 65 (June): 241–256.

Griliches, Z. 1957. Hybrid corn: An exploration in the economics of technological change. *Econometrica* 25 (4): 501–522.

Grilli, E.R., and M.C. Yang. 1988. Primary commodity prices, manufactured goods prices, and terms of trade of developing countries: What the long run shows. *World Bank Economic Review* 2 (1): 1–47.

Hirschman, Albert O. 1958. *The Strategy of Economic Development*, 1963 ed. New Haven: Yale University Press.

Hirschman, Albert O. 1967. *Development Projects Observed*. Washington, DC: The Brookings Institution.

Hirschman, Albert O. 1981. The rise and decline of development economics. In *Essays in Trespassing: Economic to Politics and Beyond*, 1–24. Cambridge: Cambridge University Press.

Hirschman, Albert O. 1984. A dissenter's confession: 'The Strategy of Economic Development' Revisited. In *Pioneers in Development*, ed. Gerald M. Meier and Dudley Seers, 87–111. World Bank: Oxford University Press.

Kaldor, Nicholas. 1978. Nemesis of free trade. In *Further Essays on Applied Economics*. London: Duckworth.

Krueger, Ann O. 1986. Aid in the development process. *World Bank Research Observer*, January: 62–63.

Krueger, Ann O. 1990. Government failures in development. *Journal of Economic Perspectives* 4: 9–23.

Krugman, Paul. 1993. Toward a counter-counter revolution in development theory. *Annual Conference on development Economics 1992*, ed. 15–38. Washington, DC: World Bank.

Lewis, W. Arthur. 1954. Economic development with unlimited supplies of labour. *Machester School of Economics and Social Studies* 22 (2): 139–191.

Lewis, W. Arthur. 1955. *The Theory of Economic Growth*. London: George Allen and Unwin Ltd.

Little, I.M.D., T. Scitovsky, and M. Scott. 1970. *Industry and Trade in Some Developing Countries: A Comparative Study*. London: Oxford University Press.

Meier, Gerald M. 1989. *Leading Issues in Economic Development*. Oxford and New York: Oxford University Press.

Meier, Gerald M. 2005. *Biography of a subject: An Evolution of Development Economics*. Oxford and New York: Oxford University Press.

Murphy, K.M. A. Shliefer, and R.W. Vishny. 1989a. Income distribution, market size, and industrialization. *Quarterly Journal of Economics* 104 (3): 537–564.

Murphy, K.M. A. Shliefer, and R.W. Vishny. 1989b. Industrialization and the big push. *Journal of Political Economy* 97: 1003–1026.

Myrdal, Gunnar. 1956. *Development and Underdevelopment*. Cairo: National Bank of Egypt Fiftieth Commemoration Lectures.

Myrdal, Gunnar. 1957. *Economic Theory and Underdeveloped Regions*. London: Gerald Duckworth.

Nurkse, Ragnar. 1953. *Problems of Capital Formation in Underdeveloped Countries*. Oxford: Basil Blackwell.

Nurkse, Ragnar. 1957. Excess population and capital construction. *Malaysian Economic Review*, October: 3–5. Reprinted in Meier (1989, pp. 115–117).

Nurkse, Ragnar. 1962. *Patterns of Trade and Development* (Wicksell Lectures 1959). Oxford: Basil Blackwell.

Prebisch, Raul. 1950. *The Economic Development of Latin America and its Principal Problems*. New York: United Nations Commission for Latin America.

Rosenstein-Rodan, Paul. 1943. Problems of industrialization of eastern and south-eastern Europe. *Economic Journal* 53: 202–211.

Rosenstein-Rodan, Paul. 1955. Programming in theory and Italian practice. In *Investment Criteria and Economic Growth*. Cambridge: MIT Center for International Studies.

Rosenstein-Rodan, Paul. 1957. *Notes on the theory of the 'big push,'* 1–16. Cambridge: MIT Center for International Studies.

Rosenstein-Rodan, Paul. 1961. Notes on the theory of 'big push.' In *Economic Development of Latin America*, ed. H.S. Ellis and H.C. Wallich, 57–67. London: Macmillan.

Sapsford, David, and V.N. Balasubramanyam. 1994. The long run behaviour of the relative price of primary commodities: Statistical evidence and policy implications. *World Development* 22 (11): 1737–1745.

Shultz, Theodore. 1961. Investment in human capital. *American Economic Review* 51 (March): 1–17.

Scitovsky, Tibor. 1954. Two concepts of external economies. *Journal of Political Economy* 62: 143–151.

Sen, Amartya. 1960. Review of *The Strategy of Economic Development* by A.O. Hirschman. *Economic Journal* 70 (279): 590–594.

Sen, Amartya. 1983. Development: Which way now? *Economic Journal* 93 (December): 745–762.

Singer, Hans W. 1950. The distribution of gains between investing and borrowing countries. *American Economic Review* 40 (May): 473–485.

Smith, Adam. 1776 (1976). *An Enquiry Into the Nature and Causes of the Wealth of Nations*, ed. Edwin Cannan. Chicago: University of Chicago Press.

Streeten, Paul. 1959. Unbalanced growth. *Oxford Economic Papers* 11 (2): 167–190.
World Bank. 1987. *World Development Report*. New York: Oxford University Press.
World Bank. 1991. *World Development Report*. New York: Oxford University Press.
World Bank. 1993. *The East Asian Miracle: Economic Growth and Public Policy*. New York: Oxford University Press.
Young, Allyn A. 1928. Increasing returns and economic progress. *Economic Journal* 38 (152): 527–542.

CHAPTER 8

Paul Krugman, New Trade Theory and New Economic Geography

New trade theory emerged as an explanation of trade in the late 1970s onwards with the pioneering work of Krugman (1979, 1980, 1981, 1986, 1990), Helpman and Krugman (1985, 1989), Brander (1981), Brander and Krugman (1983) among others. The traditional explanation of trade was dominated by the comparative advantage which is measured by relative labour costs in Ricardo and by relative differences in factor endowments in Hechscher-Ohlin. In both cases it is the difference in countries which gives rise to trade. While in one case relative labour costs (or labour productivities) differ, in the other a country produces and exports a product which is intensive in a factor with which it is abundantly supplied. Adam Smith had couched his explanation of trade in terms of absolute costs (based on the division of labour and increasing returns) but his explanation got overshadowed by that of Ricardo. As noted by Krugman (1990, p. 4), since increasing returns models were considered to be mathematically messy, the theory of international trade followed the path of least mathematical resistance.

The comparative advantage theory assumes perfect competition where price equals marginal cost, and this makes these models mathematically tractable. But once one introduces increasing returns, implying economies of scale and imperfect competition, price is no longer equated with marginal cost as marginal cost pricing results in universal losses. The only

R. Chandra, *Endogenous Growth in Historical Perspective*, Palgrave Studies in Economic History,
https://doi.org/10.1007/978-3-030-83761-7_8

exception is the case where increasing returns depend on the size of the industry instead of the size of the firm. In this case, increasing returns are external to the firm but internal to the industry as a whole. During the 1970s, however, with the developments in industrial organization, there was an explosion of models of imperfect competition. When these new theoretical developments were applied to trade theory, "new trade theory" emerged. These new mathematical models made it possible not only to construct trade models based on internal economies of scale but also models with external economies where increasing returns arise in the production of intermediate goods.[1]

The new trade theory recognizes that comparative advantage is one reason for trade. But it focuses on the role of increasing returns as a source of trade. For example, trade between rich and poor countries or between manufactures and food follows comparative advantage. But trade between advanced countries themselves is based on economies of scale (or increasing returns) where manufactures exchange for manufactures.[2] Here each country specializes in a limited range of goods to take advantage of economies of scale. But since consumers have preference for variety, international trade leads to an increase in the variety of goods available. The pattern of trade here is based on specialization and increasing returns. While the pattern of trade between food and manufactures is inter-industry trade, trade between manufactures and manufactures is intra-industry trade.[3] Intra-industry trade within standard industrial classification is a substantial part of world trade and accounts for about one-fourth of world trade (Krugman and Obstfeld 2003, p. 139).[4] However, there is an element of arbitrariness to this story. To take an example of aeroplanes manufactured in Seattle, it is difficult to find an

[1] In Krugman's (1990, p. 3) opinion: "Since economics as practiced in the English-speaking world is strongly oriented toward mathematical models, any economic argument that has not been expressed in that form tends to remain invisible".

[2] It should be noted that the new trade theory equates increasing returns with economies of scale at the firm or industry level.

[3] The standard formula for calculating intra-industry trade (I) within an industry is: $I = 1 - (|exports - imports|)/(exports + imports)$. See Krugman and Obstfeld (2003, p. 139, f.n. 5).

[4] Krugman et al. (2018, p. 212) point out that the proportion of intra-industry trade in world trade has grown over the last half century. Depending on the coarseness of the industrial classification (whether into hundreds or thousands), intra-industry trade ranges from one fourth to one half of world trade.

explanation in some special attribute that Seattle's location possesses. It may just be a historical accident that the industry got concentrated there. Once established, increasing returns keep the industry there. The same is equally true for other locations such as Detroit or Silicon Valley.

Before the new trade theory came on the scene, the proposition that increasing returns could be a cause of trade in similar countries was not well understood. As Krugman (1979) notes, it was never covered in most textbooks or courses whether graduate or undergraduate. While some authors (e.g. Ohlin 1933; Balassa 1967; Kravis 1971) recognized the importance of scale economies in international trade, they received little attention in formal trade theory. "The main reason for this neglect seems to be that it has appeared difficult to deal with the implications of increasing returns for market structure" (Krugman 1979, p. 469).

Krugman (2002) credited Ohlin's (1933) *Intraregional and International Trade* with many of the insights (but not all) of the "new trade theory" and "new economic geography". For example, Ohlin was aware that increasing returns were a cause of trade but he downplayed their practical importance. Ohlin (as quoted in Krugman 2002) stated: "[I]t is certainly the differences in factor supplies that determine the course of interregional trade—unless regions are small—whereas the advantages of large-scale production are more in the nature of a subsidiary cause, carrying the division of labour and trade a little further than it would otherwise go, but not changing their characteristics". According to Krugman, Ohlin was also a bit inconsistent; after disparaging the practical importance of increasing returns in Part I of his book, in Part II he seemed to suggest that they would play a growing role over time. Samuleson was aware that Ohlin had stressed increasing returns as a subsidiary cause, but chose to stress the primary argument in his formalization of Ohlin. Others who followed Samuelson simply took their cue from him without bothering to read the original Ohlin (1933). As Krugman notes, they may have skimmed through Ohlin, but their mind was already conditioned by Samuelson's interpretation. That is how Ohlin's insights about the role of increasing returns to scale got lost over time in the neoclassical discourse on trade starting with Samuelson.

According to Krugman, even if Ohlin had stressed increasing returns more forcefully than he actually did, his insights would still have met the same fate. Although Ohlin was aware of the Marshallian distinction between internal and external economies, he was not always careful to separate the cases. Moreover, he was not entirely clear what he meant by increasing returns. If he meant internal economies, the implication is imperfect competition. If he meant external economies, we are in the world of market failure. It was only with the development of tractable monopolistic completion model that economies of scale and external-economy models became tractable. Moreover, the habit of thinking in two-goods framework gives rise to a convex production possibility curve, unless there are accidental and arbitrary increasing returns strong enough to give rise to a concave curvature. Minus this concave curvature, the only way left to think about increasing returns is their effect in modifying comparative advantage and giving advantage to large countries in scale-intensive goods.

Krugman notes that if (1) there is a strong tendency of concentration of factors—either due to external economies or due to linkages—and (2) some factors are more mobile than others, then factor mobility accentuates regional differences instead of reducing them. That is how concentrations of beautiful people in Hollywood, ambitious people in London and nerds in the vicinity of Stanford (Silicon Valley) emerged. Ohlin appears to touch on all these elements. Krugman also notes that Ohlin's description of "agglomerating" and "deglomerating" tendencies is strikingly similar to one of new economic geography's central themes of tension between centripetal and centrifugal forces. Similarly Ohlin's insight that "Inventions may by chance lead to manufacture in one country or place when others would do just as well" is akin to new economic geography's stress on historical accidents in determining industrial location. However, Ohlin was less surefooted about these insights as compared to his insight about increasing returns as a cause of trade.[5]

[5] Krugman gives three reasons for this. First, even though Ohlin recognized that there were "arbitrary elements in location" and that the "historical influence can lead to an uneconomical location of industry" his main emphasis is that location decisions are likely to be mistaken. The main point, however, is that an industry may be in the wrong place even if nobody is making a mistake. Second, Ohlin downplays the endogeneity of factor location attributing regional differences in natural resources as the cause rather than the effect of location of industry. This may be true of Europe but not in America where the manufacturing belts owed their existence to early starts rather than to resource advantages. The location of activity in America in the 1920s was driven by the logic of self-reinforcing concentration. Third, unlike the integration of increasing returns with comparative advantage which reinforced his basic vision, the integration of increasing returns with factor mobility went counter to this vision. While in the former case the integration leads to convergence of factor prices, in the latter case it leads to their divergence.

This chapter will first discuss the role of economies of scale and external economies in new trade theory. It will also discuss new economic geography or the so-called geographical turn in economics. Next, the chapter takes up the role of strategic trade policy in the context of sophisticated arguments for governmental intervention and whether free trade is passé. Krugman's contribution to trade theory is also taken up. Finally, we make a critical assessment of the new trade policy and new economic geography.

The Role of Economies of Scale

Krugman and Obstfeld (2003, Chapter 6) discuss the role of economies of scale and external economies in trade theory. Comparative advantage models assume constant returns to scale and perfect competition. In practice, many industries are characterized by increasing returns or economies of scale where doubling of industry inputs more than doubles the industry's output. When increasing returns operate, large firms usually have an advantage over smaller ones, and the market may be dominated by a single firm (monopoly), a few firms (oligopoly), or a larger number of differentiated firms (monopolistic competition). Pure monopoly is rare in practice as a firm making high profits attracts competitors. The usual market structure is characterized by oligopoly with several firms where each firm is large enough to affect prices but none is an uncontested monopoly. Besides, pricing policies of firms under oligopoly are interdependent where the firm will consider not only the expected responses of consumers but also of competitors while setting prices. These responses in turn depend on what the competitors' perception of how the firm in question will behave. It is therefore a complex game in which each firm is trying to second-guess the others' strategies. A special case of oligopoly is monopolistic competition, a model which is easier to analyze, and has become popular with the trade theorists in the 1980s.[6] To bypass the problem of interdependence, two crucial assumptions are made: (1) each

[6] Krugman and Obstfeld (2003, p. 131) note that there are few industries in practice which are well described by monopolistic competition. The most common market structure is likely to be "small-group oligopoly" where only a few firms actively compete. Thus the key assumption of monopolistic competition model that each firm behaves like a true monopolist is likely to be violated. Interdependence of firms will come into play. There are two kinds of behaviour in oligopoly which are excluded by assumption in the monopolistic competition model. First is collusive behaviour to charge high prices or a tacit understanding to allow one firm to act as a price leader for the industry. Second is

firm produces a differentiated product (a product which is somewhat different of its rivals, and (2) each firm, though facing competition from its rivals, behaves like a monopolist by ignoring the impact of its own prices on other firms (i.e., each firm assumes the prices charged by others as given). Automobile production in Europe is a good example of monopolistic competition where a number of producers such as Ford, General Motors, Volkswagen, Renault, Fiat, Volvo, Peugeot, and Nissan offer different but competing automobiles. However, the main appeal of the monopolistic competition model is not its realism but its simplicity in explaining how economies of scale give rise to mutually beneficial trade.

Under monopolistic competition, the industry consists of a number of firms producing differentiated products, i.e., products that are not the same but substitutes for one another. Each firm is a monopolist in the sense that it is the only firm producing that particular product (or brand). But the demand for its good depends on the availability of similar products as well as the prices on which they are offered. Taking cost and price on the vertical axis, and the number of firms on the horizontal axis, market equilibrium under monopolistic competition will be determined by the intersection of the upward sloping supply curve and downward sloping demand curve. That is, at equilibrium both the number of firms as well the average price they charge are determined. Equilibrium describes the maximum number of firms the industry can support at zero profits. If the market size increases, the supply curve will shift outwards to the right, and the equilibrium price will be lower and the number of firms larger. Consumers would prefer to be in a larger market where they can benefit from lower price as well as larger variety of products. Larger market can also result from international trade where each country specializes in a restricted range of products to reap economies of scale and also benefit from the larger variety of goods. Thus, there are gains from international trade both in terms of larger variety and lower price.

To illustrate how economies of scale interact with comparative advantage to determine the pattern of international trade, let us consider an example. Suppose there are two countries in the world, Home and Foreign and two factors, labour and capital. Further suppose that Home has higher capital-labour ratio (i.e., is a capital-abundant country) than Foreign. Let us also imagine two industries—manufactures and food, with

strategic behaviour where, for example, a firm may build extra capacity to deter potential rivals from entering the industry.

manufactures being more capital intensive. The presence of economies of scale ensures that neither country can produce the full range of manufactures by itself. Although each can produce some manufactures, they produce different goods. If manufactures was not a differentiated product, Home will produce and export manufactures and import food from Foreign. If, however, manufactures is monopolistically competitive, Foreign will partly produce manufactures and partly food. Home will specialize in manufactures only but these will be different from those produced in Foreign.

The world pattern of trade will be partly intra-industry (i.e., exchange of manufactures for manufactures) and partly inter-industry (i.e., exchange of manufactures for food). While inter-industry trade reflects comparative advantage, intra-industry trade reflects economies of scale. A large part of advanced nations' (or industrial nations') trade in manufactured goods consists of intra-industry trade based on economies of scale. Over time, industrial countries have become quite similar in terms of technology, capital abundance, or skilled labour. Though economies of scale can be an independent cause of world trade, the comparative advantage still retains its importance. The pattern of intra-industry trade itself is unpredictable and has more to do with accidents and history than anything else. Krugman and Obstfeld (2003, p. 138) summarize the pattern of trade when comparative advantage and economies of scale interact:

1. *Inter-industry* (manufactures for food) trade reflects comparative advantage. The pattern of inter-industry trade is that Home, the capital-abundant country, is a net exporter of capital-intensive manufactures and a net importer of labour-intensive food. So comparative advantage continues to be a major part of the trade story.
2. *Intra-industry* trade (manufactures for manufactures) does *not* reflect comparative advantage. Even if the countries had the same overall capital-labour ratio, their firms would continue to produce differentiated products and demand of consumers for products made abroad would continue to generate intra-industry trade. It is economies of scale that keep each country from producing the full range of products for itself; thus economies of scale can be an independent source of international trade.

3. The pattern of intra-industry trade itself is unpredictable. We have not said anything about which country produces which goods within the manufactures sector because there is nothing in the model to tell us. All we know is that countries will produce different products. Since history and accident determine the details of the trade pattern, an unpredictable pattern of trade is an inevitable feature of a world where economies of scale are important. Notice, however, that unpredictability is not total. While the precise pattern of intra-industry trade within the manufactures sector is arbitrary, the pattern of inter-industry trade between manufactures and food is determined by the underlying differences between countries.
4. The relative importance of intra-industry and inter-industry trade depends on how similar countries are. If Home and Foreign are similar in their capital-labor ratios, then there will be little inter-industry trade, and intra-industry trade, based ultimately on economies of scale, will be dominant. On the other hand, if capital-labor ratios are very different, so that, for example, Foreign specializes completely in food production, there will be no intra-industry trade based on economies of scale. All trade will be based on comparative advantage.

Intra-industry trade produces additional gains from international trade over and above those from comparative advantage. This is because intra-industry trade allows countries to gain from larger markets. As noted earlier, intra-industry trade allows countries to restrict the number of differentiated products and this makes available a greater variety of goods. By producing fewer varieties, countries can gain from larger scale, higher productivity, and lower costs. Consumers also benefit from greater varieties on offer. In Hechscher-Ohlin theory, owners of abundant factors gain and owners of scarce factors lose from trade. Because of wide differences in resources, technology, and barriers to trade among countries, complete factor price equalization never takes place. So trade based on comparative advantage has strong income distributional effects. In intra-industry trade based on economies of scale, these effects are smaller and everyone tends to gain from trade. Intra-industry trade will predominate between countries of similar level of economic development. This is characteristic of advanced manufactured goods rather than traditional products like textiles and footwear.[7]

With the establishment of the European Economic Community in 1957 (Britain joined in 1973 and exited in 2020), trade within the EEC grew twice as fast as world trade during the 1960s. Growth of trade was almost entirely intra-industry, and the expected drastic dislocations did not occur. Workers of Germany's electrical machinery sector did not gain at the expense of France's electrical machinery industry; in fact workers in both sectors gained through increased efficiency of European integration. As a result, fewer political and social problems resulted from increased trade in Europe. Thus, according to Krugman and Obstfeld, intra-industry trade in manufactures has few serious income distribution effects as the European example shows.

Monopolistic competition model helps us to understand how increasing returns promote international trade. Although this model recognizes that imperfect competition is a necessary consequence of economies of scale, it does not take into account the consequences of imperfect competition for international trade. One important consequence is that firms do not charge the same price in the foreign market as in the domestic market. There may be price discrimination which in international trade commonly takes the form of dumping. This is a practice where the exported good is sold at a lower price than the same good sold domestically.[8] For dumping to occur, two conditions must be satisfied: (1) the industry must be imperfectly competitive, and (2) markets can be segmented so that domestic consumers are not able to easily purchase goods meant for exports.[9]

[7] In the US in 2009, intra-industry trade indices were high for goods such as metalwork machinery (0.97), inorganic chemicals (0.97), power generating machines (0.86) and medical and pharmaceutical products (0.85), and low for furniture (0.30), clothing and apparel (0.11), and footwear (0.10). See Krugman et al. (2018, p. 213).

[8] Price discrimination can also be of reverse type where the domestic consumer pays a lower price, but price discrimination in favour of exports is more common. Since international markets are imperfectly integrated with the domestic market because of transportation costs and protectionist barriers, domestic firms are more likely to have a larger share of the home market. This implies that foreign sales are likely to be more price sensitive than domestic sales.

[9] In many countries including the US, dumping is regarded as unfair trade practice, and firms which are injured by foreign firms can appeal through a quasi-judicial procedure. If the appeal is successful, an anti-dumping duty is imposed. In the US, the appeal is made

The possibility of reciprocal dumping was first noted by Brander (1981). Krugman and Obstfeld note that reciprocal dumping between two firms, each producing the same good, can actually give rise to international trade. Assuming transportation costs, if firms charge the same price at home and abroad, there will be no trade. Each firm will limit the quantity it sells in its home market because if it sells more it drives down the price. If the firm sells a bit more in the foreign market, it can add to its profits even if the price charged is lower abroad. By raiding the other market, each firm sells at a lower price abroad (net of transportation costs) but that price is still above marginal cost. Though international trade in exactly identical goods in both directions may appear socially wasteful, reciprocal dumping eliminates pure monopolies, leading to some competition. This may represent a benefit that may cover up for wasteful transportation. The net effect of such trade on a nation's welfare is therefore uncertain.[10]

The Role of External Economies

When economies of scale operate at the level of an industry rather than a firm, we call them external economies. When such economies operate it is possible to localize industry, i.e., concentrate production in a few locations to reduce costs even if the size of firms remains small. Alfred Marshall was struck by the phenomenon of industrial districts such as hosiery firms in Northampton or cutlery cluster in Sheffield. Marshall (1890) noted that there could be three reasons for industrial clusters: (1) specialized suppliers, (2) labour market pooling, and (3) knowledge spillovers.

Many industries use specialized equipment or support services. While an individual firm may not provide a large enough market for these

to the Commerce Department (which accepts most complaints about unfair pricing), but the actual injury is determined by the International Trade Commission (which rejects about half the cases). Economists regard dumping as a form of price discrimination and have reservations on singling out dumping as a prohibited practice. They regard charging lower price or selling at a loss in the foreign market as a normal business practice of gaining experience or breaking into a new market.

[10] Brander and Krugman (1983) present a model of reciprocal dumping where lower price abroad is not related to a higher price elasticity of demand (and therefore to accidental differences in country demands) but to systematic reasons associated with oligopolistic behaviour.

services, a localized industrial cluster consisting of many small firms can collectively provide a market large enough to support a wide range of specialized suppliers. Modern examples of such external economies include the semiconductor industry of Silicon Valley, investment banking in New York and entertainment industry in Hollywood. In Silicon Valley high technology firms are clustered because key inputs are easily available, and many firms compete to provide them. The firms then specialize in what they do best and contract out other aspects of their businesses to others. A high technology firm entering some other location would face immediate disadvantage of not being able to access Silicon Valley suppliers, and would have to produce these inputs itself. Or alternatively it will have to deal with the Silicon Valley suppliers from a long distance.

A cluster of firms can also create a pooled market of workers with highly specialized skills. This benefits producers who are saved possible labour shortages. It is also beneficial for skilled workers as they are less likely to be unemployed. If firms are located in different cities, a low demand in a particular location is likely to result in unemployment. If an industry is concentrated in a single location, high demand for labour from one firm may be offset by low demand from others. As a result, workers have a lower risk of unemployment. Besides, it becomes easier to switch employers in a place like Silicon Valley, so losing a job with one employer may not be a big catastrophe as one is very likely to get another job with a different employer.

In innovative industries, being a few weeks or months behind the cutting edge technology or design can seriously disadvantage a company. Companies can acquire technology either through their own R&D efforts or through reverse engineering the products of their competitors. A third source of technical knowledge can be the informal exchange of information among workers when an industry is concentrated in a single place. The workers from different companies then mix socially and talk freely about technical matters. Even Marshall wrote that in an industrial district with many firms mysteries of trade remain no mysteries. A new idea soon becomes known to others which when combined with their own additions becomes the source of further new ideas. In Silicon Valley, it is easier for firms to stay near the technological frontier than elsewhere. Some firms even locate their R&D centres there to keep up with the latest technology.

External economies arising out of specialized suppliers, pooled labour market, and knowledge spillovers are possible in a country with a large industrial sector. A country with large industry is more likely to reap these external economies than a country with small industry, other things remaining the same. External economies also lead to a downward sloping industrial supply curve, i.e., the larger the industry's output, the lower will be the price at which firms sell their output. This is reminiscent of Marshall's downward sloping industry supply curve where firms are small but there are increasing returns at the industry level, i.e., costs and prices are lower as the industry expands its output.

External economies play an important role in international trade. Countries can sometimes get locked into undesirable patterns of specialization, and there can even be losses from international trade. Countries that start as large producers in certain industries tend to remain large even if some other country could potentially produce that good at a lower cost. In other words, these countries enjoy first mover advantage even in the presence of cheaper producers. For example, Swiss watch industry consisting of a large number of small producers was, for historical reasons, established first. Although Thai watch industry which came up later could produce watches at a cheaper rate as Thai wages are lower, but it did not lead to Thailand taking over the world market. This is because at zero level of production, Thai costs are higher than the Swiss costs at equilibrium level of production, although in both cases long-run average cost curve is downward sloping and Thai curve is lower than Swiss curve. So although Thai industry can potentially make watches at a lower cost than Switzerland, Switzerland's head start enables it to establish its hold. This implies that historical accident plays an important role in the presence of external economies, and established patterns of trade persist even if they go counter to comparative advantage.

If Thailand were to block all trade in watches, it would be able to supply its domestic market at a lower price based on its own demand. In the presence of international trade its domestic consumers pay the world price established by the Swiss industry. This price is low enough to block entry of Thai producers who must initially produce at higher cost (when Thai output is zero). This leaves Thailand worse off in the presence of international trade than it would have been if international trade was absent. Thailand has an incentive to protect its watch industry from foreign competition, but in practice it is difficult to identify cases of external economies. This constitutes one of the main arguments against activist government policies in trade.

Knowledge spillovers in an industry may give rise to a situation where production costs depend on cumulative output rather than on current output. This is because the production costs of individual firms fall as the overall industry accumulates experience. This is shown by a downward sloping learning curve where unit costs decline with cumulative output. When costs decline as a result of cumulative output (rather than current output), this is known as dynamic increasing returns. Like ordinary external economies, dynamic external economies can also lock a country into a head start or initial advantage. The new country will be prevented from entering the industry because of initial higher costs. A new country could potentially consider temporarily subsidizing or protecting its industry experiencing dynamic external economies to enable it to gain experience. This is known as infant industry argument for protection so as to enable an industry to gain experience. However, in practice, it is just as hard to identify cases of dynamic external economies as those involving non-dynamic increasing returns.

Increasing Returns and Economic Geography

The foregoing analysis of industrial districts brings us to the concept of economic geography or the centre-periphery pattern of industrial development. Apart from new trade theory, Krugman (1991a; b) can also be credited with pioneering work in economic geography—the location of factors across space. Krugman (1991b) notes that economic geography occupies a relatively small part of standard economic analysis. This is surprising in view of the striking real world facts about economic geography. "For example, one of the most remarkable things about the United States is that in a generally sparsely populated country, much of whose land is fertile, the bulk of the populations resides in a few clusters of metropolitan areas; a quarter of the inhabitants are crowded into a not especially inviting section of the East Coast. It has often been noted that nighttime satellite photos of Europe reveal little of political boundaries but clearly suggest a center-periphery pattern whose hub is somewhere in or near Belgium" (Krugman 1991b, pp. 483–84).

Krugman (ibid., p. 484) asks the question: "Why and when does manufacturing become concentrated in a few regions, leaving others relatively undeveloped"? To answer this question, Krugman develops a simple model of "industrialized" core and an agricultural "periphery". Geographical concentration is based on the interaction between economies of scale and transportation costs. Although Marshall offered an account of localization of particular industries, Krugman's concern is to answer why manufacturing in general gets concentrated in one or a few regions of a country (manufacturing core) and the remaining regions playing the role of agricultural suppliers (agricultural periphery). Accordingly, his explanation focuses on generalized external economies rather than on those external economies specific to a particular industry. It is also assumed that the external economies which lead to the emergence of core-periphery pattern are pecuniary external economies associated with demand or supply linkages rather than pure technological spillovers.

Because of economies of scale, manufacturing will get concentrated in a few locations, preferably near large markets to minimize transportation costs. Other locations can then be served from these centrally located sites. Though some demand for manufactures will come from the agriculture sector, a major source would be the manufacturing sector itself. This creates the possibility of "circular cumulative causation" (Myrdal 1957) or "positive feedback" (Arthur 1990). That is, manufacturing gets concentrated where the market is large and the market is large where manufacturing is concentrated. To this analysis one can add Hirschman's (1958) forward and backward linkages as these linkages are likely to be the strongest where manufacturing concentrations already exist. As noted by Krugman, though this story of circular processes is not new and has been familiar to economic geographers since the emergence of the US manufacturing belt in the second half on the nineteenth century, no attempts were made to formalize it.

How far will geographical concentration proceed? It depends on the parameters of the economy—transportation costs, economies of scale, and the share of expenditure on nonagricultural goods. Thus, small changes in these parameters may have huge qualitative effects. "[W] hen some index that takes into account transportation costs, economies of scale and the share of nonagricultural goods in expenditure crosses a critical threshold, population will start to concentrate and regions to diverge; once started, this process will feed on itself" (Krugman 1991b, p. 487). And where will manufacturing concentration actually end up? Initial conditions are important. If one region has slightly more population than the other, transportation costs decline below threshold, and the region in question gains and others lose. Had the distribution of population at the critical moment been slightly different, the roles of different regions may have been reversed.

Krugman (1991c), in his paper "History versus expectations", points out that in models of external economies there could be two or more equilibria in the long run. Which equilibrium is chosen depends on the role of history versus expectations. Much literature emphasizes the role of history in setting the initial conditions, and it is this which determines the outcome. In the traditional literature (e.g., Myrdal 1957; Kaldor 1972; David 1985) the role of history is only implicit. In the formal literature (e.g., Arthur 1986; Krugman 1981, 1987a) the dynamics are formulated in such a way that history is decisive. For example, in Krugman (1981) the dynamics of capital accumulation are such that the region which starts with a slightly higher capital stock eventually occupies the dominant industrial position. An alternative view stresses the role of expectations or self-fulfilling prophesy in determining the equilibrium outcome. Rosenstein-Rodan's (1943) "big push" and its formalization by Murphy et al. (1989) are good examples of this alternative view. Krugman (1991c) presents a simple model with external economies and adjustment costs where the eventual outcome depends on the parameters of the economy. The relative importance of history and expectations depends on the underlying structure of the economy, particularly on adjustment costs. Marshall had assumed that resources move slowly in response to differences in current earnings. This implies that it is costly for them to do so. If there are zero adjustment costs history becomes irrelevant. The slower the rate at which the economy adjusts, the more likely it is that history matters. If adjustment is slow enough, history becomes decisive.

Krugman (1999) presents a Table 8.1 showing centripetal and centrifugal forces of geographical concentration. The list is by no means comprehensive but is of practical value. Krugman points out that there is a tug of war between centripetal and centrifugal forces. These forces are shown as follows.

The centripetal forces listed in the first column are three classical Marshallian sources of external economies discussed earlier. The centrifugal forces listed in the second column consist of immobile factors (land and natural resources), high land rents (due to concentration of

Table 8.1 Centripetal and Centrifugal Forces

Centripetal forces	*Centrifugal forces*
Market size effects (linkages)	Immobile factors
Thick labour markets	Land rents
Pure external economies	Pure external diseconomies

Source Krugman (1999, p. 143)

economic activity), and pure external diseconomies (such as congestion, pollution etc.). For modelling economic geography, one has to move away from the complexities of the real world and consider a more limited set of forces. Thus, most modelling since the start of the field (Krugman 1991a, b) takes the first item in each column, i.e., the interaction between linkages and immobile factors. Two strategic modelling considerations dictate this choice. First, we want to be able to avoid an approach which asserts that agglomeration takes place because of agglomeration. That is, some distance has to be created between assumptions and conclusions. Second, if location is at the heart of the problem, distance as measured by transportation costs needs to enter the picture. Since linkages and access to immobile factors are both tied to distance, modelling in a spatial setting becomes easier.

Krugman is however cautious in drawing any strong policy conclusions from new economic geography despite the temptations.[11] First, it is difficult to jump from small suggestive models to empirical models that can be used for evaluating specific policies. There has been a long debate on how to make strategic trade policy operational (discussed below). In the case of new economic geography, effects are general equilibrium rather than partial equilibrium making the task even harder. Perhaps more research is required before any strong policy conclusions are drawn.

Sophisticated Arguments for Governmental Intervention and Strategic Trade Policy

In the advanced countries during the 1980s, new sophisticated arguments emerged for governmental intervention in trade. These arguments focussed on high technology industries such as silicon chips (or semiconductors). While some of these arguments were related to market failure, a new controversial theory of strategic trade policy, based on different ideas, emerged.

[11] These temptations for governmental intervention from new economic geography literature may include: (1) the market may not get it right, (2) small policy interventions have large effects, and (3) cumulative processes of concentration produce winners and losers, so government authorities have an incentive to ensure that their country emerges as a winner.

The main problem with the market failure arguments is the problem of identifying it. In advanced countries two such failures have been identified: (1) inability of high technology firms to completely capture the benefits of knowledge spillovers to other firms, and (2) the presence of monopoly profits in highly concentrated oligopolistic industries. In the high technology industries where there are substantial externalities, there is a good case for providing a subsidy to the industry. This is akin to infant industry protection of less developed countries, but in advanced countries the argument acquires a special edge, as in high technology industries which are central to the generation of new knowledge through R&D expenditures. If other firms are able to imitate the products of innovating firms through reverse engineering, and because patent laws provide weak protection for innovators, the incentive for innovation is weakened.

The government can subsidize industries where knowledge generation is believed to take place, but this involves using the instrument bluntly. Alternatively, the government can subsidize R&D wherever it happens. But here the problem is of definition, a lose definition leading to abuse and a strict definition would favour large bureaucratic organizations (where the allocation of funds can be strictly documented) over smaller informal organizations (where original thinking is widely believed to happen). How much should be the level of subsidy? No one has a good idea of the optimal level of subsidy—whether it should be 10, 20, or 100%. Knowledge spillovers are in the nature of externalities, do not carry a market price, and are therefore hard to measure. Moreover, the benefits may spillover to firms in other countries, so appropriability at the level of a nation may be a problem even in a large country such as the US. Despite these limitations, technological spillovers argument is probably the best case one can make for an active industrial policy.

In a *Journal of International Economics* article Brander and Spencer (1985) put forward a new argument for governmental intervention which generated considerable controversy.[12] They point out that some industries are dominated by a small number of firms enjoying excess returns over and above what equally risky investments can earn elsewhere. This will lead to international competition over who gets these profits. In

[12] Other early contributions to strategic trade policy include Brander and Spencer (1981, 1983), Krugman (1984), Dixit (1984) and Eaton and Grossman (1986). See also Spencer and Brander (2008) entry on strategic trade policy in *The New Palgrave Dictionary of Economics*.

principle, the government by subsidizing domestic firms can shift these profits from foreign to domestic firms. Subsidy to domestic firms will deter foreign firms from investing in the domestic excess-returns industries, domestic firms are able to earn profits exceeding the amount of the subsidy. Ignoring the effect on the consumers, subsidy raises a country's national income at the expense of other countries.

To take a simple example to illustrate the point, suppose there are two countries—the US and Europe, and two firms which can produce a new design aircraft, namely, Boeing and Airbus. As the example is set up, either firm alone can make profits; if both produce the new design both make losses. The question is, who gets the profits? Suppose Boeing has a small head start, Airbus will have no incentive to enter. Suppose Europe is able to subsidize Airbus, this creates an advantage in favour of Airbus comparable to the strategic first mover advantage Boeing had. Critics have pointed out that the use of strategic trade policy is likely to require more information than is likely to be available. Secondly, such policies which increase domestic welfare at the cost of some other country are beggar-thy-neighbour policies, and therefore risk retaliation. The resulting trade war leaves everyone worse off. Third, the domestic politics may itself prevent the use of such subtle policy tools.[13] Special interest groups may be able to buy influence. For example, in the US contributions by business and labour had an impact (in terms of the number of votes polled) on the 1993 vote on NAFTA or 1994 vote on GATT (See Baldwin and Magee 1988).

Krugman (1987b) asks the question: is Free Trade Passé? He observes that free trade based on comparative advantage was an almost sacred tenet in economics since the publication of Ricardo's *Principles of Political Economy*. Yet, in the current context doubts are being cast on the case for free trade. This has happened not because of political pressures but due to radical changes in international trade theory which emphasize increasing returns and imperfect competition. These new models not only doubt the extent of trade which can be explained by comparative advantage but

[13] Krugman and Obstfeld (2003, p. 221) point out that in practice there is a political argument for free trade though there may be better policies in principle. Trade policy in practice is often dominated by special-interest politics rather than national costs and benefits. Though selective tariffs and subsidies can sometimes be shown to increase national welfare, but in practice a sophisticated programme of trade intervention is subject to capture by interest groups and there may be redistribution of income in favour politically influential sectors.

also make out the case that import restrictions and subsidies under some circumstances may increase national welfare.

Krugman points out that the positive conclusions of the new trade theory that much of trade reflects increasing returns and that many international markets are imperfectly competitive have been readily accepted by the profession. However, the normative conclusion that this justifies a greater degree of governmental intervention in trade has been sharply criticized including by those who created the new theory. The critique partly reflects the politics of trade policy which was mentioned earlier. "There are, however, three economic criticisms. First, critics suggest that it is impossible to formulate useful interventionist policies given the empirical difficulties involved in modeling imperfect markets. Second, they argue that any gains from intervention will be dissipated by the entry of rent-seeking firms. Third, it is argued that general equilibrium considerations radically increase the empirical difficulty of formulating interventionist trade policies and make it even more unlikely that these policies will do more good than harm" (ibid., p. 139).

Thus political economy concerns as well as the economic criticisms combine for the reemergence of free trade as a rule of thumb. Also, when the expected gains from intervention become sufficiently diluted, the political economy argument becomes overriding. Krugman points out that the reemergence of free trade is a "sadder but wiser" argument especially "in a world whose politics is as imperfect as its markets". It is therefore possible to believe that while comparative advantage as a model is incomplete, free trade nevertheless is a good practical policy. The conclusion is:

> [F]ree trade is not passé, but it is an idea that has irretrievably lost its innocence. Its status has shifted from optimum to reasonable rule of thumb. There is still a case for free trade as a good policy, and as a useful target in the practical world of politics, but it can never again be asserted as a policy that economic theory tells us is always right (ibid., p. 132).

Krugman's Contribution

Krugman (2008a) in his Nobel Prize lecture places his contribution to new trade theory and new economic geography in perspective. He describes "new trade theory" as an unfortunate phrase. For one thing, what was once new has already become old. For another, the increasing returns revolution in trade and geography may have already peaked, and the world may be more classical today than when the revolution in the trade theory began. For example, the index of regional manufacturing specialization based on Krugman (1991a) reached its peak during the interwar period and has since declined dramatically. After WWII, the manufacturing belt began to dissolve, and after the 1950s industry spread to the sunbelt. The role of increasing returns, as opposed to comparative advantage, in trade was applicable after 1950 when similar-similar trade between advanced countries increased. However, during the last few decades similar-similar trade is giving way to trade between rich and poor low-wage countries like China. Krugman (2008b) proposes an indicator of this shift—the average hourly compensation of workers in top US trading partners as a percentage of US compensation. The indicator which stood at 76 in 1975 slightly rose to 81 in 1990, and by 2005 had fallen to 65 largely reflecting the rapid increase of trade with China and Mexico. In 2006, for the first time, the US trade with developing countries exceeded that with advanced countries. Krugman (2008a, pp. 346–47) concludes:

> And nobody doubts that trade between the United States and Mexico, where wages are only 13 percent of the US level, or China, where they are about 4 percent, reflects comparative advantage rather than arbitrary scale-based specialization. The old trade theory has regained relevance... Both new geography and new trade, then, may describe forces that are waning rather than gathering strength. Yet they are hardly irrelevant. And even the fact that they may be losing force is itself an important insight... Whether the influence of increasing returns on trade and geography is rising or falling, one thing is clear: much was learnt from the intellectual revolution that brought increasing returns to the heart of how we think about the world economy.

In his first year as an assistant professor when Krugman began working on international trade theory, he was dissuaded by his colleagues as they thought that the theory was complete and there was nothing interesting left to do. However, Krugman was aware that there was an undercurrent of dissatisfaction with the conventional trade theory as exemplified by Balassa (1966), Gruber and Lloyd (1975) among others. Besides, there was huge similar-similar trade between similar countries as exemplified by two-way trade in automotive products between the US and Canada. Still in 1980, it was a new phenomenon and trade was dominated by comparative advantage between dissimilar countries. Balassa (1966) was quite clear that countries specialized in a narrow range of products, importing the rest from others, because this helped produce machinery and intermediate products and reap economies of scale. Yet such ideas of similar-similar trade were incomprehensible because economies of scale at the firm level implied imperfect competition, and there were no readily usable general equilibrium models of imperfect competition. This led Harry Johnson (1967) to remark that the theory of monopolistic competition had virtually no impact on the theory of international trade. But when new models of monopolistic competition were put forward by Spence (1976), Dixit and Stiglitz (1977), and Lancaster (1979), it became obvious that these new "gadgets" could be used to explore the role of increasing returns in a number of ways including intra-industry trade. In the works of Norman (1976), Krugman (1979), and Lancaster (1980), it became obvious that one could use monopolistic competition models to bypass comparative advantage. In this setting, countries with similar resources and technology specialize in different products and obtain the rest through trade as consumers prefer variety. An extension of this approach by Dixit and Norman (1980) and Helpman (1981) sought to bring back comparative advantage by assuming that all differentiated products were produced using the same factor proportions. One could then explain inter-industry trade in terms of Hechscher-Ohlin, with the overlay of intra-industry specialization due to increasing returns.

Balassa (1966) pointed out that trade liberalization among industrial countries had proved to be largely non-disruptive as Europe's industrial landscape had not changed much after the formation of the common market and nor were there any serious income distribution effects. This was because the trade had taken the form of intra-industry specialization rather than inter-industry specialization. Krugman (1981) tried to capture this phenomenon by showing that Stolper-Samuelson theorem where trade hurts a country's scarce factor is strictly valid if comparative advantage is strong and/or economies of scale weak. In case of intra-industry trade between industrial countries, trade was win–win for all parties. There was another important insight from the application of Dixit and Stiglitz (1977) type models to trade. Krugman (1980) shows that increasing returns provide an incentive to concentrate production in one location to minimize transportation costs. Production is concentrated near the largest market and this location then is used to supply other locations.

Helpman and Krugman (1985) tried to recreate Samuelson's insight that factor price equalization theorem could only work if specialization and trade took place as if in an integrated world economy. They tried an approach to trade which combined both increasing returns and comparative advantage. The key insight, in an integrated economy framework, was that all goods subject to economies of scale be located in a single country. This approach also made it clear that increasing returns reinforce, rather than call into question, the gains from trade. Although it is possible to conjure up examples where trade under increasing returns leads to losses, this approach points to gains from trade even under increasing returns, an outcome which is better than what was previously thought.

Krugman points out that monopolistically competitive models gave an impetus to new trade theory, but it did not remain confined to those models. By the mid-1980s, approaches involving external economies, oligopolies, and even contestable markets were applied to new trade theory. What made this possible was a shift in the attitude of trade theorists. First, there was a change in focus from proving general results (based on some upfront assumptions) to special cases. Second, attention shifted from detailed prediction—which country produces what—to the aggregate description of the pattern of trade.

Krugman observes that since the publication of Ohlin's (1933) *Intraregional and International Trade*, the motives for the shipment of goods within countries are similar to those between countries. One might have expected that international trade theory and economic geography theory to have developed in tandem. However, the truth is that trade theorists paid little attention to trade within national boundaries or location of production across space. Despite Marshall, in his *Principles of Economics*, devoting a whole chapter on "The concentration of specialized industries in particular localities", the subject stayed away from the standard economics curriculum. The reason, as Krugman notes, was the centrality of increasing returns in geographical concentrations. "As long as trade theorist shied away from increasing returns in general, economic geography wasn't an inviting field" (Krugman 2008a, p. 342). Further, work in urban economics led economists to gibes like "agglomeration takes place because of agglomeration economies". Particularly, thinking about spatial reach of agglomeration economies posed a problem. Fujita (1988) used monopolistic competition models to derive endogenous externalities, but his assumption that monopolistically produced goods are completely nontradable once again meant that the problem of spatial limits of spillovers remained unresolved.

The character of US geography, Krugman points out, underwent a phase change in mid-nineteenth century and the nation became differentiated between farm and manufacturing belts. The features of this change were the rise of large-scale production (economies of scale), railroads (lower transportation costs) and declining share of agricultural production (more mobile production). Krugman's (1991b) "core-periphery" model was the starting point of new economic geography. It was essentially a model of agglomeration, and it became obvious that one also needed models to deal with other aspects of geography such as regional specialization of different industries and the system of cities. By assuming a few things such as increasing returns in intermediate as well as final production, it became possible to address many of these issues. The willingness to focus on tractable special cases, as was the case in trade theory, became important. For example, in Fujita et al. (1999), increasing returns models of Dixit-Stiglitz type are combined with "iceberg" transportation costs that are proportional to fob prices; use simple adaptive dynamics to arrive at equilibria, and numerical simulations to deal with complex calculations. The method has been described as "Dixit-Stiglitz, icebergs, evolution, and the computer".

There was renewed interest in Marshall's trinity of reasons for local specialization. The original new trade models only modelled specialized suppliers, but with the emergence of new economic geography the other two reasons, namely knowledge spillovers and labour market pooling, also received attention. Also, there was an explosion of empirical work after 1990. Economists became interested in cross-city comparisons to shed light on such subjects as externalities, innovation, and growth.

Critical Appraisal

Comparative advantage theory assumes constant returns to scale and perfect competition. Given these assumptions, trade can arise as a result of differences in tastes, technology, or factor endowments. The Ricardian theory emphasizes differences in technology, while Hechscher-Ohlin-Samuelson model focuses on differences in factor endowments. As a result of these differences, trade is shown to be mutually beneficial to the participating countries. Comparative advantage theory makes free trade an almost sacred idea in economics. Thoughtful economists have long known that comparative advantage is an incomplete story in trade. But the development of theory which could incorporate increasing returns was long held up because of the difficulties in modelling imperfect market structure. The developments in industrial organization theory solved this problem when these models were applied to trade theory. The new trade theory, which emerged in the late seventies and early eighties, emphasizes increasing returns and imperfect competition. Here trade arises not because of dissimilarities between countries but due to economies of scale. Intra-industry trade takes place between industrial countries at a similar level of development. A case is made out for sophisticated arguments for protectionism and also for the use of strategic trade policy under certain circumstances.

We noted several shortcomings of the new trade theory. First, the pattern of intra-industry trade is itself unpredictable. History and accident determine the details of intra-industry trade. Second, evidence suggests that similar-similar trade between advanced countries may be giving way to trade between the rich (high wage) countries and poor (low wage) countries.[14] Also, new trade theory and new economic geography may be waning forces. Although these forces have hardly become irrelevant, the world itself may have turned more classical. Third, although sophisticated arguments for intervention argue that intervention may be welfare enhancing under some conditions, these welfare effects may be exaggerated. Once the net benefits of interventionism are sufficiently whittled down, political economy arguments take over and call for free trade as a practical policy that avoids succumbing to special interest groups and lobbies. But the idea of free trade has lost its earlier innocence—free trade may not always be right, contrary to what the economic theory tells us.

The main shortcoming of the new trade theory perhaps lies in its supply-side view of the matter. It looks at increasing returns as an important source of trade, but the original authors of increasing returns such as Smith (1776) thought of increasing returns as the effect of trade. By increasing the size of the market, international trade carries the division

[14] Krugman et al. (2018, pp. 47–48) point out that till the 1970s, developing countries mainly exported primary products, but since then are moving rapidly into manufactured exports. During 1960–2001 there has been a complete reversal of relative importance of agricultural goods and manufactures in developing countries exports. While agricultural exports as a percentage of developing countries' exports declined from about 60% to about 10%, manufactured exports increased from about 10% to over 65%. China's manufactured exports now constitute more than 90% of its total exports.

of labour in a country to utmost perfection. In terms of cumulative causation framework, as propounded by Young (1928), increasing returns are as much the effect of trade as its cause. Moreover, these authors had a generalized (or macroeconomic) notion of increasing returns rather than a notion confined to particular firms or industries. Young had also talked about an imperfect market structure as closer to reality, but for him imperfections arose because of the imperfect working of competitive process in practice. Thus, imperfect competition for him was a part of the real world competition where each producer tried to be a bit different from others and where selling costs were not to be thought as social wastes but competitive investments. Threat of entry put a limit on the prices charged by producers and hence on their profits.

Deraniyagala and Fine (2001, p. 812) see new trade theory as basically neoclassical economics but incorporating four innovations. These innovations are market imperfections, strategic behaviour, new growth theory, and political economy arguments. Though the policy of intervention is allowed for, the main thrust is on free trade mainly arising from political economy (or rent seeking) arguments. However, these political economy arguments are not very convincing:

> If there are underlying economic and political interests in favour of trade policy, why should they allow trade liberalization to proceed? And, if they have no choice, might they not engage in even more costly forms of pursuing their advantage? This is exactly what is perceived to have happened, if not anticipated, in the wake of the Uruguay Round, with trade policy pursued by other means and, most notably, through antidumping measures which have become the new form of (privatized) trade policy in the WTO era. (ibid., p. 816)

Derniyagala and Fine point out that the neoclassical consensus in favour of trade liberalization has done a double disservice both by undermining interventionist trade policy and its integration with other policy areas. After surveying the empirical literature on trade liberalization, they conclude: "First, there is little to suggest that trade policy is itself an important determinant of industrial performance... Secondly, at least as important as trade policy have been the other elements of industrial policy, such as R&D, and the impact of technology transfer and the scale and growth of domestic markets... Thirdly, trade policy involves a very wide variety of complex instruments with an equally varied set of outcomes depending upon how trade policies interact with other policies... Consequently, trade policy should not be seen in isolation from other policies and as a bias in one direction or the other" (ibid. p. 820).

Ron Martin (1999), while welcoming the new found interest by economists in geography, points out that thus far geographers have not been particularly impressed with this "geographical turn" in economics. The new economic geography has very little resonance with the theoretical and empirical concerns of economic geography proper. It represents reworking of regional science and urban economics models—approaches which were discarded by geographers long ago. Their preoccupation with mathematical modelling leads to neglect of real geography. The results of these mathematical models are not particularly novel and the empirical applications trivial. Thus, the conclusion reached is: "the 'new geographical economics' represents a case of mistaken identity: it is not that new, and it most certainly is not geography" (ibid., p. 67).

References

Arthur, W. Brian. 1986. Industry location patterns and the importance of history. Center for Economic Policy Research, Paper No. 84. University of Stanford.

Arthur, W. Brian. 1990. Positive feedbacks in the economy. *Scientific American* 262 (February): 22–99.

Balassa, B. 1966. Tariff reductions and trade in manufactures among industrial countries. *American Economic Review* 56 (3): 466–473.

Balassa, B. 1967. *Trade Liberalization Among Industrial Countries: Objectives and Alternatives*. New York: McGraw-Hill.

Baldwin, Robert E., and Christopher S. Magee. 1988. Is trade policy for sale? Congressional voting on recent trade bills. National Bureau of Economic Research, Working Paper No. 6376.

Brander, James A. 1981. Intra-industry trade in identical commodities. *Journal of International Economics* 11: 1–14.

Brander, James A., and Barbara J. Spencer. 1981. Tariffs and the extraction of foreign monopoly rents under potential entry. *Canadian Journal of Economics* 14: 371–389.

Brander, James A., and Barbara J. Spencer. 1983. International R&D rivalry and industrial strategy. *Review of Economic Studies* 50: 707–722.

Brander, James A., and Barbara J. Spencer. 1985. Export subsidies and international market share rivalry. *Journal of International Economics* 18: 83–100.

Brander, James A., and Paul Krugman. 1983. A reciprocal dumping model of international trade. *Journal of International Economics* 15: 313–321.

David, Paul. 1985. Clio and the economics of QWERTY. *American Economic Review* LXXV: 332–337.

Deriyagala, Sonali, and Ben Fine. 2001. New trade theory versus old trade policy: A continuing enigma. *Cambridge Journal of Economics* 25: 809–825.

Dixit, A.K. 1984. International trade policy for oligopolistic industries. *Economic Journal* 94 (Supplement): 1–16.

Dixit, A.K., and V. Norman. 1980. *Theory of International Trade: A Dual, General Equilibrium Approach*. London: Cambridge University Press.

Dixit, A.K., and J.E. Stiglitz. 1977. Monopolistic competition and optimum product diversity. *American Economic Review* 67 (3): 297–308.

Eaton, J., and G.M. Grossman. 1986. Optimal trade and industrial policy under oligopoly. *Quarterly Journal of Economics* 101 (May): 383–406.

Fujita, M. 1988. A monopolistic competition model of special agglomeration: A differentiated product approach. *Regional Science and Urban Economics* 18: 87–124.

Fujita, M., Paul Krugman, and A. Venables. 1999. *The Spatial Economy*. Cambridge: MIT Press.

Gruber, H.G., and P.J. Lloyd. 1975. *Intra-Industry Trade: The Theory and Measurement of International Trade in Differentiated Products*. London: Macmillan.

Helpman, Elhanan. 1981. International trade in the presence of product differentiation, economies of scale and monopolistic competition. *Journal of International Economics* 11: 305–340.

Helpman, Elhanan, and Paul Krugman. 1985. *Market Structure and Foreign Trade*. Cambridge: MIT Press.

Helpman, Elhanan, and Paul Krugman. 1989. *Trade Policy and Market Structure*. Cambridge: MIT Press.

Hirschman, Albert O. 1958. *The Strategy of Economic Development*. New Haven: Yale University Press.

Johnson, Harry. 1967. International trade theory and monopolistic competition theory. In *Monpolistic Competition Theory – Studies in Impact: Essays in Honour of Edward H Chamberlin*, ed. R.E. Kuenne, 203–218. New York: Wiley.

Kaldor, Nicholas. 1972. The irrelevance of equilibrium economics. *Economic Journal* 82: 1237–1255.

Kravis, I. 1971. The current case for import limitations. In *United States Economic Policy in an Interdependent World*. Commission on International Trade and Investment Policy, Washington: Government Printing Office.

Krugman, Paul. 1979. Increasing returns, monopolistic competition, and international trade. *Journal of International Economics* 9 (November): 469–479.

Krugman, Paul. 1980. Scale economies, product differentiation, and the pattern of trade. *American Economic Review* 70: 950–959.

Krugman, Paul. 1981. Intraindustry specialization and gains from trade. *Journal of Political Economy* 89: 959–973.

Krugman, Paul. 1984. Import protection as export promotion: International competition in the presence of oligopolies and economies of scale. In *Monopolistic Competition and International Trade*, ed. H. Kierzkowski. Oxford: Oxford University Press.

Krugman, Paul, ed. 1986. *Strategic Trade Policy and New International Economics*. Cambridge: MIT Press.

Krugman, Paul. 1987a. The narrow moving band, the Dutch disease, and the competitive consequences of Mrs. Thatcher: Notes on trade in the presence of dynamic economies of scale. *Journal of Development Economics* XXVII: 41–55.

Krugman, Paul. 1987. Is free trade passé? *Journal of Economic Perspectives* 1 (2): 131–144.

Krugman, Paul. 1990. *Rethinking International Trade*. Cambridge: MIT Press.

Krugman, Paul. 1991. *Geography and Trade*. Cambridge: MIT Press.

Krugman, Paul. 1991. Increasing returns and economic geography. *Journal of Political Economy* 99: 483–499.

Krugman, Paul. 1991. History versus expectations. *Quarterly Journal of Economics* 106 (2): 651–667.

Krugman, Paul. 1999. The role of geography in development. *International Regional Science Review* 22 (2): 142–161.

Krugman, Paul. 2002. Was it all in Ohlin? In *Bertil Ohlin – A Centennial Celebration (1899-1999)*, Part IV, ed. R. Findlay, L. Jonung, and M. Lundahl. Cambridge: MIT Press.

Krugman, Paul. 2008a. The increasing returns revolution in trade and geography, 335–348. Prize Lecture, December 8. www.nobelprize.org.

Krugman, Paul. 2008b. Trade and wages reconsidered. *Brooking Papers in Economic Activity*, Spring.

Krugman, Paul, and Maurice Obstfeld. 2003. *International Economics*, 6th ed. Boston: Addison Welsley.

Krugman, Paul, Maurice Obstfeld, and Marc J. Melitz. 2018. *International Economics*. Eleventh. Harlow: Pearson.

Lancaster, K.J. 1979. *Variety, Equity and Efficiency*. New York: Columbia University Press.

Lancaster, K.J. 1980. Intra-industry trade under perfect monopolistic competition. *Journal of International Economics* 10: 151–175.

Marshall, Alfred. 1890 (1920). *Principles of Economics*, 8th ed. London: Macmillan.

Martin, Ron. 1999. The new 'geographical turn' in economics: Some critical reflections. *Cambridge Journal of Economics* 23: 65–91.

Murphy, Kevin M., A. Schliefer, and R. Vishny. 1989. Industrialisation and the big push. *Journal of Political Economy* 97 (5): 1003–1026.

Myrdal, Gunnar. 1957. *Economic Theory and Underdeveloped Regions*. London: Gerald Duckworth.

Norman, V. 1976. Product differentiation and trade. *UK Economic Theory Study Group*. University of Warwick.

Ohlin, Bertil. 1933. *Intraregional and International Trade*. Cambridge: Harvard University Press.

Rosenstein-Rodan, Paul. 1943. Problems of industrialization in eastern and south-eastern Europe. *Economic Journal* 53 (June-September): 202–211.

Smith, Adam. 1776 (1976). *An Inquiry Into the Nature and Causes of the Wealth of Nations*, ed. Edwin Cannan. Chicago: University of Chicago Press.

Spence, A.M. 1976. Product selection, fixed costs and monopolistic competition. *Review of Economic Studies* 43: 217–236.

Spencer, Barbara J., and James A. Brander. 2008. Strategic trade policy. In *The New Palgrave Dictionary of Economics*, 2nd ed., Steven N. Durlauf and Lawrence E. Blume. Basingstoke and New York: Palgrave Macmillan.

Young, Allyn. 1928. Increasing returns and economic progress. *Economic Journal* 38: 527–542.

CHAPTER 9

Paul Romer and Modern Endogenous Growth Theory

Endogenous growth occurs as a result of the forces engendered within the system and not due to any forces outside the system. It can also be thought of as growth resulting from the actions of the economic agents within the system. Even technological change is the result of the actions of profit-maximizing economic agents. As Paul Romer (1994, p. 3) writes:

> The phrase 'endogenous growth' embraces a diverse body of theoretical and empirical work that emerged in the 1980s.[1] This work distinguishes itself from neoclassical growth by emphasizing that economic growth is an endogenous outcome of an economic system, not the result of forces that impinge from outside. For this reason, the theoretical work does not invoke exogenous technological change to explain why income per capita has increased by an order of magnitude since the industrial revolution. The empirical work does not settle for measuring a growth accounting residual that grows at different rates in different countries. It tries instead to uncover the private and public sector choices that cause the rate of growth of the residual to vary across countries. As in neoclassical growth theory, the focus in endogenous growth is on the behavior of the economy as a whole. As a result, this work is complementary to, but different from,

[1] Barro and Sala-i-Martin (2004, p. xv) also note: "This combination of theory and empirical work is the most exciting aspect of ongoing research on economic growth".

R. Chandra, *Endogenous Growth in Historical Perspective*, Palgrave Studies in Economic History,
https://doi.org/10.1007/978-3-030-83761-7_9

the study of research and development or productivity at the level of the industry or the firm.

Endogenous growth theory attempts to explain why per capita income in capital-abundant countries often grows faster than in capital-poor countries and defies the operation of diminishing returns. The phenomenon of increasing returns is thought to be at the root of continuing high growth in capital-rich countries and is at odds with the law of diminishing returns. Early post-war development economists emphasized the role of capital accumulation in growth. The Harrod-Domar model of growth underlined the role of a higher saving (or investment) rate in achieving a higher growth rate given a constant capital-output ratio.[2] Some authors (e.g. Solow 1956) pointed out that the assumption of a constant capital-output ratio was unrealistic as the operation of diminishing returns would eventually eliminate all per capita income growth. Krugman (1994) stated that both the East Asian and the earlier communist miracles were largely based on input growth, so would not be sustainable.[3] Thus, Romer (1989, p. 51) poses the problem: "How can one reconcile extraordinary, continuing increases in average per capita income with the notion of diminishing returns?".[4]

The neoclassical growth theory as pioneered by Solow (1956, 1957) and Abramovitz (1956), employing an aggregate production function

[2] One of Kaldor's (1961) stylized facts of growth is that capital-output ratios remain steady over long periods of time with no clear long-term rising or falling trend. Over long periods, output and capital tend to grow at the same rate.

[3] "Popular enthusiasm about Asia's boom deserves to have some cold water thrown on it. Rapid Asian growth is less of a model for the West than many writers claim, and future prospects for that growth are more limited than almost anyone now imagines" (Krugman 1994, p. 64). See also Alwyn Young (1995) who shows that factor accumulation, rather than total factor productivity, has played a larger part in the growth story of newly industrializing economies of East Asia such as Hong Kong, Taiwan, Singapore and South Korea during 1966–1990/1991. While growth rates of 6–7% per annum in these economies were unprecedented, productivity performance was not.

[4] In the 1960s, because such questions were avoided, and each of the bothersome questions was assigned an exponential trend term, growth theory came to be viewed as a sterile exercise. Growth theory had little to offer in terms of policy advice, and in models of exogenous technological change or exogenous population growth government's actions did not really matter. "Partly in reaction, development branched off as a separate endeavor, designed to offer the direct policy advice that growth theory could not" (Romer 1989, p. 51).

framework, gave a large role to exogenous technical change. The contribution of exogenous technical change, which offsets the law of diminishing returns, is obtained as a residual in growth accounting exercises. Since the residual is left unexplained it is also termed by Abramovitz (1956) as a "measure of our ignorance". This theory has little to offer in terms of policy since technical progress is given from outside, and therefore not amenable to policy. The theory also predicts convergence of living standards to a common level on the assumption of diminishing returns to capital and identical technology and preferences across countries. Romer (1989), using data of 115 market economies from Summers and Heston (1984), presents a scatter plot suggesting that there is no systematic variation between growth rates and per capita incomes across these economies.[5] Thus, he draws the conclusion: "The absence of any negative slope in this scatter plot is evidence against the assertion that low-income countries tend to grow more rapidly than high income countries and that convergence in per capita income is taking place" (Romer 1989, p. 64).

While it is true that lack of evidence on absolute convergence stimulated the emergence of endogenous growth theory, it was subsequently emphasized that Solow's model only predicts conditional (or beta) convergence. Mankiw et al. (1992) point out that in the unaugmented (or textbook) Solow model, the exogenous saving and population growth rates determine the steady state level of per capita income; while saving rate has a positive impact on income per capita, population growth rate has a negative impact. As Mankiw et al. observe, all is not well with the Solow model as it correctly predicts the direction of the effects of saving and population growth rates, but not the magnitudes. In the unaugmented model, the effects of saving and population growth rates are too large. Once the Solow model has been augmented by including accumulation of human as well as physical capital, the estimated effect of saving and population growth rates is lowered. Mankiw et al. (1992, p. 408) explain:

[5] More recently, Barro and Sala-i-Martin (2004, p. 516), based on a sample of 112 countries, draw scatter plot between the log of per capita GDP in 1960 on the horizontal axis and the growth rate of per capita GDP during 1960–2000 on the vertical axis, and find that the correlation between the two is weakly positive at 0.19. "Thus there is no evidence from the broad cross-country sample of absolute convergence".

> To test the augmented Solow model, we include a proxy for human-capital accumulation as an additional explanatory variable in our cross-country regressions. We find that accumulation of human capital is in fact correlated with saving and population growth. Including human-capital accumulation lowers the estimated effect of saving and population growth to roughly the values predicted by the augmented Solow model. Moreover, the augmented model accounts for about 80 percent of the cross-country variation in income. Given the inevitable imperfections in this sort of cross-country data, we consider the fit of this simple model to be remarkable. It appears that the augmented Solow model provides an almost complete explanation of why some countries are rich and other countries are poor.

Thirlwall (2006, p. 158) summarizes evidence of conditional convergence based on six studies on macrodeterminants of growth: Barro (1991); Mankiw et al. (1992); Knight et al. (1993); Barro and Wha Lee (1993); Levine and Renelt (1992); and Levine and Zervos (1993). Regressing growth of per capita income on various variables such as initial level of per capita income, savings (investment) ratio, population growth, education etc., all these studies find evidence of conditional convergence, holding all other factors affecting per capita income growth constant except the initial level of per capita income where the relationship is found to be significantly negative. The evidence on conditional convergence "delights the neoclassical economists because it is interpreted as a rehabilitation of the neoclassical growth model with diminishing returns, but this may be hasty judgment" (Thirlwall 2006, p. 155). There is a body of literature[6] suggesting that economic growth may be negatively related to the initial level of per capita income because more backward the country, the more the scope for "catch-up".

The new growth literature, which took off with Romer (1986, 1987a) and Lucas (1988), has grown enormously over the years.[7] A sample of this literature consists of Romer (1989, 1990, 1994), Shaw (1992), Krugman (1990, 1993), Murphy et al. (1989a; b), Grossman and Helpman (1991), Pack (1994), Thirlwall and Sanna (1996), Ruttan (1998), Temple (1999), Aghion and Howitt (1998, 2009), Aghion and Durlauf (2005), and Barro and Sala-i-Martin (2004). This literature often cites Adam Smith,

[6] See, for example, Gomulka (1971, 1990), Abramovitz (1986), Dowrick and Nguyen (1989), Dowrick and Gemmell (1991), and Amable (1993).

[7] One of the first attempts to endogenise technical progress was made by Arrow (1962) in his 'learning by doing' model.

Alfred Marshall, and Allyn Young, the original contributors, as the starting point of endogenous growth. But since their presentation was verbal, and not adequately rigorous, the modern endogenous growth theorists then claim to explain what they had in mind with more rigour, clarity, and depth.[8]

Modern growth theory aims to explain eleven stylized facts of growth. Kaldor (1961) had presented a set of six stylized facts about growth which any growth model should satisfy.[9] These were: (1) Output per worker shows continuing growth with no tendency for a falling rate of growth of productivity, (2) capital per worker shows continuing growth, (3) the rate of return on capital is steady, (4) the capital-output ratio is steady, (5) labour and capital receive constant shares of total income, and (6) there are wide differences in the rate of growth of productivity across countries.[10] While endorsing these facts, Romer (1989) added five more to this list making a total of eleven. These are: (7) in the cross-section, the mean growth rate shows no variation with the level of per capita income, (8) growth in the volume of trade is positively correlated with the growth in output, (9) population growth rates are negatively correlated with the level of income, (10) the rate of growth of factor inputs is not large enough to explain the rate of growth of output, i.e., growth

[8] Thirlwall (2006, p. 157) points out that Kaldor's technical progress function, as a critique to the neoclassical production function, precisely anticipates the "new" growth theory. The technical progress function relates the rate of growth of output per worker (on the vertical axis) to the rate of growth of capital per worker (on the horizontal axis). The position on the function depends on the exogenous rate of technical progress which is embodied in capital. Along the 45^0 line, the capital-output ratio is constant. An equilibrium is reached at the intersection of the technical progress function and the 45^0 line. In Thirlwall's (ibid., p. 157) words: "Kaldor's technical progress function is the true progenitor of endogenous growth theory". Thrirlwall (1987, p. 175) further states: "Kaldor rejected the notion that it is possible to distinguish, at least empirically, between movements along a production function (the substitution of capital for labour) and movements in the whole function due to technical progress. There cannot be capital deepening without some technical progress embodied in new capital, and most new ideas need capital accumulation for their embodiment. Society's ability to absorb new knowledge depends on capital accumulation".

[9] Solow (1970) in his book *Growth Theory: An Exposition* stated that while his model of growth satisfied five of the six facts, the last one, namely, wide dispersion of growth rates, was a problem for him.

[10] Romer (1989) observes that Kaldor's fact five that capital's share in total income is constant has increasingly been disputed. He conceded that after accounting for the uncertainties involved, capital's share may be falling.

accounting exercise finds a residual, and (11) both skilled and unskilled labour tends to migrate towards high-income countries.

The Origins of Endogenous Growth Theory

Romer (1994) recounts two versions of the origins of endogenous growth: (1) convergence controversy, and (2) the search for a viable alternative to perfect competition at the aggregate level theory. The first story got a boost with the creation of data sets for many countries over long periods of time, for example, by Maddison (1982) and Heston and Summers (1991). Working with the Maddison data-set, Baumol (1986) found that during 1870–1979, poor countries such as Japan and Italy substantially closed the per capita income gap with advanced countries (e.g. USA and Canada). However, two shortcomings of this analysis were noticed. First, convergence emerged only after WWII, and before that per capita incomes tended to diverge (Abramovitz 1986). Second, the Maddison data-set has bias for convergence because it includes only those countries which were successful in industrializing by the end of the data period (De Long 1986). Thus, in effect, there was no convergence.

The attention therefore shifted to the broad sample of countries in the Heston-Summers data-set. Romer (1994), plotting income per capita relative to the US in 1960 on the horizontal axis and average annual growth rate of per capita income on the vertical axis during 1960–1985, shows that convergence fails in this broad sample of countries. In another plot, taking the share of investment in GDP on the vertical axis this time, and using the equation of the type $Y = K^{1-\beta} L^{\beta}$ where β captures the aggregate social impact of employment (including private as well as the external effect), Romer (1994) found that the effect of investment rate on growth was positive and that of initial income was negative. This result has received special attention in the light of the lack of convergence in the first plot. Romer (1987b) estimated the value of β to be in the vicinity of 0.25, which Barro and Sala-i-Martin (1992) subsequently showed to be of the same order whether one takes cross-country data or cross-states data within the US. Convergence does occur but at a very slow rate. If one introduced capital mobility into the model convergence would be harder to explain.

In a third approach, taken by Mankiw et al. (1992) alluded to earlier, a low value of β can be justified in the pure version of the closed economy neoclassical model (which assumes technology level to be the same in each country) if one allows for human capital along with physical capital in the model. Here the value of β is reduced from 0.6 to 0.33 and is consistent with the data on income shares as total wage payments include payments to human capital as well as unskilled labour.

The above neoclassical mode of analysis however neither gives up the assumption of perfect competition nor can it address the complicated issue involved in the diffusion of technology, information, or knowledge. In Romer's (1994) opinion, the convergence controversy is only a part of the full story behind endogenous growth theory. Although it may encompass a large fraction of recently published literature, it represents a digression from the main story, and may give a misleading message that the data are the only scarce resource in economic analysis. As he sums up:

> This history has many elements in common with many stories about the development of economics. The story starts with the emergence of new data. These present anomalies that lead to new theoretical models, some of which differ markedly from previous, well accepted models. Then a more conservative interpretation emerges that accommodates the new evidence and preserves much of the structure of the old body of the theory. In the end, we have refined the set of alternatives somewhat, but seem to be left in about the same position where we started, with too many theories that are consistent with the same small number of facts. (ibid., p. 11)

The second version of the origins of endogenous growth starts from the fact that there was always enough evidence to reject the available growth models in 1950s, 1960s, and 1970s; the only thing lacking was the availability of good aggregative models. The evidence about growth can be summed up in five basic facts:

First, there are many firms in a market economy. Second, discoveries differ from inputs in the sense that while inputs are rival, discoveries are non-rival (i.e., many people can use discoveries at the same time). Third, it is possible to replicate physical activities. If the production function is: $Y = AF(K,H, L)$, then it is assumed to be homogenous of degree one with respect to its conventional inputs K, H, and L. That is, doubling all rival inputs (K, H, and L) will double output (Y). There is no need to double non-rival inputs represented by A as the existing level of A suffices even when output is scaled up. Fourth, technological advances come from things people do. Even if discoveries are accidental side effects of some other activity or if market incentives play no role in encouraging an activity, the aggregate rate of discovery will still be determined by things that people do. Fifth, Many individuals and firms have market power over discoveries and earn monopoly rents on them. Information from discoveries is not a pure public good as discoveries are partially excludable or excludable for some period of time. Because people and firms have some control over discoveries, they can charge monopoly profits.

The neoclassical model as developed by Solow and others was a big advance in formal growth modelling, but it captured facts 1, 2, and 3 and postponed consideration of 4 and 5. It treats knowledge as a non-rival and non-excludable good and combines it with the simplicity of perfect competition. But it is inconsistent with fact 5 that individuals and firms earn profits from their discoveries. It was useful as an interim modelling strategy till excludability could be formulated. Endogenous growth models take a step further and accommodate fact 4. Many try to follow Arrow (1962) in emphasizing the role of private sector activities in technological advance rather than public sector funding for research. Some of these models accommodate both facts 4 (that technological advance is the result of things people do) and 5 (that there is an existence of monopoly rents). These are sometimes referred to neo-Schumpeterian models as Schumpeter had emphasized the importance of temporary monopoly power in the innovative process.

The endogenous growth theory, in Romer's opinion, would ultimately have to take step 5 by introducing imperfect competition. But initial efforts were confined to step 4 only. Both Romer (1986) and Lucas (1988) included fact 4 without taking the final step of fact 5. In both, technical change is endogenous as it results from the private investment decisions. From the point of view of users, technology is a pure public good as in the neoclassical model. The result is that firms are price takers and equilibrium with many firms can exist. A model of some form of aggregate increasing returns with many firms was first introduced by Marshall (1890 [1920]) in his *Principles of Economics*. Marshall had drawn a downward sloping industry supply curve and had introduced a notion of increasing returns which are external to a firm but are internal to the industry. This was consistent with his supply–demand apparatus where increasing returns and price taking behaviour can both coexist.

The emergence of neo-Schumpeterian models required two steps. The first was to give up perfect competition in the presence of external effects and adopt imperfect competition. By the end of 1970s there were aggregative models with many firms each of which could have a market power. Main examples were Dixit and Stiglitz (1977) and Ethier (1982). Ethier showed how Dixit and Stiglitz model of preferences over several goods could be interpreted as a production function with a large number of inputs. The second step involved the evolution of A(t). The equation in a steady state can be expressed as $\dot{A} = gA^{\varphi}$, where $\dot{A}$ is time derivative of A, g is a constant, and the exponent $\varphi = 1$. Mathematically, this kind of formulation is not robust; if φ is even slightly greater than 1, the stock of technology goes to infinity in finite time. If φ is less than 1, growth eventually stops. Because of the knife edge character of the equation, economists stayed away from $\varphi = 1$ and assumed φ to be strictly less than 1. Romer (1983, 1986) constructed spillover models and paid a lot of attention to the robustness problem. By modifying other functional forms elsewhere in the model, growth stayed finite for values of φ strictly greater than 1. For values slightly less than one, growth eventually stopped but could persist for long periods.

By the late 1980s, economists like Judd (1985) and Grossman and Helpman (1989) were working with models of monopolistic competition and stayed away from a case where $\varphi = 1$. While Judd invoked exogenous technical progress to keep the economy growing, Grossman and Helpman investigated the link between trade and growth. Romer (1987a, 1990) constructed two models of sustained growth accommodating all the five facts noted above. While Romer (1987a) did not evoke any spillover effects, Romer (1990) combined spillovers with monopoly power, that is, incomplete intellectual property rights. In each of these models $\varphi = 1$. Models with monopoly profits motivating innovation have progressed rapidly since, and unexpected connections between market size, international trade, and growth have been uncovered.

Romer (1994, p. 19) concludes by saying that in each of the areas of growth, development, international trade and economic geography, "we have gone through a progression that starts with models based on perfect competition, moves to price taking with external increasing returns, and finishes with explicit models of imperfect competition". The pattern is likely to repeat itself in other areas of economics such as macroeconomic fluctuations. This has far reaching implications. Free trade and markets are good not because of perfect competition or Pareto optimality but because something more interesting and complicated is going on. This includes intra-industry trade between developed nations; little trade between the North and the South; while some developing countries have forged ahead, others have lagged behind; technological change is not a “manna from heaven” but based on things what people do; and the number of locally made goods depends on the extent of the market in the vicinity.

In Romer’s opinion, future developments in endogenous growth have to go beyond cross-country regressions and convergence controversy where the neoclassical models rule the roost and where market incentives and government policies have no effect on discovery, diffusion, and technological advance. If one makes use of all available evidence, one can progress towards a more complete understanding of the determinants of long-run growth, and participate in policy debates on tax exemptions and subsidies on private research, anti-trust exemptions on joint research ventures, the link between trade policy and innovation, intellectual property protection, the link between private firms and universities, costs and benefits of an explicit government-led technology policy, and the like. In advanced countries like the US the relevant question is to find the best institutional arrangements for the production and use of new knowledge. In a developing country like Philippines, the question may be to arrive at the best institutional arrangements for gaining access to the knowledge that already exists in advanced countries.

Some Basic Growth Paradigms

Aghion and Howitt (2009) present four basic growth paradigms to explain various facts and puzzles about growth: (1) the neoclassical growth model, (2) the AK model, (3) the product-variety model, and (4) the Schumpeterian model. This section follows their lead.

The Neoclassical Model

The neoclassical model is described as parsimonious which has only two equations. The first is the product equation making output (Y) a function of inputs of capital (K) and labour (L):

$$Y = AK^{\alpha}L^{1-\alpha}$$

where A is the productivity parameter, and $\alpha < 1$ so that there are diminishing returns to capital.

The second is a law of motion showing how capital accumulation ($\dot{K}$) depends on investment (or aggregate savings) and capital depreciation:

$$\dot{K} = sY - \delta K$$

where sY is aggregate savings and δK is the aggregate depreciation of capital.

In this model the long-run economic growth does not depend on economic conditions or on policy. In the long run, per capita income cannot grow unless productivity A grows over time. This growth in productivity is termed as "technical progress" which can neither be explained nor rationalized. One therefore needs a framework in which productivity growth is endogenous and depends on the economic environment without which decreasing returns to capital and labour would eventually halt all growth. This is provided by the AK model.

The AK Model

The AK model is the first version of the endogenous growth theory and does not make any explicit distinction between capital accumulation and technical progress.[11] In effect both are lumped together in the form of physical and human capital. When different forms of capital accumulates, its marginal product is not driven down to zero. Formally, the AK model can be termed as the neoclassical model without diminishing returns. We assume a linear homogenous aggregate production function of the type:

$$Y = AK$$

[11] Aghion and Howitt (1998) point out that an early variant of the AK model is the Harrod-Domar model, which assumes that labour grows automatically in proportion to capital. The other variant is Frankel (1962) which assumes that it is technological knowledge, rather than employment, which grows automatically with capital. It is based on the idea that technological knowledge is a kind of capital good. He derives the aggregate model from the micro production functions using a scale factor. As capital increases output increases in the same proportion even in the presence of full employment because knowledge automatically increases in proportion. However, Frankel's contribution went unnoticed till the basic idea of the AK model was rediscovered by Romer (1986). Romer made use of Ramsey's (1928) model of intertemporal utility maximization by an individual, and the assumption that individuals do not internalize externalities associated with the growth of knowledge. Romer's contribution was popularized by Lucas (1988), and became a benchmark in the modern endogenous growth theory.

where A is a constant. If capital accumulates as before:

$$\dot{K} = sY - \delta K$$

The economy's long-run growth (as well as short run) growth rate is

$$g = \frac{\dot{K}}{K} = sA - \delta$$

According to the AK paradigm, a higher rate of growth can be sustained by a higher saving rate s some of which will be used to finance higher rate of technological progress. This theory represents "one size fits all" view of the growth process, and applies to both advanced (where capital has already accumulated) and poor countries (where capital accumulation is lagging behind). This model looks at the growth process which is independent of the developments in the rest of the world except when international trade changes the rate of capital accumulation. But it is useful in situations where a sharp distinction between capital accumulation and innovation is of secondary concern.

The Product-Variety Model

"Innovation-based" models emerged in the second wave of the endogenous growth theory. One way in which innovation can be modelled is through product variety as in Romer (1990). In this, new varieties, which are not necessarily improved varieties, emerge for innovation to cause productivity growth. This emerged out of the new international trade theory which emphasizes the role of technology spillovers. The starting point is the Dixit and Stiglitz (1977) production function of the form:

$$Y_t = \sum\nolimits_0^{Nt} K_{it}^{\alpha}\, di$$

where there are N_t different intermediate product varieties each produced using K_{it} units of capital. The aggregate capital stock K_t is equally divided evenly among N_t varieties. The production function can then be re-expressed as:

$$Y_t = N_t^{1-\alpha} K_t^{\alpha}$$

The degree of product-variety N_t is the economy's aggregate productivity parameter and represents the long-run growth rate of per capita output. The larger the product varieties, the larger is the economy's production potential as the given stock of capital gets spread over a larger number of uses each of which exhibits diminishing returns. The researcher-entrepreneurs, motivated by monopoly rents, undertake R&D investments leading to new innovations and hence new varieties. Here there is just one innovation resulting in the same kind of new product. Also there is no role for exit or Schumpeterian "creative destruction". Indeed increased exit may drive down product varieties and reduce a country's GDP. However, this model is useful where competition and turnover considerations take the back seat, for example, in analyzing persistent cross-country productivity differences or in analyzing the relationship between risk, diversification, and growth.

The Schumpeterian Model

Another way of modelling innovations, developed by Aghion and Howitt (1992, 1998), is commonly referred to as Schumpeterian growth theory because of its focus on quality-improving innovations that render old products obsolete through the process of creative destruction.[12]

The production function is specified at the industry level:

$$Y_{it} = A_{it}^{1-\alpha} K_{it}^{\alpha},\ 0 < \alpha < 1$$

where A_{it} is the productivity parameter in terms of the most recent technology of industry i at time t. K_{it} is the intermediate output of this sector. Aggregate output is the summation of industry specific outputs Y_{it}.

As new innovators enter with the most recent intermediate output, they displace the old ones, and improve the productivity parameter A_{it}. Thus, faster growth is generally associated with higher rate of firm turnover as the process of creative destruction implies entry of new and exit of

[12] As Aghion and Howitt (1998, p. 1) in their book *Endogenous Growth Theory* explain: "The approach put forward in this book is based on Joseph Schumpeter's notion of creative destruction, the competitive process by which entrepreneurs are constantly looking for new ideas that will render their rivals' ideas obsolete. By focusing explicitly on innovation as a distinct economic activity with distinct economic causes and effects, this approach opens the door to a deeper understanding of how organizations, institutions, market structure, market imperfections, trade, government policy, and the legal framework in many domains affect (and is affected by) long-run growth through their effects on economic agent's ability to engage in innovative (or more generally knowledge-producing) activities".

old innovators. The theory is focussed on individual industries and is concerned with the microeconomics of industrial competition. But since industries are assumed to be identical in ex ante sense, aggregate per worker output is obtained as a function of aggregate capital K_t:

$$Y_t = A_t^{1-\alpha} K_t^{\alpha}$$

where A_t is unweighted sum of sector-specific A_{it}s. As in the neoclassical theory, the long-run growth is driven by A_t which in this case is determined endogenously on the economy-wide rate of innovation.

The growth rate of innovations (g_t) can be derived as:

$$g_t = \frac{(A_{t+1} - A_t)}{A_t = \mu_n(\Upsilon - 1) + \mu_m(a_t^{-1} - 1)},$$

where $a_t = A_t/\bar{A}$ and μ_n is the frequency of leading-edge innovations and μ_m is the frequency of imitations. $\bar{A}$ is the global technology frontier or the stock of global technological knowledge.

Here there are two types of influences on innovations—the private expenditures of innovators and the stock of innovations that already exist. So two cases are included: (1) that of leapfrogging, where the new innovation is some multiple Υ of the preexisting value, and (2) that of catching-up (or convergence), where the new innovation catches up to the global technology frontier $\bar{A}$.

Paul Romer's Contribution

Romer (1986) presents a fully specified model of the long-run growth in which knowledge is an input in production exhibiting increasing marginal productivity. It is an essentially competitive equilibrium model where technological change is endogenous rather than exogenous as in the neoclassical model. The per capita output can grow without bound possibly at a monotonically increasing rate over time. The long-run growth is primarily driven by the accumulation of knowledge by forward-looking and profit-maximizing agents. However, the production of knowledge itself is subject to diminishing returns, i.e., doubling the inputs into research would not double the production of new knowledge. The production of knowledge by a firm has a positive external effect as knowledge itself cannot be patented or kept secret. "These three elements – externalities, increasing returns in the production of output, and decreasing returns in the production of new knowledge – combine to produce a well-specified competitive equilibrium model of growth. Despite the presence of increasing returns, a competitive equilibrium with externalities will exist. This equilibrium is not Pareto optimal, but is... capable of explaining historical growth in the absence of government intervention" (ibid., pp. 1003–4).

Romer stated that his model differed from the aggregate growth models of Ramsey (1928), Cass (1965), and Koopmans (1965) where the rate of growth of per capita output is a decreasing function of the level of per capita capital stock. Over time wage rates and capital-labour ratios in these models are expected to converge across countries. Thus, there is no long-run effect of initial conditions or current disturbances on the level of output or consumption. Based on the assumption of diminishing returns, and in the absence of technological change, per capita output tends to converge to a steady state value with no per capita income growth. Romer's (1986) model offers an alternative view of the long-run growth prospects. The per capita output in different countries need not converge, and in developing countries growth may either be slow or may fail to take place at all. The crucial point of departure is the assumption of diminishing returns.

Romer (1986) thought that the ideas of Smith (1776), Marshall (1890 [1938]), and Young (1928) on increasing returns could be given a competitive equilibrium interpretation in the presence of externalities. "The idea that increasing returns are central to the explanation of long-run growth is at least as old as Adam Smith's story of the pin factory. With the introduction by Alfred Marshall of the distinction between internal and external economies, it appeared that this explanation could be given a consistent, competitive equilibrium interpretation. The most prominent such attempt was made by Allyn Young in his 1928 presidential address to the Economics and Statistics section of the British Association of the Advancement of Science... Subsequent economists (e.g., Hicks 1960; Kaldor 1981) have credited Young with a fundamental insight about growth, but because of the verbal nature of his argument and the difficulty of formulating explicit dynamic models, no formal model embodying that insight was developed" (Romer 1986, pp. 1004–5).

Aghion and Howitt (1998, pp. 27–28) take a special case of the Romer model. They derive the following steady state growth rate under constant social returns to capital ($\alpha + \beta = 1$), where the economy sustains a finite growth rate (g):

$$g = \frac{(\alpha A - \rho)}{\varepsilon}$$

or taking the technology parameter A to be equal to the total (rather than average) stock of accumulated capital:

$$g = \frac{(L^{1-\alpha} A\alpha - \rho)}{\varepsilon}$$

The implications are summarized as follows. First, the larger the number of firms (L), the more the knowledge externalities in the economy, the faster is the growth rate. The growth rate is positively correlated with the scale effect L. This scale effect also implies that trade liberalization may be growth enhancing. The discount rate ρ negatively impacts the growth rate. Second, as individuals and firms do not internalize the effects of capital accumulation, the equilibrium growth rate is less than the optimal. Although growth has been endogenized, it relies entirely on unremunerated external effects of knowledge accumulation. Imperfect competition was later incorporated in Romer (1987b, 1990). Fourth, variations in α and ρ result in permanent differences in cross-country growth rates. Thus, the simple AK approach does not predict conditional convergence. Fifth, in AK technology, marginal product of capital is constant, so there is no dynamic inefficiency howsoever large the capital stock may be, unlike in the neoclassical model.

However, Romer (1986) actually took $\alpha + \beta > 1$, i.e., increasing social returns to capital. In this case growth accelerates indefinitely. In the case of $\alpha + \beta < 1$, growth will vanish asymptotically without technological progress as in Solow or Ramsey.

Romer (1987a, 1989) presents models of increasing returns arising out of specialization based on fixed costs. Therefore, one need not rely on the beneficial external effects of knowledge. Marshall (1890 [1920]) had talked of competitive equilibrium in the presence of external economies. He also talked of the growth of subsidiary trades in a localized industrial district which used "highly specialized" machinery. In Romer (1987a, 1989) the first effect of spillovers of knowledge is ignored, and the second effect of the role of specialization due to fixed costs is taken up.[13] As Aghion and Howitt (1998, pp. 35–36) explain:

> This second [Romer 1987a] model of Romer formalizes an old idea that goes back to A. Young (1928), namely that growth is sustained by the increased specialization of labour across an increasing varieties of activities: As the economy grows, the larger market makes it worth paying the fixed cost of producing a large number of intermediate inputs, which in turn raises the productivity of labour and capital, thereby maintaining growth. In this model, as in the earlier Romer model [Romer 1986], the growth in A is directly attributable to the growth in K, but those who accumulate capital are not rewarded for having caused A to grow.

The model employs product-variety idea of Dixit and Stglitz (1977), and its interpretation given by Ethier (1982). Ethier suggested that Dixit and Stiglitz utility function could be interpreted as a production function to capture preference for variety. In Romer (1987a) there is a continuum of intermediate goods over [0, A], and each good is produced by a local monopolist. The growth of knowledge A results not from learning externalities of individual firms but from an increase in the variety of inputs. The final output is produced using labour and intermediate goods:

$$Y = L^{1-\alpha} \int_0^A X_i^{\alpha}\, di, 0 < \alpha < 1$$

where x_i is the input of the ith intermediate good. In a symmetric equilibrium, $x_i = x^*$ for all i. For each monopolistic producer, x^* is determined by the equality of marginal cost and marginal revenue. Intermediate production is subject to free entry, so there are zero profits in equilibrium,

[13] Describing his Marshall-Young-Romer model of growth, Romer (1989, p. 108) stated: "The degree of specialization, or equivalently, the number of different firms that are available at any point in time or location, is limited by the presence of fixed costs. In this model, these different goods are assumed to be intermediate inputs into production, and the technology is such that having more available goods is useful. Surely a large part of what distinguishes Silicon Valley from the cross-roads in Nebraska is the set of specialized goods and services immediately available for sale at each point… Although Marshall and Young choose to describe specialization in terms of competitive equilibrium with externalities, it is now clear that a more rigorous way to capture the effects they had in mind is in a model with fixed costs. In an equilibrium with non-negative profits, price must exceed marginal cost to be able to recover these fixed costs, so the model must therefore contemplate some form of market power".

and monopolistic (rather than oligopolistic) competition with product differentiation prevails. Romer shows that the equilibrium value of A is $[(2 - \alpha)/2\ h]K$, where h is the fixed cost of each intermediate good and K is the total stock of capital. The aggregate production function can be written as:

$$Y = bL^{1-\alpha} A^{1-\alpha} K^{\alpha},$$

where b is a positive coefficient. There are increasing returns to scale in L and K once A is replaced by its equilibrium value noted above. This model is different from Romer (1986) because of the introduction of imperfect competition or monopoly rents. Each firm engages in research activities to create new knowledge, and gets compensated through monopoly rents if the innovation is successful.

Romer (1990) extended the model by assuming sunk costs in the intermediate sector.[14] Again these costs are recovered through monopoly rents, and the intermediate good sector is subject to increasing returns and monopolistic competition. Final good is again produced using labour and the intermediate good, but labour gets divided between manufacturing final good (L_1) and intermediate good (L_2), such that $L = L_1 + L_2$. A refers to the current number of designs or the number of intermediate inputs. The production for the final good is:

$$Y = (L_1)^{1-\alpha} \int_0^A X_i^{\alpha}\, di$$

The above also includes sunk cost for producing x units of a given intermediate input, or P_A for corresponding design (or license). The rate of growth of designs ($\dot{A}/A$) is:

$$\dot{A}/A = \delta L_2$$

There are two major sources of increasing returns in Romer (1990): specialization or product differentiation (as in Romer 1987a) and research

[14] Jones (2019) considers Romer's 1990 paper as a watershed. "It stands as the most important paper in growth literature since Solow's Nobel-recognized work" (p. 859). Further, the paper makes three key contributions. "1. It identifies the non-rivalry of ideas as crucial to economic growth; (2) it highlights the role of profit-maximizing entrepreneurs and imperfect competition; (3) it places the key AK linearity in the idea production function" (p. 864).

spillovers (as in Romer 1986). The steady state growth rate is derived as:

$$g = \frac{(\alpha\delta L - \rho)}{(\alpha + \varepsilon)}$$

That is, growth rate g increases with productivity of research activities (δ) and the size of the economy as measured by total labour supply (L), and decreases with rate of time preference (ρ). Since intermediate firms do not internalize their contribution to product diversity and researchers do not internalize research spillovers, the equilibrium growth rate is always less than the social optimum.

One important limitation of this approach based on product variety, as noted by Aghion and Howitt (1998, p. 39), is that it assumes away obsolescence of old intermediate inputs. If old intermediate inputs were to become obsolete over time, the rate of growth of A would not increase systematically, and hence the growth destroying forces of diminishing returns may not be warded off. To formalize technical obsolescence, one needs to move away from horizontal models of Dixit and Stiglitz (1977) type to vertical models of quality improvements or models of growth through "creative destruction".[15]

Policy Implications

G. K. Shaw (1992) spells out the policy implications of the new endogenous growth theory. As he notes, it is useful to begin with the Harrod-Domar model as a starting point. In developing countries budgetary surpluses came to be regarded as a substitute for domestic saving, and therefore the government had an important role to play. Development agencies gave prominent role to the raising of saving ratios in line with the mainstream development thought [e.g., Lewis (1954), Rostow (1960) and Fei and Ranis (1964)] before an economy could take off into self-sustaining growth. Similarly, in advanced market economies easy money policies (along with strict fiscal discipline) were advocated for economic growth.

[15] In Schumpeterian models, since innovation is associated with creative destruction, new firms are created and old destroyed in the process of growth. Recently this dynamic, as also noted by Jones (2019), has been explored incorporating the firm level data by Aghion et al. (2014, 2017), Akeigit and Kerr (2018) and Atkeson and Burstein (2019) among others.

An antidote to excessive emphasis on capital accumulation was provided by the neoclassical model of Swan (1956) and Solow (1956). In these one sector models, the ultimate determinant of growth rate is the autonomously determined rate of growth of population. Fiscal policy was rendered largely irrelevant though it could still play a part in the attainment of esoteric goals like golden rules or golden ages.

A third ingredient to growth common to both Harrod-Domar and neoclassical models was provided by exogenous technical progress which, as Solow (1957) showed, was the dominant element of the growth equation. As the exogenous technical change was left unexplained in the neoclassical growth theory, there was no role for the government to play. Perhaps the only possible role contemplated for the government was in returning the economy to steady state should it diverge from it due to some temporary disturbance.

Solow's growth accounting exercise showed that in the US during 1909–1949, while the gross output per man had doubled, as much as 87.5% came from technical change and 12.5% from the increased use of capital. Abramovitz (1956) and Kendrick (1973) confirmed these findings and it became obvious that more than half the US growth came from increased efficiency in the use of productive inputs rather than from a mere increase in those inputs. Technical progress, derived as a residual after deducting the contributions of factor inputs, was itself unexplained, as noted earlier, and there was no adequate theory to account for these efficiency gains.

Arrow's (1962) learning by doing model and its extension by Levhari (1966a; b) and Sheshinski (1967) made technical change endogenous through the use of intangible input knowledge, and increasing returns were reconciled with competitive equilibrium (and hence marginal productivity theory of distribution), but in the steady state the rate of growth was determined by exogenously given rate of growth of labour force. Since knowledge is a public good, Arrow's conclusion was that too little is socially invested and produced. So while the level of investment is sub-optimal, the ultimate determinant of economic growth is outside the scope of policy action. An increase in the rate of investment (through private sector savings ratio or fiscal intervention) may have a "level effect" through the upward shift in the production function, but it fails to have a "growth effect". A model by King and Robson (1989) in this tradition links productivity growth directly with investment, and since multiple steady state paths exist, tax policy can affect the ultimate growth path attained by the economy.

A variant of the learning by doing models is Romer (1986) where knowledge is an input in the production function and competitive equilibrium is made consistent with aggregate increasing returns due to externalities. Here, as we noted, per capita income can grow without limit, and new knowledge is the ultimate determinant of long-run growth. New knowledge is itself produced by an investment in research technology which is subject to diminishing returns. The assumption of diminishing returns in the production of new knowledge imposes an upper limit on the investment activity undertaken by profit-maximizing private agents. They are therefore expected to respond to appropriate tax and fiscal incentives.

A striking implication of Romer's increasing marginal productivity assumption is that there may be divergence instead of conventional convergence. The gap between the rich and poor countries may widen as poor countries may experience slower growth rates than advanced economies. Indeed capital and investment may flow from poor to rich countries due to increasing marginal productivity of capital in the latter. Increasing returns to knowledge may imply economic integration, common markets, and economic unions.

Another way to endogenize technical change is provided by Uzawa (1965), Romer (1990), and Lucas (1988). The essential feature here is to identify a sector specializing in the production of ideas (see Stern, 1991). The emphasis is on human capital in the growth process.[16] In Romer (1990), the research sector produces ideas or improved designs for making producer goods for the final goods production. A new design allows the production of new intermediate input; it also increases the productivity of human capital in research sector through increased stock of knowledge. Thus the benefits of a new design are only partially excludable. By introducing partial excludability, profit-maximizing agents are able to reap quasi rents. In the Lucas (1988) model, on the other hand, knowledge emerges as a public good which is non-rival and non-excludable as in Arrow (1962). Since all or some benefits of research are freely available to all, the implication is that the production of research

[16] As Warsh (2006) notes, Lucas greatly simplified the mathematics of Romer's Ph.D. dissertation (p. 243) and replaced his knowledge variable (which has externalities) with human capital (p. 257) which has spillovers.

would be sub-optimal, and there is a role for the government in subsidizing research. The difficulty however lies in identifying the relevant R&D sectors; in that case subsidizing the acquisition of human capital may generally be the second best option. Mention may also be made of King and Rebelo (1990), who building on Uzawa (1965) and Lucas (1988), emphasize the role of tax policy. In open economies with access to international capital markets the adverse effects of small changes in tax policy get magnified—generating development traps (zero-growth steady states) as well as growth miracles.

We now come to policy implications for the developing countries. Potentially, they should benefit from freer international trade as they can gain from the stock of world knowledge. However, policies at the country level are important to be able to do so. If a country possessing comparative advantage in R&D subsidizes research, world growth will increase. On the other hand, if an economy more efficient in manufacturing were to subsidize innovation, world growth would decline. Trade policy, ceteris paribus, will affect the transfer of resources from research to manufacturing in policy active countries and in the opposite direction in policy inactive countries. However, the issue is far from being clear cut. The opening of trade may affect adversely countries with a high ratio of skilled labour to non-skilled labour like the US with the sudden appearance of cheap Mexican skilled labour. This may affect the incentive to produce non-rival inputs and slow down growth in high ratio countries. Traditionally new products are produced in advanced economies where R&D is well developed. Later, with the transfer of technology or imitation, these goods come to be produced in less advanced countries with lower wages. So the international product cycle may lead to constantly evolving international trade where the advanced countries now import the same very goods they earlier exported. However, within the context of the product cycle model, subsidizing innovation is growth enhancing in both advanced and less advanced countries. In advanced countries, migration of production to less advanced countries frees up more resources for product development. In less advanced countries, more resources may be available for new product development than for adapting the imported techniques to their requirements.

Finally, the role of trade policy is not one of unlimited optimism. The identification of knowledge producing sectors itself poses a major difficulty. Conclusions arrived from models are easily overturned with changes in assumptions, thus weakening one's confidence in growth prescriptions.

Interdependence of policy actions of different countries would point to coordination of these actions or to consideration of the second best options.

Critical Assessment

Various critiques of the endogenous growth theory have emerged over the years. For example, Ben Fine (2000) and Anthony Thirlwall (2003) point out that there is hardly anything new in the endogenous growth theory. It appears more a case of an old wine in a new bottle. Fine, while assessing the theory in the perspective of new developments in the economics discipline, has suggested that the endogenous growth theory draws heavily as well as strengthens the traditional microeconomic foundations of neoclassical economics. As he explains: "A number of contributors have reasonably argued that most of the ideas deployed are not new and are to be found in the old neoclassical growth theory or other schools of thought. The originality lies more in bringing these ideas to the fore and packaging them in the most advanced form of mathematical models. At a more mundane level, the claim to newness resides, at least terminologically, in substituting endogenous for exogenous. What was previously taken as given is now explained" (Fine 2000, p. 248). Further: "endogenous growth theory has been heavily influenced by microeconomics. Indeed, like much macroeconomics in the most recent period, it can be thought of as microeconomics parading as macroeconomics, especially in the context of representative economic agents whether serving as producers or consumers" (ibid., p. 252).

Similarly, Thrilwall (2003, pp. 44–45) finds nothing much new in the theory's stress on externalities and knowledge spillovers of human capital and R&D investments as these factors were already highlighted by scholars in the 1950s and 1960s, for example, by Shultz (1961), Denison (1967) and Griliches (1957).[17] Schultz (1961, p. 1) highlights the importance of human capital in growth thus: "Although it is obvious that

[17] "What is new is that the ideas are being modeled in a more rigorous way for a different purpose. The purpose is not to supplant the neoclassical growth model as a conceptual framework for the analysis of growth, but rather to rehabilitate the neoclassical model to make it compatible with the observation that living standards in the world are not converging. Most new growth theorists are neoclassical economists in disguise e.g. Barro, Mankiw, Lucas and Romer (for a survey of early studies see Thirwall and Sanna1996)" (Thirlwall 2003, p. 45).

people acquire useful skills and knowledge, it is not obvious that these skills and knowledge are a form of capital, that this capital is a substantial part a product of deliberate investment, that it has grown in Western societies at a much faster rate than conventional (nonhuman) capital, and that its growth may well be the most distinctive feature of the economic system. It has been widely observed that increases in national output have been large as compared with the increases of land, man-hours, and physical reproducible capital. Investment in human capital is probably the major explanation of this difference".

Sandilands (2000) takes issue with Romer's (1989) emphasis on fixed costs in his Marshall-Young-Romer model of growth. Romer had stated that the degree of specialization (or the number of different firms in a location) is limited by the presence of fixed costs. Sandilands pointed out that this was a big advance but did not fully capture what Young (1928) had in mind. "Young did not say that specialization is limited by the presence of fixed costs though he did say that specialization increasingly took the form of greater roundaboutness in the economy as a whole. In his theory fixed costs and increased roundaboutness are not so much a constraint on growth as its consequence" (Sandilands 2000, p. 315). Further: "[I]t is true that since a larger market promotes more roundabout, capitalistic methods of production, fixed costs would increase. Nonetheless, Young does not claim that this will cause monopoly (in which profit maximization implies that price is above marginal cost) to be the normal outcome, nor even that the average size of firm necessarily increases... Young's point was that a larger market size permits more of the infinite potential stages of production to be undertaken by a larger number of specialist firms, big or small" (Sandilands 1990, pp. 318–19).

Although Young had stated that economies of increasing returns are basically the economies of capitalistic and roundabout methods of production but they are limited by the size of the market. Thus the market size was a greater concern for Young than the presence of fixed costs. He also stated that increasing returns are not available for the taking by adopting rational economic reforms such as mass production, rationalization, or economies of large-scale production. Such things cannot be divorced from the size of the market. Marshall had also talked about indirect and roundabout methods of production. But he was clear that not all will be adopted; only those which were more remunerative or pay in practice. Clearly, therefore, neither fixed costs nor capital accumulation by itself can be regarded as independent engines of growth divorced from the market size.

Sandilands (2000) also questions the stress on "new" knowledge in the modern endogenous growth literature in contrast with the greater diffusion of "existing" knowledge as the size of the overall market expands. As he explains: "Youngian endogenous growth relates to that part of growth that depends on growth itself, and the way it permits and encourages the fuller exploitation and adaptation of existing knowledge. He draws a distinction between this and what has come to be the focus of much of modern neoclassical endogenous growth theory, namely growth that is dependent on the discovery of new knowledge by research and development teams motivated by a rational calculus of costs and benefits of such research. Thus the modern literature in this respect neglects or misrepresents Young's concept of increasing returns in the process of self-sustaining growth" (ibid., p. 325).

Similarly, Chandra and Sandilands (2005) find that the modern endogenous growth theory misrepresents Young in a number of ways. It is essentially an extension of the neoclassical supply-side production function approach where, in addition to the conventional inputs, new inputs such as human capital and R&D are also introduced. Young's theory, on the other hand, is based on real demand (or Sayian reciprocal demand) where the division of labour and size of the market are preponderant influences. These, in turn, are interlocked in a cumulative causation framework. Moreover, the aggregate production function framework retains all the properties of microeconomics where it is assumed that the whole is simply the sum of its parts, and aggregate output is a unidirectional function of inputs including human capital and new knowledge. A fallacy of composition may therefore be involved in these models. Endogenous growth theory discusses integration with world markets but only because larger markets induce more research inputs. It is assumed that growth arises because of new knowledge, but the role of larger market in making more effective use of existing knowledge is largely neglected. Finally, the theory recommends patents, intellectual property rights, and other protectionist privileges to induce more R&D and innovation so that monopolistic (or oligopolistic) firms are able to recoup the costs of their investments. Young had also talked of imperfect competition, but for him this meant imperfect working of competition rather than its absence. An entrepreneur who is the first to innovate can reap supernormal profits but as others enter the field these disappear and may reappear in some other area. Imperfect competition in Young may emerge from the normal competitive growth process, but from this one cannot conclude that policy-induced market power is a sound way to promote growth. In the Smith–Young framework competition and growth are seen as mutually reinforcing.

Modern endogenous growth theory has also been criticized on empirical grounds. Howard Pack (1994) expresses scepticism whether it offers a better guide to explaining the actual growth experience. Most empirical research generated by endogenous growth theory has tested earlier models rather than testing endogenous theory itself. Most research has used cross-country data imposing extremely strong assumptions regarding international production functions. "Unless there is some demonstration forthcoming that the theory is useful in explaining the growth pattern over time of national economies, it will remain a rich expansion of existing growth theory rather than powerful organizing framework for thinking about actual growth phenomena" (ibid., p. 55).

We noted that most studies on macrodeterminants of growth invariably show conditional convergence of per capita income with respect to the initial level of income when all other factors affecting growth are kept constant. We also noted Alwyn Young's (1995) conclusion that much of East Asian growth was attributable to factor accumulation rather than productivity growth. Charles Jones (1995) pointed out that most OECD countries had seen permanent policy changes in terms of trade liberalization, increases in average years of schooling, higher investment rates, and substantial increases in R&D levels, but there has not been any commensurate payoff in growth rate or productivity growth.[18]

References

Abramovitz, Moses. 1956. Resources and output trends in the United States since 1870. *American Economic Review, Papers and Proceedings* 46 (May): 5–23.

Abramovitz, Moses. 1986. Catching up, forging ahead and falling behind. *Journal of Economic History* 46 (2): 385–406.

Aghion, Philippe, and S. Durlauf, eds. 2005. *Handbook of Economic Growth.* Amsterdam: Elsevier North-Holland.

[18] Aghion and Howitt (1998, pp. 407–16), however, claim that this finding does not challenge the augmented Schumpeterian model presented by them.

Aghion, Philippe, and Peter Howitt. 1992. A model of growth through creative destruction. *Econometrica* 60: 323–351.

Aghion, Philippe, and Peter Howitt. 1998. *Endogenous Growth Theory*. Cambridge: MIT Press.

Aghion, Philippe, and Peter Howitt. 2009. *The Economics of Growth*. Cambridge: MIT Press.

Aghion, Philippe, U. Akeigit, and Peter Howitt. 2014. What do we learn from Schumpeterian growth theory? In *Handbook of Economic Growth*, Vol. II, ed. P. Aghion and S.N. Durlauf, Chapter I, 515–563. Amsterdam: North-Holland.

Aghion, Philippe, A. Bergeau, T. Boppart, P.J. Klenow ,and H. Li. 2017. Missing growth from creative destruction. NBER Working Paper No. 24023.

Akeigit, U., and W.R. Kerr. 2018. Growth through heterogeneous innovations. *Journal of Political Economy* 126: 1374–1443.

Atkeson, A., and A. Burstein. 2019. Aggregate implications of innovation policy. *Journal of Political Economy* 127 (6): 2625–2683.

Amable, B. 1993. Catch-up and convergence: A model of cumulative growth. *International Review of Applied Economics*, 7 (January): 1–25.

Arrow, Kenneth J. 1962. Economic implications of learning by doing. *Review of Economic Studies* 29: 155–173.

Barro, Robert J. 1991. Economic growth in a cross-section of countries. *Quarterly Journal of Economics* 106 (May): 2–407.

Barro, Robert J., and Xavier Sala-i-Martin. 1992. Convergence. *Journal of Political Economy* 100 (2): 223–251.

Barro, Robert J., and Xavier Sala-i-Martin. 2004. *Economic Growth*, 2nd ed. Cambridge: MIT Press.

Barro, Robert J., and J. Wha Lee. 1993. Losers and winners in economic growth. *Proceedings of the World Bank Conference on Development Economics*. Washington, DC: World Bank.

Baumol, William J. 1986. Productivity growth, convergence and welfare. *American Economic Review* 76 (5) (December): 1072–1085.

Cass, David. 1965. Optimum growth in an aggregative model of capital accumulation. *Review of Economic Studies* 32 (July): 233–240.

Chandra, Ramesh, and Roger J. Sandilands. 2005. Does modern endogenous growth theory adequately represent Allyn Young? *Cambridge Journal of Economics* 29: 463–473.

De Long, J. Bradford. 1986. Productivity, growth, convergence and welfare: Comment. *American Economic Review* 78 (5): 1138–1154.

Denison, E. 1967. *Why Growth Rates Differ: Post-war Experience in Nine Western Countries*. Washington, DC: Brookings Instittution.

Dixit, Avinash, and Joseph E. Stiglitz. 1977. Monopolistic competition and optimum product diversity. *American Economic Review* 67 (3): 297–308.

Dorwick, S., and N. Gemmell. 1991. Industrialisation, catching-up, and economic growth: A comparative study across the world's capitalist economies. *Economic Journal* 101 (March): 263.
Dorwick, S., and D.T. Nguyen. 1989. OECD comparative economic growth 1950–85: Catch-up and convergence. *American Economic Review* 79 (December): 1010–1030.
Ethier, W.J. 1982. National and international returns to scale in the modern theory of international trade. *American Economic Review* 72: 389–405.
Fei, J.C.H., and G. Ranis. 1964. *Development of the Labor Surplus Economy: Theory and Policy*. Homewood: Irwin.
Fine, Ben. 2000. Endogenous growth theory: A critical assessment. *Cambridge Journal of Economics* 24 (2): 245–265.
Frankel, M. 1962. The production function in allocation and growth: A synthesis. *American Economic Review* 52: 995–1022.
Gomulka, S. 1971. *Inventive Activity, Diffusion and Stages of Economic Growth*. Aarhus: Aarhus University Press.
Gomulka, S. 1990. *The Theory of Technological Change and Economic Growth*. London: Routledge.
Griliches, Z. 1957. Hybrid corn: An exploration in the economics of technological change. *Econometrica* 25 (4): 501–522.
Grossman, Gene, and Elhanan Helpman. 1989. Product development and international trade. *Journal of Political Economy* 97 (6): 1261–1283.
Grossman, Gene, and Elhanan Helpman. 1991. *Innovation and Growth in the Global Economy*. Cambridge: MIT Press.
Heston, Alan, and Robert Summers. 1991. The Penn world table (mark 5): An expanded set of international comparisons, 1950–88. *Quarterly Journal of Economics* 106 (May): 327–368.
Hicks, John R. 1960. Thoughts on the theory of capital: The Corfu conference. *Oxford Economic Papers* 12: 123–32.
Jones, Charles I. 1995. R&D based models of economic growth. *Journal of Political Economy* 103: 759–784.
Jones, Charles I. 2019. Paul Romer: Ideas, nonrivalry, and endogenous growth. *Scandinavian Journal of Economics* 121 (3): 859–883.
Judd, K.L. 1985. On the performance of patents. *Econometrica* 53 (3): 567–585.
Kaldor, Nicholas. 1961. Capital accumulation and economic growth. In *The Theory of Capital*, ed. F. Lutz. London: Macmillan.
Kaldor, Nicholas. 1981. The role of increasing returns, technical progress and cumulative causation in the theory of interntional trade and economic growth. *Economic Appliquee* 34 (4): 593–617.
Kendrick, J. 1973. *Postwar Productivity Trends in the United States 1948–1969*. New York: National Bureau of Economic Research.

King, Merwyn, and Mark Robson. 1989. Endogenous growth and the role of history. Discussion Paper No. 63. London: LSE Financial Markets Group.

King, Robert G., and Sergio Rebelo. 1990. Public policy and economic growth: Developing neo-classical implications. *Journal of Political Economy* 98: S126–S150.

Knight, M., N. Loayza, and D. Villanueva. 1993. Testing the neoclassical theory of economic growth. IMF Staff Papers, September.

Koopmans, T.C. 1965. On the concept of optimal economic growth. In *The Econometric Approach to Development Planning*. Amsterdam: North-Holland.

Krugman, Paul. 1990. *Rethinking International Trade*. Cambridge: MIT Press.

Krugman, Paul. 1993. Towards a counter-counterrevolution in development theory. *Proceedings of the World Bank Annual Conference on Development Economics*, 15–38. Washington, DC: World Bank.

Krugman, Paul. 1994. The myth of Asian miracle. *Foreign Affairs* 73 (6): 62–78.

Levhari, David. 1966. Further implications of learning by doing. *Review of Economic Studies* 33: 31–39.

Levhari, David. 1966. Extensions of "Arrow's learning by doing." *Review of Economic Studies* 33: 117–132.

Levine, R., and D. Renelt. 1992. A sensitivity analysis of cross-country growth regressions. *American Economic Review* 82 (September): 942–963.

Levine, R., and S. Zervos. 1993. What we have learned about policy and growth from cross-country regressions. *American Economic Review*. Papers and Proceedings, May.

Lewis, W. Arthur. 1954. Economic development with unlimited supplies of labour. *The Manchester School of Economics and Social Studies* 22 (2): 139–191.

Lucas, R.E. 1988. On the mechanics of economic development. *Journal of Monetary Economics* 22 (1): 3–42.

Maddison, Angus. 1982. *Phases of Capitalist Development*. New York: Oxford University Press.

Mankiw, N.G., D. Romer, and D.N. Weil. 1992. A contribution to the empirics of economic growth. *Quarterly Journal of Economics* 107 (May): 407–437.

Marshall, Alfred. 1890 (1920). *Principles of Economics*, 8th ed. London: Macmillan.

Marshall, Alfred. 1890 (1938). *Principles of Economics*. London: Macmillan.

Murphy, K.M., A. Schleifer, and R. Vishny. 1989. Income distribution, market size and industrialization. *Quarterly Journal of Economics* 104 (3): 537–564.

Murphy, K.M., A. Schleifer, and R. Vishny. 1989. Industrialization and the big push. *Journal of Political Economy* 97 (5): 1003–1026.

Pack, Howard. 1994. Endogenous growth: Intellectual appeal and empirical shortcomings. *Journal of Economic Perspectives* 8 (Winter): 55–72.

Ramsey, Frank. 1928. A mathematical theory of saving. *Economic Journal* 38: 543–559.

Romer, Paul M. 1983. *Dynamic Competitive Equilibria with Externalities, Increasing Returns and Unbounded Growth*. Unpublished Ph.D Thesis. Chicago: University of Chicago.

Romer, Paul M. 1986. Increasing returns and long-run growth. *Journal of Political Economy* 94: 1002–1038.

Romer, Paul M. 1987. Growth based on increasing returns due to specialization. *American Economic Review* 77 (2): 56–62.

Romer, Paul M. 1987. Crazy explanations for the productivity slowdown. In *NBER Macroeconomics Annual*, ed. S. Fischer, 163–202. Cambridge: MIT Press.

Romer, Paul M. 1989. Capital accumulation in the theory of long-run growth. In *Modern Business Cycle Theory*, ed. Robert J. Barro. Cambridge: Harvard University Press.

Romer, Paul M. 1990. Endogenous technological change. *Journal of Political Economy* 98 (5): S71–S102.

Romer, Paul M. 1994. The origins of endogenous growth. *Journal of Economic Perspectives* 8 (1): 3–22.

Rostow, W.W. 1960. *Stages of Economic Growth: A Non-communist Manifesto*. Cambridge: Cambridge University Press.

Ruttan, V. 1998. New growth theory and development economics. *Journal of Development Studies* 35 (December): 1–26.

Sandilands, Roger J. 1990. *The Life and Political Economy of Lauchlin Currie*. Durham and London: Duke University Press.

Sandilands, Roger J. 2000. Perspectives on Allyn Young in theories of endogenous growth. *Journal of the History of Economic Thought* 22 (3): 309–328.

Shaw, G.K. 1992. Policy implications of endogenous growth theory. *Economic Journal* 102 (412): 611–621. Reprinted in Snowdon and Vane (1997, pp. 616–627).

Sheshinski, E. 1967. Optimal accumulation with learning by doing. In *Essays on the Theory of Optimal Economic Growth*, ed. K. Shell. Cambridge: MIT Press.

Shultz, Theodore. 1961. Investment in human capital. *American Economic Review* 51 (March): 1–17.

Smith, Adam. 1776 (1976). *An Enquiry Into the Nature and Causes of the Wealth of Nations*, ed. Edwin Cannan. Chicago: University of Chicago Press.

Snowdon, Brian, and Howard R. Vane. 1997. *A Macroeconomics Reader*. London and New York: Routledge.

Solow, Robert M. 1956. A contribution to the theory of economic growth. *Quarterly Journal of Economics* 70 (February): 65–94.

Solow, Robert M. 1957. Technical change and aggregate production function. *Review of Economics and Statistics* 39 (August): 311–320.

Solow, Robert M. 1970. *Growth Theory: An Exposition*. New York and Oxford: Oxford University Press.
Summers, Robert, and Alan Heston. 1984. Improved international comparisons of real product and its composition: 1950–1980. *Review of Income and Wealth* 30 (June): 207–262.
Stern, N.H. 1991. The determinants of growth. *Economic Journal* 101: 122–133.
Swan, T.W. 1956. Economic growth and capital accumulation. *Economic Record* 32: 334–361.
Temple, J. 1999. The new growth evidence. *Journal of Economic Literature* 37 (March): 112–156.
Thirlwall, Anthony P. 1987. *Nicholas Kaldor*. Washington Square: New York University Press.
Thirlwall, Anthony P. 2003. Old thought on new growth theory. In *Old and New Growth Theories: An Assessment*, ed. Neri Salvadori. Cheltenham and Northampton: Edward Elgar.
Thirlwall, Anthony P. 2006. *Growth and Development*, 8th ed. Basingstoke: Palgrave Macmillan.
Thirlwall, Anthony P., and G. Sanna. 1996. New growth theory and macrodeterminants of growth: An evaluation and further evidence. In *Employment, Economic Growth and Tyranny of the Market: Essays in Honour of Paul Davidson*, Vol. 2, ed. P. Arestis. Cheltenham and Brookfield: Edward Elgar.
Uzawa, H. 1965. Optimum technical change in an aggregate model of economic growth. *International Economic Review* 6: 18–31.
Warsh, David. 2006 (2007). *Knowledge and the Wealth of Nations: A Story of Economic Discovery*. New York and London: W. W. Norton and Company.
Young, Allyn. 1928. Increasing returns and economic progress. *Economic Journal* 38 (152): 527–542.
Young, Alwyn. 1995. The tyranny of numbers: Confronting the statistical realities of the east Asian growth experience. *Quarterly Journal of Economics* 110 (August): 641–680.

CHAPTER 10

Endogenous Growth: Concluding Remarks and Policy Conclusions

Allyn Young (1990) observed that there is no area in economics where there is so much confusion as increasing returns. There appear to be misconceptions on the true source of increasing returns. Most literature takes the view that increasing returns arise in manufacturing and therefore this sector needs to be promoted. Some of this literature thinks that increasing returns arise because of economies of scale at the firm (or plant) level. Adam Smith's pin-factory example is cited to show that economies of scale arise when the scale of production at the microeconomic level expands. This leads to a related question whether the market power created by scale economies is the true source of increasing returns. Also, what is the role of external economies? In the modern endogenous growth literature, investment in new knowledge is emphasized. At the same time it is big firms who are able to invest in R&D; and to recoup the costs, some artificially created market power in the form of patents, monopolies, and protectionism is recommended. If artificially created market power is necessary to reap increasing returns, then what exactly is the role of competition? What role does external competition (or international trade) play in the realization of increasing returns? Smith had argued that international trade widens the market and therefore promotes the division of labour. This leads to the question of the relative importance of the role of demand factors vis-à-vis supply factors in

R. Chandra, *Endogenous Growth in Historical Perspective*, Palgrave Studies in Economic History, https://doi.org/10.1007/978-3-030-83761-7_10

growth. These are some of the issues we discuss in this chapter in the light of various conceptions of endogenous growth discussed earlier (in Chapters 2–9). We also discuss some of the various policy conclusions emerging from these conceptions.

Are Increasing Returns Confined to Manufacturing?

Some influential literature (Rosenstein-Rodan 1943, 1961; Kaldor 1966, 1972, 1975; Murphy et al. 1989; Krugman 1993) argues that increasing returns are sector-specific rather than generalized. Particularly they see increasing returns confined to the industrial sector. Rosenstein-Rodan talked about simultaneous industrialization over a wide number of wage goods industries in his theory of the big push. Kaldor interpreted Adam Smith and Allyn Young in terms of sectoral increasing returns. He also believed in the empirical validity of Verdoorn's Law which posited a strong relationship between productivity growth and output growth in manufacturing. In terms of a two-sector framework, the industrial sector (which was the increasing returns sector) was sought to be promoted even in a country like Britain where the industrial revolution took place without protection. Murphy et al., building on Rosenstein-Rodan, saw the big push as taking an economy from bad equilibrium to a good industrial one. While no industry on its own can break even, simultaneous industrialization of many sectors can be profitable. Krugman (1993), while resurrecting some core ideas called "high development theory" which had been swept away by the neoclassical counterrevolution, presented a streamlined version of Murphy et al.'s (1989) big push model.

Smith, it is true, had stated that the division of labour is better carried out in manufacturing. The nature of agriculture, on the other hand, did not permit as complete a specialization as in manufacturing. The same person acts as the ploughman, harrower, sower of seed, and reaper of the crop at different times of the year. If specialization opportunities in agriculture are limited, it did not mean Smith wanted to favour manufacturing over agriculture. In fact he was against a policy of restraints and preferences. Any artificial direction of economic activity was anathema to him. As Buchanan and Yoon (2000) point out, the Smithian proposition regarding the division of labour and market size does not require any distinction between various sectors. In its minimalist formulation, a larger exchange nexus is preferred to a smaller one because it is more efficient.

Allyn Young (1928), building on Smith, defined market in an inclusive sense as an aggregate of productive activities tied together by trade. He saw various sectors of the economy in a reciprocal exchange relationship where different sectors grow at different rates depending on the elasticities of demand and supply. So nothing should be done to upset these intersectoral relationships as growth would be affected. Young believed in the togetherness of the economic phenomenon and saw industrial relations as an "interrelated whole". He put forward a macroeconomic notion of increasing returns, and pointed out that increasing returns lie under our eyes but we are likely to miss them if we focus too much on individual firms or industries. Thus in this macroeconomic conception of increasing returns, the market size and competition are preponderant influences which policy has to keep in mind.

If increasing returns are generalized rather than sector-specific what exactly is the role of a leading-sector strategy in growth? Does not a leading-sector strategy conjure up notions of favourable treatment to the chosen sectors? As we saw, Currie's (1974) leading-sector strategy is consistent with the Smith-Young framework of "no favours, no handicaps". It is not based on the logic of sector-specific increasing returns but on the logic of sectoral handicap removal. If some sectors suffer from institutional barriers vis-à-vis rest of the economy, then removal of those barriers will stimulate those sectors and the rest of the economy would then follow in response. Currie pointed out that the housing sector (as the internal leading sector) was inhibited by inadequate institutional finance, and the export sector (as the external leading sector) suffered because of the chronic overvalued exchange rate. If suitable financial products are made available, and the exchange rate is made more realistic, these leading sectors can take off pulling the other sectors behind them. This strategy does not consider industry and agriculture as the leading sectors; but once the chosen leading sectors such as exports and construction have been stimulated, agriculture and industry can then follow in response. By getting the sequence right, Rosenstein-Rodan's big push over a wide front automatically becomes a reality. Thus, Currie's leading-sector strategy is consistent with the macroeconomic or generalized notion of increasing returns.

Do Increasing Returns Arise Because of Internal Economies of Scale?

Most literature (e.g. Romer 1986; Stigler 1951; Krugman 1993; Warsh 2007) has misinterpreted Smith's (1776) pin-factory example to suggest that increasing returns are due to internal economies of scale. Smith used the pin-factory example for illustrative purposes only as all the operations of pin-making can be observed under one roof. Smith's main purpose was to show how the division of labour (or job specialization) at the firm level leads to dramatic improvement in total output as well as productivity. Smith was not trying to illustrate the advantages of large-scale production at the firm level or any relationship between fixed and variable costs. What the literature (especially the modern growth literature) generally misses is that Smith had talked about a broader process of the social division of labour. As the size of the market expands, not only new trades come into being but existing trades split up into a number of sub-trades (or specialisms) like different types of smiths or different types of weavers. Smith also stated that to produce even an ordinary commodity like a woolen coat, different arts and crafts had to join hands. Thus, for Smith, it was this broader process of social division of labour which was more important.[1]

Do increasing returns arise from the relationship between fixed and variable costs in the sense that as the output expands, fixed costs of a firm get spread over a larger output leading to a reduction in cost per unit? Allyn Young (1990, p. 54) maintained that increasing returns do not arise because of any relationship between supplementary (fixed) and prime (variable) costs but due to other causes. He was of the view that it was "large production" (at the macroeconomic level reflecting a large market) rather than "large-scale production" (at the microeconomic level reflecting the size of a firm) which permitted increasing returns. Increasing returns are more commonly realized in industries which are not consolidated. As the market size increases, an industry splits up into

[1] Buchanan (1994), points out that Smith's pin-factory example has proved to be misleading. "Adam Smith's familiar illustration has been misleading because it draws attention away from the phenomenon of economy wide increasing returns and toward increasing returns to scale of operation within the single producing unit, in his case, the pin factory... The focus is shifted away from the limitless range of potentially advantageous specialization of inputs in a complex economic network and to the simple division of tasks among workers on something like an assembly line" (ibid., p. 5).

a number of specialist firms and industries. It is this process of industrial differentiation rather than integration which is more important for the realization of increasing returns. This also implies that the scale of a firm or industry is only incidental to the broader phenomenon of increasing returns. In some cases scale might increase if the product is standardized and operations are routinized. But in most cases, because of the dominance of industrial differentiation, the size of specialized firms or industries is relatively small. In any case, the size of a firm (or industry) is not entirely a matter for it to decide as the scale at which it is able to operate is not independent of the size of the market. Each firm or industry is adjusted to the overall market. Thus the size of the market emerges as a crucial determinant of specialization and hence increasing returns.

Is specialization limited by the presence of fixed costs? Romer (1989, p. 108) posited that the degree of specialization, or equivalently, the number of firms which are available at any given time or location, is determined by the presence of fixed costs. He also stated that to recover these fixed costs, the model has to contemplate some form of market power. The point missed by Romer is that endogenous growth is a process which draws forth the required resources needed for fixed costs. Fixed costs are more a consequence of growth than its cause. Young did not link the degree of specialization to the presence of fixed costs but to the overall size of the market. As the market expands, processes and methods became more roundabout and capital intensive. Production becomes more indirect and the number of processes (or stages) between raw materials and the final product increases. But the important point is that increasing roundaboutness is limited by the size of the market not by fixed costs.

Warsh (2006, chapter 4) points out that there is a contradiction between Adam Smith's pin factory and his principle of the invisible hand. To reduce costs, the pin factory has to operate on a large scale making monopolization inevitable. This comes in conflict with the invisible hand which represents competition:

> The problem is that the two fundamental theorems of Adam Smith lead off in quite different and ultimately contradictory directions. The Pin Factory is about falling costs and increasing returns. The Invisible Hand is about rising costs and decreasing returns. Which is the more important principle? When Paul Romer read back over the literature, he found that one of his teachers had seen the dilemma perfectly clearly as a young man. In 1951 George Stigler had written, 'Either the division of labour is limited by the

> extent of the market, and, characteristically, industries are monopolized; or industries are characteristically competitive, and the [Pin Factory] theorem is false or of little significance.' According to Stigler, they cannot both be true. (Warsh 2006, p. 46)

Is there really a contradiction between the pin factory and the invisible hand? The contradiction arises if specialization is interpreted in terms of economies of scale or increasing size at the firm level. For Young, increase in scale or monopoly is not inevitable. Evolution was not based on any one principle. Some firms producing standardized products may become large-scale, but most of the specialized firms are small or medium and not big. Young (1990) pointed out that in the real world competition was the rule rather than an exception. In most cases, if a firm grew beyond a point, disadvantages accumulated faster than advantages. So a capitalistic monopoly was not to be found beyond the short term. Young was of the view that it is not possible to sustain an artificial monopoly against competitive forces unless there was an underlying natural monopoly. In case of natural monopolies like railways or public utilities, there was no point in running them on competitive lines. Young regarded imperfect competition, the field lying between pure competition and pure monopoly, as closer to reality than the two extremes. Here the presence of product differentiation, brand names, advertising, selling costs, goodwill, etc. means that each producer tries to be bit different from others to rise above the dead level of competition. The monopoly elements were more apparent than real. Competitive forces still operate relentlessly under the surface. Competition now takes the form of non-price competition; it works through substitutes, supplementary service, or better terms of payment. For Young, imperfect competition was a part of the broader competitive process. Young stated that except for electric power, gas, telephone, water, and street car service an average consumer was not much aware of monopoly. In fact, Young felt that competition had increased over the years rather than diminished (see Ely et al. 1930, pp. 216–18; Chandra 2020, pp. 249–53).

Alfred Marshall (1890) also thought that the economy was dominated by small and medium firms rather than big ones. In his *Principles* he did not consider joint stock companies seriously as they did not constitute significant proportion of the economy.[2] His frequent tours to factories (*wander-jahre*) revealed to him that most of the economy consisted of family based firms.[3] The presence of external economies and his life cycle theory of firms meant that firms did not grow beyond a point after which they start declining like the trees in a forest. As Hart (2006, p. 403) notes "Marshall's biological analogy was intended to explain why monopolization was not the inevitable outcome of internal economies". Marketing difficulties and the combined fear of spoiling a particular market meant that "the ability of business firms to exploit the efficiency gains arising from increasing returns to scale is limited by the size of the market" (ibid., p. 403). In *Industry and Trade*, Marshall (1919) considered joint stock companies in a framework of open markets characterized by competition between the small and big where the market structure was subject to evolutionary changes. Large firms had advantages in marketing and in exploiting existing technology. However, as firms grew, effective management problems arose such as "excessive management scope" and "mechanical methods of administration" which might hinder "elasticity and initiative". The small businesses also had their strong points in greater initiative and flexibility and in developing new technology. Small businesses were also best educators of initiative and versatility, the main sources of economic progress. It may be noted that Marshall's firm, big or small, is not a static or equilibrium firm. "Business size was the outcome of processes that were irreversible in time and which were not independent from forces operating within business organizations. Placed in the context of twenty-first century economic analysis, Marshall's discussion of forces that determine business size fits most comfortably within the boundaries of evolutionary economics" (Hart 2006, p. 405).[4]

[2] See, for example, Whitaker (2003, p. 145) who points out that joint stock companies constituted one tenth of the total business in the UK which "seems a remarkably small fraction".

[3] Marshall in a letter to Alfred William Flux, dated 7 March 1898, mentioned that "one of the chief purposes of my Wander-jahre among factories, etc., was to discover how Cournot's premises were wrong". See Whitaker (1996, II, pp. 227–28). According to Cournot, if a firm reaps economies of scale, it becomes a monopoly. Marshall on the other hand wanted to reconcile increasing returns with competition in an evolutionary framework.

[4] Hart (2003, p. 171) points out that Marshall (1890) used the concept of free competition, and he identified perfect competition with the assumption of perfect knowledge. Therefore his definition of free competition excludes perfect knowledge. "Marshall's

In an evolutionary setting, economies of scale need not be antagonistic to broader process of competition.[5] However, in the static or equilibrium concept of a firm, economies of scale become antagonistic to perfect competition which requires rising marginal and average cost curves to reach equilibrium. It is important to realize that both Marshall and Young did not use the words "perfect competition". For them competition was the real world competition with all its imperfections. Moreover, competition was viewed as a process and not as an end-state conception. Here monopoly elements are consistent with competition but are regarded as temporary. With the entry of other firms, availability of close substitutes, and given time for adjustment, these elements wither away. Young pointed out that long-run profits, after adjusting for bad years against good years, are probably zero. In that case society's entrepreneurial function gets performed at virtually no cost to society. He opined that profits are mixed incomes like quasi or short-term rents, return on the entrepreneur's own land, capital and labour, and partly pure profits. They arose because competition worked imperfectly in the real world due to the forces of inertia and friction. However, most of these surpluses get eliminated in the long run. He viewed pure profits as rewards of competition; "But it is more important that pure profits should be obtainable than obtained" (see Ely et al. 1923, pp. 518–19; Chandra 2020, pp. 152–56).

treatment of competition was much closer to Adam Smith, where competition did not coincide with a particular 'situation' but represented an active process, than to that of his contemporaries" (Hart 2003, p. 171).

[5] Some commentators take the view that Marshall failed in his project of combining evolution with the long-run equilibrium of industry. For example, Loasby (1991, pp. 15–16) writes: "Adam Smith's explanation of economic progress linked development with co-ordination. Though he certainly used a concept of equilibrium, both development and co-ordination resulted from competitive processes (Richardson 1975). Marshall associated development with evolution and co-ordination with equilibrium, and attempted to incorporate both equilibrium and evolution within a single body of analysis; but he failed". Hart (2003) calls the problem arising from Marshall's analysis of increasing returns in Appendix H where he points to the limitations of static theory outlined in Book V as the "reconciliation problem". "The reconciliation problem centres on the difficulties associated with representing, within an equilibrium framework, outcomes of 'evolutionary' processes identified directly with the increasing returns and thus the long-period industry supply schedule (derived from the representative firm)" (ibid., p. 168).

The Role of External Economies

Marshall distinguished between internal and external economies. External economies are those external to a firm but become available to it with the growth of an industry as a whole. His concept of localization of industry or industrial districts is based on this concept where a large number of specialized firms are able to coexist and grow. "External economies" is also an important concept in Young's theory of growth. In the first place, he pointed out, it should be a safeguard against the common error of assuming that whenever increasing returns take place there is an effective tendency towards monopoly. Secondly, increasing returns take the form of pecuniary external economies (or reduced costs and prices) which are transmitted more effectively in a competitive market system. The process is cumulative in Young as cost and price reductions lead to an increase in the size of the market; an increase in the size of the market in turn leads to further reductions in costs and prices. Marshall used the device of the representative firm, which has access to both internal and external economies, to arrive at the long-run industry supply curve. While Young used the concept of external economies in his growth theory based on cumulative causation, Marshall's objective was to obtain an industry's equilibrium of demand and supply in the long run.

Pecuniary external economies are seen as a sign of well-functioning market system in Young, but the post-war development economists saw them as a sign of market failure. Scitovsky (1954) made an important distinction between pecuniary and technological external economies. He pointed out that while examples of technological external economies are rare, as they have to do with such examples as bees and orchards, pecuniary external economies are widespread. Therefore from development point of view "pecuniary external economies" is the more relevant concept. But, as noted by him, market prices reflect the situation as it is and not as it will be. So market prices and profits "are a bad guide to economic optimum as far as investment and industrial expansion are concerned" (ibid., pp. 149–50). Thus there is a market failure involved; centralized investment planning or some additional communication system to supplement the market is required. Similarly, Rosenstein-Rodan (1961, p. 58) was of the view that pecuniary external economies cause a possible divergence between the private and social marginal net product, and therefore the price system does not put an economy on an optimum path. This implies that the entire industrial sector needs to be planned and created like a huge firm or trust.

It is one thing to use government intervention to strengthen the market system and its institutional framework to make it work better but another to replace it with control and command mechanisms. First type of intervention helps facilitate the realization pecuniary external economies so important in the context of growth and development. For example, investment designed to integrate the market internally through transport and communication links, and establishment of a legal-institutional framework to enforce contracts and control the growth of monopoly can help better realize pecuniary external economies. But what the post-war development economists were suggesting was an anti-market intervention designed to replace the market with centralized decision mechanisms. Moreover, they also recommended an import-substitution model behind tariff and quantitative protection. Such a system leads to the development of a command economy insulating the economy from competitive pressures particularly from international trade, and hence is detrimental to the adequate realization of increasing returns.

More recently Krugman (1991a, b, 1997) and Krugman and Obstfeld (2003) have highlighted the role of external economies in economic geography. Building on Marshall (1890), who highlighted the role of specialized suppliers, labour market pooling, and knowledge spillovers in the industrial districts where there is localization of industry, Krugman and Obstfeld point out that such economies are possible in a country with a large industrial sector. Here the industrial supply curve is downward sloping highlighting the fact that costs and prices are lower at a higher level of output. In such situations, countries may get locked into undesirable patterns of specialization, historical accidents may become decisive, and established patterns of trade may persist even if they go counter to comparative advantage. Krugman and Obstfeld give the example of Swiss watch industry which got established first, and despite higher costs could not be displaced by Thailand's newly established watch industry. The Thai producers were blocked because of higher initial costs. Thai watch industry could have benefited from protection, but in practice it is difficult to identify cases of external economies. Just as intra-industry trade based on economies of scale is difficult to predict and therefore policy is of little use here, likewise policy is of little help in industry clusters based on external economies as they are difficult to identify a priori. Even cases of dynamic external economies (due to knowledge spillovers) are difficult to identify where production costs depend on cumulative output (or cumulative experience).

Krugman (1991b) points out that because of external economies as well as the fact that some factors are more mobile than others, there is a tendency for factors to get concentrated in a few geographical locations. For example, beautiful people may get concentrated in Hollywood, ambitious people in London, and nerds in Silicon Valley. Here historical factors play an important role in geographical concentration just as in Swiss watch industry. Krugman also developed core-periphery model to explain geographical concentration of manufacturing in general (unlike Marshall's localization phenomenon in a few industries) in a few geographical locations or belts called the industrial core with other regions playing the role of agricultural periphery. He bases these patterns on generalized external economies (i.e., pecuniary external economies) rather than those specific to particular industries. Concentrations may develop near large markets to minimize transportation costs, and other locations may be served from there. Some demand may come from agriculture, but the major source is manufacturing itself. The concept of pecuniary external economies can be applied to cumulative causation models (e.g., Murphy et al. 1989; Krugman 1993) where these economies result in multiple equilibria. Krugman points out that similar processes are at work in Arthur's (1990) concept of "positive feedback" or Hirschman's (1958) "forward and backward linkages".

Krugman, however, is wrong in suggesting that pecuniary external economies arise primarily due to economies of scale at the plant level. He maintained that economies of scale at the firm level translated into increasing returns at the macroeconomic level through the vehicle of pecuniary external economies. In Krugman the sequence is from economies of scale at the firm level to pecuniary external economies at the generalized level. In Young, by contrast, the sequence is more from the pecuniary external economies to specialization at the firm and industry level through the process of industrial differentiation. Economies of scale at the firm level do not constitute an essential feature of Young's theory. As the size of the market expands, so do pecuniary external economies, and this results in specialist firms emerging which need not be large. Most of them are small and medium as both Marshall and Young noted.

Moreover, reduced costs and prices are transmitted better in a more competitive system, not in a monopolized system where economies of scale predominate. According to Marshall-Young view competition still rules the roost; monopoly elements are temporary and tend to disappear through freedom of entry and availability of close substitutes. As Young noted, common public does not perceive of monopoly in any real sense except in railways and other public utilities like electric power or gas supply. So according to Smith-Marshall-Young conception competition is the rule rather than an exception.

The Role of Demand vis-à-vis Supply Factors in Growth

Post-war development economists diagnosed the problem of development as resulting from an acute shortage of physical capital. Capital was regarded as the missing component which, if applied in proper amounts, would help break vicious circles of poverty. Thus the key to enhanced productivity lay in greater use of capital, and the supply of capital could be increased by increasing the rates of saving and investment. Rosenstein-Rodan's (1943, 1961) big push (or simultaneous industrialization over a wide range of industries) also needed large domestic resources as well as foreign aid. Ragnar Nurkse (1953) analysed the problem of capital formation in underdeveloped countries both from the demand side as well as the supply side. His conclusion was that supply side of the problem was more important than the demand side. Arthur Lewis (1954), a Nobel Prize winning development economist, thought that the key to development lay in understanding how a country could be converted from a low saving economy (where saving and investment rates were only 4–5% of GDP) to a high saving one where these rates are 12–15% of GDP. In Lewis model, the capitalist surplus (out of profits) plays a key role in creating new employment opportunities till the entire labour surplus in the traditional sector disappears. This is the famous thesis of "economic development with unlimited supplies of labour".

As is obvious from the preceding paragraph, this was largely a supply based view of growth where demand considerations were either not considered important or ignored. Rosenstein-Rodan and Nurkse did talk about the vicious circle of poverty on the demand side, but their solution was either big push (requiring large domestic and foreign resources) or synchronized application of capital (or balanced growth) over a wide front. So they only paid lip service to the demand problem, that is, to the problem of how to expand the real market size in the sense of Adam Smith or J. B. Say. The post-war development economists also recommended anti-market policies (like high import protection and centralized planning to decide the size and composition of investment) which curbed the overall market instead of enhancing it.

Another supply-side explanation is provided by the Harrod-Domar model where the rate of growth is given by the investment rate divided by the incremental capital-output ratio. Given a constant incremental capital-output ratio, the rate of growth is determined by the investment (or saving) rate. The neoclassical theory continues this supply-side tradition. Invoking Cobb–Douglas aggregate production function with constant returns to scale but diminishing returns to each input such as labour and capital, Solow (1956, 1957) and Abramovitz (1956) obtain a rate of growth which is determined by the rate of growth of population and exogenous technical progress. Government policy has no role as technological progress, which accounts for most growth, is given from outside. Modern endogenous growth theory came into being partly to explain technical progress which was left unexplained by the neoclassical model and partly to garner a policy role for itself. Also, the neoclassical theory predicted convergence of living standards between the rich and poor countries because of diminishing returns to capital, but evidence finds no absolute convergence. Thus the new growth theory attempts to explain why the capital-abundant countries continue to grow faster than capital-poor countries. The modern endogenous growth theory does not abandon the supply-side production function framework of the neoclassical theory but introduces new features such human capital and R&D expenditures. Thanks to the externalities exhibited by these new inputs, and endogenous improvements in productivity due to technical progress (which is now endogenised), the aggregate production function is now made to exhibit increasing returns to scale rather than constant returns to scale as earlier. As pointed out by Thirlwall (2003, p. 45), the purpose of the new growth theory was not to supplant the neoclassical growth model but to make it compatible with observed lack of convergence of living standards. "Most new growth theorists are neoclassical economists in disguise e.g. Barrow, Mankiw, Lucas and Romer" (ibid., p. 45).

As against these supply-side theories, Adam Smith (1776) and Allyn Young (1928) provide a demand-side explanation of growth. For Smith, the chief explanation of growth was the division of labour. But the division of labour is limited by the size of the market. Since the use of capital facilitates the division of labour by employing more productive labourers and by providing them with better tools and equipment, capital accumulation by itself cannot be regarded as an independent engine of growth. Young (1928) cast Smith's relationship between the division of labour and market size in terms of cumulative causation. He defined market in an inclusive sense as an aggregate of productive activities tied together by trade which, in other words, implies that the total market size is given by the total volume of production. This suggests that capacity to buy depends on the capacity to produce, and Adam Smith's theorem can be restated as "the division of labour depends in large part on the division of labour". Here Young makes use of Say's law where supply creates its own demand such that general overproduction in the aggregate is not possible. This also means that an expansion of a sector creates demand for the products of other sectors, and expansion of other sectors fuels growth in the original sector. Thus growth is based on the principle of reciprocal demand.

It needs to be emphasized that the concept of demand in Young is different from Keynesian aggregate demand. In Young demand means reciprocal demand in the Sayian sense rather than monetary demand in the Keynesian sense. Nicholas Kaldor and Lauchlin Currie, two of Young's students, developed Youngian ideas further but the important difference was that while Kaldor thought that increasing returns were confined to manufacturing, for Currie they were generalized. This leads to totally different policy conclusions. While for Kaldor[6] manufacturing was the leading sector (although he did not use the term), and could be promoted by a policy of favours. For Currie, on the other hand, the leading-sectors could be promoted by a policy of handicap removal. Moreover, Currie regarded housing and exports as the leading sectors and manufacturing as a following sector.

Adam Smith had emphasized the need to enlarge the market to promote growth. This could be done by integrating the domestic market by investing in transport and communication, and opening up the domestic market to foreign trade. Smith thought that businessmen were monopolists in spirit, and therefore they should be made to compete

[6] For a critical assessment of Kaldor's growth ideas and his policies, see Chandra (2019) and Chandra and Sandilands (2021).

through domestic as well as international competition. Smith regarded competition conducted in accordance with the laws of justice as the most important ingredient of growth. Smith also emphasized the institutional arrangements for a competitive exchange economy—for example, protection of private property, strong law and order, administration of justice, enforcement of contracts, legal and moral codes. Without this minimal institutional-moral framework, no exchange economy can work.[7] Young also emphasized the same basic ingredients of market size and competition to promote growth. In the Smith-Young framework winners and losers emerge from the competitive race, and cannot be picked and promoted a priori for policy purposes. The field is leveled for everyone in a "no favours, no handicap" framework.

In the Smith-Young demand based view, the role of market is emphasized in the growth process. A large and growing market provides the opportunities for growth. Here supply of inputs of labour, capital, technology, human capital, or R&D inputs are not seen as constraints on growth. An economy is viewed not so much as resource constrained as opportunity constrained. This implies that the "economics of opportunity" is a more dominant paradigm than the "economics of scarcity". If resources are viewed as scarce, they then are thought to pose a formidable constraint in the satisfaction of human wants. In the production possibility frontier framework more of guns means less of butter. Post-war development economists were so much weighed down by the problem of scarcity that they posed the problem of growth in terms of various constraints such as saving, foreign exchange, or wage goods. In the Smith-Young demand side view resources are scarce but for that very reason they are productive as well. Young stated that whether earnings of capital are

[7] Smith stated that institutional arrangements should ensure two things—liberty and security. After analysing various systems of political economy, he came to the conclusion that these are best provided in a system of natural liberty where the government is confined to a few basic tasks it can do well. For Young, institutional development depended on the stage of society. The advent of war (WWI), monopoly capitalism, and business cycles meant that newer institutional mechanisms had to be created to deal with these. For example, an independent central bank was required to control credit—which he thought was an unstable component of money supply in line with Hawtrey—to moderate business cycles. Anti-trust laws and institutions were required to deal with the growth of monopoly. Advent of WWI meant that the state machinery had to be used not only to move men and materials for the war effort but also for post-war reconstruction. Also, the statistical machinery had to be created or strengthened for more effective steps in these directions. See Chandra (2021).

due to their productivity or relative scarcity, it means the same thing. For him scarcity and productivity were two sides of the same coin. At the microeconomic level, under ceteris paribus assumptions, factors of production are subject to diminishing returns. But at the macroeconomic level, the fact that growth takes place implies that increasing returns are real, and they are not negated by their costs. Even a small trading country without many resources can transform its growth possibilities through international trade. It appears that Young was attempting a new vision of the economic process—a vision which sees economics more in terms of opportunities than in terms of debilitating scarcity (see Chandra 2020, pp. 310–11).

The Role of International Trade

Adam Smith had placed much emphasis on the role of international trade in the realization of increasing returns. In fact his theory of domestic growth and that of international trade are both based on the importance of the division of labour and can be viewed as two sides of the same coin. International trade, by widening the narrow domestic market, not only helps a country to attain the highest level of perfection in the division of labour but also keeps the domestic monopolies in check. The consumer also benefits in terms of lower price and better quality. Young viewed the creation and expansion of markets as a precursor to the industrial revolution. In his view, it was the commercial revolution which preceded the industrial revolution. The so-called inventions of the industrial revolution and improvements in techniques and methods of production were made possible because markets had been enlarged and deepened. Thus, for Young, technical change mostly follows enlarged production. Producers do not enlarge production in the blind hope that markets will somehow be found. Young stated that industry does not impose its will on the market (or commerce). It does not dispose of a "surplus product" in the Marxian sense, but plans for a "potential product" for a "potential market" (Young 1928, pp. 536–37).

In Smith, international trade is based on absolute costs. A country specializes and exports those products where these are lower. In the Ricardian theory, a country specializes and exports those products where comparative costs (in terms of labour units) are lower. The Ricardian theory is an advance on Smith's theory in the sense that a country suffering absolute disadvantage in the production of all commodities could still specialize and trade on the basis of comparative advantage. While Smith's theory was dynamic and related to the division of labour, Ricardian theory was static, but had a greater influence on the subsequent trade theory. It is possible that Ricardo saw comparative advantage as an additional argument for free trade especially in the context of corn-laws controversy in Britain. However, the subsequent literature made it the focal point of trade.

As we saw, many of the post-war development economists viewed trade with suspicion. Nurkse (1962) did not doubt that trade had acted as an engine of growth in the nineteenth century but this engine had become unavailable in the contemporary context of his time. Added to this were the doctrines of export pessimism and declining terms of trade for primary goods producers. Thus the mainstream view which emerged was that developing countries should industrialize behind high tariff and non-tariff barriers, and follow an inward-looking model of growth. However, Balassa (1980) showed that this strategy of import substitution was alright as long as it did not deviate much from comparative advantage and confined to the first stage of import substitution. But when carried into the much more difficult second stage, it was like travelling up the staircase and involved higher capabilities in terms of technology and skills beyond the reach of many developing countries. Those countries of South Asia, Latin America and Africa which followed this path of second-stage import substitution suffered a low economic performance.

The new trade theory (e.g. Krugman 1990), made increasing returns as the basis of intra-industry trade between similar countries. In this theory, countries specialize in products in which they enjoy economies of scale and obtain other varieties (since consumers have a preference for different varieties) through trade. While inter-industry trade between food and manufactures is based on comparative advantage, intra-industry trade between manufacturers and manufacturers is based on economies of scale. But the pattern of intra-industry trade (or which country will export what products) is left unspecified. Industrial clusters are formed on the basis of external economies (like the Swiss watch industry) are also viewed as historical accidents where policy does not have much role to play. While in Smith-Young conception, trade is the cause of increasing returns, in the new trade theory trade is caused by increasing returns. In a cumulative causation framework the process is two way but it would be fair to say that trade is as much the cause of increasing returns as increasing returns are the cause of trade. Krugman admits that intra-industry trade based on economies of scale may now be giving way to trade between low-wage developing countries (e.g. China and Mexico) and high-wage advanced countries (e.g. USA).

In his article "Is free trade passé?", Krugman (1987) mostly favours free trade as a practical necessity but not because theory tells us so. He cites the political economy argument of rent-seeking sectional interests which can only be countered by a policy of free trade. Otherwise, in his opinion, some case can be made for strategic trade policy where a country's gain is at some other country's loss. But he admits that such a beggar-thy-neighbour policy is likely to invite retaliation. So for Krugman free trade is not passé not because of any economic theory, but because of practical imperatives. He feels that free trade argument based on theory had lost its earlier innocence. Krugman's qualified support for free trade perhaps arises from the fact that he views increasing returns as the source of trade, and has not paid much attention to the Smith-Young reverse relationship of international trade as the source of increasing returns.

Role of Knowledge in Growth

Adam Smith does not directly talk about the role of knowledge in growth. He stated that one of the advantages of the division of labour was the improvement of skill and dexterity of workers. This appears akin to "learning by doing"—a result similar to one obtained by Arrow (1962) in his learning-by-doing model of growth. According to Eltis (1975, p. 427), in modern growth theory, Arrow comes closest to Smith's results with his "learning by doing" model where the rates of growth of labour productivity and wages per head depend on the rate of growth of employment opportunities provided by new machines. If a strong interconnection between investment and growth lies at the centre of the development process, Smith's theory of growth must be rated highly for it is one of the very few where investment has highly favourable long-term effects.[8]

[8] It is true that there may be a strong association between capital accumulation and growth (as, for example, noted by Sen 1983; DeLong and Summers 1991, 1992) but correlation does not prove causality. Considerable evidence suggests that the causation may be from economic growth to capital accumulation rather than from capital accumulation to economic growth. For this evidence see Chapter 6.

As the division of labour advances, the production of knowledge in Smith becomes a specialized activity. As we noted in Chapter 2, not all improvements in machinery are made by workmen. Some are made by philosophers or men of speculation when speculation itself becomes a separate trade. As the society advances, like the various trades which get subdivided, there are subdivisions within philosophy itself. Loasby (1999, pp. 8, 37–38) observes that Schumpeter was not much impressed with Smith's contribution to economics, but what impressed him was his essay on "History of astronomy" in which he talks of a psychological theory of scientific progress which anticipated Kuhn (1962) by two centuries in arguing that perception of new anomalies was a necessary stimulus to the production of new knowledge. Marshall, in his *Principles*, believed that such stimuli were important in developing human imaginative faculties through exercise. However, as Loasby notes, routines are also important not only in economically preserving the successful products of imagination but also by stimulating thought towards further innovation.

Marshall regarded knowledge as the most important requirement for production. He linked knowledge with capital and economic organization which is of various types. As Marshall (1890, pp. 138–39) explains:

> Capital consists in great part of knowledge and organization: and of this some part is private property and other part is not. Knowledge is our most powerful engine of production; it enables us to subdue Nature and force her to satisfy our wants. Organization aids knowledge; it has many forms, e.g. that of a single business, that of various businesses in the same trade, that of various trades relatively to one another, and that of State providing security for all and help for many. The distinction between public and private property in knowledge and organization is of great and growing importance...and partly for that reason it seems best sometimes to reckon Organization apart as a distinct agent of production.

Allyn Young also emphasized knowledge but greater diffusion of existing knowledge was at least as important (if not more) than the creation of new knowledge. For Young, there were no limits to increasing returns even with a stationary population and in the absence of new knowledge: "Even with a stationary and in the absence of new discoveries in pure and applied science there are no limits to the process of expansion except the limits beyond which demand is not elastic and returns do not increase" (Young 1928, p. 534). Young admitted that different industries will grow at different rates depending on the reciprocal elasticities of demand and supply, but these elasticities are related to the market. Thus, contrary to the new growth theory, Young regarded market size (and its growth) as the important factor which makes more effective use of existing and new knowledge. In fact the greater the market size, the greater would be the production of new knowledge. For this reason he was against artificial monopolies in the form of patents or protectionist privileges.[9] For Young the diffusion of existing knowledge was at least as important as the creation of new knowledge. Young thought that scientific knowledge was the common property of mankind, and those who contributed to it often got no commensurate pecuniary rewards. It came into being for the love of creativity, not for any reward (see also Chandra 2020, p. 159).

Like Marshall, Kaldor (1957, 1961) also viewed knowledge (and technology) embodied in capital. To illustrate this he put forward the concept of the "technical progress function" which is based on the idea that capital accumulation and technical progress cannot be separated, and therefore the concept does away with the artificial neoclassical distinction between shift of the production function and movement along with it. As Thirlwall (2003, p. 46) elucidates:

> Kaldor's explanation lay in his innovation of the technical progress function (to replace the neoclassical production function with its artificial distinction between movements along the function and shifts in the function), relating the growth of output per man to the rate of growth of capital

[9] Young favoured reform of the patent system to avoid lasting domination and preemption of future improvements. "Reforms of the patent system are undoubtedly sorely needed. It should not be possible for any one company to secure lasting domination of an industry by getting control of so many patents that future improvements and inventions affecting the industry have no market and no value except to the one company already in control. A situation like this virtually perpetuates the life of patents long beyond the years which the law contemplates. It is likely that some day we shall have to come to a system by which the users of important patent rights shall be licensed by the government, which will administer the patent system in such a way as to eliminate the evils of artificial monopoly" (Young 1929; Mehrling and Sandilands 1999, p. 249). Today patents in most countries, including US and Europe, are for 20 years. Under the WTO framework, product patents have been instituted in addition to process patents, but poor countries can take recourse to compulsory licensing provisions under certain circumstances. In line with Youngian thinking, perhaps the time period of patents can be reduced, compulsory licensing provisions can be made more liberal (for example, in case of Covid vaccines), and further moves to making the system more stringent (for example, from process patents to product patents in the past) can be halted.

> per man, the slope and position of which determines the long-run equilibrium growth of output. The basic idea is that capital accumulation and technical progress cannot be separated. If investment gets ahead of technical progress, the productivity of capital falls and investment is cut back. If technical progress proceeds faster than investment, the productivity of capital rises which encourages further investment. In other words, capital accumulation adjusts to changes in technical dynamism preserving the rate of profit and the capital/output ratio. New endogenous growth theory is precisely anticipated. (see also Palley 1996)[10]

The modern endogenous growth theory includes new knowledge as one of the inputs while preserving the neoclassical supply-side aggregate production function. It also talks about integration with world markets only because this yields more new knowledge inputs. The role of market size or competition find no mention.[11] By contrast, as we noted above, in Youngian conception there are no virtual limits to increasing returns even if new knowledge is not increasing. His stress is on the increased use of existing knowledge as the size of the market expands. While the new growth theory stresses grant of monopolistic privileges like patents, protectionism, and subsidies to generate more research inputs in the system, the Smith-Young framework stresses the market size and competition as important considerations. Young recognized that in the real world there was imperfect competition and took the form of product differentiation, brand names, advertising and selling costs, etc. but for him all this was a part of broader competition where each producer tried to be a bit different from others to rise above the dead level of competition. But competition still prevailed and put an effective lid on profits through close substitutes and entry of new firms. The prevalence of imperfect competition did not justify grant of artificial monopolies to promote knowledge accumulation or growth. His conception of competition was closer to

[10] Thirlwall (2003) also points out that Kaldor's explanation preserves a steady capital-output ratio, one of Kaldor's stylised facts which any growth model has to satisfy.

[11] Sandilands (2000) notes that in Romer's (1989) "Marshall-Young-Romer" model, growth is made more rapid by giving investment subsidies when trade is restricted by transport and other barriers. This will be the case if the society chooses less consumption today, and saves and invests more. "But this could run up against another demand constraint. Why invest more when consumption is being restrained?" (Sandilands 2000, p. 319).

Marshall (1919, p. 397) for whom imperfections and monopolies were temporary and, given time, tended to disappear[12]:

> [T]hough monopoly and free competition are ideally wide apart, yet in practice they shade into one another by imperceptible degrees: that there is an element of monopoly in all competitive business: and that nearly all the monopolies, that are of any practical importance in the present age, hold much of their power by an uncertain tenure; so that they would lose it ere long, if they ignored the possibilities of competition, direct and indirect.

Further: "Stress must be laid on the fact that absolute monopolies are of little importance in modern business as compared with those which are 'conditional' or 'provisional': that is, which hold their sway only 'on condition' that, or 'provided' that, they do not put prices much above the levels necessary to cover their outlays with normal profits. If they did, then competition would probably make itself felt; unless stayed by authority, as is the case with patents, copyrights, and some rights of way" (ibid., pp. 397–98).[13] Marshall further points out that competition would be wasteful and also intolerable in public utilities such as water, gas, or electricity as it would involve encroachments and disturbances on roads and other public spaces so much so "that it could not be tolerated" (ibid., p. 398).[14]

[12] As noted by Quéré (2003, p. 192), Marshallian competition (Marshall 1919, p. 653) had three elements: "'friendly emulation' where the major purpose is to share resources with the aim of organizing co-operative agreements among companies and of making feasible the common discovery of new productive opportunities; 'ordinary business competition' corresponds to a context where the usual price competition mechanisms prevail; and 'competition with destructive aims' is a situation where the explicit purpose of companies is to establish a monopoly position and to drive the other incumbents from the market". So competition in Marshallian conception is not always cut-throat or destructive; it has elements of cooperation as well.

[13] Young was of the view that the case against monopoly was overstated and a monopolist did not charge as high a price as theory sometimes suggested. If a monopoly has cost curves where increasing returns exist, a monopolist takes a longer time period in view and does not maximize his net returns in the short term. The longer the time period he takes, the lower the price he will set. Also, a monopolist was not aware of his demand and supply functions, and this made him raise prices slowly, if at all. Moreover, he cared for public opinion and feared regulation by the government. See Chandra (2020, p. 134).

[14] Becattini (2003, p. 22) sees Marshallian competition in the context of industrial districts as individual interest pursued within a group where every labourer engaged in

Policy Conclusions

Before intelligent policies are designed to promote growth it is important to understand how growth takes place on its own. From the Smith-Young framework it is obvious that the relationship of the division of labour and market size lies at the heart of growth. Policies designed to aid this process are likely to promote growth rather than intrusive policies which hinder aggregate exchange. Also, competition emerges as the inescapable policy conclusion as the key to growth. In this context, the Smith-Young framework leads to a policy of "no preferences, no handicaps". In natural liberty the field is leveled for everyone, and winners and losers emerge from the competitive race itself and cannot be picked and promoted on a priori grounds. Any attempt to do so results in Clapham's (1922) "empty economic boxes". That this is so springs from the fact that increasing returns are generalized rather than sector-specific, and arise from pecuniary external economies rather than internal economies of scale whether at firm or industry level.[15]

Policies to encourage knowledge sectors through subsidies, patents, protectionist privileges go against the concept of competition.[16] These anti-market policies distort the market, and as Young showed, growth mostly takes place on the basis of existing knowledge rather than new knowledge. Emphasis should be on measures to enhance the size of the

social production has opportunities for moral and technical self-education. "The perception of individual interest as a part of a group interest can, under certain conditions, not only produce commodities but also foster the rise of a civic consciousness. And what is the district if not the ideal place for that self-educating process?"

[15] In the Youngian conception even agriculture experiences increasing returns. The fact that it experiences the fruits of technical improvements and grows over time testifies to this. But since it has a lower demand elasticity, it grows slowly as compared to say manufacturing. So Young did not make a distinction between diminishing returns sectors and increasing returns sector (which are empty economic boxes anyway), only between those with lower and higher demand elasticities as their respective growth rates would differ. Because agriculture has lower demand elasticity, its relative share declines over time and productive resources (e.g., labour, land, food, and raw materials) are released for other uses.

[16] Although the modern endogenous growth theory seeking to promote knowledge sectors claims to represent the ideas of the original authors of endogenous growth—Smith, Marshall and Young—with greater clarity, rigour and depth, it actually appears closer to Schumpeterian theory of creative destruction based on "innovation" and "monopoly profits" as noted by Aghion and Howitt (1992, 1998). For a brief discussion of the Schumpeterian theory see Chapter 1.

market which then leads to more effective use of existing as well as new knowledge. Imperfect competition in the real world does not justify policy-induced monopolies to promote growth. Besides, such a policy encourages rent-seeking and lobbying among various interest groups or potential beneficiaries. It is not the job of the state to favour one group at the cost of another and thereby encourage rent-seeking.

International trade plays very prominent role in the realization of increasing returns. Some authors (e.g., Krugman) see increasing returns as the source of trade, but the reverse relationship of increasing returns as an outcome of free (or freer trade) is forgotten. Indeed Smith saw international trade as fostering the division of labour (or increasing returns). Since the division of labour depends on the size of the market, he advocated public investment in transport and communication to integrate the market domestically and international trade to widen it externally. For Smith domestic economic growth and international trade were two sides of the same coin. Even Krugman recognizes the importance of free trade as a practical policy tool which can avoid rent-seeking among vested interests.

If some sectors need to be promoted, this can be done on the basis of handicap removal. Currie's (1974) leading-sector strategy of growth, as it was shown, is consistent with the Smith-Young stress on competition and "no favours, no restraints" policy framework. Currie advocated construction and exports as the leading sectors not because they were increasing returns sectors but because they had latent demand waiting to be actualized and the fact that they can be stimulated independently of the overall rate of growth. Once the institutional barriers holding these sectors back are removed—overvalued exchange rate for exports and suitable financial products for housing—these sectors can then take off pulling rest of the economy including agriculture and industry behind them. The logic of handicap removal can be extended to the entire economy and need not remain confined to the leading sectors (Chandra 2006, 2020).

Any attempt to promote increasing returns sectors (e.g. manufacturing) through subsidies, protection, dual exchange rates, selective employment tax and other anti-market policies upsets reciprocal exchange between sectors, turns the terms of trade against agriculture, and depresses agricultural incomes which in turn poses a demand constraint on industry itself. Studies on effective rates of protection show that the actual (or effective) protection to industry is much higher than what the nominal rates suggest. Further, the larger the variation of tariffs among final goods (as well as inputs), and the larger the gap between inputs and final output tariff, the larger is the distortion caused by tariffs. Thus a moderate uniform tariff on all inputs and final outputs is the least distortionary. The studies on effective protection rates also suggest that protection to industry constitutes disprotection to agriculture and exports, and retards their growth. Generally an outward-oriented policy framework, where the incentive structure is neutral between production for the domestic market and production for exports, is a good policy to follow (see, for example, World Bank 1987).

Promotion of industries in developing countries can be justified on infant protection grounds, but protection has to be moderate (eschewing quantitative means like import licensing, quotas and exchange controls, etc.)[17] and has to be for limited period only till a country's true pattern of comparative advantage emerges. After all, no country has industrialized without protecting its industries with the exception of Britain and Hong Kong. The late comers like Germany and USA could only industrialize after following a policy of protection. But, as Balassa (1980) has shown, if inward orientation is carried too far into the second stage, the results are adverse in terms of economic performance and efficiency of resource use. So it is best to confine import substitution to the easy first stage where the extent of protection is not much out of tune with the dictates of comparative advantage.

Finally, what should be the role of the state? The state can play an important role in aiding the market forces and in developing legal-institutional-moral framework for the market to work better. The state can work towards strengthening the market system and its institutions. For example, it can ensure strong law and order, protect private property, enforce contracts, develop suitable infrastructure to integrate the domestic market, ensure freer trade (if not free trade) with moderate protection (preferably a uniform rate of tariff for all inputs and final outputs), a stable macroeconomic framework where inflation is moderate and exchange rate is better aligned with the market forces of demand and supply, appropriate legal-institutional framework for the proper conduct of monetary and fiscal policies, and competition laws and institutions to

[17] In any case, quantitative restrictions and exchange rate manipulation go against the current WTO framework, and therefore are a strict "no-no".

check the growth of monopoly.[18] However, the government needs to concentrate on getting the basics right and should not venture into areas in which it does not have a comparative advantage like running businesses, taking allocation decisions through centralized planning, and intrusive interference in the market mechanism through price controls, rationing, and other illiberal policies.[19] We therefore conclude with a quote from Marshall (1919, pp. 647–48):

> [T]he state is the most precious of human possessions; and no care can be too great to be spent on enabling it to do its special work in the best way: a chief condition to that end is that it should not be set to work, for which it is not easily qualified, under the conditions of time and place.

References

Abramovitz, Moses. 1956. Resources and output trends in the United States since 1870. *American Economic Review, Papers and Proceedings* 46 (May): 5–23.

Aghion, Philippe, and Peter Howitt. 1992. A model of growth through creative destruction. *Econometrica* 60: 323–351.

Aghion, Philippe, and Peter Howitt. 1998. *Endogenous Growth Theory*. Cambridge: MIT Press.

Arrow, Kenneth J. 1962. Economic implications of learning by doing. *Review of Economic Studies* 29 (3): 155–173.

Arthur, W. Brian. 1990. Positive feedbacks in the economy. *Scientific American* 262 (2): 92–99.

Balassa, B. 1980. The process of industrial development and alternative development strategies. Princeton University International Finance Section, *Essays in International Finance*, No. 141: 4–12.

[18] Young thought that monopoly capitalism was not as widespread as it was thought to be. It was largely confined to a few sectors which were natural monopolies like railways and public utilities. Forces of competition were still strong and were growing. In any case the remedy for concentration did not lie in arbitrarily leveling down of fortunes but in ensuring "equality of competitive opportunity" through the democratic process. He was against discriminating privileges for the few; the system has to work for all. See Chandra (2020, pp. 160–61; 249–53).

[19] See also Krueger (1990) for the argument that the state should not venture beyond its areas of comparative advantage.

Becattini, Giacomo. 2003. The return of the white elephant. In *The Economics of Alfred Marshall*, ed. Richard Arena and Michel Quéré. Basingstoke and New York: Palgrave Macmillan.

Buchanan, James M. 1994. Return to increasing returns: An introductory summary. In *Return to Increasing Returns*, ed. James M. Buchanan and Yong J. Yoon. Ann Arbor: The University of Michigan Press.

Buchanan, James M., and Yong J. Yoon. 2000. A Smithian perspective on increasing returns. *Journal of the History of Economic Thought* 22 (1): 43–48.

Chandra, Ramesh. 2006. Currie's 'leading sector' strategy of growth: An appraisal. *Journal of Development Studies* 42 (3): 490–508.

Chandra, Ramesh. 2019. Nicholas Kaldor on Adam Smith and Allyn Young. *Review of Political Economy* 31 (3): 445–463.

Chandra, Ramesh. 2020. *Allyn Abbott Young*. Cham: Palgrave Macmillan.

Chandra, Ramesh. 2021. Adam Smith, Allyn Young, Amartya Sen and the role of the state. *History of Economics Review* 78 (January 10): 14–43 (published online).

Chandra, Ramesh, and Roger J. Sandilands. 2021. Nicholas Kaldor, increasing returns and Verdoorn's law. *Journal of Post Keynesian Economics* 44 (2): 315–339.

Clapham, J.M. 1922. On empty economic boxes. *Economic Journal* 32: 305–314.

Currie, Lauchlin. 1974. The leading sector model of growth in developing countries. *Journal of Economic Studies* 1 (1): 1–16.

DeLong, J. Bradford, and L. Summers. 1991. Equipment investment and economic growth. *Quarterly Journal of Economics* CVI: 445–502.

DeLong, J. Bradford., and L. Summers. 1992. Equipment investment and economic growth: How strong is the nexus? *Brookings Papers on Economic Activity* 2: 157–211.

Eltis, Walter. 1975. Adam Smith's theory of economic growth. In *Essays on Adam Smith*, ed. Andrew Skinner and Thomas Wilson. Oxford: Clarendon Press.

Ely, Richard T., Thomas S. Adams, Max O. Lorenz, and Allyn A. Young. 1923. *Outlines of Economics*. New York: The Macmillan Company.

Ely, Richard T., Thomas S. Adams, Max O. Lorenz, and Allyn A. Young. 1930. *Outlines of Economics*. New York: The Macmillan Company.

Hart, Neil. 2003. From the representative to the equilibrium firm: Why Marshall was not a Marshallian. In *The Economics of Alfred Marshall*, ed. Richard Arena and Michel Quéré, 158–181. Basingstoke and New York: Palgrave Macmillan.

Hart, Neil. 2006. Business size. In *The Elgar Companion to Alfred Marshall*, ed. Tiziano Raffaelli, Giacomo Becattini, and Marco Dardi, 401–406. Cheltenham and Northampton: Edward Elgar.

Hirschman, Albert O. 1958. *The Strategy of Economic Development*. New Haven: Yale University Press.

Kaldor, Nicholas. 1966. *Causes of the Slow Rate of Economic Growth in the United Kingdom*. Cambridge: Cambridge University Press.
Kaldor, Nicholas. 1957. A model of economic growth. *Economic Journal* 67 (December): 591–624.
Kaldor, Nicholas. 1961. Capital accumulation and economic growth. In *The Theory of Capital*, ed. F.A. Lutz and D.C. Hague, 177–222. London: Macmillan.
Kaldor, Nicholas. 1972. The irrelevance of equilibrium economics. *Economic Journal* 82: 1237–1255.
Kaldor, Nicholas. 1975. What is wrong with economic theory. *Quarterly Journal of Economics* 89 (3): 347–357.
Krueger, Anne O. 1990. Government failures in development. *Journal of Economic Perspectives* 4 (3): 9–23.
Krugman, Paul. 1987. Is free trade passé? *Journal of Economic Perspectives* 1 (2): 131–144.
Krugman, Paul. 1990. *Rethinking International Trade*. Cambridge: MIT Press.
Krugman, Paul. 1991a. *Geography and Trade*. Cambridge: MIT Press.
Krugman, Paul. 1991b. Increasing returns and economic geography. *Journal of Political Economy* 99: 483–499.
Krugman, Paul. 1993. Towards a counter-counterrevolution in development theory. *Proceedings of the World Bank Annual Conference on Development Economics 1992*, 15–38. Washington, DC: World Bank.
Krugman, Paul. 1997. *Development, Geography and Economic Theory*. Cambridge and London: MIT Press.
Krugman, Paul, and Maurice Obstfeld. 2003. *International Economics*, 6th ed. Boston: Addison Welsley.
Kuhn, T.S. 1962. *The Structure of Scientific Revolutions*. Chicago: University of Chicago Press.
Lewis, W. Arthur. 1954. Economic development with unlimited supplies of labour. *Manchester School of Economics and Social Studies* 22: 139–191.
Loasby, Brian. 1991. *Equilibrium and Evolution: An Exploration of the Connecting Principles in Economics*. Manchester and New York: Manchester University Press.
Loasby, Brian. 1999. *Knowledge, Institutions and Evolution in Economics*. London and New York: Routledge.
Marshall, Alfred. 1890 (1920). *Principles of Economics*, 8th ed. London: Macmillan.
Marshall, Alfred. 1919. *Industry and Trade*. London: Macmillan.
Mehrling, Perry G., and Roger J. Sandilands. 1999. *Money and Growth: Selected Papers of Allyn Abbott Young*. London and New York: Routledge.
Murphy, K.M., A. Schleifer, and R. Vishny. 1989. Industrialization and the big push. *Journal of Political Economy* 97 (5): 1003–1026.

Nurkse, Ragnar. 1953. *Problems of Capital Formation in Underdeveloped Countries*. Oxford: Basil Blackwell.
Nurkse, Ragnar. 1962. *Patterns of Trade and Development* (Wicksell Lectures 1959). Oxford: Basil Blackwell.
Palley, Thomas. 1996. Growth theory in a Keynesian mode: Some Keynesian foundations for new endogenous growth theory. *Journal of Post Keynesian Economics* 19 (1): 113–135.
Quéré, Michel. 2003. Increasing returns and competition: Learning from Marshallian perspective. In *The Economics of Alfred Marshall*, ed. Richard Arena and Michel Quéré, 182–201. Basingstoke and New York: Palgrave Macmillan.
Richardson, G.B. 1975. Adam Smith on competition and increasing returns. In *Essays on Adam Smith*, ed. Andrew Skinner and Thomas Wilson. Oxford: Clarendon Press.
Romer, Paul M. 1986. Increasing returns and long-run growth. *Journal of Political Economy* 94: 1002–1038.
Romer, Paul M. 1989. Capital accumulation in the theory of long-run growth. In *Modern Business Cycle Theory*, ed. Robert J. Barro. Cambridge: Harvard University Press.
Rosenstein-Rodan, Paul. 1943. Problems of industrialization in eastern and south-eastern Europe. *Economic Journal* 53 (June–September): 202–211.
Rosenstein-Rodan, Paul. 1961. Notes on the theory of 'big push.' In *Economic Development of Latin America*, ed. H.S. Ellis and H.C. Wallich, 57–67. London: Macmillan.
Sandilands, Roger J. 2000. Perspectives on Allyn Young in theories of endogenous growth. *Journal of the History of Economic Thought* 22 (3): 309–328.
Scitovsky, Tibor. 1954. Two concepts of external economies. *Journal of Political Economy* 62: 143–151.
Sen, Amartya. 1983. Development: Which way now? *Economic Journal* 93 (December): 745–762.
Smith, Adam. 1776 (1976). *An Enquiry Into the Nature and Causes of the Wealth of Nations*, ed. Edwin Cannan. Chicago: University of Chicago Press.
Solow, Robert M. 1956. A contribution to the theory of economic growth. *Quarterly Journal of Economics* 70 (February): 65–94.
Solow, Robert M. 1957. Technical change and aggregate production function. *Review of Economics and Statistics* 39 (August): 311–320.
Stigler, George. 1951. The division of labour is limited by the extent of the market. *Journal of Political Economy* 59 (3): 185–193.
Thirlwall, Anthony P. 2003. Old thoughts on new growth theory. In *Old and New Growth Theories: An Assessment*, ed. Neri Salvadori. Cheltenham and Northampton: Edward Elgar.

Warsh, David. 2006 (2007). *Knowledge and the Wealth of Nations: A Story of Economic Discovery*. New York and London: W. W. Norton.

Whitaker, John K., ed. 1996. *The Correspondence of Alfred Marshall Economist*, 3 Vols. Cambridge: Cambridge University Press.

Whitaker, John K. 2003. Alfred Marshall's *Principles* and *Industry and Trade*: Two books or one? Marshall and the joint stock company. In *The Economics of Alfred Marshall*, ed. Richard Arena and Michel Quéré, 137–157. Basingstoke and New York: Palgrave Macmillan.

World Bank. 1987. *World Development Report*. New York: Oxford University Press.

Young, Allyn A. 1928. Increasing returns and economic progress. *Economic Journal* 38 (152): 527–542.

Young, Allyn A. 1929. Combination and monopoly. In *The Book of Popular Science*, 3971–3980. New York: The Grolier Society. Reprinted in Mehrling and Sandilands (1999, pp. 244–251).

Young, Allyn A. 1990. Nicholas Kaldor's Notes on Allyn Young's LSE Lectures 1927–29. *Journal of Economic Studies* 17 (3/4): 18–114.

Author Index

R. Chandra, *Endogenous Growth in Historical Perspective*, Palgrave Studies in Economic History,
https://doi.org/10.1007/978-3-030-83761-7

Subject Index

R. Chandra, *Endogenous Growth in Historical Perspective*, Palgrave Studies in Economic History,
https://doi.org/10.1007/978-3-030-83761-7

C

F

J

K

L

GPSR Compliance
The European Union's (EU) General Product Safety Regulation (GPSR) is a set of rules that requires consumer products to be safe and our obligations to ensure this.

If you have any concerns about our products, you can contact us on

ProductSafety@springernature.com

In case Publisher is established outside the EU, the EU authorized representative is:

Springer Nature Customer Service Center GmbH
Europaplatz 3
69115 Heidelberg, Germany

www.ingramcontent.com/pod-product-compliance
Ingram Content Group UK Ltd.
Pitfield, Milton Keynes, MK11 3LW, UK
UKHW020154290926
15471UKWH00005B/857
9783030837631